S0-ADJ-559

Family in America

Family in America

THE COLONIAL AMERICAN FAMILY

Collected Essays

ARNO PRESS & THE NEW YORK TIMES
New York 1972

Reprint Edition 1972 by Arno Press Inc.

LC# 76-169359
ISBN 0-405-03880-1

Family in America
ISBN for complete set: 0-405-03840-2
See last pages of this volume for titles.

Manufactured in the United States of America

Publisher's Note: This edition was reprinted from the best available copies.

CONTENTS

AN

ESSAY

ON

MARRIAGE;

OR,

The lawfulneſs of DIVORCE,

IN CERTAIN CASES,

CONSIDERED

ADDRESSED TO THE FEELINGS OF MANKIND.

PHILADELPHIA:

PRINTED BY ZACHARIAH POULSON, JUNIOR, ON THE WEST SIDE OF FOURTH-STREET, BETWEEN MARKET AND ARCH-STREETS, MDCCLXXXVIII.

PREFACE

THE writing of the following pages was occasioned by seeing a paragraph in a news paper, relative to a woman in the city who had destroyed herself on account of some infelicity in marriage. The author reflecting how many there might probably be, who were completely wretched, and who, notwithstanding, did not plunge themselves into another world to avoid the miseries of this, thought it might be a subject worthy the consideration of every humane person; and therefore has, in the subsequent pages, set forth the misery of marriage in those who are unsuitably united together, and endeavoured to show the causes of such infelicity, and the lawfulness and necessity of divorce, in other cases beside those at present admitted. And although no essay on this subject has yet appeared in this country, that he has seen, yet this does not prove it unnecessary; and, whatsoever may be the merits of the work, if it opens a way for abler discussion of the subject, the writer will not think his labour entirely lost.

ALL that he can say of his performance, is, that he was induced to undertake it from a strong sympathetic feeling for the weakness and distresses of human nature; and has endeavoured to execute it in a manner most likely to communicate the same to his Readers. He has chiefly aimed at brevity and perspicuity, and if he has advanced any thing new, it is in the way of opinion only, and therefore requests the attention of his Readers to the matter, and not to the manner, of his remarks. But if any should think any thing in the former worthy of making objections to, the writer has more to say, but in regard to the latter, he only requests of the Public a favourable reception.

AN ESSAY ON MARRIAGE;

OR,

The lawfulneſs of DIVORCE,

IN CERTAIN CASES, CONSIDERED.

CHAPTER I.

AMERICA has been famous for her love of liberty, and hatred of tyranny of every kind; ſhe has not only by arms expelled her foreign foes, but generouſly extended her liberality, in a great meaſure, even unto the African ſlaves. Therefore, it is hoped, the ſame ſpirit of indulgence will extend ſtill further—to thoſe unhappy individuals, mixed among every claſs of mankind, who are frequently united together in the worſt of bondage to each other; occaſioned by circumſtances not in their power to foreſee, or prevent, at the time of their union; which ſhould entitle them to relief from humane legiſlators and the reſt of mankind. We believe it will be readily admitted, that there is no circumſtance in life, on which our happineſs ſo much depends, as being ſuitably united together in marriage; and that no foreſight that people are capable of, at that time, is ſufficient to foreſee, or prevent, the many cauſes that are likely to deſtroy the felicity of that union; and that it is equally certain, that various cauſes do deſtroy it, and render

render them completely miserable; from hence arises the necessity of divorce in such situations, under such restrictions as may be deemed necessary.

The large portion of moral essays generally taken up in lectures on the subject of marriage, shows of what consequence that single, important action of our lives is esteemed to be to mankind; which could not be of so much importance if we were allowed to rectify past errors by future experience. But the whole of our instruction, on that head, generally amounts to little more than if such instruction as this should be given to a traveller in a strange country: that in the midst of the highway, that he must unavoidably pass, there is a deep and dreadful pit, curiously covered from view, into which, if he falls, he can never extricate himself therefrom, but must inevitably die a miserable death. And truly such is the marriage lot at present to many, and to more than can easily be conceived, because the greatest sufferers thereby, for the most part, conceal their situation, to keep themselves from being despised by the rest.

We shall recite, in the first place, the probable causes of such infelicity; in the next place, the miserable prospect of an unhappy couple, and the evil they are the occasion of, not only to themselves but others; and lastly, of the lawfulness and necessity of divorce. The cases we shall briefly state, by way of example, will be taken from the middling class of mankind, as the nearest representation of the others. And we shall only mention the leading and principal dispositions, and leave the judicious reader, from observations and reflections in his own mind, to pursue the description more minutely.

In the first place, the unsuitableness arising from circumstances: as when a gentleman from the country, or farmer's son, marries a young woman educated in the city, perhaps of smaller fortune, but of genteel family, he takes her home; after the first formality of visiting being over, the appearances of every thing around displeases her; she cannot help, after a while, making remarks; sometimes, perhaps, such as these: of his want of neatness in his dress, of the furniture of his house, of the requisites that are wanting on his table, of the indecency of his servants and domestics, of the rusticity of his neighbours and acquaintance. He thinks himself justified in retaliating, in some degree, in remarks on the needless formality, appearances, dress and address, of the citizens; for the present it passes off, but the scene is again often renewed with more dislike than before on each part: from remarks they go to dispute, after a while to jest, ridicule and contempt, and these, by imperceptible degrees, from

time

time to time, as occasion occurs. The servants, neighbours and relatives of the husband, mock and sneer at all the wife says or does; she has the dairy, poultry and housewifery to manage and conduct in a manner she never saw in her life, and is unable to perform; her husband complaining of her doing needless things and leaving the necessary undone, which equally displeases him. They disagree in their humours about dress, table, recreations, servants and every thing. From the repetition of disputes (which are the effect of their different feelings only) passions are exited in each, which were before unknown to either. They then mutually torment, thwart, plague, revile, and hate one another; and this, perhaps, takes place in no long time after marriage. I need not add more. It is easy to conceive a great many different degrees of unsuitableness, arising from the same cause, that is, in the manner of their education, that sooner or later has the same effect. But if they are well-bred people they conceal their situation from the world as much as possible.

If a gentleman of good rank and education marries a woman of mean birth, but superior fortune, the case is no better: she despises him for his notions of dignity and elegance that she cannot comprehend; and he reproaches her for her mean, low conceptions and appearances, in every thing; she censures him for his want of wealth, and he retorts upon her for the want of every thing else.

Secondly, those who marry of different professions in religion, although they may not be so zealous themselves as to differ about it much at first; yet, when the warmth of their passion has abated, they will each of them feel their former prejudices, and their respective relatives, on each side, in all their separate conversations with them, will imperceptibly, without design, inspire each of them by degrees, with disapprobation, dislike, and contempt of the manners, customs, appearances and principles of each other; and each of them will be more and more inclined to vindicate their own. All the errors, faults, and misfortunes will be magnified and misrepresented, and charged upon each other by the friends of each party; which will, by degrees, create reflections; sourness, dislike and contempt will encrease, especially if there is any harshness of temper in either party, and falshood, for the most part, will not be wanting on one side or other to keep up a ferment, until a steady hatred ensues.*

Thirdly, if a young couple marry without consent of parents on each side, the consequence is nearly the same as the last;

* A steady hatred will always begin, as soon as the pain they receive from each other is greater than the pleasure.

laſt; the animoſity of the friends of each party is greater; they refuſe to aſſiſt their children in a ſettlement in the world, but reflect on each other, and foment uneaſineſs and ſourneſs in their children, which encreaſes with their ſtrait circumſtances in the world; each of them become weary of their ſituation; their company grows painful with each other, for the ſame reaſon as in the laſt caſe; they conceive an averſion to each other they know not why, and their tempers are ſoured towards others they know not for what; this creates enemies; poverty, contempt and averſion follows.

Thus it is with the paſſions of the human ſoul, as with the ſtrings of a muſical inſtrument: one being diſordered, ſpoils the muſick of the whole, and produces nothing but diſharmony.

Fourthly, when a couple, with mutual affection, and naturally good diſpoſitions, agree to unite in marriage; but, through warmth of paſſion, or affection, that would not perhaps wait until a ſettlement, or means of a living, could be provided; they miſconduct, or make what is called a miſſtep: they are then without remedy not only diſowned, but expoſed to the world; and now they are not only looked upon as children of ſin and diſobedience, but as malcontents and enemies to the ſociety in which they were educated. In this ſituation, deprived of the confidence of their fellow citizens, they are left to provide for themſelves;—their parents* chooſe rather to give or truſt their property in the hands of children who have conducted better; a coldneſs and ſhyneſs takes place among all their acquaintance; they ſeem as if they belonged to nobody, and nobody to them; they muſt aſſociate with inferiors, or none at all. Viſits are made into the neighbourhood, and enquiries into every part of their conduct, and how they behave, and if they are like to make out in the world. And thoſe viſitors being fully prepoſſeſſed with the above opinion, they operate as ſieves, or

* Though as children have nothing but what they receive by nature and education from their parents, tutors and companions, the infamy reſts ultimately on their parents and thoſe who have the care of their education, (eſpecially when they live among thoſe of their own profeſſion) and not on themſelves, who are ignorant of their own weakneſs and of the evil conſequences that will attend, until it is too late to prevent them. The Chineſe laws make communities anſwerable for offences committed within their reſpective authorities; parents for the miſbehaviour of their children; concluding that they muſt have neglected their education, and magiſtrates are ſeverely puniſhed for thoſe crimes committed within the diſtricts of their authority. Modern Univerſal Hiſtory, vol. viii. p. 153, 172. Antient Univerſal Hiſtory, vol. viii. p. 266.

or ſkimmers; they take away all the droſs, and leave the good behind; their characters are too reſpectable to be queſtioned; they ſow their tares as they go, the opinion of the world is ſoon formed in regard to their worthleſſneſs, and they are accordingly treated with contempt.

The unthinking couple cannot help murmuring at thoſe from whom they receive unmerited affronts; this never fails of creating a number of real enemies, who conſtantly magnify their faults, and miſrepreſent all they ſay or do; they find themſelves not only deſerted by their acquaintance, but their neareſt and deareſt friends are hoſtily armed to do them every injury.

In this ſituation, unconſcious of any fault, they reflect on each other as the cauſe of their misfortune, by ſome indiſcretion or other. They tire each other with complaints they cannot relieve, and in this ſtate of ſourneſs and diſcontent, every tale of calumny and falſhood, makes deep impreſſion on them; and lowneſs of ſpirits, and inactivity of body enſues, when the contrary is moſt requiſite for their ſupport; then poverty and ill-humour, and all the train of evils and calamities that can befal human creatures in diſtreſs, attend them to the end of their days.* For the honour of human nature we could wiſh the above repreſentation was entirely groundleſs; yet we believe this will not be found an imaginary deſcription by thoſe who will be at the pains to examine what becomes of many of thoſe who are thus diſowned.

And here we cannot help making a reflection, though not immediately relating to the ſubject.

O ye paſtors of flocks and heads of ſocieties, what ſentence do you expect to receive at the laſt day, for making theſe numerous ſacrifices of your moſt innocent lambs? The powers of nature are ſtrong in the moſt perfect parts of the creation; youth may plead ignorance of the conſequence, but age cannot; you know well, by experience, what you are about and what will be the conſequence of your doings; neither does it deter from theſe offences, becauſe they know not their puniſhment until it arrives, nor even then from whence it ſprings. Their crime certainly hurts not you; but it is not the ruin and deſtruction of their periſhable beings and livings here alone you ſeek or effect; but perhaps of their precious, immortal ſouls for ever hereafter, at leaſt as far as you are capable of effecting it.

How differently did the Saviour and Judge of mankind ſentence the woman taken in adultery: "Neither do I condemn

* See page 12, 13, 14.

demn thee, go and sin no more," was all his reproof to her, when she told him no man had condemned her. Not so his sentence when he pronounced condemnation, and so many woes, on the teachers of that day, that bound grievous burdens on other men's shoulders that themselves would not move with one of their fingers; think to yourselves if this be not a parallel case, and how you will answer for it; think where the rich man lifted up his eyes in torment, and how you will abide a like situation, if the scene should be changed for you. But if you are more innocent than these victims, heaven will regard you, and this reflection will not hurt you.

But to return from this digression: the observations we shall make next, are, upon unsuitableness of temper. If a man of a subtil, proud, unforgiving temper, marries a woman of a passionate, provoking, unreserved disposition, he accidently affronts her; she immediately, in the most unreserved manner, affronts him in return; he conceals his resentment, but will frequently afterwards sting her with his witty sneers, in a manner she cannot guard against nor easily bear; her anger is over; she bears it for a while; but at last she affronts him still worse where he can least bear it: he now never omits any opportunity of exercising his malicious wit upon her; they soon grow intolerably weary and hateful to each other.

There are many other bad tempers and dispositions that would tend to make any unhappy if indulged to extreme: such as incessant scolding, abusive and indecent language, cruelty to children, excessive fretfulness and impatience about things unavoidable; many of these qualities would become moderated on a change of companions, so as to become agreeable accomplishments: as when a compassionate man of fortune marries a tender and weakly woman that is ever complaining; he affectionately sympathizes with her in all her complaints, and exercises a very sensible and peculiar pleasure of his own, in giving her those constant proofs of his affection, in the attention he shows to her wants; and receiving hers in return, which he could not do in a woman otherwise constituted. Also a very good-natured man married to a passionate, severe-tongued, though otherwise good wife; when she is suddenly provoked, he is remarkably pleased with those sudden sallies of her wit and eloquence, although it should be directed against himself; he looks upon them as marks of her wit and spirit, and attention to her business.

A very passionate couple that sometimes vent their full rage at each other on certain occasions, having fully satisfied their resentment, their affection returns again to each other, like

like a tide, with more fondnefs than before, and rather en-creafes than abates affection.

Cruelty to children is fo unnatural, one would be tempted to think it could not exift, did not experience evince it; it muft proceed from affections wholly mifplaced on objects quite diftinct from the human being, and themfelves tormented with fome kind of paffions or defires unlawful, unfatisfactory, or impoffible to be enjoyed; or what will be found to be the fame thing, when kind and natural affection in companions to each other is loft, and bitternefs and cruelty fucceed.

A liberal and a mercenary, a polite and an impolite, a candid and a deceitful difpofition, are unhappy united together; but happy if their qualities are alike. But more unfuitable ftill are thofe of religious and irreligious principles when they are united together.

A couple kept low in the world by the hand of Providence only, go through a feries of trials, hardfhips and difficulties together in raifing a family; their affections and attachments encreafe, like two caft away feamen, or unfortunate foldiers, that have been companions, and fhared the fame toils, travels, dangers, and diftreffes together, and mutually affifted each other for a long feries of time, have a greater attachment to each other than they can poffibly have to any elfe whatever.

Moreover there are incidental circumftances that will entirely deftroy the happy marriage-union; lying, that father and mother of all wickednefs, becaufe it fcreens and protects it, is yet unreftrained and unpunifhed by any law, civil or religious; and hateful as it is to God and man, doubtlefs prevails among fome of thofe efteemed the beft, as well as the worft of mankind: I fay lying is in full practice among us, and one judicious, well framed tale, by a malicious perfon, will excite fuch fecret jealoufy, uneafinefs, and doubts of each other, and open the way for fo many more of the fame kind, of whatever kind they may be; they feldom or never are got over, but foment, by degrees, to the greateft hatred and rancour.

Some are compelled to marry through the force, fraud, deception, or artifice of their friends or others, and conceive the greateft averfion immediately. We do not fay thefe will not ever be reconciled to each other, but that much fmaller matters of difturbance, fuch as we have defcribed, will render them thoroughly irreconcilable.

The

B

The laſt inſtance we ſhall mention, is, a violent, unchangeable affection for ſome other perſon beſides thoſe unto whom they are married. William Penn, ſomewhere ſays, marry a woman thou loveſt, or thou wilt love a woman thou never married; this may be equally true when we ceaſe to love thoſe unto whom we are married.

It may be thought needleſs, perhaps, to mention thoſe incidents that ſo ſeldom happen, but we believe it very often happens, ſometimes to our certain knowledge, perhaps much oftener than can eaſily be conceived; and when that is the caſe very great diſturbance muſt enſue; in public places they are likely to happen moſt frequently, but it is not likely they ſhould often come to any ones knowledge, much leſs to the public: more eſpecially when we conſider the powerful effect of ſhame, and the propenſity it has to conceal what is thought to be a diſgraceful paſſion. Read the accounts phyſicians ſometimes give of modeſt women, of otherwiſe unblemiſhed character, actually expiring in child-birth, in the moſt excruciating tortures, rather than own their ſituation, although earneſtly urged to it with promiſes of ſecrecy, and this is becauſe they were unmarried, and thought it would be a diſgrace they could never ſurvive.

Plutarch relates an anecdote of the Mileſian virgins, which merits the attention of the philoſopher: " Multitudes fell by their own hands, doubtleſs in that trying age when nature, giving birth to reſtleſs and turbulent deſires, inflames the imagination, and when the heart, aſtoniſhed at new wants which virtue forbids to gratify, feels pining melancholy ſucceed to the ſportful tranquillity of child-hood. Nothing could ſtop the contagion; a law was made condemning the firſt who ſhould be guilty of ſelf-murder, to be brought naked and expoſed in the market place; thoſe young women were not afraid of death, but they were afraid of ſhame even after death. Not one of them, henceforth, made an attempt on her life."

It had more became the wiſdom and goodneſs of the legiſlature to have prevented, if poſſible, the temptation, than to have inflicted a puniſhment worſe than death, on a crime that proceeded from the powerful effect of nature only, and that in its moſt innocent ſtate and ſtage of life.

We have had accounts lately of the Reverend Mr. Hackman, falling violently in love with a Miſs Ray; a lady who lived ſixteen years in the family of lord Sandwich. by whom ſhe had nine children; he grew ſo inſupportable to himſelf, that he meditated the deſtruction of both her and himſelf; he loaded two piſtols, and as ſhe was entering a coach he

diſcharged

discharged one at her and shot her dead, and the other at himself, without effect; then delivered himself up to justice and was executed. This appears to have been the case by his confession, in the pathetic speech he made at his trial.

And here we might fill a chapter with quotations, but as they generally mislead the Reader, we will omit them. But to what other account can we so reasonably attribute the strange disturbance of mind we see people undergo, without knowing the cause: the many disorders besides melancholy, dejection of spirits, distraction and suicide, physicians tell us, proceed from a disturbance of mind. All our passions encrease with age though more concealed; this, as well as others; and we believe the most gentle, mild and friendly dispositions, are the most likely to be liable thereto.

Thus we have recited a great many causes;* any one of them may be sufficient to destroy the felicity of marriage, and render perfectly miserable that union, that should, of all things in this world, yield us the most perfect enjoyment; or, at least, sweeten the bitter potion that so frequently falls to the lot of human nature.

But it often happens that many of these causes do unite and join in one and the same effect, and proportionably encrease the mischief they tend to create; and when that is the case, who can conceive the disturbance they may probably give, or a remedy equal to the disease, other than a separation.

And now we are come to the second part of our observations.

CHAP. II.

Of the miserable Prospects of an unhappy Couple.

BUT it may not be improper, in the first place, to set forth the blessings and advantages of an happy union in marriage, in order that the different consequences may appear more distinctly in the comparison.

When each party with sincere, mutual affection, and good dispositions, nearly equal in fortune, and with the approbation of parents and friends, the same in education and way of life and religion; are fortunately joined together in marriage, all things seem then to strengthen the union and not destroy it; such appear to every one as if actuated by one soul, a most consum-

* More causes might be enumerated, especially in second marriages, but those we have recited are sufficient for our present design.

conſummate pleaſure, joy, and ſatisfaction appear in the countenance of each; their preſence, and all their behaviour to each other, ſeem to inſpire a kind of inexpreſſible pleaſure to the beholder, like the joys of the bleſſed; for good, as well as evil, is communicative by ſympathy or example, and ſuch being perfectly happy themſelves, it gives full and free exerciſe for all the gentle, kind and friendly diſpoſitions of the human ſoul toward themſelves and others, even of their enemies, if they have any; but as their friendlineſs appears on all occaſions, there is none but thoſe perfectly overcome with evil diſpoſitions themſelves, have any inclination to injure them, but on the contrary, a kind of zeal to do them good. Their relatives by marriage, on each ſide, inſtead of detracting from, are commending them to each other, and aſſiſting them in the world; and the bulk of mankind appear to them as the moſt upright and friendly beings in nature. And as their paſſions and deſires are moderate, they ſee things nearly as they are, and plan their conduct more wiſe accordingly; and as they feel their ſpirits lively, they are active in buſineſs, and if their circumſtance is but middling in the world, their gains are ſure and conſtant, and in a few years are encreaſed beyond expectation.

Their good example not only ſpreads a kind of luſtre round them, and communicates its likeneſs every where, but operates as an impenetrable guard to their character; if malice or ill-will ſhould raiſe a tale of calumny againſt them, it dies where it begins, and its author is deteſted. Their children partake of the good qualities of the parents, both by nature and example. Thus it will appear, if the above caſe is truly ſtated, that happineſs cauſes virtue and not virtue happineſs, as is generally ſuppoſed; and whoever will be ſufficiently attentive to what paſſes in his own breaſt, will be ſatisfied of the truth of the obſervation.

But now let us reverſe the ſcene: a man and a woman of good diſpoſitions naturally, but who unfortunately marry under one, or all, of the before-mentioned diſadvantages, have all the evils reſulting from them; their little comforts leave them one, by one, and peace and tranquillity become ſtrangers to their breaſts; and finding themſelves miſerable at home, they muſt and will ſeek enjoyment ſomewhere; we have mentioned the danger of an unchangeable affection where it cannot be indulged, and ſurely we need not mention the many wandering imaginations and deſires of every kind; the many paſtimes, amuſements, and, perhaps, vices that muſt and will enſue; the continual increaſe and exerciſe of all the vicious,

irri-

irritating paſſions and pleaſures; we need not be particular, the bad example they ſet to others, and the many innocent people they draw into their practices; the loſs of time, neglect of œconomy, diſregard of their worldly intereſts; or, if reſtrained from theſe by religion, the fear of looſing their reputation, or of excommunication; then melancholy, extreme avarice, or paſſionate deſires after worldly poſſeſſions and honours alone, as their only enjoyment, frequently take place: here they have the men of the world to contend with and oppoſe; intereſt againſt intereſt, and honour againſt honour; a thouſand croſſes and diſappointments, unavoidably interfere and irritate them; every affront makes an incurable wound; every virtuous feeling is ſacrificed for the ſmalleſt gain; the greateſt ſeverity is uſed in their families to gain an eſtate, and the greateſt oppreſſion and diſhoneſty abroad; in either caſe their vices are ſo conſpicuous that the virtuous part of mankind become their enemies; their enjoyments are precarious, unnatural and unſatisfactory, and their ſouls ſtill wandering in ſearch of what they cannot find, and being extremely wretched themſelves, they cannot help ſtriving to make others ſo by detraction, from envy, ſelfiſhneſs and views of competition: all mankind are intereſted in oppoſing them in their own kind, and do it accordingly; which makes the whole maſs appear to them as a race of devils, and the unhappy wretch is viewed in the ſame light by others. Their children are miſ-uſed and miſ-taught, both by precept and example; and all the evil they intend others is generally returned back on themſelves tenfold. As old age advances and naturally draws them toward their latter end, their pleaſures of ſenſe are abated; they can only exerciſe reflection on what is paſt and what is to come; weakneſs and diſeaſes encreaſe, and give them warning the awful period is not far off, when their being and exiſtence here muſt ceaſe, and they muſt give way to another generation. Alas, on what can they reflect but on a long life paſt of extreme wretchedneſs and pain, amidſt ſurrounding felicity? On the many ways and means they have uſed to afflict others, and others them, more eſpecially thoſe who ſhould have been the dear companion of their lives? and alſo of the manifold ſins and tranſgreſſions they have committed, in conſequence thereof? And laſtly, on what is to come? How ſhall we deſcribe it, ſeems it not like a dark and hedious monſter ſtretching forth her dreadful jaws to cloſe upon the trembling wretch forever? And this is the final end and final hope of him, or her, who but a few years before thought, that binding themſelves in the

bands

bands of wedlock, was leaping into the lap of Paradise, and entering in the sure road to heaven and happiness, and the joy of angels. And yet, unwelcome as this prospect of final dissolution appears, it seems it is more welcome, oftentimes, than a being in this world under the before-mentioned disagreeable circumstances. But nevertheless, we do not pretend to say, that all this is the certain consequence of infelicity in marriage; but only that it most frequently is so. Notwithstanding constant private devotion, frequent conversation with sincere friends, or engagement in some very pleasing study or employment, will in a good degree supply the deficiency of marriage bliss, and prevent, in a measure, the evil consequences. But are we to expect every one wise, or fortunate enough to obtain them? if they are not, their misfortunes are without remedy. And here the scene is changed; misfortunes produce vice, instead of vice producing misfortunes, as is mostly supposed; or rather that they go hand in hand, and promote each other.

Thus, if the foregoing observations are just, there appears to have been one general mistake, that teachers in religion, moralists, and mankind in general have adopted; that is, that reason doth, or ought, to preside over our affections, when the fact in reality is otherwise; our reason, commonly so called, neither can, doth, nor ought to govern our affections, but only regulate them, and govern our actions and contrive and contribute means to indulge them; if our affections did not rule, neither man nor woman would ever marry, or propagate their kind, labour for posterity, or hazard their lives in defence of their friends without reward, or do any thing through pity, compassion, or disinterested regard to their kind; or, in other words, be good or virtuous; but exceed beasts in savageness and yet be less wise. And our affections, if strong, will be found, in reality, rather to encrease, in proportion to the endeavours we use to suppress them; because it causeth us to meditate on the object of our affection or aversion, and by constant meditation to fix our love or hatred more durable than before: neither can we easily expel from our thoughts, the object of our attention, if a lively sensation of the good or evil we have received from them be often present. And it is the duty of rulers and instructors, to lead and direct our good affections, and to indulge them in good and worthy objects, and not to force them, otherwise they will be found to exert themselves like forced waters and break the strongest bounds; or secretly undermine the works of the workman, to their great damage and hurt. For our evil affections

fections are frequently no other than our good affections forced, or misled from their proper objects; and this indulgence of our good affections is the only sure way of preventing our evil ones, otherwise one mischief begets another, and we punish misfortune instead of vice; it is like an unskilful surgeon that cuts off a limb he can not cure, to hide his ignorance and save his credit.

And now we are come to the last part of our essay.

CHAP. III.

Of the lawfulness and necessity of Divorce, and the Benefits deriving therefrom.

THE reflections that naturally and unavoidably arise from the above recited facts and considerations, are: doth God require this sacrifice of our happiness, or in other words, accomplishment of our destruction? or, would not this supposition be more applicable to the enemy of mankind, who, they say, goes about like a roaring lion seeking whom he may devour? If our Creator seeketh or rejoiceth in our infelicity, for what purpose did he pour forth in the creation such a profusion of ornaments and delights? delightful objects for sensation and reflection; such multitudes of fruits and and flowers, meats and drinks, pleasing objects for the eyes, and sounds for the ears, and grateful smells for the nostrils, and ten thousand pleasing subjects of contemplation for the understanding; and herbs for food and for medicine, and remedies for almost every disease, so various and numerous, that it is impossible to enumerate them in every part of the creation.

The pangs of child-birth are to give life and joy to the child and parent; the pains of sickness and wounds to confine the patient to his bed until he is healed, and to warn him to take especial care of that tender frame his Maker hath been pleased to give him, and his sensations of pain and pleasure are his motives to action and means of happiness. But for what end was unhappy matrimony instituted or compelled to be born, when there is an easy remedy always at hand, and not denied to the meanest slave, that of changing his or her master?

And as slave-keeping is justly becoming detestable in this country, it may not be improper, in this place, to make a comparison between a slave and an unhappy, married free person: so that a relief may appear as necessary to the one as to the other, if the married person, as such, may be esteemed equally worthy of our attention and regard.

Slaves,

Slaves,* almoſt always, by complaint or remonſtrance to their maſter or others, may change their maſter, until they have found out the moſt moderate. And although always at call to come and go, yet their common portion of labour is ſeldom equal to that of a free perſon; they moſtly eat the ſame kind of food with their maſter, their cloaths are ſufficient to keep them from ſuffering; they are relieved from the care and concern of providing for themſelves and families: bodily correction they can moſtly avoid by ſubmiſſion and fair promiſes, and this they often regard no longer than it ſmarts, which is ſoon over; they are not confined to their maſter's apartment, to be always tormented and abuſed; they have frequent holidays of ſport, recreation, and paſtime, at which they contrive to crib for a feaſt, and revel the whole night in merriment; where the moſt unreſtrained liberty and joy abounds; they are under no reſtraint from religion, morality or fear of loſing their reputation, or of excummunication; their love is all delight; they feel no dread from future conſequences; they marry with whom, and for as long as they pleaſe, and no longer.

They are all of one ſentiment in morality and religion; they are always eſteemed by their maſters and others, if they perform their ſervice faithfully, and when age comes on they are ſure of ſubſiſtance for life, as good and much eaſier than when young.

But where is there any relief to the miſerable, hen-pecked huſband, or the abuſed, and inſulted, deſpiſed wife? We forbear to recite the many ways and means they take to afflict and torment one another.† They are not only confined like a criminal to their puniſhment, but their confinement muſt laſt till death.

But perhaps it may be ſaid, that if mankind were at liberty to ſeparate and marry again, the matrimonial tie would become leſs binding; one ſeparation would make way for another, and men and women would change from one to another like beaſts and their families and kindred would be unknown and unprovided for, and their names and deſtinctions loſt.

We

* Alluding to the ſlaves of Pennſylvania and New-Jerſey.

† That the pains of the mind exceed thoſe of the body we may learn from hence: heroes, martyrs and thoſe perſecuted for religion, receive the greateſt bodily torments not only with patience, but tokens of pleaſure, and ſeek occaſions of receiving them when they think the cauſe they are ſuffering for redounds to their honour or glory. But the moſt delicate fare of the moſt voluptuous perſon, yields him not the leaſt pleaſure whenever ſo little galled or fretted in his mind.

We ſhould not propoſe to ſet men and women wholly at liberty to ſeparate and marry at pleaſure; but only on complaint of each or either party, and the cauſe inquired into, and their children, if any, provided for out of their eſtate equally, and liberty given to marry again and their eſtate divided between them; but not at liberty to repeat the like often. This much might ſerve for a trial. But we do not ſuppoſe an inclination to part would often happen, or any inconvenience ariſe, if they were left wholly at liberty in this reſpect.

For we ſee, in the order of the creation, thoſe creatures who bring forth their young quite helpleſs into the world, where the female alone is unable to defend and provide for them, nature has impelled them, by ſecret and powerful inſtinct, to pair together in couples for their mutual defence, and ſupport, without which it would be impoſſible for them to exiſt; as we ſee remarkably in birds and ſome beaſts, that are helpleſs when young; it is not ſo in cattle that are able to ſhift and provide for themſelves immediately.

And mankind, in a ſtate of nature, all of one religion, cuſtom, and manners, never incline to ſeparate, although not compelled to remain together; there appears to have been no incitement thereto, as has ariſen through the various ſtages and changes of our civilized ſtate, without a change of cuſtom, as was neceſſary in this reſpect; civilization having, in a manner, changed our natures, by introducing new kinds of ſenſations, as deſcribed in the foregoing part of this eſſay.

And as there is no creature nearly ſo helpleſs as the human ſpecies in infancy, ſo neither is their any nearly ſo violently attached to each other; not in the way of ſudden paſſion, but unchangable affection. Providence having wiſely proportioned their affections, in ſuch a degree as the neceſſity of their nature and ſituation requires, in order to go through and bear a ſeries of trials, troubles, anxieties, and cares, needful to raiſe and ſupport their otherwiſe helpleſs offspring.

And when the human ſpecies are confined, in their choice, to thoſe of the ſame way of life, manners, religion, or education, and unite through mutual affection, they are directed by ſecret inſtinct to thoſe whoſe tempers, qualities and diſpoſitions are moſt ſuitable to their own. Or if it does not, it is moſtly owing to ſome ſeparate views, ſuch as the proſpect of an eſtate or other circumſtances, or perhaps, when too much confined in their choice, as is the caſe with ſome young people reſtrained by their parents, (to uſe my former ſimilie) like confined waters breaking bounds, too ſudden a flow of paſſion

passion ensues toward those objects whom chance presents to their view and acquaintance, and overcomes and precipitates them into a union, before they have time to examine their own breasts; or, in other words, passion overcomes their judgment, when both should unite together in forming the happy connection.

Living together as man and wife, is, doubtless, as old as the creation; but many ages passed away before any form of marriage was instituted, and the man took the woman with the parents' consent, and lived with her, and she became his wife.

Thus we read of Abraham sending his servant to take a wife for his son Isaac; he did according to his instructions and brought her home with the consent of her parents, and Isaac received and took her into his Mother's tent, and he loved her and she became his wife; and this was all the ceremony; the whole of the transaction is very particularly related by the historian, and so material a circumstance as marriage would not have been left out. It was nearly the same with Jacob; he agreed to serve Laban seven years for his daughter Rachel, and they seemed to him but a few days for the love he had to her, and at the end of the time he said, give me my wife, for my days are fulfilled.

Moses allowed a man to put away his wife at pleasure, yet we do not find that it was often practised; but on the contrary, they had the greatest difficulty to separate those who married into strange nations in the time of the Jewish captivity, as may be seen in Ezra, chapters ix. and x. and we read in Nehemiah, on the same occasion, in the xiii*th*. chap. and 25th. verse, that he contended with them; and cursed them, and smote certain of them, and plucked off their hair, and caused them to swear by God, saying, you shall not give your daughters unto their sons, nor take their daughters unto your sons, or for yourselves. So sensible were the Jews of the impropriety of strange marriages; yet we do not read that a separation was really effected. These instances show how little danger there is of separations becoming too frequent.

But it is probable they will become more necessary, and frequent as our manners shall become changed and varied from those of the primitive ages: but never, in no age or nation, was marriage esteemed any other than a civil contract, or any thing so divine, holy, or sacred in it that it might not be dissolved by the parties contracting, until Christianity took place, which leads us naturally to consider of Christ's command in this respect: if there was any thing in the

Christian

Christian doctrine that would tend to destroy the peace and happiness of mankind, we should be apt to reject it entirely, as something that had got in by mistake. But perhaps it may appear otherwise.

The Pharisees came unto him, tempting him; saying, *Is it lawful for a man to put away his wife for every cause?* The question is doubtful in every sense, for they came to him, tempting him. It is impossible, without hearing the words spoken, to determine the full meaning of the question, for if the emphasis of the speaker should be placed on the words *lawful;* the question would then be, not concerning who might put her away, or for what cause, but if a separation at all was *lawful.* If the emphasis of the speaker should be placed on the word *man,* the question would then be, not concerning the lawfulness of the separation, or for what cause, but if the *husband* alone, without consent of his wife or any other person, might put her away.

But if the emphasis should be placed on the word *cause,* the question would then be, not concerning who might put her away, or the lawfulness of the separation, but whether she might be put away for *every cause,* or only *some causes,* and as the question is doubtful, so is the answer. He tells them, in the beginning God created male and female, for which cause a man should leave father and mother, cleave unto his wife, and they twain should be one flesh; what therefore God hath joined together let not man put asunder. That Moses indulged them in putting away their wives on account of their hard hearts; that it was not so in the beginning, that whosoever put away his wife, except for fornication, and married again, committed adultery.

In the fore part of his discourse he undoubtedly referred to that secret and powerful instinct, or strong mutual affection, that joined men and women together as at the beginning, in a state of nature; such as we before observed united Jacob unto Rachel when seven years seemed but as a few days, for the love he had unto her, and these he calls those whom God hath joined together; and such let not man put asunder, he could not mean the priest, the magistrate, or themselves, for they are not God.

In the next place, he forbids the cruel custom of the husband alone putting away his wife for every cause; without regarding her feeling or situation, and declares, such as do and marry again, commit adultery.

The whole of the discourse amounts to this, that such as are joined together by strong, mutual affection, let none cause

their

their ſeparation, and let the huſband alone put away his wife for no cauſe but fornication.

Neither of which declarations affects our argument in the leaſt, that men and women may not part by mutual conſent, or laws of the land, or when mutual hatred has taken place, and marry again when God ſhall join them together as at the beginning. But it ſeems as if this paſſage had been the occaſion of all thoſe ſcruples, concerning the ſeparation of man and wife, in the early ages of Chriſtianity, and handed down to us until this day.

And ſo it ſhould ſeem from the three ſucceeding verſes of of the ſame chapter, Matthew xix. from verſe the 10th. to the 13th. compared with Matthew, chapter v. from the 27th. to the 31ſt. verſe, as if emaſculation was adviſed; and as ſuch, ſome of the firſt fathers of the church believed it, and received it; but ſurely ſuch doctrines need not a ſerious refutation.

And here we ſubmit to the judicious Reader, what merit is due to thoſe (the greater part of mankind) who implicitly follow guides; and what to thoſe who reject them, in many caſes, in favour of common ſenſe and their own underſtandings.

If our Creator, as we before obſerved, ſeeketh or requireth our infelicity, he hath then no longer the attribute of a God, but of a devil. But if our good affections are miſled by our inſtructors, they are converted into evil affections, and drawn from their proper objects, while we ourſelves have eyes to ſee and hearts to underſtand, then is our Creator guiltleſs. For if we, having eyes and underſtanding, freely give them to our guides and walk without, then are our ſelves only accountable for our ſtumbling and the pains and bruiſes we feel in conſequence thereof.

It will be next ſaid, what has been the univerſal cuſtom for ſo many ages, muſt have had ſome great advantage or benefit ariſing therefrom; found out by the experience of paſt ages that we cannot immediately apprehend, but upon a trial, otherwiſe would be found extremely injurous to ſociety. This obliges us, as far as we know, to relate the cuſtoms of other countries.

The Indians of America and Negroes of Africa, and ſavage nations of various kinds, live according to nature, that is, they unite or part, as pleaſes them, without compulſion; generally unite and live as man and wife, and are faithful to each other as long as they live agreeably to natural inſtinct.

In France and Italy every man has but one wife, but every wife has, if ſhe pleaſes, a lover that conſtantly viſits and attends her, with her huſband, to all public places, and the

the hufband looks upon him as his friend, and efteems his wife in proportion to the rank and quality of her lover; this gives him no uneafinefs, becaufe he acts in the fame capacity to another lady, if he pleafes.

In England, it is faid, the nobility marry to add to their rank and eftates, but indulge feparate pleafures afterwards, at plays, balls, mafquerades, dancing matches, and other diverfions, without offence taken on either fide.

In Turkey a man may have four wives and as many concubines as he pleafes, but if a complaint comes to a magiftrate that he doth not perform the duty of an hufband once a week, he is obliged to put fome of them away. In Perfia a man takes as many wives as he pleafes, and for what time they agree.

In India the women are compelled, by the cuftom of the country, to burn themfelves alive with their difeafed hufband, in honour to their memory.* This is fulfilling the text literally, what God hath joined together, let no man put afunder; and fhows the impropriety of adhering too ftrictly to the letter, in matters of great importance to our welfare.

Here are two extremes, and it is moft probable, that there are different degrees of practice between them. And if we may judge reafonably here, as in moft other cafes, the beft mark to ftop at is the middle way, for the powers of nature in all animate, as well as inanimate bodies, gravitate to a middle line, like the vibrations of a pendulum, whofe center of gravity is equidiftant from the extremes of its motion, and our prefent practice is but one degree diftant from the laft mentioned worft extreme.

From the above-mentioned inftances it doth appear, the fentiments of mankind in general are very different from thofe of our prefent practice, and that there are no inconveniences arifing to the public from one cuftom more than another, except the happinefs the parties may receive themfelves, and thereby communicate to others; which furely themfelves ought to be the beft judges of.

Then the queftion will finally terminate here, are they, or are they not, judges of their own happinefs? If they are, why are

* As fome of our Readers may incline to doubt the truth of this account, we refer them to Doctor Hurd's Hiftory of the Religion of different Nations, where they may fee the practice largely and particularly related. Alfo Marius D'Alligny, in his Hiftory of the Heathen Deities, faith it is a cuftom of the Indians in Afia to this day to facrifice and bury the deareft wives of Princes with them; for they believe in the immortality of the foul, and therefore fend fuch perfons as have been dear to them, to ferve them in another world, and keep them company; but later accounts fay the practice is falling into difufe all over Indoftan.

are they reſtrained by law and religion from exerciſing it? if they are not, why are they allowed the liberty of exerciſing it in other things? why are they not compelled to follow the ſame calling, live on the ſame land, and poſſeſs the ſame property they have received by gift or purchaſe during their lives, or the duration of ſaid property? are not the reaſons for the one as ſtrong as for the other?

We would not, by any means, be underſtood, by propoſing divorce, that we deſire to leſſen the ſolemnity of marriage, or weaken the ſacredneſs of the marriage promiſe in any reſpect, during their union; but only, that a ſincere union of hearts do accompany a union of hands, from which alone, all our other enjoyments, as from a ſecret ſource, are derived: as ſtreams flowing from a ſweet, clear, and pure fountain, without which every thing is lifeleſs, inſiped and diſagreeable; and that in proportion to the diſharmony that ſubſiſts here, or on the contrary, all is pleaſing.

And here we beg leave to communicate our ſentiments on marriage in the lines of that elegant and ſublime poet, who is ſaid once to have employed his pen in vindicating the ſame cauſe we do now.

"Hail wedded Love, miſterious law, true ſource
Of human offspring, ſole propriety
In Paradiſe of all things common elſe.
By thee adult'rous luſt was driv'n from men
Among the beſtial herds to range; by thee
Founded in reaſon, loyal, juſt, and pure,
Relations dear, and all the charities
Of father, ſon, and brother firſt were known.
Far be it, that I ſhould write thee ſin or blame,
Or think the unbefitting holieſt place,
Perpetual fountain of domeſtic ſweets,
Whoſe bed is undefil'd and chaſte pronounc'd,
Preſent, or paſt, as ſaints and patriarchs us'd.
Here love his golden ſhafts employs, here lights
His conſtant lamp, and waves his purple wings,
Reigns here and revels; not in the bought ſmile
Of harlots, loveleſs, joyleſs unindear'd,
Caſual fruition; nor in court amours,
Mix'd dance, or wanton maſk, or midnight ball,
Or ſerenate, which the ſtarv'd lover ſings
To his proud fair, beſt quited with diſdain."

But all the arguments hitherto uſed in favour of divorce to procure matrimonial bliſs, will doubtleſs militate greatly againſt us with a great number of devout perſons, who believe

lieve that the rewards they will receive in another life, will be in proportion to the voluntary punishment they shall receive in this. To such we must freely own that all our wits are exhausted, and arguments are at an end; we can only leave them to enjoy what they take to be their greatest good, and assure them, they will not be envied or molested in their so doing, if they do not molest others in the enjoyment of what they take to be their good.

We beg the Reader's pardon for making one more quotation, from that solemn and much admired poem, Young's Night Thoughts.

" Pleasure's the mistress of the etherial powers;
For her contend the rival Gods above:
Pleasure's the mistress of the world below;
And well it is for man, that pleasure charms;
How would all stagnate, but for pleasure's ray!
How would the frozen stream of action cease!
What is the pulse of this so busy world?
The love of pleasure: that through every vein,
Throws motion, warmth; and shuts out death from life,
Is nought but virtue to be prais'd, as good?
Why then is health prefer'd before disease?
What nature loves is good, without our leave,
And where no future drawback cries, " beware"
Pleasure, tho' not from virtue, should prevail.
'Tis balm to life and gratitude to heaven;
How cold our thanks for bounties unenjoyed!
The love of pleasure is man's elder born,
Born in his cradle, living to his tomb;
Wisdom, her younger sister, tho' more grave,
Was meant to minister, and not to mar,
Imperial pleasure, queen of human hearts.
Pleasure came from heaven,
In aid to reason was the Goddess sent;
To call up all its strength by such a charm.
Pleasure, first succours virtue, in return,
Virtue gives pleasure an eternal reign.
What but the pleasure of food, friendship, faith,
Supports life; natural, civil and divine?
'Tis from the pleasure of repast we live;
'Tis from the pleasure of applause we please;
'Tis from the pleasure of belief we pray.
All prayer would cease if unbeliev'd the prize.
It serves ourselves, our species, and our God;
And to serve more, is past the sphere of man.

Glide,

Glide, then, forever, pleasure's sacred stream!
Thro' Eden as Euphrates ran it runs,
And fosters ev'ry growth of happy life;
Makes a new Eden where it flows."

The above must be understood to mean virtuous pleasure, in common occurrences and occasions of life, as well as those of religion; and if such are its salutary effects, what must be the effect of the contrary, I leave the Reader to judge, by attending to his own feelings in some unhappy moments he may have experienced.

We believe it will be readily admitted, that there is no portion of the lives of mankind so extremely pleasant; as when about to take possession of a lovely and agreeable companion: except the enjoyment they may receive afterward, in finding their expectations fully satisfied: until some untoward circumstance, incident, or misfortune puts an end to their felicity. And yet this blessing, according to our present practice, can never be enjoyed by one of the parties, but once in a life-time. And if their joys should chance to be short, all the rest is little better than distraction. In vain will they strive to find them again in wealth, honours, or promotion; they may kindle the fires of hell, and ransack nations, or destroy neighbours, according to their respective situations and capacities in life, yet they will still meet with nothing but disappointment in their enjoyments. Or if there is any thing in this world, that would excite virtuous and amiable dispositions in men and women, it is the thought and ambition of recommending themselves to virtuous and amiable companions; more especially when in distress with one that is otherwise. The expectation of such good fortune if it should never happen, would make them incline more to good, virtuous, and worthy actions than otherwise they would do.

If divorce was declared not only lawful by the legislature, but honourable by the ministers and elders of religious bodies, (without which, the law would not have its full effect) it would probably remove one of the most melancholy misfortunes of the human being—suicide.* For certainly it is a most odious reproach

* We may observe, our Creator in framing the passions of the human soul, has wisely preserved a balance between our private and public affections; in order to secure the duty we owe to others as well as ourselves; for where there is a strong propensity to private affection, there is one equally strong to the public—a love of reputation. And when a strong private affection, no way interfering with the good of the public, is rendered infamous by means of law and religion; then the soul is exceedingly agitated by different impulses; and strongly impelled different

proach to the rulers of any people, to see their subjects go distracted and destroy themselves on account of their mis-government, or misfortunes that might easily be removed.

Cruel men and women would then be afraid to misuse and abuse their good, worthy partners, whom they know to be better than themselves; but would be induced to act the lover instead of acting the tyrant.

It would probably prevent fraud and deception in courtship. It would tend greatly to industry, as men and women would exert themselves much more to support those they loved, than those they did not; this is plain in the change we often see in young people, for the better or worse after marriage.

Parents might not then forever lament the loss of an only son, or an only daughter, by an imprudent, precipitate marriage. Many bachelors might not then remain so long unmarried, and disgrace religion and mankind with their vices. Many young women would then become virtuous wives and mothers; comfortable to their friends, useful and ornamental to society, who, as circumstances are at present, do frequently bring disgrace upon themselves and their sex, and a burden on others. And we believe the like of these would not so often be forsaken by those who have deceived them, if the ideas of perpetual bondage did not intimidate them. Every plea whatever for unlawful commerce between the sexes would then be taken away. If reasonable liberty of parting was given, the desire of it would be frequently removed. Continual enmity and ill-will between the relatives of the respective parties disagreeing in marriage would cease. It would inculcate more friendly and beneficent ideas of the wisdom and goodness of Divine Providence in the disposition of human affairs, and dispose mankind more sincerely to reverence and adore the great Author of their being.

 If

different ways and greviously tormented. And if the sensation is violent it will occasion involuntary watching or waking, and when this is the case, body and mind reciprocally act as a stimulus upon each other, encreasing their sensations; until the soul, inflamed with furious impatience, instantly bursts the strongest bands and bounds of nature, and flings herself into the ocean of spirits from whence she sprang. And the disaster speaks aloud to the world, in the most pointed, explicit language, that may not be mistaken; that the laws of men have perverted the laws of Providence, and these catastrophies are as beacons set upon a hill that cannot be hid, to warn foreigners and all others of the danger of breathing the tainted air of such a soil: for although the body may escape destruction the soul or mind may not, if we may presume the same causes to have the same effect, on the same kind of beings; and we believe if the number of these in this country, were strictly taken and made public, they would greatly exceed what can easily be imagined.

If the number of objects that wish for a change are but few, their liberty can do no harm; if many, they ought to be the more regarded, and attention paid to their situations.

The offspring of happy matches would be, by nature as well as by education and example, less viciously inclined. For we believe the qualities and dispositions that are contracted by habit, are propagated afterwards by generation, as is visible in the wildness and tameness of young animals from their respective parents: also in the ferocity and docility of those persons descended from free or enslaved nations: likewise the uncivilized nature of young savages, longing to live the same sort of life of their parents, although otherwise educated.

Perhaps it might be a step towards restoring the golden age so much desired, for certainly those countries approach the nearest to it where there are no wars, but where agriculture and population are in their highest perfection, as in China, where their customs are very different from ours in this respect.

Perhaps none would oppose this alteration but those who were conscious of having companions better than themselves, and who might be apprehensive such would become dissatisfied with their situation.

No distinction of preference in favour of either sex ought to be made when nature has made none.

Thus, free citizens of America, we have briefly and without any ornament of stile, represented to you such of the many truths, relative to our situation in respect to marriage, as must strike the apprehension of the most indifferent observer. It would be doing injustice to your humanity and feelings, as men and as Christians, to suppose you will not take the subject under your serious consideration, and communicate your sentiments to each other; and finally propose such alterations and amendments in the laws and customs of our country, as will tend to the benefit of those unhappy individuals who have never wilfully, in this respect, transgressed the laws of God or man; or, done any thing to incur your resentment or displeasure, and whose infelicity calls yet louder for relief than their failings call for censure; and that you will not let other matters so much engross your care and attention, that you cannot sympathize with, and feel for, the afflictions and distresses of such of your worthy fellow-citizens, who are united to you by the strongest ties of affinity and affection, and also as neighbours, friends, and members of the same community with yourselves; neither suffer them to remain under that contempt and disregard that ever is the

lot

lot of the unfortunate; nor let ignorance, bigotry and superstition, any longer govern your understanding, by suffering one doubtful text of scripture (which is evidently misunderstood) a means of destroying the happiness of multitudes, without a prospect of redress, for endless generations; therefore, we trust, that you will generously show an example of liberality and wisdom to the rest of the Christian nations, by immediately setting at liberty all those who suffer under the severe restrictions of cruel, tormenting partners; which would make them valuable and worthy members of society; a comfort to themselves and their friends, and an ornament to human nature; and by so doing you will doubtless receive the grateful thanks of such, and the honour and approbation of all good men.

We shall now conclude, with addressing a few words to those on whose behalf we have been writing this essay.

O ye unhappy people, unto whom the bands of wedlock has entailed wretchedness instead of joy! Perhaps your situations may be without remedy; it is so, doubtless, without you seek it, which it is your duty to do both for yourselves and for posterity. But it is not without hope if you exert yourselves according to your ability; be not ashamed of your situation; it is your misfortune and not your fault; either of you might have been completely blest and happy with another partner, had it been your good fortune to have united with one suitable to your disposition and circumstances: but it is never too late to try to be revenged on fortune. Let your situation in life be what it may, your circumstances high or low, if you can but be thoroughly reconciled to those who where once your fond choice, and renew the days of courtship and felicity you once felt, not only by avoiding every thing that is found to be disagreeable to your spouses, but also exerting yourselves in every thing that is serviceable, generous, kind and freindly; you will then be revenged on fortune, and heaven will have blessings yet in store. But if this is not practicable, as is most commonly the case, apply decently to the legislature for redress, to pass such laws for your relief, and others in the like situation, as they shall think necessary and proper; they certainly cannot refuse so reasonable a requisition who have granted relief to a less respectable class of mankind, without request, in a less painful situation. But nevertheless, as sudden innovations from customs long established in any country, are not easily obtained, more especially where it is a part of the established religion of the people. Those of some rank and character in the world, who shall have virtue and resolution enough, to set some exam-

ples

ples of separating and marrying again, great part of mankind would be more indebted to them for their liberty and happiness, than unto those who delivered this country from British oppression. For their virtuous courage, resolution and magnanimity, would break the way for others to follow; and a law would at last be obtained in their favour. Thus we see the first advocate for the liberty of slaves in America, Benjamin Lay,* a worthy and good man, gave away great part of his substance, when in Jamaica, to relieve them; and wrote and testified, in all places, violently against the practice of slave-keeping; and, when in America, would sometimes enter meeting-houses, and sprinkle blood upon the people, and tell them the blood of the slaves was in like manner upon their heads, if they did not repent and free their slaves.

It was by such remarkable exertions as these, that almost every sect in religion has been established, without which the attention of mankind are not roused or excited, but every thing goes on in its former course, and glides down the stream of time unnoticed; and the misfortunes of a few are unregarded and unrelieved; or, according to the expression of a poet, on another occasion,

"Unrespited, unpitied, unreprieved ages of hopeless end."

* Succeeding writers have ungenerously passed over this worthy person's name in silence, and given the honour of the testimony to those people who excommunicated him from their society, for this very conduct. See his own writings.

F I N I S.

ELIZABETH *in her Holy Retirement.*

An ESSAY To Prepare a Pious WOMAN FOR HER Lying in.

OR,

MAXIMS and METHODS of PIETY,

To Direct and Support an HANDMAID OF THE LORD, Who Expects a Time of Travail.

On Gen III. 16.

Luthers [and Mankinds.] Exclamation

O *most Miserable Misery!*

The Divine Relief;

I. Tim. II. 16. *Notwithstanding, she shall be Saved in Child bearing*

BOSTON in *N. E.* Printed by *B. Green*, for *Nicholas Boone*, at his Shop in Corn Hill. 1710

The PREFACE.

THE *Occasion* & *Intention of the* ESSAY *now before us, is to be declar'd.* *The Writer thought it One part of* Pastoral *Diligence* & *Vigilance, to allow a Proportion of Seasonable Visits, unto Such of his Flock, as he was informed from time to time, were near their* Lying in; *and therein to Address them with such* Admonitions of Piety *as were most suited unto their* present Condition, & *such as their* Pregnant Condition *most Reasonably Awaken them to hearken to. It was part of* Timothies *charge;* To intreat such, with all Purity. *He remembred, who they were whom* David follow'd, *when he was a* Shepherd; & *whom the Glorious LORD will* Gently Lead, *when He* feeds His Flock. *He Pondered the Tenderness, which the Great GOD our Saviour, has Expressed for* Women with Child, *in many other Passages of His Bible, besides the* XXI Chapter *of* Exodus. *He was in* Pain, *to think, that a* Sudden Destruction, & *a fearful and endless One, should* come as

Trava

Travail upon a Woman with Child. *upon any who* draw near a Time of Travail. *He found his Addresses Acceptable and Serviceable. At length he resolved upon a further Method, of more Effectually* [illegible]*ing at many, whom he cannot have Opportunities Personally to Speak unto. He* [illegible]*eads*, Exod. I. 21. The MIDWIVES [illegible]eared God. *It is to be hoped, They gene*[illegible]*ally do so. He therefore Publishes this* [illegible]SSAY, *and furnishes the Pious* Midwives [illegible]*ith Some Numbers thereof, that they may* [illegible]*end or Give, the Little BOOK, unto those, by* [illegible]*hom they know an* Hour of Travail and [illegible]rouble *to be Expected. Certainly the* Hand[illegible]aids of the Lord, *will receive this as a* [illegible]essenger *from HIM unto them! When the* [illegible]*oly* ELIZABETH *Retired for so many* [illegible]onths, *into the* Hilly Country, *you may* [illegible]*stly conceive, that she was Employ'd in Ex*[illegible]*ci*[illegible]*s of the same Tenour and Tendency with* [illegible]*ch as are here Prescribed. None but Filthy* [illegible]*d Hard.* Scoffers, *will cast Contempt on the* [illegible]*er of Prescriptions, that are so adapted unto* [illegible]*e of the most* Frequent, *and yet* One *of* [illegible]*e most* Solemn, *Occasions in the World.*

THI[illegible]

THE

Duties and the Supports OF One Expecting an Hour of Travail.

AN Addreſs is now to be made unto an *Handmaid* of the LORD, who Expects e're long the arrival of a Time, when her *Loins* will be *filled with Pain, Pangs will take hold on her, the Pangs of a Woman, which travaileth.* 'Tis *Now,* Sure, if ever, a Time, wherein it may be Expected, that ſhe will hearken to the Counſils of God *This,* if any, is the Time, wherein the Methods and Motions of Divine Grace, will *find her*; And if ever you will *hear the Voice of God* at all, *To Day you will hear His Voice.*

The

The Hazards and Hardships undergone by the *Travailing* Daughters of *Eve*, make a Considerable Article of the *Curse*, which the *Transgression* where-into she was *Deceived*, has brought upon the miserable World. But our Great Redeemer has procured this Grace from God, unto the *Daughters of Zion*, that the *Curse* is turn'd into a *Blessing*. The Approach of their *Travails* proves to them an Occasion and an Excitement for those Exercises of *Piety*, that Secure to them, and prepare them for, Eternal *Blessedness*; and they may Say, *Tis Good for me that I have been Afflicted*. Unto this it is very much owing, that tho' thro' the Evident Providence of God watching over Humane Affairs, there is pretty near an equal Number of *Males* & *Females* born, yet the Number of the *Males* who are apparently *Pious*, and partakers of a *New Birth*, is not so great as that of the *Females*. Indeed, it will argue a wonderful stupidity of Soul, and Obstinacy in sin, if the Dangers and Sorrows whereto you are now obnoxious, do not make you Serious, and cause you Seriously

ously to Consider on your Condition, and bring you to a Considerate, Sollicitous, Effectual Preparation for Eternity: if you are not now ready to hear the *Admonitions of God your Saviour.* You are now Addressed, with some Advice from Heaven, in hopes, that *This is the Time*, for you to be more than ever *Made Wise unto Salvation.*

And the first thing, to be propounded unto you, is; That you do not indulge an indecent *Impatience* or *Discontent*, at the State, which you find ordered for you. It will be a very blameable Indecency and Indiscretion in you, to be *Dissatisfyed* at your State of *Pregnancy.* Froward Pangs of *Dissatisfaction*, harboured, and humoured, in you, because you See that *in Sorrow you are to bring forth Children*, may displease Heaven, and bring yet more *Sorrow* upon you. It will indeed look too *Unnatural* in you, to complain of a State, whereinto the *Laws of Nature* established by God, have brought you. The will of the Great God, has been declared in these Terms, 1 Tim. V. 14. *I will that the Younger Women*

ven, *Marry, bear Children.* When you
nd that a Conception has brought you
nto *Child-bearing* circumstances, Let
our Submission to the *Will* of God there-
n, be full of Satisfaction, and Resigna-
ion. Let this Thought now carry you
Cheerfully thro' all the *Uneasiness*, which
s now become Unavoidable : *Great*
GOD ; I am thine ; And I am willing to be,
ll that thou wilt have me to be ! Indeed,
t is to be esteemed *a Mercy* of God, that
One principal End of *Marriage*, is thus
ar in an *Honourable way* of being answe-
ed with you. It was acknowledged as
*a Mercy, in the Old Time, by the Holy Wo-
men, who trusted in God.* They Look'd
on themselves as *Mercifully Visited of God*,
when they had conceived. It was en-
ertained, as a Gracious *Promise* of God
unto His People, *That they should have an
Offspring.* It was esteemed, The *taking
away of a Reproach.* *Barrenness* was Threatened, and Bewayled, as a *Calamity* : A
Punishment for a *Michol.* The Saints
made it a frequent Petition in their
Prayers, That *God would bestow Children
upon them.* I shall Speak but in a Language

guage which your Sex of Old would have allow'd of, if I now tell you; *That God has Look'd upon His Handmaid, and Remembred her, and not forgotten her, but given her to Conceive.* For I must go on to tell you, That upon your giving up your self unto the Lord, Your Children become the *Children of God. They are my Children,* Saith your God: It is a *Child of God,* that you have now within you: What a Consolation! 'Tis a Subject and a Servant of a Glorious CHRIST, whose *Bones are now growing in the Womb, of her that is with Child*: It is, a *Member* of His Mystical Body, which is now *Shaping in Secret*, and *Curiously to be wrought.* An Excellent Gentlewoman, who had a Strong presage, which prov'd a True One, of her *Dying* by her Travail, yet you read in her *Legacy* Written for her unborn Child, her *Desire of God, that she might be a Mother to One of His Children.* I add, You are to bring forth a Creature of Excellent Faculties; and One from whom the Lord will have glory for Eternal Ages. You don't know, what an Instrument of Good this Child may

prov

prove in the World. As mean a *Mother* as you, has brought forth an *Hero*. Nor do you know, what a *Possession*, what an *Enjoyment*, this Child may prove unto *You* particularly. Who can foresee, how far, *This Same shall comfort you!* This is the first *Lesson of Piety*, to be urged upon you: Whatever *Sickness* you now labour under, be not *Sick* of your present State. Rebuke, Repress, Restrain, all Disquiet of Mind; *Why art thou cast down, O my Soul, and why art thou disquieted within me? Hope in God!* It is all for the best. O *Builder up* of the Church of God in the World; Say, and Pray, *O my God, Help me always to like the State, wherein thou performest the thing, that is appointed for me.*

But now, the *Next* thing to be propounded, is; That you hasten into a State of *Safety* for *Eternity*: Yea, This is the very *First* Thing that you have to do, upon your being Sensible of a *Conception*. For ought you know, your *Death* has entred into you, and you may have conceived That which determines but about Nine Months more at the most, for you to Live in the World. **Preparation for Death** is that Most Reasonable and Most Seasonable thing, to which you must now Apply your self. It will do you *no Hurt.* You will Dy not One Minute the Sooner for it. And being *Fit to Dy*, you will be but the more *Fit to Live.*

Daughter of Sorrows; Will you give a Great and Just Attention? *Set your Heart unto these things*; They are *not Vain Things*; Your Everlasting *Life* is concerned in them.

You must in the first Place be very sensible, That Except you are *Born again*, it had been *Good for you that you had never been born*; Except you have Experience of a true *Conversion* to God, you unavoidably *Perish.* The *Sorrows* of *Child-birth*, will be to you, but the *Beginning of Sorrows*, and of such as know no *End.* Think with your self, *If the Pains of my Travail, which I hope, will be quickly over, were to last a thousand years, how wretched, Oh how wretched were I! And yet, if my Peace be not made with the Holy God, I may fear to be more terribly dealt withal! Oh! Tis a fearful*

fearful thing to fall into the Hands of the Living God! Some Women that have been in *Horror of Conscience*, have declared, that all the Anguish of bringing more than Seven Children into the World has been much more tolerable, than that horrible Anguish of their Mind. How Intolerable then, Oh! how Insupportable, will be the Anguish, in the Conscience of a Sinner, banished from God, fearfully Scorched and Tortur'd with Impressions from the Wrath of God; and cast into a *Place of Torments*, into the *Place of Dragons*! Let the Thought of this, mightily Quicken and Hasten your *Flight from the Wrath to come*. In this Flight you must first, Acknowledge; *O Holy Lord, I am not Able to Turn unto thee.* You must also Acknowledge; *O Holy Lord, I am not Worthy, that thou shouldest help me to Turn.* Without this *Humiliation*, you will never *Turn*. But then, go on with proper Acknowledgments of *Sovereign Grace*, to beg of the Gracious Lord; *O Glorious One, Turn thou me, and I shall be turned.* Proceed now, and Ponder, on your Sinful and Woful circumstances before the Lord; Ponder,

Ponder, and Confess; *O Great God, I have Sinned, and Perverted that which is Right! I have Sinned, and I have done very foolishly!* Examine your past Life; Reflect on all the Errors and Follies of your Life. Look back with Bitterness of Soul, upon every Sin, that you can charge your self withal; Every Violation of the *Ten Commandments*, on each of which you should make a Pause; Every Miscarriage, in every *Condition*, in every *Relation*, in every *Employment*. Be as much afraid of Leaving any Sin unconfessed, as you would be of having the *After-birth left in you*, after your Travail. And because you have not *Observed*, and have not *Remembred* Thousands of your Sins, bewail this *Inadvertency* also, as not the least of your Sins. With Astonishment cry out, *O Holy God, I am a most Polluted Creature! My Life has been a very course of Sin. Innumerable Evils compass me about; My Sins, my Sins are Numberless. My Heart fails me, when I think upon them!* At the same time, Go up as far as the *Original Sin*, which is the *Fountain* of all your Sins: The Terrors of *Child-bearing* which are now upon you, do very properly lead you to bewail your Share in the *Sin of your First Parents*; and to bewail with Bitter Tears, that *Corrupt Nature*, which by a Derivation from your *Next Parents* you brought into the World with you. Think, *Lord, I was conceived in Sin; I was born a Leper; and my poor Child will be so too!* But herewithal, you must very deeply affect your self, with the horrid and heinous Evil, which there is in every Sin. Afflict your self, with it; *What have I done? O Great God, How wickedly have I Deny'd thee, and Defy'd thee, and Despised the Blood of my Saviour, and Hearkened unto Satan before my Saviour, and chose Earth and Hell, before the Joyes of Heaven, as often as I have Sinned against thee! I have been a Fool that have made Light of Sin. This, This has been an heavy Aggravation of all my Sin.* Go on then to an amazing View of the Deplorable State into which you are fallen by your Sin Think with Amazement; "Wo is unto me, that I have Sinned! The Infinite God is angry with "me; And who knows the Power of His "Anger! The Devil demands me as his "Captive; I am a Prey to the Terrible "one.

"one. Sin Tyrannizes over me; I am
" held in chains of Darkness. If I dy, as
" I am, what will become of me! Who
" can dwell in those Everlasting Burn-
" ings, which will be the Doom of those
" who dy unpardoned! O Wretched one
" that I am; who shall deliver me!
Being brought into the *Contrition* of this
Distress. NOW, Behold the admirable
SAVIOUR provided for you; The JE-
SUS, who is *God Manifest in Flesh*, God
and Man in One Person: The *Saviour*,
who is *Able to Save you unto the Uttermost*;
the *Saviour* who bids you *Look unto Him
and be Saved*. Oh! Take the Encouragement of that Sweet Word, Joh. VI. 37.
*Him that comes unto me I will in no Wise cast
out*. Cry to Him, *O my dear Saviour, Draw
me to thee; Oh! make me thine, and Save
me*. Let no Apprehension of your own
Vileness make you despair to find Acceptance with Him; Nor let any Good in
your selves Embolden your Hope & Plea,
that you may be Accepted. Come under no Recommendation but that of your
own dreadful *Necessity*, and *Confusion*, and
the *Triumphs of Grace*, which arise from
 the

the Salvation of such a *Loathsome Sinner !*

NOW Behold the *Sacrifice* of your Saviour, and Plead, " O Great God, let the " Blood of thy Son, cleanse me from all " my Sin. Be Reconciled unto me, be- " cause my JESUS has been my Sacrifice! Behold the *Righteousness* of your Saviour, and Plead, " O Great God, Thy Son has " answered thy Law, as a Surety for me. " My Advocate Shews His Righteous- " ness for me ; therefore deliver me from " going down to the Pit. That this your *Precious Faith* in the *Sacrifice* & *Righteousness* of your Saviour may be *Justified* with a Good *Evidence* to the Sincerity of it, Resign your self up to the *Holy Spirit* of your Saviour ; Consent that the *Spirit of Holiness* take Possession of you. Yield the consent of a Conquered Soul ; " O " Spirit of the Holy One ; I am willing, " Oh! do thou make me willing, that " thou come and Renew me in the Spi- " rit of my Mind ; make me a New " Creature ; Produce the Holy & Love- " ly Image of God upon me. Embitter " all my Sin to me ; Enable me to bear " every Cross thou appointest for me.

" Wean

" Wean me from this World; Reign in " my Heart; Oh! Dwell there, as in " thy Temple. Guide me by thy Coun- " sil; Bring me to thy Glory. So in the Promised Strength of Heaven, take up *Resolutions* of Universal and Perpetual Piety. Come to that Piety; Psal. CXIX. 57. *Thou art my Portion, O Lord; I have said, That I would keep thy Words.* Thus the *New birth* is carried on! Thus you have gone through the Work, that will disarm *Death* of all its *Terror*; that may Enable you to Sing, *O Death, where is thy sting!* If you should now be *Treating* with your *Death*, yet you may keep *Rejoycing in the Hope of the Glory of God.* When the Handmaid of the Lord, had the Proposals of Heaven made unto her, She complied; Luk. I. 38. *Behold, The Handmaid of the Lord; be it unto me according to thy Word*; and she became in a *Transcendent Sense* owner of a CHRIST immediately. O Handmaid of the Lord, The Great Saviour, who condescended once to make a Virgin, *The Tabernacle of God*, proposes this to you; *Shall I be thy Saviour; and Heal thee, and Lead thee, and* ale thee for ever more? Let your Answer be, *Behold, the Handmaid of the Lord; be it unto me according to thy Word.* In an Agreeable sense you become owner of a CHRIST immediately. Now, if you Dy, To *Dy will be gain!*

You would have the Great Saviour hear your *Calls* unto Him for His Help, when in *your Travail you have Sorrow, because your Hour is come.* You will then, with Agony *Cry out, Oh! my God, Help me.* And will be in a Sad case, if He turn a *Deaf Ear* upon your cry. There is all possible *Reason*, that you should *Now* hear His *Calls* to you; and by Obedience to His Gospel, prevent the Execution of that Threatning; *As He cryed, and they would not Hear, so they cried, and I would not Hear, saith the Lord of Hosts.* He calls, *Abhor thy Sins*; Let your Answer be, *Lord, I Abhor them!* He calls, *Renounce all Trust in thy own Worth or Strength*; Let your Answer be, *Lord, I Renounce it!* He calls, *Embrace thy offered Redeemer in all His Offices*; Let your Answer be, *Lord, I Embrace Him.* O *Effectually called* One; say now, Mic. VII. 7. *I will wait for the God of my Salvation; my God will hear me!*

Were the Event of your *Travail*, much less uncertain than it is, yet the main Provision which you have to make against your *Lying in*, should be, That in the *Day of Judgment* your *Account* may be made *with Joy, and not with Grief.* In order to this, you must then be capable of saying, "O my Glorious Judge, The Sacrifice "and the Righteousness which is my Plea "for Everlasting Life, is in the Judg-"ment-Seat. Lord, Thou art it. My "Judge is my Advocate. Lord, I did, "by a Faith of thy Direction, Engage "thee to be So. That this *Faith* may not then be Rejected as a *Counterfeit* you must then be capable of Saying: "Lord, "Thou hast infused a principle into my "Soul, which tells me, That all Sin must "be Repented of. I could not come to "my Redeemer, without such a Princi-"ple But I have heartily and Earnest-"Repented of all my Sins; yea, as far "as I could find them out, I have parti-"cularly done so. And now, in order to that, it were desireable for you, to take a Catalogue of things *Forbidden* and *Required* in the *Ten Commandments* of the *Two*

Tables

Tables; and pass a *Judgment* on your selves according to the Discoveries which that *Glass* will give you of your self. That word is of a Vast Importance; 1 Cor. XI. 31. *If we would Judge our selves, we should not be Judged.* But it must then be found that this your *Faith* was not only *Sorry* for your *Evil Works*, but also, which will necessarily follow, *Zealous of Good Works.* O Anticipate the awful Transaction. Place your selves now as before the *Judgment-Seat of God.* Think, *When He Visits, what shall I answer Him!*

[illegible] you have managed your *Grand Concern.* What is to be next Propounded unto you, is, in the Words of the Apostle; Tim. II. 15. *She shall be Saved in Child-bearing, if they continue, in Faith, and Charity, and Holiness, with Sobriety.*

You see Holiness is a point of Great Consequence for the *Child-bearing Woman.* And what is *Holiness*, but a *Dedication unto God?* May God assist you now to *Dedicate* your self unto Him. Study, and contrive, *How to be the Lords*; In what methods you may Employ all your *Powers* to *Glorify the Lord.* Come into the *Covenant vant* of God ; and Kneeling before the Lord, thus Declare unto Him ; " O " Great God, Thou shalt be my God, " and Portion. Heavenly Father, make " me One of thy Children. O Son of " God, Thou shalt be my Shepherd ; O " Spirit of God, Thou shalt be my Quick- " ner. Lord, I Resolve to be thy Ser- " vant. I will Enquire after my Duty, " and persist in thy Service all my Days. If the Breach of the *Old Covenant* be that which has brought the Difficul[illegible] your *Travail,* with all other misch[illegible] upon you, what can you do better [illegible] as far as you can under the Wi[illegible] *New Covenant* ? But then when you bring your selves under this *Consecration* unto the Lord, you must bring your *Children* into it with you.

Tis particularly to be done, even for the *Unborn Child.* When 'tis become Sensible to you, that you have conceived you will do well, without any Delay to carry even this *Embryo* unto the Lord, and in some such manner as this *Devote* it unto Him. " O God of the Spirits of all " Flesh ; I bring to thee, even my Hoped " Offspring.

"Offspring. Oh! Let thy Holy Spirit
" now take an Early Possession of it.
" Oh, Form it, and Fill it, and make it an
" Everlasting Instrument of thy Praises
" in the World.

But you must Remember, that a *Detestation of all Sin*, is a thing wherein your *Holiness* is to shine, with a very convictive Splendor. *Holiness* is that *which cannot Look upon Iniquity*. The *Griefs* which you are now Suffering in your Body, are the *Frui*[illegible] *Sin*. Let your *Griefs* for all your *Si*[illegible]cited and Sharpened by them. [illegible] One of your frequent Indispositions: May you become disposed thereby to a greater *Loathing* of *Sin*, than you have yet had raised in you. This is, to be *Chastened, and made Partaker of Holiness*. Think on that Word; Jam. I. 15. *When Lust hath conceived, it brings forth Sin, and Sin when it is finished, brings forth Death.* And say, O *my Soul, Do not that abominable thing, which the Soul of God abominates: Let me chuse rather to Dy, than to Sin against the Holy One!*

Tis to be further Noted, That *Meditations*, assiduous and affectuous Meditations,

tions, on a Glorious CHRIST, are both *Instances* and *Incentives* of *True Holiness*. It is the most astonishing thing that ever was in the World; Gal. IV. 4. *God sent forth His Son, made of a Woman.* Oh, Meditate much on it, and with much Astonishment. " O Great Saviour, O Bright
" Emmanuel; How gloriously didst thou
" Humble thy self! Was there a Sinless
" Man conceived in a Virgin! Did the
" Son of God vouchsafe to Assume and
" Unite this Man, into His o[illegible]
" Person! Is there now lyin[illegible] Bo-
" som of the Eternal Son of God. [illegible],
" who was once an Infant in the Womb
" of a Virgin! A Man born of a Wo-
" man, who is more than a Man! God
" manifest in Flesh. A Man bred, and
" born, and nursed by a Woman; but
" this Man-Child caught up unto God
" and His Throne; and become the Lord
" of Angels, and of Worlds, and the Judge
" to whom all must give an Account. We
" are Sav'd thro that Illustrious Child
" bearing! O the Dignity put upon our
" poor Sex, in the Birth of such a Redee-
" mer! O the Assurance which the
" Distress

" Distressed Handmaids of the Lord have
" to find Help with such a Redeemer in
" their Time of Need! Yea, you may
improve this Consolation, in your Supplication for a *Safe Deliverance*, in the Hour
that is coming upon you. Plead, " O
" Good God, The Humiliation of my
" Saviour in the circumstances [illegible] His
' Nativity, has purchased this for me that
' I should be Saved in Child bearing; Oh,
' Save me graciously! O my Saviour,
' [illegible] thou wast born of a Woman, cer-
" [illegible] child bearing Women, may cry
" [illegible] for thy Protection, thy Assistence.
" I hope in thee for it; such Salvation
" belongs unto thee, O Lord!

You shall note this One thing more. 'Tis a Description of *Holiness*; Gal. IV. 19. *Little Children, Of whom I travail in birth again, until Christ be formed in you.* You have a *Child formed in you.* But, Oh! That you might have a CHRIST *formed in you*! Now, if you take up Right Thoughts of a Glorious CHRIST; if you have such a *Mind* as in a *Christ* you may see a Pattern of; if your *Walk* be such as a *Christ* has left you a Pattern of: Or,

Or, if you Love what a CHRIST Loves, and Hate what a CHRIST hates, and bear Afflictions and Abasements, with a CHRIST-like Patience, and are Crucified unto the World, in which a CHRIST was Crucified; Then you have a CHRIST *formed in you.* A CHRIST will be gloriously concerned for the welfare of such *Holy Women.*

But Sobriety must accompany this your *Holiness.* Indeed, the *Unborn Infant* will be *Naturally* and Powerfully and Profitably affected, by the *Sobriety* of an *Holy Mother.* The *Passions,* or the *Surfeits* of the *Mother,* make a strange Impression on the Infant; yea, on the Soul of it. Be *Temperate in all Things.* Keep your *Mind* in all the undisturbed Serenity that is possible. In your *Meats, Drinks, Rest,* use enough; but, *Nothing too much.* This *Temperance,* will dispose you to *Wait upon God,* in a due Frame for His Favours, and your *Offspring* will Enjoy the good Effects of it. Let the Conscience of the *Sixth Commandment,* make you Tender of your *Health.* If such Counsil had not been of some Consequence for the *Infant* also, the

 Ange'

Angel would not have Counselled the Wife of *Manoah*, as you remember he did. If also the *Intemperate Longings* of Women, are (as the Learned say) some unhappy *Signatures* of the Womans First Sin, left upon their Sex, this ought to render you as cautious as may be, of admitting them.

I said but now, To *Wait upon God*. And this you are to do, by pouring out your incessant **Prayers** unto Him. It is to be hoped, that you have been used unto *Prayers* all your Dayes. But certainly your *Pregnant Time*, should be above all a *Praying Time*. If you have never yet *Prayed Earnestly*, 'tis now a Time to do so; NOW a Time to have it said, *Behold she Prayes!* --- and to Lament it Penitently before the Lord, that you have been so hardly brought unto it. You will now Retire to Daily and Frequent and Fervent *Prayers*, for all the *Blessings of Goodness*. Your *Prayers*, must be *Cries*; *For thy Names sake, O Lord, Pardon my Iniquity, for it is great!* And, *O Lord, order my Steps in thy Word, and let not any Iniquity have Dominion over me.* And, *O Shew me*

thy

thy Marvellous Kindness in thy Strong City, and the Goodness thou hast laid up for them that Fear thee! With the *Pangs* and *Throwes* of a Distressed Soul, in your Prayers, you will *Cry* for such things, and *Lift up your Voice for such things.* But then you will more particularly Employ your *Prayers*, for an Happy and an Ea[sy] *Delivery*, in your Approaching *Trav[ail].* In your Prayers for this Mercy, [a Mercy, which is *Big* with a Thousand Mercies !] you will Plead the *Power* of God. Think on the Word Spoken to the Handmaid of the Lord ; Luk. I. 37. *With God nothing shall be unpossible.* Plead the *Mercy* of God. Think on the word wherewith she of Old comforted her Soul ; Lam. III. 25. *The Lord is Good unto them that wait for Him, to the Soul that Seeks Him.* Remember, that the Name of God is, *O Thou that hearest Prayer.* You know how to turn these things into *Prayer* ; how to make them the *Plea's* of your *Pra[yers].* But, Oh! Don't Forget now to Plead the Mediation of the *Saviour*, who was pleased to be, and Sometimes to call Himself, *The Son of the Hand-maid of the Lord.*

Let such as these be your *Groans*, before the Lord. "O most Powerful God, I "know, Thou canst do every thing. "There is nothing that can stand before "the Power of thy Almighty Arm. Lord, "If thou wilt, thou canst give me a Good "Time, in the Time of Trouble, that is "before me. According to the Greatness of thy Power, preserve One, that "is appointed to dy, if thou doest not "powerfully Step in to uphold and "Stengthen her. O Father of Mercies, "Deal Mercifully with thy Distressed "Hand-maid; Look Mercifully, and "with Pitty, on the Miseries, which the "Sin of the World has entailed upon "me. God be Merciful to me a Sinner. "Oh! Behold thy Beloved JESUS who "was made a Curse, that so we might "either not feel the Curse, or else get "Good out of the Curse. For the Sake "of thy JESUS, the Son of Man, who "is the Son of God, and whom thou "Lovest above all the Works of thy "Hands, and for the Sake of whom thou "Lovest all that fly unto Him; Oh! be "Favourable to me!

Let

Let your *Prayers* be those, Psal. XXXVIII. 21, 22. *Forsake me not, O Lord; O my God, be not far from me. Make Haste to help me, O Lord my Salvation.* Or these; Psal. XXII. 11. *Be not far from me: for Trouble is near; and there is none to Help.*

In these your *Prayers,* it would be of admirable Advantage, for you, to Search and find out the *Precious Promises* of God that may most of all Suit your Conditio[n] Present those *Promises* before the Lor[d] as containing and engaging of Blessing[s] which the *Blood* of the Lamb of God ha[s] bought for you. And Say, "Therefor[e] "has thy Hand-maid found in her Hea[rt] "to Pray this Prayer unto thee: O Lor[d] "God, Thou art that God, and these b[e] "thy Words, and thy Words be true, an[d] "thou hast Promised this Goodness unt[o] "thy Hand-maid; Therefore now l[et] "it please thee to Bless the House of th[y] "Hand-maid; For thou, O Lord Go[d] "hast Spoken it.

Behold, Some of the *Promises* and C[or]*dials,* that you have to Live upon.

Psal. XXXIV. 22.

None of them who trust in the Lord shall [be] Desolate.

Psal. LV. 22.

Cast thy Burden on the Lord, and He shall Sustain thee.

Psal. LVI. 3.

At what time I am afraid, I will Trust in thee.

Isa. XLI. 10.

Fear thou not, for I am with thee; Be not dismay'd, for I am thy God: I will Strengthen thee; yea, I will uphold thee, by the Right Hand of my Righteousness.

Heb. XIII. 5, 6.

He hath said, I will never leave thee, nor forsake thee. So that we may boldly say, The Lord is my Helper.

Isa. LXVI. 9.

Shall I bring to the Birth, and not cause to bring forth, saith the Lord!

Job V. 19.

He shall Deliver thee in Six Troubles, yea, in Seven there shall no Evil touch thee.

And now, *Having these Promises,* go Plead them with God; and let your Experience, be that which is related concerning an *Hand-maid of the Lord,* Praying for a Child; 1 Sam. I. 15, 15, 18. *She said, I am a Woman of a Sorrowful Spirit,* but

but have poured out my Soul before the Lord.--- *So the Woman went her way, and her Uneasiness continued no longer.*

That you may be the better furnished and quickened for your *Prayers*; you wil do well to *Read the Scriptures*: 'Tis you Duty, to *Search the Scriptures*. In th Scriptures, you may especially Single ot the *Book of Psalms*, for your Companio and Counsellour & Comforter. *Luth* Religious Wife, Said, That she had nev known the meaning of many Passages the *Psalms*, if *Afflictions* had not Expoun ded them unto her. Your *Afflictive* a *Anxious* condition, will make many pass ges in the *Psalms*, exceeding Relish and Agreeable. The Pious Author the Book Entituled, *A Present for Teem Women*, propounds to you, That y should Sing the *Psalms* considerately al by your self; because you will find, *Voice* quicken your Heart-affecting M ditation on the *Matter*; and he adds, *sides, it is most unquestionably Pleasant those Good Angels, who are Ministring rits to attend you for Good.* Accordi them; for the *Songs*, by which you

Harmonize with Heaven, and call in the Help thereof I commend unto you, Multitudes of Passages, which ly Scattered all over the Psalter; especially in the III Psalm; the IV the XVIII. the XXIII. the XXV; the XXVII; the XXXI; the XXXIX; the XLIII; the LI; the LXXI; the LXXXVI; the XCI; the CXVI; the CXVIII; the CXIX; the he CXXVII; the CXXX; the CXXXVIII; the CXLII. To which ou may add, the Prayer of *Jonah*; the ong of *Hannah*; and the Song of *Mary*. Nor are *Psalms* only, but *Alms* also, to accompany your *Prayers*. The XLI Psalm, ill tell you, what you are to think of iem. Our Saviour, how frequently, ow earnestly does He insist upon them! *y, Thy Merits, O my Saviour; are my only ;es; I shall never imagine my Alms to have y; But thy Commands, O my Saviour, ve directed them; therefore by my Alms I ill prepare for thy Mercies.* This is Pure igion. The *Prayers* have a distinguishing cacy, when it may be said, *Thy Prayers thy Alms are come up as a Memorial be-God.* You are taught, *That the Merciful*

ful shall obtain Mercy. It is a Sweet Word, Psal. XVIII. 25. *With the Merciful, thou wilt shew thy self Merciful.* Especially, when you Set apart your *Whole Dayes for Prayer* (which you will some-times do, as you shall be able to bear it,) you will on these Days dispense your *Alms*, with a particular *Liberality*. *Is not this the Fast that I have chosen*, Saith the Lord? And what if in the Dispensation of your *Alms*, your should have a Special Eye, to *Poor Child-bearing Women*, if you can hear of any Such, in Wants, and Straits, and grievous Necessities? You will have yet a more Special Eye, to such *Poor* as can *Pray* for you; and you will engage them to do it, with a *Daily Remembrance* of you.

What remains, is, for you to Enquire, Whether you have *Omitted no Duty*, the Omission whereof may be uneasy to you in a *Dying Hour*. Such a Duty often, is that of *Joining to a Particular Church*, and So, coming to the *Table* of the Lord, and there Laying Hold on His *Covenant*. If you have hitherto Delay'd this Duty, 'tis *now* High Time to do it. Wherefore *Now* first Secretly and Sincerely come into the

Co

Covenant of Life, by an Hearty Consent unto every Article of it. And then proceed Openly to *Seal* your Act and Deed in this way of God. Be *Heartily Willing* to be Delivered from all the Maladies and Miseries of your Soul; which is the first *Mark* of the Regenerate State: and then, Look on the *House of the Lord*, as an *Hospital* for a *Sin Sick Soul*; Give not way to Discouragements, by the Sight of what is *Amiss*, but not *Allow'd*, in your Heart and Life; but approach the Table of the Lord, with a Soul *Hungring* and *Thirsting* after the *Righteousness* that will be the Cure of it. Make sure of this Qualification, *That you have given up your self to the Lord, as well as you can; and that you Desire to be His and glorify Him; and that you Resolve alwayes to Pursue this Blessedness.* Then come; Come, out of Obedience to the Lord, who sayes, *Do This*; Come, and be not Afraid. Be able to Say, *Ah, Lord, I would come to thy Table with all the Grace, that may assure me of thy Love; I desire to Fear thy Name. But, if I can't come* With *it, I will come* For *it; Oh! Take Pitty on me!*

If

If any thing else be necessary to Settle the *Good State*, either of your *Soul*, or of your *House*, *Do with your might what your Hand finds to do.*

And now, Your FAITH! You Read, Heb. XI. 11. *Thro' Faith, Sarah was delivered of a Child.* In the Renewed, and often Repeted Exercise, of a Lively *Faith*, keep *Looking for the Mercy of our Lord* JESUS CHRIST, unto *Life*, both Temporal and Eternal. By *Faith*, keep continually committing your self, into His Glorious Hands; who said unto a Godly Woman when her *Faith* began to fail her; Joh. XI. 40. *Said I not unto thee, that if thou wouldest believe, thou shouldest see the Glory of God?* Were your *Husband* able to give you an Happy *Travail*, how willing would he be to do it! Yea, (were there any Goodness in him!) tho' it were to be by bearing your Trouble for you, as a rare *Sympathy* has caused Some to do! But by *Faith* you make Sure of your *Saviour* to be your *Husband*. The Voice of your *Faith* is, *O my Saviour, I am thine; Do thou Possess me; And by thee let me bring forth Fruit unto God!* And now, by *Faith* depend

pend on your most Mighty, and most Gracious *Husband*. Say to Him, Cry to Him; *O my Saviour, How canst thou cast me off!* Hope in Him, to see the Fulfilment of a Word that once dropp'd from Him; Joh. XVI. 21. *A Woman when she is in Travail, hath Sorrow, because her Hour is come; but as soon as she is Delivered of the Child, she remembers no more the Anguish; for Joy that a Man is born into the World.*

Yet by *Faith* Submit unto His Holy Will. We read of *Rachel*; Gen. XXXV. 16, 18. *She Travailed, and she had hard Labour; Her soul departed, and she died.* We read of another; I. Sam. IV. 19, 20. *She was with Child, near to cry out; She travailed, her Pains came upon her; it was the Time of her Death.* Suppose this may, by the Sovereign Lord of Life, be the Portion appointed for you: yet by *Faith* triumph over the *Fear of Death*; By *Faith* Resign your self into the Hands of the Glorious Lord, *Lord Jesus, Receive my Spirit!* And so, *Rejoyce in the Hope of the Glory of God.* When your Time arrives, meet it with an honourable *Courage*; bear it with an honourable *Patience*. But in the Minutes

of

of your Anguish, Let your Cry be of that importance; Psal. XXVI. 11. *Oh! Redeem me, and be Merciful unto me.* Or, Psal. XXX. 10. *Hear me, O Lord; Have Mercy upon me; Lord, Be thou my Helper.* Your Omnipotent Redeemer, is One who *Commands Deliverances*, for them who *Weep and Make Supplication*; That is, He *Commands* His Good Angels, to bring and work *Deliverances*; *Deliverances* come as the Effects of His *Commands* unto His *Ministers*. No *Mid-wives* can do, what the *Angels* can!

While you are in a Doubtful Expectation of your *Travail*, you will do well to avoid all *Rash Vowes*; which usually prove the *Snares of Souls*: But yet Entertain some Holy *Resolutions*, of a more Exact, a more Watchful, a more Fruitful *Walk with God*, when He shall have *Delivered* you. And being Delivered, your *Next Work* will be, to consider, *What you shall render to the Lord*. Oh! Think, as in Ezr. 9. 13, 14. *Seeing thou, O my God, hast given me such a Deliverance as this, Should I again break thy Commandments, wouldst thou not be Angry with me, till thou hast consumed me?* But then, Go on to think, *What* you will do, that you may maintain more Communion with God, in the *Religion of the Closet*: Think, *What* you will do, that you may be a greater Blessing in your Family, and to your several Relatives: Think, *What* you will do in Abating of your Superfluities, that you may Employ the more upon Pious Uses; Perhaps, to Clothe poor Widows, like another *Dorcas*. Beg the Help of the Divine Grace, that you may Do such Things; and Glorify your Saviour, with a *Reasonable Service.*

One of the First Things to be done, is to Give up your *New-born Child* unto the Lord, in His Holy *Baptism*. Thus rescue the Child, from the *Great Red Dragon*, who is watching to Devour it. Let the *Child* be either *Male* or *Female*, this is a matter to be left entirely unto the *Wisdom* of the Glorious GOD. Either of them if it be a *Perfect Child*, brings ten Thousand Mercies with it. And, if it may be a *Child* of God the Father, a *Subject* of God the Son, a *Temple* of God the Spirit, think, *This is enough; Lord, I have enough:*

brought One of thy Children into the World.

As a Declaration of this Intention in you, Send the Child abroad, unto the Congregation of the Faithful, where it shall be *Washed*, and *Blessed* in the Name of the Glorious One, and laid under Everlasting *Bonds* to be the Lords. But at the same time, Look on your self as laid under *Bonds*, to bring up the Child for Him; and *in the Nurture and Admonition of the Lord.*

You will *Suckle your Infant your Self* if you can; Be not such an *Ostrich* as to Decline it, meerly because you would be One of the *Careless Women, Living at Ease*. Of such we read, They are *Dead while they Live.*. But if you have the Calamity of *Dry Breasts*; or your Health will not permit you to *Give Suck*; Entertain it with Submission to the will of God; but as a *Calamity*.

Finally; Being well Recovered, you will Rejoyce in your Fresh Opportunities to Repair unto the Worship of God in His *Congregations*. Thither you will now Repair with such Dispositions as these;

[Pid.

[Psal. CXVI: 16, 17, 18.] O *Lord, Truly I am thy Handmaid, I am thy Handmaid; Thou hast Loosed my Bonds. I will offer to thee, the Sacrifice of Thanksgiving, and I will call upon the Name of the Lord. I will pay my Vows unto the Lord, now in the Presence of all His People.*

FINIS.

Given to be Lent, when and where it may be seasonable.

THE

SCHOOL

OF

Good Manners.

Composed for the Help of Parents in Teaching their Children how to carry it in their Places during their Minority.

BOSTON:

Printed and Sold by JOHN BOYLE in Marlborough-Street. 1775.

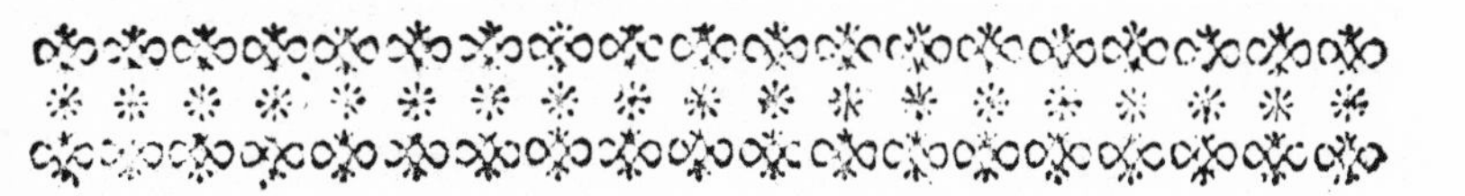

THE

PREFACE.

IT is acknowledged by almoſt every One, that a *Good Carriage* in Children, is an Ornament not only *to Themſelves*, but alſo to *Thoſe whom they deſcend* from. When *David* while he was but a Lad or Youth behaved himſelf wiſely, the KING obſerving of him ſaid, *Whoſe Son is this Youth? Enquire whoſe Son the Stripling is*, 1 Sam. XVII. 55, 56. So that his Parents were honoured by his good Carriage. Whereas Children of but a mean careleſs or *ill Breeding* bring *Diſgrace* on their *Parents*, as well as *Contempt* on *Themſelves*. This Little Book is compoſed for the Help of Parents, in Teaching their Children how to carry it in their Places, during their Minority. (And 'tis humbly recommended to *School-Masters* to introduce it into their Schoo's, as what is (*thought by some*) proper to be Taught there, and might be very *Profitable.*) For we read Prov. XXII. 6. *Train up a Child in the Way he should go, and when he is Old he will not depart from it.*

The following Institutions were compiled (*chiefly*) by Mr. *ELEAZAR MOODY*, late a famous *School-Master* in *Boston*, several Editions thereof have been P.inted and Sold; and 'tis *hoped* that Parents will *so* befriend this *Edition also*, as to *Inculcate* and *Encourage* their Children in the *Observation* of what is here emitted.

THE SCHOOL OF Good Manners.

CHAP. I.

Containing Twenty Mixt Precepts.

FEAR GOD and believe in CHRIST.

2 Honour the King.

3 Reverence thy Parents.

4 Submit to thy Superiors.

5 Despise not thy Inferiors.

6 Be Courteous with thy Equals.

7 Pray Daily and Devoutly.

8 Converse with the Good.

9 Imitate not the Wicked.

10 Hearken diligently to Instruction.
11 Be every desirous of Learning.
12 Love the School.
13 Be always Neat and Cleanly.
14 Study Virtue and Embrace it.
15 Provoke no Body.
16 Love thy School-Fellows.
17 Please thy Master.
18 Let not Play entice thee.
19 Restrain thy Tongue.
20 Covet future Honour, which only Virtue and Wisdom can procure.

CHAP. II.

Containing One Hundred and Sixty Three Rules for Childrens Behaviour, viz. *At the Meeting House; at Home; at the Table; in Company; in Discourse; at the School; when Abroad; and when among other Children; With an Admonition to them.*

I. *Of their Behaviour at the Meeting-House.*

1 DECENTLY walk to thy Seat or Pew, run not, nor wantonly.

2 Sit where thou are ordered by thy Superiors, Parents or Masters.

3 Shift not Seats, but continue in the Place where your Superiors order you.

4 Lend thy Place for the easing of any one that stands near thee.

5 Keep not a Seat too long that is lent thee by another, but being eased thy self, restore it to him that lent it to thee.

6 Talk not in the Meeting-house, especially in the Time of *Prayer* or *Preaching*.

7 Fix thine Eye upon the Minister, let it not widely wander to gaze upon any *Person or Thing*.

8 Attend diligently to the words of the Minister; Pray with him when he prayeth, at least in thy Heart; and while he preacheth listen that thou mayest remember.

9 Be not hasty to run out of the Meeting-house when the Worship is ended, as if thou wer't weary of being there.

10 Walk decently and soberly Home, without Haste or Wantonness; thinking up-what you have been hearing.

II. *Of Childrens Behaviour when at Home.*

1 MAKE a Bow always when you come Home, and be immediately uncovered.

2 Be never covered at Home, eſpecially before thy Parents or Strangers.

3 Never Sit in the Preſence of thy Parents without bidding, tho' no Stranger be preſent.

4 If thou paſſeſt by thy Parents, at any Place where thou ſeeſt them, when either by themſelves or with Company, Bow towards them.

5 If thou art going to ſpeak to thy Parents, and ſee them engaged in diſcourſe with Company, draw back and leave thy Buſineſs until afterwards; but if thou muſt ſpeak, be ſure to whiſper.

6 Never ſpeak to thy Parents without ſome Title of Reſpect, *viz.* Sir, Madam, *&c.* according to their Quality.

7 Approach near thy Parents at no time without a Bow.

8 Diſpute not, nor delay to Obey thy Parents Commands.

9 Go not out of Doors without thy Parents leave, and return within the Time by them limited.

10 Come not into the Room where thy Parents are with Strangers, unleſs thou art called, and then decently; and at bidding go out; or if Strangers come in while thou art with them it is Manners, with a Bow to withdraw.

11 Uſe reſpectful and courteous, but not inſulting or domineering Carriage or Language towards the Servants.

12 Quarrel not nor contend with thy Brethren or ſiſters, but live in love, peace & unity.

13 Grumble not nor be diſcontented at any thing thy Parents appoint, ſpeak or do.

14 Bear with Meekneſs and Patience, and without Murmuring or Sullenneſs thy Parents Reproofs or Corrections: Nay, tho' it ſhould ſo happen that they be cauſleſs or undeſerved.

III. *Of Childrens Behaviour at the Table.*

1 COME not to the Table without having your Hands and Face Waſhed, and your Head Combed.

2 Sit not down till thou art bidden by thy Parents or other Superiors.

3 Be ſure thou never ſitteſt down till a Bleſſing be deſired, and then in thy due Place.

4 Offer not to carve for thy ſelf, or to take any thing tho' it be that which thou doſt greatly deſire.

5 Aſk not for any thing, but tarry till it be offered thee.

6 Find no fault with any thing that is given thee.

7 When thou haſt Meat given thee, be not the firſt that begins to eat.

8 Speak not at the Table: If thy Superiors be diſcourſing, meddle not with the Matter; but be ſilent, except thou are ſpoken unto.

9 If thou wanteſt any Thing from the Servants, call to them ſoftly.

10 Eat not too faſt, or with greedy Behaviour.

11 Eat not two much, but moderately.

12 Eat not ſo ſlow as to make others wait for thee.

13 Make not a Noise with thy Tongue, Mouth, Lips or Breath, either in eating or drinking.

14 Stare not in the Face of any one (especially thy Superiors) at the Table.

15 Grease not thy Fingers or Napkin more than Necessity requires.

16 Bite not thy Bread, but break it; but not with slovingly fingers, nor with the same wherewith thou takest up thy Meat.

17 Dip not thy Meat in the Sauce.

18 Take no Salt with a greasy Knife.

19 Spit not, Cough not, nor blow thy Nose at the Table, if it may be avoided; but if there be necessity do it aside, and without much Noise.

20 Lean not thy Elbow on the Table, or on the back of thy Chair.

21 Stuff not thy Mouth so as to fill thy Cheeks, be content with smaller Mouthfuls.

22 Blow not thy Meat, but with Patience wait until it be cool.

23 Sup not Broth at the Table; but eat it with a Spoon.

24 Smell not of thy Meat, nor put it to thy Nose: Turn it not the other ſide upward to view it upon thy Plate or Trencher.

25 Throw not any thing under the Table.

26 Hold not thy Knife upright in thy Hand, but ſloping; and lay it down at thy right Hand, with the Blade upon thy Plate.

27 Spit not forth any thing that is not convenient to be ſwallowed, as the ſtones of Plumbs, Cherries, or ſuch like; but with thy left hand, neatly move them to the ſide of thy Plate or Trencher.

28 Fix not thine Eyes upon the Plate or Trencher of another, or upon the Meat on the Table.

29 Lift not up thine Eyes, nor roll them about while thou art Drinkin

30 Foul not the Napkin all over, but at one corner only.

31 Bend thy Body a little downwards to thy Plate, when thou moveſt any thing that is Sauced to thy mouth.

32 Look not earneſtly on any one that is Eating.

33 Foul not the Table-Cloth.

34 Gnaw not Bones at the Table but clean them with thy Knife (unleſs they be very ſmall ones) and hold them not with a whole Hand, but with two Fingers.

35 Drink not nor ſpeak with any thing in thy mouth.

36 Put not a bit into thy mouth till the former be ſwallowed.

37 Before and after thou drinkeſt, wipe thy Lips with thy Napkin.

38 Pick not thy Teeth at the Table, unleſs holding up thy Napkin before thy mouth with thine other hand.

39 Drink not till thou haſt quite emptied thy mouth, nor drink often.

40 Frown not, nor Murmur if there be any thing at the Table which thy Parents or Strangers with them eat of, while thou thy ſelf haſt none given thee.

41 As ſoon as thou ſhalt be moderately ſatisfied; or whenſoever thy Parents think meet to bid thee, riſe up from the Table, though others thy Superiors ſit ſtill.

42 When thou risest from the Table having made a Bow at the side of the Table where thou fattest, withdraw.

43 When Thanks are to be returned after Eating, return to thy Place, and stand reverently till it be done; and then with a Bow withdraw out of the Room, leaving thy Superiors to themselves (unless thou art bidden to stay.)

IV. *Of Childrens Behaviour when in Company.*

1 ENTER not into the Company of Superiors without command or calling, nor without a Bow.

2 Sit not down in Presence of Superiors without bidding.

3 Put not thy hand in the presence of others to any part of thy Body, not ordinarily discovered.

4 Sing not nor hum in thy mouth, while thou art in Company.

5 Stand not Wriggling with thy Body hither and thither, but steady and upright.

6 Play not wantonly like a Mimick, with thy Fingers or Feet.

7 In Coughing or Sneezing, make as little Noise as possible.

8 If thou canst not avoid Yawning, shut thy Mouth with thine Hand or Handkerchief before it, turning thy face aside.

9 When thou blowest thy Nose, let thy Handkerchief be used, and make not a noise in so doing.

10 Gnaw not thy Nails, pick them not, nor bite them with thy Teeth.

11 Spit not in the Room, but in the Corner, and rub it with thy Foot, or rather go out and do it abroad.

12 Lean not upon the Chair of a Superior standing behind him.

13 Spit not upon the Fire, nor sit too wide with thine Knees at it.

14 Sit not with thy Legs crossed, but keep them firm and settled, and thy Feet even.

15 Turn not thy Back to any, but place thy self so that none may be behind thee.

16 Read not Letters, Books nor other Writing in Company, unless there be necessity, and thou askest leave.

17 Touch not, nor look upon the Books or Writings of any one, unleſs the Owner invite or deſire thee.

18 Come not near when another reads a Letter or any other Paper.

19 Let thy Countenance be moderately chearful, neither Laughing nor frowning.

20 Laugh not aloud, but ſilently Smile upon occaſion.

21 Stand not before Superiors with thine hands in thy Pockets; ſcratch not thy head, wink not with thine Eyes, but modeſtly be looking ſtrait be ore thee.

22 Walking with thy Superior in the Houſe or Garden, give him the Right (or Upper) Hand, and Walk not even with him, *Check-by jole*; but a little beind him, yet not ſo diſtant as that it ſhall be troubleſome to him to ſpeak to thee, or hard for thee to hear.

23 Look not boldly or wilfully in the Face of thy Superior.

24 To look upon one in Company and immediately whiſper to another, is unmannerly.

25 Whiſper not in Company.

26. Be not among Equals froward and fretful, but gentle and affable.

V. *Of Childrens Behaviour in their Discourse.*

1 AMong Superiors speak not till thou art spoken to, and bid to speak.

2 Hold not thine hand, nor any thing else, before thy mouth when thou speakest.

3 Come not over near to the Person thou speakest to.

4 If thy Superior speak to thee while thou sittest, stand up before thou givest any answer.

5 Sit not down till thy Superior bid thee.

6 Speak neither very loud, nor too low.

7 Speak clear, not stammering, stumbling nor drawling.

8 Answer not one that is speaking to thee until he hath done.

9 Loll not when thou art speaking to a Superior, or spoken to by him.

10 Speak not without, *Sir*, or some other Title of Respect, which is due to him to whom thou speakest.

11 Strive not with Superiors in Argument or Discourse; but easily submit thine Opinion to their Assertions.

12 If thy Superior speak any thing wherein thou knowest he is mistaken correct not nor contradict him, nor grin at the hearing of it; but pass over the Error without notice or interruption.

13 Mention not frivolus or little things among grave Persons or Superiors.

14 If thy Superior drawl or hesitate in his words, pretend not to help him out, or to prompt him.

15 Come not too near Two that are whispering or speaking in secret, much less may'st thou ask about what they confer.

16 When thy Parent or Master speak to any Person, speak not thou, nor hearken to them.

17 If thy Superior be relating a Story, say not I have heard it before, but attend to it, as if it were to thee altogether new: Seem not to question the truth of it: If he tell it not right, snigger not, nor endeavor to help him out, or add to his Relation.

18 If any immodeſt or obſcene thing be ſpoken in thy hearing, ſmile not, but ſettle thy Countenance as though thou did'ſt not hear it.

19 Boaſt not in Diſcourſe of thine own wit or doings.

20 Beware thou utter not any thing hard to be believ'd.

21 Interrupt not any one that ſpeaks, though thou be his Familiar.

22 Coming into Company, whilſt any Topick is diſcourſed on, aſk not what was the preceeding talk but hearken to the remainder.

23 Speaking of any diſtant Perſon, it is rude and unmannerly to point at him.

24 Laugh not in, or at thy own Story, Wit or Jeſt.

25 Uſe not any contemptuous or reproachful Language to any perſon, though very mean or inferior.

26 Be not over earneſt in talking to juſtify and avouch thy own Sayings.

27 Let thy words be modeſt about thoſe things which only concern thee.

28 Repeat not over again the words of a Superior that asketh thee a Question, or talketh to thee.

VI. *Of Childrens Behaviour at the School.*

1 BOW at coming in, pulling off thy Hat; especially if thy Master or Usher be in the School.

2 Loiter not, but immediately take thine own Seat; and move not from one Place to another, till School-time be over.

3 If any Stranger come into the School, rise up and bow, and sit down in thy Place again; keeping a profound Silence.

4 If thy Master be discoursing in the School with a Stranger, stare not confidently on them, nor hearken to their Talk.

5 Interrupt not thy Master while a Stranger or Visitant is with him, with any Question, Request or Complaint; but refer any such matter untill he be at leisure.

6 At no time Quarrel or Talk in the School, but be quiet, peaceable and silent. Much less may'st thou deceive thy self, in

trifling away thy precious time in Play.

7 If thy Master speak to thee, rise up and bow; making thine Answer standing.

8 Bawl not aloud in making Complaints. A Boy's Tongue should never be heard in the School but in answering a Question, or saying his Lesson.

9 If a Stranger speak to thee in School, stand up and answer with respect and ceremony, both of word and gesture, as if thou spakest to thy Master.

10 Make not haste out of School, but soberly go when thy turn comes, without noise or hurry.

11 Go not rudely home thro' the Street, stand not talking with Boys to delay thee, but go quietly home, and with all convenient haste.

12 When it is time to return to School again, be sure to be there in season, and not loiter at home whilst your Master's at School.

13 Divulge not to any Person whatsoever elsewhere, any thing that hath passed in the School, either spoken or done.

VII. *Of Childrens Behaviour when Abroad.*

1 GO not Singing, Whiſtling nor Hollowing along the Street.

2 Quarrel not with any Body thou meeteſt or oſt overtake.

3 Affront none, eſpecially thy Elders, by word or deed.

4 Jeer not any Perſon whatſoever.

5 Always give the Right Hand to your Superiors, when either you meet or walk with them; and mind alſo to give them the Wall, in meeting or walking with them; for that is the Upper Hand, tho in walking your Superior ſhould then be at your Left Hand. But when Three Perſons walk together, the Middle place is the moſt Honourable: And a Son may walk at his Father's Right Hand, when his Younger Brother walks at his Left.

6 Give thy Superior leave to paſs before thee in any narrow place, where Two perſons cannot paſs at once.

7 If thou go with thy Parents, Maſter or any Superior, go not wantonly, nor even with them; but a little behind them.

8 Pay thy Reſpects to all thou meeteſt of thine Acquaintance or Friends.

9 Pull off thine Hat to Perſons of Deſert, Quality or Office; ſhew thy Reverence to them by bowing thy Body when thou ſeeſt them; and if it be the King, a Prince, Noble, Governor, Magiſtrate, Juſtice of the Peace, Miniſter or Deacon, *&c.* ſtay thyſelf until they be paſſed by thee.

10 If a Superior ſpeak to thee in the Street anſwer him with thy Head uncovered; and put not on thy Hat until he either go from thee, or bid thee once and again be covered; take not leave at the firſt bidding, but with a bow, (*by no means, Sir.* modeſtly refuſe it.

11 Run not haſtily in the Street, nor go too ſlowly; wag not to and fro, nor uſe any antick or wanton poſture, either of thy Head, Hands, Feet or Body.

12 Stare not at every unuſual Perſon or Thing Which thou ſeeſt.

13 Throw not any thing in the Street, as Dirt, Stones, *&c.*

14 If thou meeteſt the Scholars of any other School, jeer not nor affront them, but ſhew them love and reſpect, and quietly let them paſs along.

15 Eſpecially affront not the Maſter of another School, but rather, if thou knoweſt him, or if he live near either thine Houſe or School, uncover thy head to him, and bowing paſs by him.

VIII. *Of their Behaviour among other Children.*

1 AS near as may be converſe not with any but thoſe that are good, ſober and virtuous. *Evil Communications corrupt good Manners.*

2 Be not Quarrelſome, but rather patiently take, than miſchievouſly occaſion any Wrong.

3 Reprove thy Companions as oft as there ſhall be occaſion, for any evil, wicked unlawful or indecent Action or Expreſſion.

4 Give always Place to him that excelleth thee in Quality, Age or Learning.

5 Be willing to take thoſe words or actions as Jeſting, which thou haſt reaſon to

believe were designed for such ; and fret not at thy Companions innocent Mirth.

6 If thy Companion be a little too gross or sarcastical in speaking, yet strive not to take notice of it, or be moved at all therewith.

7 Abuse not thy Companion either by word or deed.

8 Deal justly among Boys thy Equals as solicitously as if thou wert a Man with Men, and about Business of higher importance.

9 Be not Selfish altogether, but kind, free and generous to others.

10 Jog not the Table or Desk on which another writes.

11 At play make not thy Cloaths, Hands or Face dirty or nasty, nor set upon the ground.

12 Avoid sinful and unlawful Recreations, and all such as prejudice the welfare of Body or Mind.

13 Scorn not, laugh not at any for their natural infirmities of Body or Mind ; nor because of them affix to any a vexing Title of Contempt and Reproach, but pity such

as are ſo viſited, and be thankful that you are otherwiſe diſtinguiſhed and favoured.

14 Adventure not to talk with thy Companion about thy Superiors, to raiſe diſcouſe reflecting upon, or touching another's Parents or Maſters; to publiſh any thing of thine own Family or Houſhold Affairs. Children muſt meddle only with the Affairs of Children.

IX. *Containing an Admonition to Children.*

CHildren, Theſe are the chief of thoſe Rules of Behaviour, the Obſervation whereof will deliver you from the diſgraceful Titles of Sordid and Clowniſh, and intail upon the mention of you, the honor of Genteel and well bred Children. For there is ſcarce a ſadder ſight, than a Clowniſh and Unmannerly Child. Avoid therefore with the greateſt Diligence ſo vile an Ignominy. Be Humble, Submiſſive and Obedient to thoſe whoſe Authority by Nature or Providence hath a juſt claim to your Subjection. Such are Parents, Maſters or Tutors, whoſe Commands and Laws have no other ten dency than your truest Good: Be always obsequious and respectful, never bold, insolent or saucy, either in Words or Gestures. Let your Body be on every occasion pliable, and ready to manifest in due and becoming Ceremonies, the inward Reverence you bear towards those above you. By this means, by a timely and early accustoming yourselves to a sweet and spontaneous Obedience in your lower Station and Relations, your minds being habituated to that which is so indispensibly your Duty; the task of Obedience in further Relations will be performed with the greater Ease and Pleasure. When it shall please God that you come to riper Years, and under the circumstance of Servants, pay Homage to your Masters and Mistresses; and at length if it seem good to the Divine Providence, that you arrive at Manhood, and become Members of the Common-Wealth, there will remain in your well managed Minds no presumptuous Folly, that may prompt or tempt you to be other than faithful, obedient and loyal Subjects.

Be kind, pleaſant and loving, not croſs o churliſh to your Equals. And in thus beha ving yourſelves, all perſons will exceedingl deſire your familiar Acquaintance: Ever one will be ready and willing (upon oppor tunity) to ſerve and aſſiſt you. Your Friend will be no fewer than all that know you, an obſerve the excellence and ſweetneſs of you deportment. This practice alſo (by inducin an habit of obliging) will fit you for Con verſe and Society, and facilitate and advantag your dealing with Men in riper Years.

Be meek, courteous and affable to you Inferiors, not proud or ſcornful. To b courteous to the meaneſt is a true Index of great and generous Mind. [But the inſult ing and ſcornful Gentleman, uſually hat been himſelf originally low, ignoble o beggarly; makes himſelf to his Equal ridiculous, and by his Inferiors is repaid with ſcorn and hatred.]

By carefully obſerving theſe methods o Life, your Superiors will indeed eſteem you your Infe. ors honor and admire you: you

Equals delight in and love you; all that know and obſerve you, ſhall praiſe and reſpect you: Your Example ſhall be propounded as a Pattern of Ingenuity and obliging Behaviour. You ſhall be valuable and well eſteemed in every Time, Station and Circumſtance of your lives: You ſhall be bleſt with the Names of good Children, good Scholars, good Servants, good Maſters, good Subjects; Praiſe ſhall be your Attendant all your Life long, and your Names ſhall out-live the Envy of the Grave; the Encomium of every Survivor ſhall embalm your Memory.

CHAP. III.

Containing good Advice for the Ordering of their Lives, with a Baptiſmal Covenant.

I. *Good Advice to Children.*

BELIEVE without Doubt that there is a GOD, that He is moſt Holy, hating Sin, and that never any ſhall ſee Him and taſte of His Sweetneſs, unleſs they walk Holy before Him.

2 Be aſſured that the Sacred Scriptures (the Written Word of God) are True; and that the things contained therein, will be found to be real things.

3 If God do open your Eyes and bring you to Salvation, it will be by light let in by the Word.

4 Therefore read it, and muſe upon it, and never read it without looking up to God to ſpeak ſomewhat to you out of it

5 And when you go to hear the Word preached be ſure go to hear God, and liſten with Diligence to every Word that is ſpoken.

6 Make it one main work, and try at it again and again, to Meditate,and in Meditation to conclude what your State is; and to aſk both the LORD and your own Conſciences concerning your State; and give no reſt to either, till you put that great Queſtion out of Queſtion, where you ſhall ſpend your Eternity.

7 Be ſure that Sin is the greateſt Evil in the World; and that no Affliction can hurt us if Sin do not.

8 Examine what your most Especial Sin is, which you shall know from its most frequent rising out of your Heart, and bring that before GOD, and Pray against it Day and Night; and resolve against it: For there will be no communion with GOD if this Sin reigns in you.

9 Study to know JESUS CHRIST every way, and give God no rest until He reveals Christ as the most glorious thing to you; and until you can say Now I see that all other things are but loss in comparison of Christ.

10 Make a serious Dedication of your self to Him, to be His, and chuse Him to be Yours, Write your own Covenant and subscribe it, and satisfy yourself with Christ though you have nothing else, and give up your self to be ruled by Him, and then say thou art my Lord, help me now in the Time of my straits.

11 Pray Morning and Evening without fail, and that with all Seriousness; for those things that you want, and against those things that you fear.

12 Be faithful in your Place and Calling, and let there not the least Unrighteousness lie upon your Consciences.

13 Be diligent to improve Time, and suffer not precious Hours to run away without improvement.

14 Be assured you have awful work to do, till you get Pardon of Sin and Heaven assur'd.

15 Make it part of your Daily Work to call your Heart to an Account; and do not any momentary Business without proposing of some grounded End that will bear you out in it, let the Event be even what it will.

16 And if you love your Life, beware of Evil Company, a deadly Mischief; rather none than ill ones, which there be in every place, have no fellowship with them, do not keep with them if possible, for the Devil has poison'd many a man thus. *Keep yourself pure.*

17 Now is the Time for you to offer to the Lord the First Fruits, the Morning of your Age, the Prime of your Days.

18 Labour to approve your self honest before God and men. The way to be up

right is to walk before God. Set God before you as One that feeth and trieth not only visible, but fecret thoughts and fecret works.

II. *A fhort Baptifmal Covenant, to be fubfcribed unto, and kept by Young Perfons for their Ufe and Comfort; which if ferioufly and often reflected upon and well confidered of, would tend to the prevention of much Evil, and be a means to promote much Joy and Comfort to their Souls.*

I TAKE GOD the FATHER, to be my Chiefeft Good and Higheft End.

I take GOD the SON, to be my Prince and Saviour.

I take GOD the HOLY GHOST, to be my Sanctifier, Teacher, Guide and Comforter.

I take the WORD of GOD, to be my Rule in all my Actions.

And the PEOPLE of GOD, to be my People in all Conditions.

I do likewife devote and dedicate unto the LORD my whole Self, all I am, all I have, and all I can do.

And this I do deliberately, and as far as I know my own Heart, sincerely, freely, and for ever more; depending always on the *Sovereign Grace of God and Merits of the Lord JESUS CHRIST* alone, for Assistance and Acceptance.

CHAP. IV.

Containing Eight wholesome Cautions.

Caution I. *Of taking GOD's Name in Vain.*

THIS is a Sin that Children are addicted unto; to say, *O Lord, O God, O Jesus, O Christ, &c.* in their Common Talk, upon every trivolous Occasion; but it is expressly forbidden in the Third Commandment: The words of which Command are these, *Thou shalt not take the Name of the Lord thy God in vain: For the Lord will not hold him guiltless that taketh His Name in vain.* Therefore be warned to take heed of this Sin.

He will not hold him guiltless. That is, He will surely hold him *guilty.* To be held guilty before God, notes two things,

1 To be under the Merit of Everlaſting Wrath: By taking God's Name in vain, you deſerve the Wrath of the Great and Infinite GOD.

2 Guilt notes an Obligation to Wrath: taking God's Name in vain, binds you over to the Judgment of the great Day; when thou comeſt to appear before God's Tribunal, and it be demanded of thee Guilty or not Guilty? This Sin alone will prove you to be really Guilty.

And certainly, however the breakers of this Command may eſcape puniſhment here, yet they ſhall find there is a Judgment.

Caution II. *Of Vain, Idle and Naughty Words.*

THIS is another Sin that Children are addicted to and are to be warned againſt. Mat. xii. 36. *That every idle Word that Men ſhall ſpeak, they muſt give an account thereof in the Day of Judgment:* Do you believe this, Children, and will you yet ſpeak idle words, vain words, naughty words: O have a care of this evil.

Caution III. *Of the Sin of Lying.*

THIS is another Sin that Children are addicted unto and are to be warned against. A Lie is a speaking an Untruth wittingly and willingly, with a purpose to deceive. Of Lies there are three sorts, *viz.*

An Officious Lie.
A Sporting Lie.
A Pernicious Lie.

1 An Officious Lie, is that which is intended to prevent some danger, or to procure some good, either to our Selves or Neighbours. Thus *Rahab* lied. *Josh.* ii. 4. And that Woman mentioned in 2 *Samuel,* xvii. 20.

2 A Sporting Lie, or Lie in Jest, is that which is made to make one merry, or to pass away precious Time.

3 A pernicious Lie, is that which is made for some evil, hurtful, dangerous intent against our Neighbour. All these sorts of Lying are Sinful.

A lying Tongue is one of the things that are an Abomination to the Lord, Prov. vi.

16, 17. *A Proud Look, a Lying Tongue,* &c. And again, Prov. xii. 22. *Lying lips are an abomination to the Lord.* And Lying is the mark of the Devil's Children, John. viii. 44. *Ye are of your Father the Devil.—He abode not in the truth because there is no truth in him; when he speaketh a Lie, he speaketh of his own; for he is a Liar and the Father of it.* Liars are reckoned among the grossest of Sinners, and must go to the same Hell that they are going to. We are told Rev. xxi. 8. *The Fearful and Unbelieving, and the Abominable, and Murderers, and Whoremongers, and Sorcerers, and Idolaters, and all LIARS, shall have their part in the Lake which burneth with Fire and Brimstone.*

A Liar is abhorred both of God and Man; he is abhorred of God, as you were before told, *Lying lips are an abomination to the Lord,* Prov. xii. 22. He also is abhorred of Man: *David* could not endure a Liar in his sight, Psal. ci. 7. *He that worketh deceit shall not dwell within my house: He that telleth lies shall not tarry in my sight.* 'Tis said of *Pom-*

tonius that he never used Lying, neither could he with Patience lend his ear to a Liar. *Tenendo* was so strict in Judgment, that he caus'd an Ax to be held over the Witnesses Head, to execute them out of hand, if they were taken in a Falshood. If one accustom himself to Lying, he is scarce believed when he speaks True. The Devil's Breast (saith *Luther*) is very fruitful with Lies. *Austin* hath a Tractate about an Officious Lie: To tell a Lie for no hurt, but for good (says he) we are not to do it, tho' it were to save all the World. Though some Saints and holy Servants of God have used the Officious Lie, as *Rebecca* and *Jacob*, Gen. xxvii. 18, 19. And Abraham, Gen. xx. 2. Yet their Faults were not recorded for our Imitation, but for our Caution.

Caution IV. *Of obscene and wanton Speeches, and filthy and lascivious Songs and Ballads.*

THIS is another Sin that Children are addicted to, and to be warned of: This is a Sin that doth greatly corrupt

Youth. The Apostle *Paul* cautions you against it, Eph. iv. 29. *Let no Corrupt Communication proceed out of your mouth.* And Chap. v. 4. *Neither Filthiness, nor foolish Talking, nor Jesting,* &c. Have a care of lascivious Speeches, and unchaste and wanton Songs or Ballads: Take heed, Children, of these things; for the Practice of them will greatly debauch you: Therefore you should much rather improve your time in reading the Bible, and other Books of Piety, which have a tendency to make you wise unto Salvation.

Caution V. *Of Prophane and Rash Swearing.*

THIS is another Vice whereunto Young Men are too much addicted: But expresly forbidden by our Saviour, Mat. v. 34. *Swear not at all,* (*i. e.* Prophanely or Rashly) *but let your Communication be yea, yea: Nay, nay: For whatsoever is more than these, cometh of evil;* that is, of the Devil that evil One. Have a Care of Swearing by Faith, and Troth; much more of Swearing by the Name of GOD.

Caution VI. *Of Prophaning the Sabbath-Day.*

SAbbath-Breaking is another Sin which Children are too generally prone unto. The fourth Commandment is, *Remember the Sabbath-Day to keep it Holy.* But how contrary hereto is the Practice of very many Children and elder Persons too? Oh! then, have a care of Playing upon the Lord's-Day, which is the Christian's Sabbath-Day; but do you spend the whole day in religious Exercises. That famous Judge, Sir *Matthew Hale,* who in a Letter to Children in which he gives them Directions for the Sanctification of the Lord's-Day; says, That he often found that the due Observation of the duty of this Day, had ever joined to it a Blessing on the rest of his Time; and the Week so began was blessed and prosperous to him: But if on the other side, he had been negligent in the duties of this Day, the rest of the Week was unhappy; so that he could easily make an Estimate of his Successes, by the manner of his passing this Day: And this (says he)

I do not write lightly, or inconſiderately, but upon long and ſound Obſervation and Experience.

A late Writer tells us, that a Friend of his, obſerving a Woman expoſing Fruit to Sale on the Lord's-Day, adviſed her to leave that Practice and to attend the Public-Worſhip, and to ſerve God on His Day. The Woman replied, that ſhe took more Money on the Lord's-Day, than on any day of the Week, and that ſhe could not live, if ſhe did not do thus. To whom it was replied, If you would leave off this Practice, and keep the Lord's-Day holy, attending the Public-Worſhip; and when you come home ſpend the time in reading the Scripture, and in Prayer to God and praiſing Him for his Mercies, God will ſend a Bleſſing on your labors on the reſt of the Week, which you cannot expect ſo long as you make a Market of His Sabbath. The Woman hearkned to his Advice, and ſome time after thanked him for it: Saying ſhe found his words true; for ever ſince ſhe kept the Sabbath-Day, ſhe ſold more on Mondays and Tueſdays than ſhe uſed to do all the Week before. But there is greater things to be obtained by Obſerving this Holy Day, than Temporal Bleſſings, viz. Spiritual and Eternal Bleſſings.

And conſider alſo the Judgments which have overtook thoſe who have profaned that Day · One ſpeaks of Fourteen Young Perſons who on the Lord's-Day in the winter time would go to play at Foot-Ball on the ice; but that broke under them, and they were all drowned. 'Tis reported that two Young Men belonging to *NewEngland*, would be ſo Profane as to ride a Race on the Lord's-Day; but when they were on their Horſes Backs, God ſmote them with a ſtrange kind of Palſey, of which they both died, after they had been for ſeveral Months in a very miſerable Condition. But Sabbath-breakers expoſe themſelves to that which is worſe than any Temporal Judgments, viz. to Spiritual and Eternal Judgments.

Caution VII. *Of Stealing.*

THIS is another Sin which Children are prone unto : tho' 'tis forbidden in the Eighth Commandment. The Eighth Commandment is, *Thou ſhalt not Steal.* To Steal is to take that which is another's without their Leave. Oh ! Children, be caution'd againſt the ſin of Stealing : Steal not the Value of a Pin from any one ; eſpecially from your Parents or Maſters, for to ſteal from them is a great ſin, tho' ſome may count it none at all. A Thief is reckon'd up among thoſe ſinners that ſhall be ſhut out of heaven, 1 Cor. vi. 9.—*Know ye not that the Unrighteous ſhall not inherit the kingdom of God. Be not deceived, neither fornicators, nor idolaters, nor adulterers, nor effeminate,* (*i. e.* Self Polluters,) *nor abuſers of themſelves with mankind, nor* THIEVES, (which are placed in the middle of thoſe ungodly ones, as if they were the worſt of them all.) *nor covetous, nor drunkards, nor revilers, nor extortioners, ſhall inherit the kingdom of God.*

Caution VIII. *Of Disobedience to Parents.*

DIsobedience to Parents, is another sin too common among Children, and indeed 'tis a great sin. Obedience to Parents is that which is expresly required of Children in the Fifth Commandment, which is *Honor thy Father and thy Mother.* But alas, how many Children do violate this great Commandment? Disobedience to Parents is so foul a sin, as that it is put into the black Catalogue, Rom. i. 29, 30, 31. *Being filled with all unrighteousness, fornication, wickedness, covetousness, maliciousness, full of envy, murder, debate, deceit, malignity, whisperers, backbiters, haters of God, despiteful, proud, boasters, inventers of evil things.* DISOBEDIENT to PARENTS, *covenant breakers, without natural affection, implacable, unmerciful.* Many that have come to an untimely Death, and that both in the days of old and in our days, in the Land of our forefathers Sepulchres and in the Land where we have liv'd (when the terrors of Death have been upon them, and they just ready to launch out into an awful Eternity) bitterly lamented and very much bewailed that God-provoking Sin, *viz. Disobedience to their Parents.* Let Children take heed they be not found among such : But let them always remember that word, Eph. vi. 1. *Children, Obey your Parents in the Lord; for this is right.*

CHAP. V.

Containing a short, plain, and Scriptural CATECHISM.

Quest. 1. D*O you know who is God, and who made you and us all?*

Answ. I know that the Lord He is God, that He made us and not we our selves, (*a*)

Q 2. *Who is he that hath preserved you from the Womb hitherto?*

A. The Lord hath upheld me from the Womb hitherto, (*b*)

Q 3. *Whom then are you bound to worship and serve?*

A. The GREAT GOD, that hath made and preserved me, (*c*)

(*a*) Psal. c, iii. Isa. xliv. 2. (*b*) Psal. lxxi. 5, 6.
(*c*) Psal. c. 2, 3.

Q. 4. *When are you to ſet your ſelf to this happy work of Serving God?*

A. While I am a Child, in the days of my Youth. (*d*)

Q. 5. *What Rule have you to direct you how to ſerve the Lord?*

A. The word of God, contained in the Old and New Teſtament, is the only Rule to direct me how to ſerve the Lord. (*e*)

Q. 6. *What is God?*

A. God is a moſt Holy, Wiſe, Merciful, Juſt and Mighty Spirit, yea, He is Almighty. (*f*)

Q. 7. *Are there more Gods than One?*

A. Our God is but One; the Father, of whom are all things; the Son, Jeſus Chriſt the Saviour, by whom are all things; and the Holy Spirit of Truth, whom the Father ſends in the Son's Name to Sanctify and Comfort. (*g*)

Q. 8. *What Works hath God done?*

(*d*) 2 Tim. iii. 15. Eccl. xii. 1. (*e*) Eph. ii. 20 (*f*) Joſh. xxiv. 19. 2 Tim. i. 17. Ex. xxxiv. 6 Gen. xvii. 1. John iv. 24. (*g*) 1 John v. 7 1 Cor. viii. 6. 1 Tim. ii. 5. John xiv. 16.

A. GOD made the Heavens, and the Earth, and the Waters; and all that in them is. *(h)*

Q. 9. *Whether did God at first, make all things good or bad?*

A. God made all things very good. *(i)*

Q. 10. *How then came Sin, Sorrow and Death into the World?*

A. By *Adam*'s Fall, in whom we all sinned and came short of the glory of God. *(k)*

Q. 11. *What is Sin?*

A. Sin is any want of Conformity unto, or Transgression of the Law of God. *(l)*

Q. 12. *What do you and I deserve for committing Sin?*

A. The Wages of Sin is Death and the Wrath of God. *(m)*

Q. 13. *What hopes have you of being deliver'd from Sin, and so from Death and the Wrath of God?*

(h) Gen. i. 1. *and* Chap. ii. 1. Exod. xx. 11. *(i)* Gen. i. 31. *(k)* Rom. iii. 23. *and* Chap. v. 12. *(l)* 1 John iii. 4. *(m)* Rom. vi. 23. Gal. iii. 10.

A. The Love of God, who gave his only begotten Son, that whosoever believeth in him should not perish, but have everlasting Life. (*n*)

Q. 14. *What did Christ the Son of God do in order to the Redeeming Mankind?*

A. Christ became our Surety unto God, so he undertook the Curse in our stead, and died to redeem us from Sin and Wrath. (*o*)

Q. 15. *Who are they that shall share in the Benefits purchased by Christ?*

A. Such as are convinced of Sin, of Righteousness and of Judgment; and that receive Jesus Christ as their Prophet, Priest & King. (*p*)

Q. 16. *How must you live if you hope to be saved by Jesus Christ?*

A. I must live in all purity, cleansing myself from all filthiness of the flesh and spirit, perfecting holiness in the fear of God. (*q*)

Q. 17. *How are you to worship and serve the great God?*

(*n*) John iii. 16. (*o*) Heb. vii. 22, 25. Gal. iii. 13. 1 Cor. xv. 3. (*p*) John xvi. 8. Rom. iii. 19, 23. John i. 11, 12. Col. ii. 6. (*q*) 1 John iii. 2, 3. 2 Cor. vii. 1. *and* Chap. v. 17, 18.

A. I muſt worſhip and ſerve God in ſpirit and in truth; with all my heart and with all my ſoul, and with all my might. (*r*)

Q. 18. *What is the beſt Evidence of your Love to God?*

A. The keeping his Commandments, and counting the doing of them a pleaſure. (*ſ*)

Q. 19. *How many Commandments are there?*

A. There are Ten Commandments. (*t*)

Q. 20. *What excellent Sum have you of the Chriſtian Faith?*

A. That which uſually goes under the name of the Apoſtles Creed. [Which let the Child now repeat.] (*u*)

Q. 21. *What is the moſt perfect form of Prayer?*

A. That which Jeſus Chriſt taught his Diſciples. [Repeat the Lord's Prayer.] *w*)

Q. 22. *What are the Sacraments of the New-Teſtament?*

D

(*r*) John iv. 24. Deut. vi. 5. (*ſ*) John xiv. 15. 1 John v. 3. (*t*) Exod. xx. 1—17. Chap. xxxiv. 28. Deut. v. 7—21. (*u*) I believe in GOD the Father, &c. (*w*) Mat. vi. 9. 13. Our Father which art in Heaven, &c.

A. Baptism, as entering into the Churc of Christ; and the Lord's Supper, as confirming and comforting us there. (*x*)

Q. 23. *What will become of the wicked after Death?*

A. They must be turned into Hell, with all those that forget God. (*y*)

Q. 24. *What also becomes of the godly, or those that fear God and serve Him?*

A. They all go to Heaven, and are for ever solaced in rivers of pleasure at God's right Hand. (*z*)

(*x*) Mat. xxviii. 19, 20. Acts ii. 42. 1 Cor. xi. 24, 25, 26. (*y*) Psalm ix. 17. (*z*) Psalm xvi. 11. Mat. xxv. 34, 46. Rev. ii. 10.

CHAP. VI.

Containing Principles of the Christian Religion; in which there is a double advantage to Youth. First, *In that all the while they are reading of them, they learn to Read as well as by reading any other Matter.* Secondly, *In that thereby they are instructed in the Grounds and Principles of Religion.*

One GOD.

HAVE we not One Father? Hath not One GOD created us? *Mal.* ii. 10.

But be not ye called Rabbi: For one is your Maſter, even CHRIST; and all ye are Brethren: For one is your Father which is in Heaven. *Mat.* xxiii. 8, 9.

The LORD He is GOD; and there is none elſe beſides him. *Deut.* iv. 35.

Hear, O Iſrael, the LORD our GOD is one Lord. *Deut.* vi. 4.

I am the LORD, and there is none elſe beſides me. *Iſa.* xlv. 5.

An Idol is nothing in the world, and there is none other God but One. To us there is but One God, the Father, of whom are all things. 1 *Cor.* viii. 4.

For there is One God, and there is none other but He. *Mark* xii. 32.

Seeing it is One God, which ſhall juſtify the Circumciſion by Faith. *Rom.* iii. 30.

Now a Mediator is not a Mediator of One; but God is One. *Gal.* iii. 20.

One Lord, one Faith, one Baptiſm; one God and Father of all, who is above all, and thro' all, and in you all. *Eph.* iv. 5, 6.

For there is one God, and one Mediator between God and men, the man Chriſt Jeſus. 1 *Tim.* ii. 5.

But the Lord he is the true God, he is the living God, and an everlaſting King. *Jer.* x. 1.

Three Perſons in the Godhead, i. e. the Father, the Son, and the Holy Ghoſt.

GO ye therefore and teach all Nations, baptizing them in the name of the Father, Son, and Holy Ghoſt. *Mat.* xxviii. 19.

There are Three that bear record in Heaven, the Father, the Word, and the Holy Ghoſt: and theſe three are one. 1 *John* v. 7.

And Jeſus when he was baptized, went ſtraightway out of the water; and lo, the Heavens were opened unto him, and he ſaw the Spirit of God deſcending like a Dove, and lighting upon him. And lo, a voice from Heaven, ſaying, This is my beloved Son, in whom I am well pleaſed. *Mat.* iii. 16, 17.

The Grace of our Lord Jesus Christ, and the Love of God, and the Communion of the Holy Ghost, be with you all, Amen. 2 *Cor.* xiii. 14.

And I will pray the Father, and he shall give you another Comforter, that he may abide with you for ever: Even the Spirit of Truth.——*John* xiv. 16, 17.

Of the Attributes of GOD.

I. *Of* GOD's *Eternity*.

BUT now is made manifest, and by the Scriptures of the Prophets, according to the Commandment of the everlasting God, made known to all Nations for the obedience of Faith. *Rom.* xvi. 26.

Hast thou not known, hast thou not heard, that the everlasting God the Lord, the Creator of the ends of the Earth, fainteth not, neither is he weary? There is no searching of His understanding. *Isa.* xl. 28.

Who hath wrought and done it, calling the generations from the beginning? I the Lord, the first, and with the last, I am He. *Isa.* xli. 4.

Before the mountains were brought forth or ever thou hadst formed the earth and the world: Even from everlasting to everlasting Thou art God. *Psalm* xc. 2.

The eternal God is thy refuge, and underneath are the everlasting arms, *Deut* xxxiii.2

Now unto the King eternal, immortal, invisible, the only wise God, be honor and glory for ever and ever, Amen. 1 *Tim.* i. 17.

And Abraham planted a grove in Beersheba, and called there on the Name of the LORD, the everlasting GOD. *Gen.* xxi. 3

For thus saith the High and lofty One that inhabiteth eternity, whose name is holy, I dwell in the high and holy place, with him also that is of a contrite and humble spirit, to revive the heart of the contrite ones. *Isa.* lvii. 15.

II. *Of GOD's Omnipotency.*

AND when Abram was ninety years old and nine, the Lord appeared to Abram, and said unto him, I am the Almighty God; walk before me, and be thou perfect. *Gen.* xvii. 1.

I am Alpha and Omega, the Beginning and the Ending, ſaith the Lord, which is, and was, and which is to come, the Almighty. *Rev.* i. 8.

And I heard as it were the voice of a great multitude, and as the voice of many waters, and as the voice of mighty thunderings, ſaying, Allelujah! For the Lord God Omnipotent reigneth. *Rev.* xix. 6.

And I appeared unto Abraham, unto Iſaac, and unto Jacob, by the Name of GOD ALMIGHTY, but by the Name of JEHOVAH was I not known to them. *Exod.* vi. 3.

His eyes ſhall ſee his deſtruction, and he ſhall drink of the wrath of the Almighty. *Job* xxi. 20.

Ah, Lord God, behold thou haſt made the Heaven and the Earth, by thy great Power and ſtretched out Arm, and there is nothing too hard for Thee. The great, the mighty God, the Lord of Hoſts is his Name, great in Counſel and mighty in Work. *Jer.* xxxii. 17—

Now unto him that is able to do exceeding abundantly above all that we aſk or think, according to the Power that worketh in us, unto Him be Glory in the Church by Christ Jesus, throughout all Ages, World without End, Amen. *Eph.* iii. 20, 21.

III. *Of* GOD'*s Omnipresence.*

BUT will God indeed dwell on Earth? Behold the Heaven, and Heaven of Heavens cannot contain Thee, how much less this House that I have built? 1 *Kings* viii. 27.

Can any hide himself in secret Places that I shall not see him, saith the Lord. *Jer* xxiii 2

Whither shall I go from Thy Spirit? Or whither shall I flee from Thy Presence? If I ascend up into Heaven, Thou art there; if I make my bed in Hell, behold Thou art there. If I take the wings of the Morning, and dwell in the utmost parts of the Sea, even there shall Thy Hand lead me, and Thy Right-Hand shall hold me. If I say surely the Darkness shall cover me, even the Night shall be light about me. Yea, the Darkness hideth not from Thee, but the Night shineth as the Day; the Darkness and the Light are both alike unto Thee. *Psalm* cxxxix. 7 to 12.

And ſhe called the Name of the Lord that ſpake unto her, Thou God ſeeſt me: For ſhe ſaid, Have I alſo here looked after him that ſeeth me. *Gen.* xvi. 13.

Thy Father which ſeeth in ſecret ſhall reward thee openly. *Mat.* vi. 4.

Which is his Body, the fullneſs of him that filleth all in all. *Eph.* i. 23.

IV. *Of* GOD's *Omniſcience.*

AND thou, *Solomon* my Son, know thou the God of thy Father, and ſerve Him with a perfect heart, and with a willing mind: For the Lord ſearcheth all the hearts and underſtandeth all the Imaginations of the thoughts: If thou ſeek Him, he will be found of thee; but if thou forſake Him He will caſt thee off for ever. 1 *Chron.* xxviii. 9.

Then hear Thou in Heaven Thy dwelling-place, and forgive, and do, and give to every man according to his ways, whoſe heart thou knoweſt; for Thou, even Thou only knoweſt the hearts of all the Children of men. 1 *Kings* viii. 39.

Neither is there any Creature that is not manifest in His sight: But all things are naked and open to the Eyes of Him with whom we have to do. *Heb.* iv. 13.

Thou knowest my down-sitting and mine uprising, Thou understandest my thoughts afar off. Thou compassest my path, and my lying down, and art acquainted with all my ways. For there is not a word in my tongue, but lo, O Lord, thou knowest it altogether. *Psalm* cxxxix. 2, 3, 4.

Known unto God are all His Works from the beginning of the World. *Acts.* xv. 18.

V. *Of the Wisdom of* GOD.

GREAT is our Lord, and of great power, His understanding is infinite. *Psal.* cxlvii. 5

O the Depth of the Riches, both of the Wisdom and Knowledge of God! How unsearchable are His Judgments, and His Ways past finding out! *Rom.* xi. 33.

To God only Wise, be Glory through Jesus Christ for ever. Amen. *Rom.* xvi. 27.

VI. *Of the Holineſs of GOD.*

AND one cried unto another, and ſaid, Holy, Holy, Holy, is the Lord of Hoſts, the whole Earth is full of His Glory. *Iſa.* vi. 3.

And the four Beaſts had each of them ſix wings about him, and they were full of eyes within; and they reſt not Day and Night ſaying, Holy, Holy, Holy, Lord God Almighty, which was, and is, and is to come. *Rev.* iv. 8.

Becauſe it is written, Be ye holy, for I am Holy. 1 *Pet.* i. 16.

But Thou art Holy, O Thou that inhabiteſt the praiſes of Iſrael. *Pſalm* xxii. 3.

Who ſhall not fear Thee O Lord, and glorify Thy name? For Thou art Holy. *Rev.* xv. 4.

VII. *Of the Juſtice of GOD.*

HE is a Rock, His work is perfect: For all His Ways are Judgments: A God of Truth, and without Iniquity, Juſt and Right is He. *Deut.* xxxii. 4.

Shall not the Judge of all the Earth do Right? *Gen.* xviii. 25.

But let him that glorieth, glory in this, that he understandeth and knoweth Me that I am the Lord, which exercise loving kindness, Judgment, and Righteousness in the Earth: For in these things I delight saith the Lord. *Jer.* ix. 24.

——And that by no means will clear the guilty; visiting the Iniquity of the Fathers upon the Children, and upon the Childrens Children, unto the third, and to the fourth Generation. *Exod.* xxxiv. 7.

He shall judge the World in Righteousness, He shall minister Judgment to the People in uprightness. The Lord is known by the Judgment He executeth: The Wicked is snared in the Work of his own Hands. Higgaion, Selah. The Wicked shall be turned into Hell, and all the Nations that forget God. *Psalm* ix. 8—16, 17.

God shall wound the Head of His Enemies: And the hairy Scalp of such a one as goeth on still in his Trespasses. *Psalm* lxviii. 21.

VIII. *Of the Truth and Faithfulneſs of GOD.*

A GOD of Truth, and without Iniquity, Juſt and Right is He. *Deut.* xxxii. 4.

His Truth endureth to all Generations. *Pſalm* c. 5.

Which made Heaven and Earth, the Sea, and all that therein is: Which keepeth Truth for ever. *Pſalm* cxlvi. 6.

Now I Nebuchadnezzar praiſe and extol and honor the King of Heaven, all whoſe Works are Truth and His ways Judgment, and thoſe that walk in Pride He is able to abaſe. *Daniel* iv. 17.

All Thy Commandments are Truth, *Pſalm* cxix. 151.

Thou wilt perform the Truth to Jacob, and the Mercy to Abraham, which Thou haſt ſworn unto our Fathers from the Days of Old. *Micah* vii. 20.

And hath raiſed up an horn of Salvation for us, in the Houſe of His Servant David: As He ſpake by the mouth of His holy Prophets, that have been ſince the World begun, That we ſhould be ſaved from our Enemies, and from the Hand of all that hate us. To perform the Mercy promiſed to our Fathers, and to remember His Holy Covenant: The oath which He ſware to our Father Abraham, *Luke* i. 69, 70, 71, 72, 73. Thy Faithfulneſs reacheth unto the Clouds. *Pſalm* xxxvi. 5.

I will make known Thy Faithfulneſs to all Generations.—Thy Faithfulneſs alſo in the Congregations of the Saints. But my Faithfulneſs and my Mercy ſhall be with Him. *Pſalm* lxxxix. 1, 2, 5, 24. Thy Faithfulneſs is unto all Generations. *Pſalm* cxix. 90.

IX. *Of the Mercy of GOD.*

AND the LORD paſſed by before him and proclaimed, The LORD, The LORD GOD, merciful and gracious, long ſuffering, and abundant in Goodneſs and Truth, keeping Mercy for thouſands, forgiving Iniquity and Tranſgreſſion, and Sin. *Exodus* xxxiv. 6, 7.

O give Thanks unto the Lord, for He is good: For His Mercy endureth for ever. *Pſalm* cxviii. 1.

GOD the Creator of the World.

THOU, even Thou art LORD alone, Thou hast made Heaven, the Heaven of Heavens with all their host, the earth and all things that are therein, the Seas, and all that is therein. *Neh.* ix. 6.

And He is before all things, and by Him all things consist. *Col.* i. 16, 17.

For every house is builded by some man, but He that built all things is God. *Heb.* iii. 4.

GOD the Governor of the World, in His Works of Providence.

THE Lord reigneth, let the earth rejoice, let the multitude of isles be glad. *Ps.* xcvii. 1.

The King's heart is in the hand of the LORD, as the Rivers of Water He turneth it whithersoever He will. *Prov.* xxi. 1.

The lot is cast into the lap: But the whole disposing thereof is of the Lord. *Prov.* xvi. 33.

Upholding all things by the word of His power. *Heb.* i. 3. His Kingdom ruleth over all. *Psalm* ciii. 19. Who worketh all things after the counsel of His own will, *Eph.* i. 11.

The State of Man before the Fall.

SO God Created man after His own Image, in the Image of God Created He him, Male and Female created He them. And God blessed them, and God said unto them, Be fruitful and multiply, and replenish the earth, and subdue it; and have dominion over the fish of the sea, over the fowl of the air, and over every living thing that moveth upon the earth. *Gen.* i. 27. 28.

And have put on the New Man, which is renewed in knowledge, after the Image, of Him that Created him. *Col.* iii. 10.

And that ye put on the New Man, which after God is Created in Righteousness, and true Holiness. *Eph.* iv. 24.

Lo, this only have I found, that GOD made man upright. *Eccl.* vii. 29.

The Fall of Man.

BUT they have sought out many Inventions. *Eccl.* vii. 29.

And when the woman saw that the tree was good for food, and that it was pleasant to the eyes, and a tree to be desired to make one wise: she took of the fruit thereof, and did eat. *Gen.* iii. 6.

Wherefore as by one man Sin entered into the world, and death by sin, and so death hath passed upon all men, for that all have sinned. *Rom.* v. 12.

For since by man came Death, by man came also the resurrection of the dead: For as in Adam all die, even so in Christ shall all be made alive. 1 *Cor.* xv. 21. 22.

O Israel, thou hast destroyed thy self, but in Me is thine help. *Hos.* x. iii. 9.

Thy first Father hath sinned. *Isa.* xliii. 27.

The Way of Fallen Man's Recovery by Christ.

I Will put Enmity between thee and the Woman, and between thy Seed and her Seed; it shall bruise thy Head, and thou shalt bruise his Heel. *Gen.* iii. 15.

And she shall bring forth a Son and thou shalt call his Name Jesus; for he shall save his people from their Sins. *Mat.* i. 21.

For unto you is born this Day, in the city of David, a Saviour, which is Chriſt the Lord. *Luke* ii. 11.

For the Son of man is come to ſeek and to ſave that which was loſt. *Luke* xix. 10.

This is a faithful ſaying and worthy of all acceptation, that *Chriſt Jeſus* came into the world to ſave *Sinners*, of whom I am chief. 1 *Tim.* i. 15.

Neither is there ſalvation in any other: for there is none other name under Heaven given among men whereby we muſt be ſaved. *Acts* iv. 12.

Of Death.

FOR the wages of Sin is Death: but the gift of God is Eternal life, thro' Jeſus Chriſt our Lord. *Rom.* vi. 27.

—For in the Day that thou eateſt thereof thou ſhalt ſurely die. *Gen.* ii. 17.

The end of thoſe things is Death. *Rom.* vi. 21.

Of the Resurrection and last Judgment.

MARVEL not at this: for the hour is coming, in the which all that are in their Graves shall hear His Voice, and shall come forth, they that have done good unto the Resurrection of Life; and they that have done evil, unto the Resurrection of Damnation, *Joh.* v. 28.29.

For we must all appear before the Judgment-seat of Christ, that every one may receive the things done in his body, according to that he hath done, whether it be good or bad.. 2 *Cor.* v. 10.

Of Heaven.

FOR we know, that if our earthly house of this tabernacle were dissolved, we have a building of God, an house not made with hands, eternal in the Heavens. *Cor.* v. 1,

Eye hath not seen, nor ear heard, neither have entered into the heart of man, the things which God hath prepared for them that love Him. 1 *Cor.* ii. 9.

Of Hell.

THE Rich man died and was buried. And in Hell he lift up his eyes, being in Torments, and seeth *Abraham* afar off, and *Lazarus* in his bosom. And he cried and said, Father *Abraham*, have mercy on me, and send *Lazarus*, that he may dip the tip of his finger in water, and cool my tongue: for I am tormented in this Flame. *Luke* xvi. 22, 23, 24.

Where their Worm dieth not, and the Fire is not quenched. *Mark* ix. 44.

And these shall go away into everlasting Punishment. *Mat.* xxv. 46.

The Blessings of the Righteous in the World to come.

1 WITH Everlasting Joy, *Isa.* lxi. 7.
2 With Everlasting Life, *Joh.* iii. 16.
3 With Everlasting Glory, 2 *Cor.* iv. 17.
4 With Everlasting Honor, *Rom.* ii. 7.
5 With Everlasting Liberty, 2 *Cor.* iii. 17.
6 With Everlasting Light, *Psal.* xcvii. 11.
7 With Everlasting Dominion, *Psal.* xlix. 14.

The Curses of the Wicked.

1 WITH Everlasting Shame, *Dan.* xii. 2.
2 Everlasting Death, *Dan.* xii. 2.
3 With Everlasting Contempt, *Job* xii. 21.
4 With Everlasting Slavery, *Job* xv. 20.
5 With Everlasting Bondage, *Isa.* iii. 11.
6 With Everlasting Darkness, *Mat.* viii. 12.
7 With Everlasting Destruction, 2. *Thes.* i. 9.

CHAP. VII.

Containing Ten short Exhortations.

1 LET thy Thoughts be Divine, Awful and Godly.
2 Let thy Talk be Little, Honest and True.
3 Let thy Works be Profitable, Holy and Charitable.
4 Let thy Manners be Grave, Courteous and Chearful.
5 Let thy Diet be Temperate, Convenient and Frugal.
6 Let thy Apparel be sober, neat & Comely
7 Let thy Will be Compliant, Obedient and Ready,

8 Let thy Prayers be devout, often & fervent.

9 Let thy Recreation be lawful, brief and seldom.

10 Let thy Meditations be of Death, Judgment and Eternity.

CHAP. VIII.

Containing Good Thoughts for Little Children, a compendious Body of Divinity, an Alphabet of useful Copies, all in Verse. &c. &c.

A Verse may find him whom a Sermon flies,
And turn Delight into a Sacrifice.

I. *Good Thoughts for little Children,* viz. *To consider their Baptism to improve it. And remember God's Commandments to observe them.*

I Was baptiz'd unto the LORD,
Who FATHER, SON and Spirit is,
I must FEAR GOD, and mind his Word,
And LOOK to CHRIST for Happiness.
The GOD of Heaven did make me,
That I to Him should subject be,
The Son of GOD is Man become,
That he to GOD might bring Man home.

If I BELIEVE in JESUS CHRIST,
Then I ſhall be for ever bleſt;
But if I ſlight that Saviour kind,
My Miſery will never end.

THE LIVING GOD, I muſt adore,
As he requires, him come before,
His Holy Name take not in vain,
His Holy Day, never prophane,
To all Superiors, Honor give,
Take care, that Neighbours well may live,
Keep clear from all Unchaſtity,
Refrain from all Diſhoneſty,
That all my Speech be Truth, take heed,
All ſhews of Diſcontentment dread.

Beg pardoning Grace for all Sins paſt,
Truſt CHRIST, *my ſoul, to ſave at laſt.*

Or thus the *Commandments may be Verſify'd.*

I. HAVE thou no other Gods but me.
II. Unto no Image bow thy Knee.
III. Take not the Name of God in vain.
IV. Do not the Sabbath-Day prophane.
V. Honor thy Father, Mother too.

VI. Take heed that thou no Murder do.
VII. From Whoredom keep thy Body clean.
VIII. Steal not, altho' thy ſtate be mean.
IX. Bear not falſe Witneſs: Shun that Blot.
X. What is thy Neighbour's Covet not.

Theſe are the Laws which GOD did Give:
Keep them by Faith in CHRIST, and Live.

II. *A compendious Body of Divinity.*

THE Scriptures of Divine Authority,
A perfect rule for all men to walk by.
From them we learn the living God to know,
And what the Duty is to Him we owe.
Three Sacred Perſons in the God-head be,
Of one Power, Subſtance and Eternity;
The Father, and Chriſt Jeſus, His own Son,
The Holy Ghoſt; and all theſe Three are One.
GOD is a moſt Pure Spirit Infinite,
In Truth abaundant, of great Power & Might.
Moſt Holy, Wiſe, Juſt, Good, Long-ſuffering,
Of *whom*, thro' *whom*, to *whom* is every thing.
He made the World, and all that is therein:
Man was made upright, but ſoon fell by Sin.

We all do from polluted Parents ſpring,
And in our *fleſh* there dwelleth no *good* thing
None righteous are; but all of every ſort,
Have ſinn'd, and of God's glory are come ſhort.
But God ſo loved us that He did give,
His only Son that we thro' Him might live:
The Son of GOD became the Son Man,
That we might be the Sons of God again.
He's God and Man; the only Mediator
Between the Sons of Men and their Creator.
He gave Himſelf for our eternal good,
And waſht away our Sins with His own blood.
What *love* was this? 'twas *love* beyond degree,
The Offended dies to ſet Offenders free.
It's God that juſtifies; who ſhall condemn?
It's Chriſt that dy'd, or rather roſe again,
Who alſo ſits at God's right hand on high;
And interceeds for us continually.
We by one Spirit through Him alone,
May have acceſs unto the Holy One.
If we believe on Him that came to ſave,
We're ſure at laſt Eternal Life to have.
There's nothing that avails with God above,
But Faith in *Jeſus Chriſt*, which works by love.

Hereby we know that we do love the Lord,
When we do keep the Precepts of His Word.
The Lord has ſhewn what He requires as good.
Deal juſtly and walk humbly with your God.
Serve *Him* with *fear*, love *Him* with *all your might*,
Speak ill of none, and give to all their right.
And when you have done all you can, confeſs
The imperfection of your Righteouſneſs.
Aſcribe the Praiſe of all the Good you do,
To Him that works the will and deed in you.
Keep conſcience pure and void of all offence:
Prepare for Death with ſpeed and diligence.
Bleſt are the dead that in the Lord do die,
Their works do follow them aſſuredly.
The day is coming when the dead ſhall hear
The voice of Chriſt and forthwith ſhall appear.
All they to life whoſe works are good and right
All they to Death who do in Sin delight.
As every man hath in the Body done,
So ſhall his Sentence at the Laſt-Day run.
The wicked ſhall be turned into Hell,
The Righteous ſhall with *Chriſt* forever dwell.

III. *An Alphabet of Uſeful Copies.*

ATTEND the Advice of the Old and the Wiſe.
Be not angry nor fret, but forgive and forget.
Can'ſt thou think it no Ill, to pilfer and ſteal!
Do the Thing thou art bid, nor be ſullen when chid.
Envy none for their Wealth, their Honor, or Health.
Fear, worſhip and love, the great God above.
Grow quiet and eaſy, when Boys ſtrive to teaze thee.
Honor Father and Mother, love Siſter and Brother.
It is dangerous Folly, to jeſt with Things holy.
Keep thy book without blot, and thy cloaths without ſpot.
Let thy hand do no wrong, nor backbite with thy tongue.
Make haſte to obey, nor diſpute nor delay.
Never ſtay within Hearing of Curſing and Swearing.
Offer God all the Prime of thy Strength and thy Time.
Provoke not the Poor, though he lies at thy Door.
Quaſh all evil Thoughts, and mourn for thy Faults.
Rule carefully thy Life, keeping free from all Strife,
Shun the Wicked and rude, but converſe with the Good.
Tranſgreſs not the Rule, at Home or at School.
Vie ſtill with the beſt, and excel all the Reſt.
When Boys are at Play, let them mind what they ſay.
X is ſuch a Letter, ſpoils my Verſe and my Metre.
Yield a little for Peace, and let Quarreling ceaſe.
Zeal and Charity join'd, make Men ious and kind.

The LORDs Prayer.

OUR Father which art in heaven, hallowed be Thy name. Thy kingdom come; Thy will be done in earth as it is in heaven; give us this day our daily bread; and forgive us our treſpaſſes, as we forgive them that treſpaſs againſt us; and lead us not into temptation, but deliver us from evil; for thine is the kingdom, the power and the glory, for ever, AMEN.

The CREED, or Chriſtian Belief.

I Believe in God the Father, Almighty Maker of heaven and earth; and in Jeſus Chriſt His only Son our Lord, who was conceived by the Holy Ghoſt, born of the Virgin *Mary*, ſuffered under *Pontius Pilate*, was crucified, dead and buried, He deſcended into hell, the third day He aroſe again from the dead, He aſcended into heaven, and ſitteth on the right hand of God the Father Almighty, from thence He ſhall come to judge both the quick and the dead; I believe in the Holy Ghoſt, the holy catholic church, the communion of Saints, the forgiveneſs of ſins, the reſurrection of the body, and the life everlaſting. AMEN.

A Prayer for Wiſdom and Knowledge, to be ſaid by a Child when going to School; or at any other Time.

O Almighty God and merciful Father, Maker of heaven and earth, who of Thy free liberality giveſt wiſdom abundantly to all, who with faith and full aſſurance aſk it of Thee: Beautify by the light of Thy heavenly grace, the towardneſs of my wit; the which, with all the powers of nature Thou haſt poured into me, that I may not only underſtand thoſe things, which may effectually bring me to the knowledge of Thee, and the Lord Jeſus our Saviour; but alſo with my whole heart and will, conſtantly follow the ſame, and receive daily increaſe through Thy bountiful goodneſs towards me, as well in good life, as doctrine: So that Thou, who workeſt all things in all Creatures, mayeſt make Thy gracious Benefits ſhine in me, to the endleſs glory and honor of Thine immortal Majeſty, Amen.

A Morning Prayer for a Child.

O Lord our heavenly Father, Almighty, and everlasting God, who hast safely brought me to the beginning of this day, defend me in the same with thy mighty power. Direct me in all my laudable and praise worthy undertakings for the best, and bless me in them. Enlighten my understanding, strengthen my memory, sanctify my heart, and guide me in my life. Let the duties of this day be cheerfully undergone by me; and give me grace so to apply myself to my learning, that I may be obedient to those who have the care of my education; to behave myself soberly, and with good manners to every one; and that I may lead an innocent and inoffensive life. Lord protect and defend all my relations and friends; and grant that none of us may fall into any kind of danger; but let all our doings be ordered by Thy governance, to do always that which is righteous in Thy sight, thro' Jesus Christ our Lord, to whom with Thee and the Holy Ghost, be all honor and glory, for ever and ever. AMEN.

A N

Appeal to the PUBLIC,

ESPECIALLY TO THE LEARNED,

WITH RESPECT TO THE

UNLAWFULNESS

O F

DIVORCES,

IN ALL CASES, EXCEPTING THOSE OF

INCONTINENCY.

THE SUBSTANCE OF THE ARGUMENT WAS PLEADED BEFORE THE CONSOCIATION OF THE COUNTY OF NEW-HAVEN, DECEMBER 9th, 1785.

TO WHICH AN APPENDIX IS SUBJOINED, EXHIBITING A GENERAL VIEW OF THE LAWS AND CUSTOMS OF CONNECTICUT, AND OF THEIR DEFICIENCY RESPECTING THE POINT IN DISPUTE.

BY BENJAMIN TRUMBULL, A. M.
PASTOR OF THE CHURCH IN NORTH-HAVEN.

"*What therefore* GOD *hath joined together, let not man put asunder.*"
JESUS CHRIST.

NEW-HAVEN: Printed by J. MEIGS.
A. D. MDCC.LXXXVIII.

The AUTHOR to the PUBLIC.

WHEREAS at a meeting of the brethren of the Church, in North-Haven, December 29th, 1785, it was voted, "That "as the plea made by Mr. TRUMBULL, against divorces, before "the Reverend Consociation of New-Haven County, lately convened "in this place, was very agreeable to our sentiments, and, in our "opinion, worthy of public notice, we desire it may be made pub- "lic:" it has been considered as a matter of respect and duty to them to publish it in the form in which it was then spoken. Besides, this seemed necessary, that our sister churches, and the public, might have information of the true grounds of our conduct relative to this subject. The author has had a special view, in this publication, to the vindication of his brethren, the satisfaction, instruction and benefit of his hearers in general, whom to oblige and edify, is the business, aim and pleasure of his life. Some enlargements have been made, especially in that part of the appeal, which contains objections and answers, since it was spoken before the consociation, and the large concourse of people present on the occasion. It was then viewed as an appeal to the public, though addressed more immediately to the consociation. As it was spoken in behalf of the author's brethren of the Church, in North-Haven, they are sometimes termed this church. When he speaks of himself and them conjointly. as he does towards the close of the appeal, we, us, &c. are used. His apology for the quotations in the learned languages. is, That he could not find the sentiments they contain, in the English language: and, that it was necessary to show that he had made a fair representation of them.

An APPEAL to the PUBLIC, &c.

REVEREND FATHERS AND BRETHREN,

THE doctrine of divorces has been ſo long adopted by law, in this ſtate, ſo eſtabliſhed by cuſtom and precedents, that to appeal againſt it muſt be very unpopular and promiſe little ſucceſs. Few men are poſſeſſed of ſo much candour and nobleneſs of mind, as fully to examine new ſentiments, and admit the conviction which they offer, even when well founded and clearly demonſtrated. To be ſure this is the caſe when they are oppoſite to preconceived opinions and prejudices, confirmed by long habit and cuſtom. Such opinions, though ever ſo erroneous and clearly confuted, will be hardly given up. As I am fully appriſed of theſe difficulties, and equally with other men wiſh for popularity, nothing could have induced me to appear againſt the general opinion but a ſtrong conviction of duty. I have a full perſuaſion, that divorces, as practiſed in this ſtate, are directly oppoſed to the authority of JESUS CHRIST, to the intereſts of his kingdom, and to the general happineſs of mankind. They are calculated to inſnare individuals, and to involve them and the public in great guilt, miſery and danger. On this point therefore the divine word, my conſcience, my duty to this people, and to the world, oblige me to be unpopular. I am conſtrained to make my appeal to the public, whether the arguments from the original inſtitution and deſign of marriage, the inſtructions and expreſs commands of CHRIST and the inſpired writers, do not demonſtratively conclude againſt divorces, in all caſes, excepting thoſe of incontinency?

WHEN the lawfulneſs of divorce is denied, in every caſe but that of incontinency, it is only with reference to thoſe who come properly *in vinculum matrimonii*, into the band of wedlock; or, who are warranted to marry by the divine word. All other marriages are, *ipſo facto*, null and void. Marriages within the limits of conſanguinity are no marriages. This is the light in which both the laws of England and of this ſtate conſider them; they therefore baſtardize all the children who are the issue of such marriages*. Blackstone tells us, That divorces in such cases are *pro salute animarum*, for the safety of the soul; and that the total divorce, *a vinculo matrimonii*, is only for canonical causes, incapacity, consanguinity and the like, which render marriage, in such cases, absolutely unlawful from the beginning.

THE settlement made by our SAVIOUR, in his sermon on the mount, and in other parts of the evangelists, demonstratively evinces the unlawfulness of divorces, in all cases whatsoever, excepting those of incontinency, when the marriage hath been legal. In these passages he hath a special reference to the law of Moses, respecting divorce. As an examination of this, may show the force of his words, more clearly fix their meaning, and elucidate the subject, it claims our first and peculiar attention.

IT is written Deut. 24. at the beginning, *When a man hath taken a wife and married her, and it come to pass that she find no favour in his eyes, because he hath found some uncleanness in her: then let him write her a bill of divorcement and give it in her hand, and send her out of his house.* That is, if, on the consummation of the marriage, she be disagreeable and finds no favor with him; KI MAZA BAH GNÆRVAT DABAR, because he had found in her *a word of nakedness*, or *some nakedness*. The Hebrew root GNARAH signifies to make *naked*, and the signification of GNÆRVAT, the substantive derived from it, is primarily *nakedness* †: or, it may bear the construction of *filthiness* of body, precipue in partibus genitalibus, or of *shame* and *reproach*‡. On this supposition, it seems, there was, by implication, a permission for him to put her away. The Hebrew text however, by no means agrees with our translation, *Let him write her a bill of divorcement*. The words are, VECATAB LAH SEPHER KERITUTH VENATAN BEJADAH VESHELCHAH MEBITO, *And he should write her a bill of divorcement and give it in her hand and send her out of his house.* This and the two next verses, in the Hebrew, are entirely hypothetical, proceeding on the supposition, That if her first husband should give her a bill, and the second should treat her in the same manner, or should be taken from her by death, that then her first husband should never take her again: *For that*, saith Moses, *is abomination before the* LORD. In this view of the text it contains, at most, but a barely implied permission for a man to put away his wife, if, on consummating his marriage, he found grounds of suspicion that she had been incontinent, or discovered in her some corporal

* Blackstone Vol. I. P. 446. State Law Book P. 136.

† The nakedness of the human body. Exod. 28. 42. Gen. 9. 22. Lev. 16. 17, 18, and onward. It is translated in Latin verenda pudenda. Nuditas corporis humani propalam turpis et pudenda censetur, maxime partium genitalium, quas natura tectas voluit. Buxtorf.

‡ The Seventy render GNÆRVAT DABAR, ASCHEEMON PRAGMA, an indecent, a shameful, or filthy thing.

corporal uncleanness of which before he had no intimation or apprehension; so that he found himself wholly deceived and disappointed in his match. This was a case in which the nakedness or immodesty discovered did not amount to actual whoredom, or if there were suspicions of it, proof could not be obtained: for if a woman either before or after her espousals, played the harlot in her father's house, she was to be stoned*. That this is a literal and fair construction of the Hebrew text, and of the law of Moses respecting divorces, I dare make my appeal to the whole learned world. Mr. Pool says "If we consult "the Hebrew words, those three first verses may seem only a supposi-"tion." The Septuagint, and the Latin translation of the Old Testament, by Tremellius and Junius, give us the same idea. Here it is important to observe that this barely implied permission to put away the wife seems only to have been at the time of the consummation of the marriage, or soon after, on the account of some new discovery then made, which, ever afterward, was likely to render the connubial state unhappy. To this time only do the words refer, and to the discovery now made. They imply no permission of putting away after the husband and wife had reaped the fruits of nuptial enjoyments in a tender offspring: not on the account of desertion, bad conduct, or any malady of body or mind which might take place after the consummation of marriage and their cohabitation as one flesh. Deuteronomy 22. 19. is a corroboration of this sentiment. Here a man is expressly forbidden to put away a wife of whose virginity there was full evidence at the time of marriage. The like precept in verse 28, respecting the man who should lie with a virgin, gives it additional strength. Beside, the prophet Malachi's reproof of the Jews for putting away their wives, after cohabitation with them, in the days of their youth, seems wholly inconsistent with the law of Moses, were that to be understood as warranting a man to put away his wife, at any other time, excepting that immediately, or soon after the consummation of the marriage. Can it be supposed that the prophet would condemn them for what Moses suffered? Or that he would have declared those very women which had been put away agreeably to his law, to be the wives of those who had put them away? It therefore seems that these were the only cases, and this the only time in which a Jew was warranted, even by the law of Moses to put away his wife. In the case of adultery the divine law provided a different relief for the injured correlate, the death of the adulterer. Lev. 20. 10. *And the man that committeth adultery with another man's wife, even he that committeth adultery with his neighbour's wife, the adulterer and the adulteress shall surely be put to death.*

Now in reference to this implied permission of Moses our SAVIOUR saith, Matth. 5. 31. 32. *It hath been said, Whosoever shall put away his wife, let him give her a writing of divorcement. But I say*

* Deut. 22. 21, 22, 23, 24.

say unto you, That whosoever shall put away his wife, saving for the cause of fornication, causeth her to commit adultery: and whosoever shall marry her that is divorced, committeth adultery. In these words the old law or permission of Moses, respecting this matter is evidently repealed by CHRIST, as contrary to the original design and institution of marriage; and all divorces on the account of any bodily disease, or suspicions of unchastity, or on any other footing than that of evident incontinency, are absolutely forbidden. Our SAVIOUR's confining divorces to the case of incontinency, and declaring every man an adulterer who should put away his wife for any other cause, or who should marry one divorced on any other, in the fairest construction, is an absolute abrogation of every other law and custom. In the 19th chapter of this gospel he hath expressed himself still more fully, on this point, in his discourse with the Pharisees, who came tempting him with this enquiry, *Is it lawful for a man to put away his wife for every cause?* To which he replies, *Have ye not read, that he which made them at the beginning, made them male and female? And said, For this cause shall a man leave father and mother, and shall cleave unto his wife: and they twain shall be one flesh. Wherefore they are no more twain, but one flesh. What therefore* GOD *hath joined together, let not man put asunder.* CHRIST here points the Pharisees to the original institution of marriage and hence argues the unlawfulness of divorces;—that the husband and wife were never to be separated, Adam and Eve were originally but one flesh and one body; and when, of his flesh and bone GOD had created her, he made them one again in the primitive institution of marriage. He created but one Eve for the one man Adam; so that he could not put her away for another. Indeed he could not put her away without frustrating both the end of her creation and the design of marriage. The first formation of the sexes, the original and divinely instituted oneness of the first pair, their peculiar circumstances, being the only *male* and *female*, of their species, upon earth, afford striking evidence that the husband and wife were never to be disjoined. Mr. Pool hath this observation on Gen. II. 24. "This first "institution shews the sinfulness of divorces and polygamy, however "GOD might upon a particular reason for a time dispense with his "own institution, or remit the punishment due to the violators of it." Hence CHRIST commands that no man, no law or ordinance of man, should ever separate those correlates whom GOD and nature have thus joined together.

ON this stating of the case the Pharisees pleaded the permission given by Moses, which they termed a command. Our SAVIOUR replied, *Moses because of the hardness of your hearts, suffered you to put away your wives: but from the beginning it was not so.* "Moses did by no means command you to put away your wives: he "barely permitted it in certain cases, on the account of your murderous and implacable tempers, and of your intolerable abuse of "your

"your wives; but I assure you that this implied permission was contra-
"ry to the original design and institution of marriage." Then as head of the Church, and judge of the world, he makes this solemn declaration, *Whosoever shall put away his wife, except it be for fornication, and shall marry another, committeth adultery; and whosoever marrieth her which is put away, doth commit adultery.* The same declaration for substance is found both in Mark and Luke*. From these passages, and our SAVIOUR's reasoning on the subject, it is most evident, that he has utterly repealed the permission of Moses for divorcement, and entered a peremptory prohibition of it, in all cases, excepting those of incontinency. His words are express, positive, and without figures. They are no less plain and positive than any of the commandments, *Thou shalt not kill, thou shalt not commit adultery, &c.* There is every appearance that they are to be taken in their true literal import. They are not words of mere course and accident; but our SAVIOUR here sets himself, on design, to treat of the subject of divorces. The Pharisees evidently understood him agreeably to the plain literal import of his words, and as teaching a doctrine contrary to Moses. They therefore, in opposition to him, alledged what he had commanded. His disciples also understood him in the same manner. His doctrine bore so hard upon them, that they could not believe that he really designed all which his words fairly implied. They therefore privately desired him to explain his real meaning. He nevertheless made no retraction, but affirmed the same things to them, which he had done before unto the Pharisees. We may therefore depend upon it, that in these passages he hath unalterably fixed the law of divorce; and it greatly concerneth all those, who own HIM as LORD, to submit to this his final settlement†.

In these parts of the scriptures he hath unalterably fixed several points.

I. That whosoever putteth away his wife, or her husband, for any other cause than that of fornication before, or of adultery after marriage, and marrieth another, committeth adultery. In short he absolutely forbiddeth all putting away, in any case, but that of incontinency. It

* Mark 10. 2, 12. and Luke 16. 18.

† Some have imagined that our SAVIOUR's whole design, in this discourse, was to decide the dispute between the two famous sects of his day, the Hillæanæ, and the Samæani. The Hillæanæ maintained, That a man might put away his wife for any thing which displeased him. The Samæani denied it, and insisted that there must be the filthiness of which Moses spake; some immodesty, at least, in words or actions, or else it could not be lawful for a man to put away his wife. Selden's Hebrew wife, page 776. That any, however, should imbibe such an opinion, is to me very strange; for our SAVIOUR, by condemning and repealing the law of Moses, and forbidding divorce, except in case of fornication, equally condemned both their opinions. Beside, the dispute was not worthy of his notice. For to put away a wife for any thing which may displease, or for any thing which a man may judge immodest in word or gesture, comes, in effect, to the same thing.

It is not only contrary to the original design and institution of marriage, but to the very nature of GOD. It is a sin which he particularly noticeth as exceedingly hateful and abominable. He here speaketh the same language with the prophet, Malachi II. 14, 15, 16. *Because the* LORD *hath been witness between thee and the wife of thy youth, against whom thou hast dealt treacherously: yet is she thy companion, and the wife of thy covenant. Therefore take heed to your spirit and let none deal treacherously against the wife of his youth. For the* LORD *the* GOD *of Israel saith, That he hateth putting away.*

Fornication does not, cannot, mean any *great crime*, any *fault* or *cause* equal to that of *incontinency*, as the papists, some gentlemen of the law, and many others pretend. It is a word of very determinate signification, both in our own, and all other languages; importing that particular species of wickedness which we term *unchastity*, or *incontinence*: either in the less or more criminal instances of it. I am not sensible that it is ever used in any other sense, unless when it may be put figuratively for idolatry, or spiritual whoredom, of which, in this discourse of our SAVIOUR, there is not the least intimation. The word PORNEIA, translated *fornication*, was used by all nations to signify acts of uncleanness only; most commonly between single persons. This Dr Whitby particularly noticeth in his annotations on the nineteenth of Matthew. He understands it here to mean incontinency before marriage. However he says, "All commentators I have met "with, by *fornication*, here do understand *adultery*, or the defiling of "the marriage bed." Agreeably to him therefore all nations and expositors understand it as expressive of uncleanness only, either in the less or more criminal instances of it. It properly signifies whoredom, and may with propriety be used either for fornication or adultery. Dr. Doddridge hath this observation. "To say as some have done, that "PORNEIA does in general signify any great crime, is very arbitra- "ry.‡" Indeed, if the most determinate language may be construed with such an arbitrary latitude, nothing can be known with any certainty either by writing or speaking. By such interpretations the scriptures may be made to say and teach any thing. In short revelation could be of no essential service to mankind. This cannot therefore be our SAVIOUR's meaning. To take such a liberty in construing so solemn, express and unfigurative declarations of scripture, I humbly conceive to be an exceedingly bold, presumptuous and profane wresting of the words of GOD.

FURTHER, it is evident that our SAVIOUR designed to give no such liberty, as that of putting away the wife for any great fault, because this would have been opening a much wider door for divorces than the permission of Moses opened to the hard hearted Israelites. This would have been contrary to all his reasoning on the subject, and to his declaration that what Moses suffered was more than the original institution

‡ Doddridge, on Divorce, Lecture 189.

institution of marriage would admit. *But from the beginning it was not so.* It would also have been acting contrary to what he hath done in all other similar cases, in which he hath construed the law in its true extent and latitude.

BESIDES, had this been his meaning, both the Pharisees and his disciples must have entirely misunderstood him. Otherwise, the one would not have opposed him, by alledging the law of Moses, nor the other come to this conclusion, *If the case of the man be so with his wife, it is not good to marry* *. They no doubt would have been contented with a liberty of putting away their wives for any considerable fault or misbehaviour. Nay, had our SAVIOUR designed any thing like this, would he not, when he saw their anxiety, have fully explained himself to them? I conceive he most certainly would.

THERE is still another consideration of great weight with respect to the present argument. It is presumed that in any other case it would be thought decisive. That is, it is an excellent, and as far as I have acquaintance, an universal maxim in law, That when an exception is made to the general law, nothing can ever extend only to that particular exception. That is universally to be understood as the only exception ever pleadable under the general law. When the legislator makes one exception to his general law, and only one, there is all imaginable reason to determine there is not another. Had there been another, it would most certainly have been made, for the same reason for which the one specified was made. But our SAVIOUR's law respecting divorce is a general law, with a particular exception. This therefore, agreeably to the universal rule and practice of construing law, is the only exception. Incontinency, and no other crime is pleadable under the general law. All other faults are excluded.

IN short, other faults, or instances of misconduct are by no means like incontinency, with respect to the marriage state. *Jealousy is the rage of a man.* Nothing so inflames the injured correlate, and so totally alienates affection. *He will regard no ransome, neither will he rest content, though thou givest many gifts*†. Nothing can give satisfaction, or heal the breach. It is a most flagrant violation of the marriage covenant, in the essential and consummating part of it, in which the perfidious correlate becomes one flesh with another. It creates the utmost confusion in families, and with respect to inheritances, reducing a man to the utmost uncertainty with respect to his children, and exposing him to make heirs of the issue of his wanton neighbours. It is, beyond all other instances of misconduct, a total subversion of the institution and principal ends of marriage. From these various considerations it appears demonstratively evident, that *fornication*, as used by our SAVIOUR, is to be understood only of the sin of incontinency, and that he hath absolutely and forever prohibited all putting away on any other footing. This, so far as I know, is the general opinion

*Matth. 19. 10.

† Prov. 6. 34, 35.

opinion of all Protestant divines. Mr. Pool's continuators say, "Our "SAVIOUR gives the true sense of the moral law. He here opposeth "the Pharisees in two points. 1. Asserting that all divorces are un-"lawful except in case of adultery. 2. Asserting that whosoever mar-"rieth her that is put away committeth adultery." They roundly affirm, That "If we take divorce for the voluntary act of the hus-"band putting away his wife, it is unlawful in any case but that of "adultery." Mr. Henry, Mr. Pool and his continuators, Doctors, Whitby, Guyse and Doddridge, Mr. Willard, the Assembly of Divines, and indeed all divines whom I have ever read on the subject, unanimously give their opinion against all voluntary putting away, except in cases of incontinency. It must however be granted that most of these authors allow, that divorces are lawful in cases of total desertion, after all proper means of reconciliation have been attempted in vain.

WHETHER there be any kind of reason or consistency in maintaining the unlawfulness of spontaneous putting away, unless it be in the case of unchastity, and yet that divorces are lawful in cases of desertion, shall be noticed hereafter. I presume this venerable council, and the ministry of this state in general, agree in sentiment, with the Assembly of Divines and the authors who have been named, with respect to the unlawfulness of the former; it will therefore be unnecessary to insist further on this point.

I proceed to observe

II. THAT CHRIST, in an equally express and preremptory manner hath determined, that whosoever shall marry her who is put away from her husband, for any other cause than that of incontinency, committeth adultery. "*And whoso marrieth her that is put away doth commit adultery.*" These words are no less peremptory and determinate with respect to the adultery of him, who marrieth the woman put away, or deserted by her husband, for any other cause than that of incontinency, than the preceding are with respect to the adultery of him, who had put her away and married another. They place them both in the same class of transgressors. The woman having been put away or deserted without any just cause, the man who marrieth her committeth adultery against her husband, whose lawful wife she is still; and she, being still his wife, is likewise guilty of adultery. This is the sense which doctors Whitby and Guyse give of the text. The words of Dr. Whitby are these. "And therefore I, who came to reduce things to their "primitive perfection, say unto you, that under the gospel dispensati-"on, whosoever shall put away his wife except for fornication, and "shall marry another, committeth adultery with that other, and who-"so marrieth her that is put away, committeth adultery with her." Dr. Guyse's paraphrase is this, "And as I am come to reduce "GOD's laws to their primitive standard, I declare, that henceforth "whosoever shall divorce his wife for any other cause than that of forni-"cation before marriage, and of adultery after it, which in its own na-

"ture

" ture dissolves the matrimonial bond, shall be chargeable with the guilt " of the adultery that is committed by her, and the man who after- " wards marrieth her. For she is still the wife of him that divorced " her: and it is unlawful for her to be married to any other, while " her former husband is living."

THAT this is the true meaning of our SAVIOUR, is evident in that he speaks here of the very woman, whom her husband had put away for some other cause than that of inconntiency. He speaks of no other woman, nor does he give the least hint of any other, but of that whom her husband had *unlawfully* put away†. He speaks of *that woman* only against whom her husband committeth adultery, in giving her a divorce and marrying another. This must of necessity be the woman who is put away without a sufficient cause: for it is altogether absurd to suppose, that CHRIST would charge the man with adultery, in putting away his wife, for that which he had allowed to be a just and sufficient cause. Against such a woman he could commit no adultery. Her flesh in law and reason, became now as distinct from his, as it was in her virginity, All that which had been done, in their marriage, is now entirely undone, and it is not possible that they should commit adultery against each other. The obligations between correlates are mutual, and when they are totally vacated, each party is wholly discharged from all covenant obligations to the other. When the King of Great Britain declared the American colonies from under his protection and waged war against them, it was the general voice of America, that they were released from all allegiance to the British crown: and when a total separation took place, America and the whole world considered Great Britain as fully discharged from all obligations to her. Great Britain owes no more protection to her, than to any other nation whatsoever. These are ideas so natural and obvious, that they cannot escape the common sense and observation of mankind.

FURTHER, the supposition that CHRIST, when he said, He that marrieth her that is put away, designed *the her*, who is justly put away, involves in it this sentiment, That the man or woman, who is justly divorced, can never marry again without committing adultery, which I humbly conceive to be a grand absurdity. I presume it hath been clearly demonstrated already, that there can be no adultery in such a case, more than in the marrying of a widow or virgin; because, when the union

† AUTEEN APOLELUMENEEN. Our SAVIOUR's sentences, in the Greek are most compactly formed, each part of the sentence bearing a most determinate relation to the other, demonstratively fixing the idea of the woman against whom adultery is committed, both in putting her away and in entering into marriage with her after she had been divorced. The construction is such as necessarily confines it to the woman unlawfully divorced. It is the AUTEEN whom the man putting away causeth to commit adultery. Matth. 5 32. The AUTEEN the HER against whom in putting her away he committeth adultery. Mark 10. 11. She is the APOLELUMENEEN, the *woman put away*, in marrying whom, whosoever doth it, is declared to commit adultery. Matth. 5. 32. 19. 9. and Luke 16. 18.

union between the correlates is legally diſſolved, they are no more related, nor are under any more obligation to each other, than if ſuch union had never been.

BESIDES, the divine law no where prohibits, but allows perſons of this character to marry. Both he, who had put away his wife, and ſhe, who had been repeatedly put away, might marry again†. In this light mankind in general view the matter, and agreeably to this do they treat it, in practice, whatever may be pleaded to the contrary. There are no laws prohibiting the marriages of ſuch perſons. Neither civilians, nor the clergy, ſo far as I know, decline marrying one correlate more than the other, where a total ſeparation has been made between them, on the footing of the divine law. Our confeſſions of faith maintain, and it is the univerſal language of Proteſtants, "That "it is lawful for all ſorts of people to marry, who are able with judg-"ment to give their conſent*" I conceive therefore that it is demonſtratively evident, that when our LORD ſaith, *And whoſoever ſhall marry her that is put away committeth adultery*, he means the woman unjuſtly put away: the woman between whom and her huſband there had been no warrantable ground of ſeparation.

HENCE

3. THIS determineth the point with reſpect to all divorces on the footing of bare deſertion. It ſhows that they are abſolutely unlawful. Deſertion, is neither fornication nor adultery; it is quite a different thing, which neither implies, nor is like either of them. As incontinency only can warrant a divorce, and as the obligations of the correlates are mutual, binding them both, till the union between them is totally diſſolved; ſo it follows, by unavoidable conſequence that he who marrieth a woman barely deſerted of her huſband, and divorced on that footing, committeth adultery, and that the deſerted woman on her ſecond marriage, committeth adultery likewiſe. Nothing can effect a diſſolution of the relation, or ſet either of the correlates at liberty but that one thing, which only is ſufficient to do it in the divine account.

BESIDE, the woman put away without a cauſe is to all intents the deſerted perſon. It makes no material difference whether a man depart from his wife and wholly deſert her, or whether he give her a bill and turn her out of his houſe. She is as much forſaken, and deprived of all marriage duty, due from her huſband, and all the ends of marriage are as effectually violated, in the one caſe as in the other. The woman may be juſt as paſſive and innocent in the one caſe as in the other. Indeed the woman whom the man divorces and ſends out of his houſe, ſeems to be the moſt harſhly treated of the two. No poſſible plea can be made for the former more than for the latter. No reaſon can be given why it ſhould be declared with reſpect to him, who marrieth her who is put away, that *he* committeth adultery, rather than with reſpect to *him*, who marrieth her, whom her huſband had deſerted in a different manner. Nothing can be pleaded in her favour who is

deſerted

† Deut. 24. 2, 3.

* *Weſtminſter* and *Savoy* Confeſſions of Faith.

deſerted, more than in hers who is put away. Should it be ſaid, that there is no fault in the woman whom her husband hath deſerted, that ſhe hath been paſſive, and that it would be hard and cruel to treat her as an adultereſs, on a ſecond marriage, for that which ſhe could by no means prevent; the ſame may be pleaded with reſpect to the woman who hath been put away without a cauſe. She was innocent and could by no means prevent her huſband's giving her a bill and expelling her out of his houſe. Our SAVIOUR however was far from judging it hard or uncharitable to declare, that whoſoever ſhould marry ſuch a woman, would commit adultery: And in this very declaration he teacheth all men, wherever his word ſhall come, to treat her as an adultereſs.

SOME have indeed made a ſhift to get rid of this declaration of our SAVIOUR, by ſuppoſing that he here ſpeaks of a divorce in which there hath been colluſion, and that the woman put away had made herſelf guilty, by taking an active and voluntary part in her divorcement. This is indeed a meer ſuppoſition. I conceive it hath not even the colour of probability, There is not the leaſt intimation of any thing like this, in what our SAVIOUR hath ſaid on the ſubject, nor in any of the preceding or ſubſequent verſes. He i evidently treating of the doctrine of divorces at large, and giving a general rule reſpecting them. The ſuppoſition therefore, that he is ſpeaking of a particular exempt caſe, is unreaſonable. This would have been contrary to all the rules of good teaching or reaſoning upon a general ſubject. Beſide, the words of our SAVIOUR, Matth. 5 32. afford demonſtrative evidence, that he had no reference to divorce in the caſe of colluſion, or in any other exempt caſe. *I ſay unto you, That whoſoever ſhall put away his wife, ſaving for the cauſe of Fornication, cauſeth her to commit adultery: and whoſoever marrieth her that is put away, committeth adultery.* It is evident that our SAVIOUR chargeth the man putting away his wife, with the fault of her committing adultery. *He cauſeth her to commit adultery.* This HE, doubtleſs, would not have done, had her being put away been matter of her own choice and contrivance. It is further obſervable, that theſe words contain univerſal propoſitions, affirming with reſpect to every man, who ſhould put away his wife, ſaving for the cauſe of incontinency, that he cauſeth *her* to commit adultery, and with reſpect to every man, who ſhould marry the woman thus put away, that he committeth adultery. If our SAVIOUR ſpoke only with reference to an exempt caſe, in which there had been colluſion, the propoſition is not true. It ought, by no means, to have been univerſal. But as it is univerſal, it muſt include every woman put away for any other cauſe, than that of incontinency. It teacheth that every ſuch woman on a ſecond marriage, is an adultereſs, and that every man, who marrieth her, is an adulterer. The reaſon is, that the woman is ſtill his wife who hath put away or deſerted her.

THE prophet Malachi and the apoſtle Paul teach the ſame doctrine. The prophet ſpeaking of thoſe very women whom their huſbands had

perfidiouſly

perfidiously deserted, and who had been weeping and covering the altar of God with their tears, declares them to be the lawful and proper wives of those wicked husbands, who had deserted, or put them away. The Hebrew text is, VAHE CHABERTECHA VAESHET BARETECHA, and yet is she thy companion, and the wife of thy covenant. The comment of Calvin and Drusius on the words is this, "*Et* "*ipsa est socia tua, (i. e. quasi dimidia tui pars: Socia vitæ, ho-* "*norum ac laborum: et consors thori, et particeps sacrorum:) et* "*uxor fæderis tui**." *Even she is thy fellow: that is, as it were, the one half of thyself: the companion of thy life, of thy honours and labours, the consort of thy bed and partner of thy vows: the wife of thy covenant.* In this high strain do the scriptures, and these great expositors, speak of the woman who is put away, or deserted by her husband.

The injunction of the apostle, I. Cor. 7. 10, 11. proceeds on the same principle. But to the married I command not, but the Lord, that the wife be not separated from her husband. But if indeed she may have been separated, let her remain unmarried, or be reconciled to her husband: and that the husband put not away his wife. This, I apprehend, is a true and literal translation of these verses. The Greek word CHORISTHEE, is in the passive voice and first indefinite, in the Subjunctive Mood, and grammatically translated is, *may have been separated.* instead of *depart*, as it i in our translation. Mr. Pool's continuators take notice of the mistranslation of this verse. Those great men say, personating Mr. Pool, "How our translators came to translate "CHORISTHEE, which is manifestly a verb passive, (if she depart) "I cannot tell.' It signifieth if she be departed, and so is as well sig- "nificative of a being parted from her husband by a judicial act of di- "vorce, as of a voluntary departing. The word is to be interpreted "as well of any legal divorce, not according to the true meaning of "the Divine Law, as concerning a voluntary secession; in which case "the apostle commandeth that she should marry to no other; the "reason is plain, because no such cause of divorce broke the bond of "marriage; she was yet the wife of her former husband, in God's "eye and account, and committed adultery if she married another, "as our Saviour had determined, Matth. 5. 32. and 19. 9†" Dr. Whitby translates the passage in the same manner, EAN CHORISTHEE, if she be separated‡. This verse therefore clearly determines against divorces in any other case than that of incontinency, and it particularly determineth against divorce on the footing of desertion. The apostle terms the deserted husband still the husband of the woman who had deserted him, considers her as his lawful wife, and commands her to be reconciled to her husband. He forbids her to marry, that she might not commit adultery against her deserted and injured correlate. The apostle speaks of the deserted husband under the same predicament

* Pool's Synopsis on Malachi, 2. 14.
† English Annotations on this verse.
‡ Annotations vol. II. P. 149.

dicament, as the prophet Malachi speaks of the wives whom their husbands had deserted, as being still their lawful wives. Hence he teacheth that no desertion can dissolve the marriage band, till one of the correlates commits dultery, by a second marriage, or by becoming one flesh with another person. He also, in as express terms as our SAVIOUR, commandeth the husband and wife not to put away, or be separated from, each other. He declares this not to be his own commandment, but the LORD's; doubtless referring to what he had said in the gospels||.

AGAINST this reasoning, I am not insensible, that it will be objected and pleaded, that the 15th verse s a full proof of the lawfulness of divorces, on the account of the desertion of one of the correlate. *But if the unbelieving depart, let him depart. A brother or a sister is not under bondage in such cases: but GOD hath called us to peace.* As this is the grand text on which men build the doctrine of divorces, and seems to be the only one to keep its advocates in countenance, it merits particular attention.

ON this it is important to observe, that the passage can be nothing at all to the purpose, only, on this supposition, that by being brought into bondage the apostle means, being brought into a state, in which the deserted brother or sister is obliged to live single, or unmarried. But this supposed construction of the word *bondage* can by no means be allowed them. It is altogether arbitrary, and it is presumed, without a single precedent from any author, themselves excepted, either sacred or profane. It does by no means comport with the word used in the sacred text to express the bondage of which the apostle is speaking. This is DEDOULOTAI, a passive verb in the preterperfect tense: so that grammatically rendered it is, *A brother or sister hath not been brought into bondage, or enslaved by such things.* That is, "The "believing

|| If desertion were a sufficient ground of divorce, in the divine view, making one twain, then the deserted husband, in the case mentioned by the apostle, could have been under no obligations to receive the woman, who had deserted him, as his wife, more than any other woman; nor could she have been, now, under any obligations, as a wife, to him, more than to any other man. Nor could there have been any propriety in commanding her to be reconciled to him, as a husband, more than to another man, nor in remaining unmarried, unless she should obtain a reconciliation. For, as the obligations of the parties are mutual, whenever that takes place, which, agreeably to the divine word, makes the one flesh two again, there is no relation between them, more than there was in their childhood, as, it is conceived hath been shewn already. The instructions and commands of the apostle, therefore, in this case, proceed entirely on this principle, that the spouses, notwithstanding any desertion, or divorce, which had taken place, stood related, and mutually bound, to each other, as husband and wife. They therefore afford demonstrative evidence, that desertion, or the defrauding of each other of the marriage duty, does not make the spouses twain again. Hence desertion can be no warrantable ground of divorce. To reconcile what the apostle has said in the 10, and 11 verses, with the liberty supposed, by many, to be given in the 15 verse, is, doubtless, impossible. This shows that the general construction put upon it is totally wrong.

"believing husband or wife, hath not, by his or her marriage, nor by
"the hatred of his or her correlate to Christianity, nor on the account
"of any peevish and unreasonable conduct respecting it, been brought
"into bondage to sin, to worship idols, violate con cience, make a
"sacrifice of all spiritual peace, hope, and joy, to please an unbe-
"lieving mate. Neither the believing husband or wife is under any
"obligations to do these things, even to prevent the departure of the
"unbelieving correlate, or to recover him or her, when separated on
"religious accounts. The gospel does not bind Christians to abandon
"their unbelieving mates, nor do the laws of marriage, require that
"they enslave their consciences, to prevent a separation, or to recover
"them when separated." This I am persuaded, is the true meaning of the Apostle. It falls in with the use and meaning of the verb DOULOO, whence DEDOULOTAI is formed, which signifies to *enslave* and *bring into cruel bondage*. Acts, 7. 6. It is used to express the bondage of the Israelites in Egypt; and 2 Peter, 2. 19, the more cruel bondage of sin. It is a proper word to signify the enslaving of the conscience, but it is never once used in the new testament to signify the marriage bond or any thing relating to it. When the apostle hath occasion to speak of this he always useth another verb, DEO to bind. Rom. 7. 2, DEDETAI, and in this very chapter, verse 27 DEDESAI, *art thou bound to a wife, &c.* Must it not be unaccountable, if the apostle speaks of the marriage bond in the 15th verse, that he doth not use the verb which he useth on all like occasions? In these views the supposition, that he speaks with any reference to it, is altogether unreasonable.

FURTHER, this interpretation of the text well agrees with what appears to have been the design of the apostle, which was, to answer a question, which it seems the church of Corinth had sent him respecting the expediency of marriage, and the duty of those who were unequally matched with infidels; whether it were lawful to continue with them in the connubial state? The Mosaic law expresly prohibited all marriages of the holy seed with infidels, Deut. 7. 3, 4; and the Jews made them null. The primitive Christians therefore were in doubt with respect to the lawfulness of cohabiting with infidels†. The apostle having given them assurance that the Lord had commanded believers not to separate on this account, it became an important question, what was to be done, if the unbelieving made a point of it, and would separate from the believer on the account of his or her faith? On this the apostle determines, that if the unbelieving would depart, after all reasonable and kind measures had been taken to conciliate him or her, that it must be suffered: a brother or sister was not required to enslave conscience, by any connivance at idolaters, or communion with them, ei-

ther

† Dr. Whitby on the 13th verse, Vol. II. P. 148.

ther to prevent a separation, or to recover the infidel when separated *. The interpretation makes the concluding clause in the verse pertinent and forcible; *but God hath called us to peace*. That is, "he hath called us "in the gospel to the enjoyment of peace, while we live peaceably and du- "tifully in our several relations, and has laid us under no obligations "to enslave our consciences, and sacrifice our present or future peace, to "please the peevish humours of men." On the other hand, it is important to observe, that on the too general interpretation of the word *bondage*, as implying an obligation to live single, it makes the concluding clause, *But God hath called us to peace*, impertinent, if not ridiculous; and makes it carry in it an implication inconsistent with the general tenor of the apostle's discourse in this chapter, if not with truth itself. In this view the sense would be this; God hath called us to peace, since the deserted brother or sister is liberated from the bondage of a single life, and hath liberty to contract a second marriage. This would seem ridiculously to imply, that Christians could not live in peace without marriage; but must be in perplexity and cruel bondage: for there is no other conceivable bondage, to which the deserted mate was, or could be subjected by the separation of the pagan husband or wife, but that of living single. Further, this seems also to imply, that an important part of that peace, to which we are called by the gospel, consists in a liberty to marry? But is it either true, that christians cannot enjoy the noblest peace, and that peace in particular to which they are called, without marriage; or that the gospel hath called them to any liberty with respect to contracting marriages, which mankind have not enjoyed in all ages? Neither of these can be pretended.

Beside, this idea of a single state as a state of bondage, is directly contrary to the representations, which the apostle had repeatedly made of it, in the preceding parts of the chapter. He introduceth it with a declaration, that in those perilous times it was *good for a man not to touch a woman*. That is, the single is much preferable to the married state; much freer from incumbrances and perplexity; of greater liberty, peace and advantages, in the service of GOD. In the 7 and 8 verses he wisheth, that all single persons were like himself, on the account of the peculiar advantages of the single state, for the enjoyment of that liberty and peace, to which they were called by the gospel. In the 32, 33, and 34 he further represents the advantages and preference of a single condition. Nay, in the 27 verse he seems to command single persons not to marry. *Art thou loosed from a wife, seek not a wife*. How could the apostle therefore, in any consistency with himself, represent a single state, as a state of bondage and perplexity? or obligations to continue in it as enslaving? For these various reasons I am fully persuaded, that the bondage spoken of by the apostle

* Dr. Guyse gives this as one sense of the text, "Much less to enslave his, or her 'own conscience to the perverse humour of the unbelieving relative, for the sake of 'preventing a separation between them."

apostle, has no reference either to the married or single state, and that this passage is nothing to their purpose, who press it into their service, to support their favourite doctrine of divorces. I know of no author, either Greek, Latin or English, excepting commentators on this passage, who represents either the connubial, or single life, as a state of bondage. What is still more to the purpose, neither the apostle himself, in any other passage, nor any of the writers, either of the Old or New-Testament, have ever represented either of these states in this point of view. It is therefore unreasonable, and contrary to all scripture analogy, to put this construction upon it in the disputed passage.

THERE are, beside, other weighty reasons against this sense of the text. It flatly contradicts what the apostle had said verse 11; it gives a much greater liberty than Moses gave, as hath been already shewn. It stands in direct opposition to the original design of marriage, as stated by CHRIST, and to his solemn declaration, *That he who marrieth her that is put away, committeth adultery*, This can therefore by no means, be the meaning of the apostle. The sense which I have given, makes the apostle consistent with himself, with CHRIST, and with the prophet, who declares, That *the* LORD *hateth putting away*. It is therefore doubtless the true sense.

HENCE the scriptures declare against all divorces, except in cases of incontinency. Dr. Whitby, on the whole, is in this opinion. He represents, that a brother or sister is not released from the nuptial bond, till "the unbelieving hath entered into another marriage, or rather "hath dissolved the former by adultery; as" saith he, "may well "be supposed of those heathens, who thus separated from their Christ- "ian mates‡. Dr. Doddridge, to be sure, toward the close of his life, was in this opinion. His comment on the 11 verse of the forequoted chapter, is in these words: "And let not the husband dismiss his wife "on any light account, or indeed for any thing short of adultery. For "whatever particular reasons Moses might have for permitting divor- "ces on slighter occasions, CHRIST, our great LEGISLATOR, who "may reasonably expect higher degrees of purity and virtue in his "followers, as their assistances are much greater, hath seen fit express- "ly to prohibit such separations, and we his apostles must guide our- "selves by the authority of his determinations." In his Lectures he hath these observations: "Divorce, except in cases of adultery, ap- "pears to be so expresly forbidden by CHRIST, that it is strange it "should ever have been disputed among Christians*." With respect to what has been pleaded from the 15 verse of the chapter so often quoted, he observes, "It is so difficult to reconcile this interpretation with "the decision of our LORD, and with what Paul saith verse 11, that "perhaps it may be more adviseable to understand the liberty spoken of "as relating to a liberty of continuing to live apart, without eagerly "solliciting

‡ Dr. Whitby's Annotations Vol. II. P. 149. on the 15 verse of the 7 Chapter of the 1st Epistle to the Corinthians. * Lecture 189.

"soliciting a return to the party, by whom the Christian had been, "on a religious account, thus injuriously dismissed." The great and learned Blackstone gives his opinion full to the point. His words are, "For the canon law, which the common law follows in this case, "deems so highly and with such mysterious reverence of the nuptial "tie, that it will not allow it to be unloosed for any cause whatsoever, "that ariseth after the union is made. And this is said to be built on "the divine revealed law, though that expressly assigns incontinence as "a cause, and indeed the only cause why a man may put away his wife "and marry another §." In the decrees or institutions of the council at Nice, in 325, it was ordained, That no bishop, presbyter, or deacon should put away his wife on the account of religion, and that they should not marry a divorced woman: and, that if any layman should put away his wife and marry another, or should marry one whom another man had put away, he should be excommunicated‡. This shows us what was the opinion and practice of the church for the three or four first centuries, and that the marrying a divorced or deserted woman, was esteemed no less criminal than the putting away or desertion of an husband or wife. The primitive churches therefore evidently understood our SAVIOUR's prohibition, and the Apostle's determination in the same sense in which I have insisted that they ought to be received.

BY the statutes of the ancient Waldenses, if a man or woman left the wife or husband and married another, the person thus offending was expelled the communion, unless he or she returned to the former marriage. Among the Norwegians, He who had been guilty of a divorce, was ever after to be kept from the Eucharist||.

FROM this view of the scriptures, and of the opinion and practice of the Christian church in the first ages, I cannot but conclude that divorces are utterly unlawful in all cases, except those of incontinency.

BUT I am not insensible, that objections will be made to the foregoing reasoning, I shall therefore attempt fairly to meet and answer them.

OBJECTION I.

THE case of divorce, and that of desertion are very different; and though our SAVIOUR hath prohibited all putting away, on any account but that of adultery, and though the apostle enters the same prohibition, yet he harmonizeth both with our LORD and with himself, in allowing a divorce on the footing of desertion. In this the forsaken correlate is wholly passive, and hath done nothing amiss. The deserting correlate violates

§ Blackf. Comm. Vol. I. P. 441.

‡ Sed ubi de Cleri uxoribus agitur, sanctio est, ne quis ex illo genere ducat ECBEBLEMENEEN, ejectam vel repudiatam. Prohibitur episcopus, presbyter et diaconus uxorem ejicere obtentu religionis. Si quis laicus uxorem suam ejiciens aliam acciperet, aut ab alio repudiatam, communione pellatur. Selden's Hebrew Wife, P. 848.

|| P. 811.

violates an eſſential part of the marriage covenant, and hence the deſerted mate is at liberty to marry to whomſoever it may be agreeable. Our SAVIOUR hath ſaid nothing reſpecting the caſe of deſertion, but left it to a future determination, as circumſtances ſhould require.

ANSWER.

THOUGH our Saviour hath not mentioned the caſe of deſertion, yet he hath fully anſwered and ſettled that point: particularly in that poſitive and repeated declaration, *that he that marrieth her that is put away, unleſs it be for the cauſe of fornication, committeth adultery.* There is no difference with reſpect to the woman put away, by her huſband, and the woman who is deſerted by him, without a juſt cauſe. The woman put away by her huſband is deſerted by him, and the woman deſerted by him is put away. It is only a different manner of putting away. Nothing can be pleaded in favour of one more than of the other. It is conceived that this hath been already demonſtrated. Hence the whole objection proceeds on the footing of miſtake. It therefore highly concerns thoſe who make this objection, to ſhow the difference in point of paſſiveneſs, innocence, injury, or any thing eſſential in the one caſe rather than the other, or elſe to make it no more. It is evident that the objection is built on a miſtake of a ſuppoſed difference, where there is none, not only from our SAVIOUR's declaration concerning the woman put away without a juſt cauſe, but from the remarks made already on the 7th chapter of the 1ſt epiſtle to the Corrinthians. Indeed is not the diſtinction between deſertion and putting awav futile, and a mere quibble?

FURTHER, it is of importance to obſerve, that there is an entire inconſiſtency in allowing, that CHRIST hath abſolutely prohibited all putting away, except in caſes of incontinency, and yet maintaining that deſertion is a ſufficient cauſe: For deſertion is not incontinency, and therefore can be no lawful ground of divorce. Our SAVIOUR chargeth no adultery upon the man that putteth away or deſerteth his wife, if he marry not another. He only cauſeth her to commit adultery; that is expoſeth her to do it. Matthew 5. 32. And as deſertion is not incontinency, ſo he, or ſhe, who getteth a bill and marrieth another on this footing putteth away, and is guilty of adultery. Deſertion, though the deſerting correlate proceed to a divorce, doth not in the divine account bar a reconciliation; nay, the apoſtle commandeth that ſuch an one ſhould be reconciled. Very different is the caſe, when that fleſh which by divine inſtitution had been made one by marriage, is ſeparated and becomes the fleſh of another in a ſecond marriage. This is a total putting away. In this caſe GOD hath prohibited a return, and declared it to be an abomination. Therefore the party proceeding to this is the party who putteth away, and doth that which the LORD the GOD of Iſrael hateth.

OBJECTION

OBJECTION II.

If incontinency be a sufficient cause of putting away, then any other crime of equal magnitude may be a sufficient cause. There is no kind of reason why one particular fault should be insisted on, as a just ground of divorce, while it is denied that another of equal criminality, and equally subversive of the marriage covenant, is not a just ground. Nothing can be pleaded in point of morality, or in the nature of things, for the prohibition of a divorce in one case, more than in the other. It is therefore a grand absurdity to suppose, that our Saviour fixed on incontinency as the sole crime on which divorces might warrantably proceed. We must rather understand him as fixing on this as a specimen of the degree of criminality, or of the violation of the marriage covenant, and of the frustration of the designs of marriage, on which divorces may be lawfully given. This is fixed on as a tantamount; any one crime, or a number of crimes amounting to an equal degree of criminality, or equally subversive of the designs of marriage, will warrant a divorce,

ANSWER.

God hath shewed us, in his word, and it is evident from the common consent aud practice of mankind, that it is not every crime of equal magnitude with adultery, or that may in some very important respects frustrate the designs of marriage, that will warrant a divorce. It cannot be pretended, that infidelity, under the light of the gospel, preached by the apostles, and confirmed by miracles, and an obstinate course of idolatry, was not a crime of equal magnitude with fornication or adultery; or that it was less subversive of the religious purposes of marriage, which are by far the most important. It is however expressly forbidden, that the husband or wife should put away the other, on this account. It was determined at the council of Nice, by what has been termed the institution of the apostles, that if a woman should leave her husband on the account of heresy, infidelity, or on any religious pretence, she should be cursed†. Blasphemy and other crimes there doubtless are, equal to incontinence, yet, in the common sense and practice of mankind, are no just causes of divorce. Is perjury, and a deliberate fixed course of falsehood, less criminal than a single instance of incontinency? yet, was this ever pleaded as a just cause of divorcement? It is therefore evident, that it is not the greatness, but the peculiar nature of the crime which makes a divorce warrantable.

Hence it is also manifest, that our Saviour did not fix on incontinency as a *specimen* or *tantamount* of the degree of criminality, on which divorces may lawfully proceed; but as a crime of a peculiar nature, in such a manner violating the marriage compact, and frustrating

† Selden's Hebrew Wife Vol. III. P. 848.

ing the designsof it, as other crimes do not. Indeed if jealousy, as hath been represented, be the rage of man, that which above all other matters awakes his indignation: if this be that, in a peculiar manner, for which he will not regard any ransome, nor rest contented with many gifts, then surely incontinency is such an infraction of the nuptial compact, and hath such a malignant aspect on the designs of it, as no other crimes can possibly have. It is totally subversive of chastity, which was one principal design of marriage. It destroys all mutual trust with respect to a point, in which it is absolutely necessary, to conjugal happiness, that the corelates should have the most entire confidence in each other. It is the grossest violation of the express engagement in the nuptial vow. It creates jealousies with respect to the offspring, and it is the only crime which can render the legitimacy of it uncertain. It destroys parental affection, filial reverence, domestic harmony and happiness. There is something therefore in morality and the nature of things pleadable with respect to the sin of incontinency, why it should be fixed upon as the only warrantable ground of divorce. It cannot be pretended that any other crime has the same effect and influence with respect to these points. What the objection therefore insinuates is not true, however ingenious and plausible it may appear.

FURTHER, it is not at all probable, that our LORD fixed on incontinence as a specimen or tantamount of the degree of criminality, on the footing of which divorces may be lawfully given, because men are not capable of determining with precision the degree of criminality in any given case, or the equality of one crime with another, with respect to its nature, tendency and consequences. Men judge exceedingly different with respect to crimes; especially with respect to the sin of incontinency. Notwithstanding its heinous nature, and the divine denunciations pointed against it, yet many esteem it a mere foible, a trick of youth, a laughable, rather than a serious matter. In some countries it is esteemed a point of civility to introduce a guest, or friend, to the mistress of the house†. Though jealousy be the rage of man, yet it doth not originate so much from a general sense of the enormity of the action which is the occasion of it, as from other circumstances It in a peculiar manner strikes at all the feelings of honour and selfishness. Though on these accounts it may be peculiarly enraging, when it toucheth self, yet when this is not the case, there is, perhaps, no crime of equal magnitude, of which mankind in general think so lightly and variously. We cannot therefore imagine, that the great teacher of men would have fixed on this, as the measure of criminality, which might warrant a divorce. After all his solemn

† In India, Salmon's Grammar, P. 461. In some of the most polite parts of Europe, little or no jealousies are entertained with respect to this matter. Indeed if we consider how many instances of divorce have been publickly given in this state, on the express footing of adultery, and that there have been no prosecutions commenced, nor punishments inflicted for this iniquity, there will be no occasion to go abroad for vouchers to the truth of these observations.

ſolemn reaſonings on the point, after all the trouble he had given himſelf, the Phariſees and his diſciples, on this ſuppoſition, he would have left it in a very looſe manner. Thoſe who eſteemed incontinency a capital fault, would not have thought themſelves warranted to put away their companions without ſuch a fault; but thoſe who eſteemed it a ſmall crime, or a mere foible, would put them away for ſmall cauſes, or for every cauſe. Notwithſtanding all which had been ſaid on the ſubject, our SAVIOUR would have left it in no better ſtate, than it was before his particular and laboured diſcuſſion. This cannot be reaſonably ſuppoſed.

THAT fornication is uſed as a ſpecimen of the degree of criminality, or as a tantamount, is a mere ſuppoſition. It hath not the leaſt countenance from the text or context. Beſides, the fixing on certain crimes as a tantamount, on which particular penalties ſhall be inflicted, is contrary to all precedent divine or human. So far is the divine word from giving countenance to any thing of this nature, that it ſpecifies all crimes to which penalties are annexed, and it warrants the execution of thoſe penalties on thoſe delinquents only, who are found guilty of the crimes ſpecified. Though the criminal be found guilty of many crimes and to a very great amount, yet if the particular crime, to which the penalty hath been annexed, be not found, he cannot, in law or juſtice ſuffer the penalty. It can, by no means, be warranted, by laws human or divine. By a general law to fix on a crime, as a meaſure of the degree of criminality, under which any other crime, or number of crimes, which ſhall be tantamount to the crime ſpecified ſhall be included, and in conſequence of which the penalties denounced in the general law ſhall be inflicted, when the crime ſpecified is not found, is contrary to the nature and deſign of law, to the liberty, ſafety, common ſenſe and practice of mankind.

It is the very nature and deſign of law to ſtate crimes and their penalties; that the ſubject may know, when he is guilty, and when he is not; that he may be protected in caſe of innocence: and that in this way, the public and individuals may be ſecured in their various intereſts. But theſe ends could not be anſwered by ſuch general law as I have mentioned above. No man could know when he was ſafe, and when not. At this rate his life might be taken from him, though he had been guilty of no murder nor any like fault, if on a ſurvey of all the faults of his life, it could be judged, that they were equal to a ſingle inſtance of murder In the ſame way, his liberty, fortune and every thing dear might be taken from him, though he had never been guilty of any particular crime, by which he had made a forfeiture of life, liber-

ty

ty or property. This, instead of securing the rights and peace of community or individuals, would at once throw every thing into a state of fear, tumult and disorder; and wholly subvert the very design of law.

It is equally contrary to the common opinion and practice of mankind in the present and in all past ages. It is presumed, there never was a code of laws enacted upon these principles; that there is not, nor ever was any community upon earth, which hath gone into this practice. Is it not therefore entirely unreasonable, and contrary to all analogy, to suppose that our great LAWGIVER fixed on fornication, as a general measure, or tantamount of the degree of criminality, or of the violation of the marriage compact? Is not the supposition an affront to the common sense and practice of mankind? It is conceived that these observations may obviate the objection in hand. Some others which I shall have occasion to make with respect to the next, will answer the same purpose.

OBJECTION III.

OTHER covenants may be dissolved on various accounts, for a violation of any of the essential parts of them, and as the marriage union is made only by covenanting, it may, like all other covenants, be dissolved various ways; by neglecting the duties or frustrating the designs of marriage, or by any gross violations of the institution. It is inconsistent with reason and all just ideas of covenanting, to maintain the contrary.

ANSWER.

IN general it may be observed, That GOD may see important reasons for his own institutions, which we cannot easily, or fully comprehend; and that his will ought to satisfy us, though the reasons of it are beyond our comprehension: That, in this case, we have clear evidence of his mind, which ought to silence our objections. Besides, it is evident from the preceding observations, that there are moral reasons why this should not be annulled like other covenants. Other weighty reasons may be given.

I. THE marriage covenant is more sacred, and constitutes an union more intimate and perfect than any other. It is not merely a human covenant, but a divine institution. It is not barely a covenant of the correlates, but of GOD himself. It is charged upon the adulterous woman, not barely that she had forsaken the guide of her youth, but that she had forgotten the covenant of her GOD†. It is a covenant in a peculiar manner witnessed and sanctified by him, from the day of man's creation; stamped with his name and authority, that it might be

† Prov. 2. 17.

be indissoluble and perpetual. Grotius saith of it, It is the province of GOD to be with you in the same covenant||. He is in it as its institutor, sanctifier, witness, guardian and avenger.

It makes a more near and perfect union than any other covenant. In this, two are made one flesh, which is not said of any other covenant. The spouses are members of each other's flesh and bones, and are bound to nourish and cherish each other, as they do their own flesh. As Calvin expresses it, One is as it were the half of the other†. As a man's flesh and bones may not be torn from him, especially the rib near his heart; as he cannot be divided, and survive the shock; so the one flesh of the husband and wife may not be disjoined. They go into such familiarities, and so entrust themselves with each other, as men do not in any other union or covenant. It ought not therefore to be dissolved like other covenants, but to be held sacred and guarded beyond any other.

2. The correlates are not made one flesh barely by covenanting; but by the marriage, or consummating, act. This is an idea clearly taught in the scripture, and was a generally received doctrine of the Jewish church. It is very observable, in the old Testament, That men are said to take wives, and afterwards to marry them. They are represented as taking them, and afterwards they are said to become their wives. Gen. 24. 67. *And Isaac brought her into his mother Sarah's tent, and took Rebekah, and she became his wife.* Deut. 24. 1. *When a man hath taken a wife and married her.* In these passages, the taking of a wife, and the marrying of her, are spoken of as things very distinct; the one implying the marriage ceremonies and covenant, the other the marriage act; or the consummation of the marriage The Hebrew word translated, married her, is BAGNAL, which, according to Buxtorf and several authorities quoted by Mr. Pool, properly signifies the marriage act§. Selden is in the same opinion, and shews that the Chaldean and Samaritan Jews, and the Jews in general, had this understanding of the word‡‡ In his chapter entitled *Deductio in thalamum. The conducting into the marriage bed,* he shews that, among the Jews, nothing which preceded the marriage act, or conducting the Spouses to the marriage bed, made, or perfected, the marriage††. The apostle establisheth this sense of the word, and of the manner in which the marriage union is made 1 Cor. 6. 16. *What, know ye not*

|| "In eodem DEI fœdere est in quo tu."

† "Quasi dimidia tui pars."

§ Synopsis on Deut. 21. 13. and 24. 1. Non *statum* sed *actum* denotat. Dominium habuit: et ad *virginem* vel *mulierem relatum,* est dominium. Buxtorf.

‡‡ He renders it maritavit eam, coiverit cum ea, concubuerit cum ea. Uxor Ebraica Vol. III. P. 629, 760.

†† "Non benedictio sponsorum fecit, seu perfecit nuptias, sed deductio in thalamum.

not that he, which is joined to an harlot is one body? For two, saith he, shall be one flesh. As the marriage oneness is made in this consummation, so it cannot be dissolved, but by an infraction with respect to that by which the twain were made completely one. This is a reason of singular weight why the marriage union should not be dissolved in any other way than by incontinency, and why the supreme LAWGIVER hath fixed on this as the only warrantable cause of divorce.

3. THIS union and relation are far more important than any merely human. It is a most important covenant to the correlates, to families and to community at large. It was important even in paradise, to the purposes of piety and social virtue; and the principal design of the continuance of it is, that earth may be a nursery for heaven: that parents and their offspring may be chaste and holy. The prophet represents the introduction and continuance of an holy seed upon earth, as dependent on the institution of marriage, and the preservation of it, in its original purity. *And did not he make one? Yet had he the residue of the spirit: and wherefore one? That he might seek a godly seed.* MEBAKESH DSÆRAGN ELOHIM. *Seeking a seed of* GOD. Malachi, 2. 15. It seems to be implied that there can be no seed of GOD, to build his *church*, and to be a peculiar treasure unto himself, but from marriages agreeable to his original institution. The violation of the law of marriage began the great and general corruption of the world before the deluge, corrupted the people of GOD in Canaan, brought perpetual infamy and almost infinite mischiefs on the family and kingdom of Solomon. The commission of one kind of gross sins leads on to the commission of all others †. The out breaking of these in parents tends to corrupt families, and this corrupts community at large. Both church and state will always wear the complexion of their component parts. If parents, therefore, are covenant breakers, adulterers, and perjured persons, as are all gross and total violators of the nuptial bond, what virtue can be expected from the offspring? What can be the consequence but a general corruption? Hence as this is a most important covenant both to the purposes of time and eternity, as the greatest interests of society and human nature are concerned in the preservation of it, it ought to be guarded beyond all other covenants, and should not be dissolved as they are.

OBJECTION IV.

IT is unreasonable and cruel to prevent persons from marrying, when, without any fault of their's, they have been injuriously deserted, and

† One vice brings in another to its aid. By a sort of natural affinity they connect and entwine themselves together; till their roots come to be spread wide and deep over the whole soul. Dr. Blair, Ser. 27, on the character of Hazael.

and therefore it cannot be ſuppoſed that God hath laid any prohibition upon them in this caſe.

ANSWER.

This objection is involved in the firſt, and hath been, in effect, anſwered already. Our Saviour has aſſured us that ſhe who is put away without any juſt cauſe, is an adultereſs, if ſhe marrieth another man, and the man who marrieth her is an adulterer; but perſons deſerted without any juſt cauſe are perſons put away without any fault of their own: And as it is written, *Thou ſhalt not commit adultery*, there is, in this caſe, a prohibition againſt marrying. What the objection ſuppoſeth God would not do, he hath in fact done, and therefore it cannot be unreaſonable or cruel. The reaſonableneſs of the precept is founded in the general good. It is the wiſdom and duty of every moral governor to ſecure the public peace and happineſs. This is not only wiſe but benevolent. Private may not therefore be pleaded in oppoſition to public good. Were a country invaded, it would be thought a weak objection againſt reſiſting for the general defence, that it was hard and cruel; becauſe ſome innocent and brave men muſt be loſt, ſome of the frontier families and towns muſt be ſacrificed. To make any thing of ſuch an objection worthy of notice, it muſt be proved, that the loſs of the frontiers and of thoſe who ſhould fall in the general defence, would be more injurious to individuals and the community, than a general ravage and ſubjugation of the country. In like manner the objectors, in this caſe, to give any weight to the objection, muſt prove, that individuals and the public will be moſt ſafe, by ſuffering divorces and marriages in all caſes, in which perſons are unjuſtly deſerted or put away; or in which any thing, which ſhall be judged a tantamount, may happen. It muſt be proved, that in this caſe there are leſs temptations to deſertion, wantonneſs and new marriages; that the honour and happineſs of families, and the public purity and ſafety are better provided for, in this way, than by a total prohibition of the ſeparation of the huſband and wife, and all future marriages of either, in any caſe but that of incontinency. But it is preſumed that the proof of this is impoſſible. The contrary, no doubt, is manifeſt. Prohibitions and penalties, in all other caſes, are thought to be matter of reſtraint and defence. Hence the prohibitions, threatenings and penalties of laws both human and divine. The divine edict, *What therefore* God *hath joined together, let not man put aſunder. Whoſoever ſhall put away his wife, except for fornication, and ſhall marry another, committeth adultery, and whoſo marrieth her that is put away doth commit adultery*, muſt have great weight with all who credit the ſcriptures, and have any tenderneſs, or even remains of conſcience. Would churches and ſtates treat them in that manner which the divine law teacheth, the ſhame and penalties even of a temporal nature would be a great reſtraint, and might prevent numerous inſtances of deſertion and divorce,

and

and guard an institution most important to human happiness. It would greatly tend to keep up in the mind that veneration for the sacred rights of marriage, with which it ought ever to be penetrated. Having it a fixed point that marriage was for life, that the correlates could not be separated without great guilt, shame and punishment, it would make persons cautious with respect to whom they should marry, guard them against irregular desires, and such instances of conduct as would make them unhappy in a connubial state. This, in numerous instances, no doubt, would prevent desertions and other evils which divorces are designed to relieve. It would therefore be not only benevolent, but politic. The greatest policy and goodness is discovered in the prevention of crimes: much greater than in punishing them, or in attempting remedies after they are committed. Beside, should differences happen between the correlates, there would in this case, be motives from conscience, fear, and shame to influence them to a reconciliation, which otherwise could have no existence.

On the other hand putting a loose construction on the divine law supposing that fornication means any great crime, a number of crimes, a tantamount, &c. has a great tendency to weaken all sense of obligation, in point of conscience, with respect to marriage, and to render it doubtful how far the correlates are bound by the marriage compact, to encourage desertion, and promote separations in families on the account of small offences. A number of these may be judged tantamount to one great crime. It at once renders the rights of marriage insecure, as it puts it in the power of the parties, whenever differences arise between them, or they wax wanton and wish for new enjoyments, by deserting each other, living apart a short season, or by contention, to obtain a final separation. A door is opened to the grossest violations of the seventh commandment, and of the greatest bonds of human society. It cannot, I conceive, by any means, be pretended, that in the latter case, the same provision is made to guard the marriage relation, that there are the same restraints in point of conscience, and embarrasments in other respects, laid on the correlates, against ill conduct and separation, as in the former. We must therefore determine in favour of the divine institution, as absolutely prohibiting divorces, in all cases, but that of incontinency, as not *cruel* but *gracious*, as the tendency of it is to prevent desertions and all other breaches of the marriage covenant, and to promote both individual and public good.

The reasoning in this case is from the common sense, observation, and experience of mankind. It hath been generally found, that determinate and severe laws faithfully executed, according to their express import, have been most effectual to prevent capital crimes, and secure the general happiness. But a lax construction of law, an abatement of the penalties against vice, and diminution of the motives to virtue, have universally had the contrary effect. Indeed were not this the case, laws would be useless. We are therefore from the nature of of things, from common ſenſe and experience, obliged to determine, that this objection is more ſpecious than ſolid.

OBJECTION V.

MARRIAGE is a civil contract ſubject to the regulations of civil ſociety. The ſtatutes of the divine LAWGIVER, relative to divorce, reſpect individuals, the huſband and wife, only, and not the makers or judges of the law. Though they may bind the conſciences of the former, yet they lay no obligation on the latter. It muſt be granted, that the legiſlature have a right to determine what ſhall be a legal marriage, and conſequently when, and for what reaſons, there ſhall be a diſſolution of the contract. Therefore the preceding arguments are not concluſive.

ANSWER.

WHETHER marriage be a civil contract or not, to me does not appear important, or at all deciſive in the preſent argument: for in what caſe ſoever GOD hath made a law, whether it reſpect a civil, or any other matter, that law is binding on all to whom the knowledge of it is come. As HE therefore hath given laws reſpecting marriage, and, in certain caſes, prohibited divorce, no legiſlators, or judges, can, in ſuch caſes, have any right to make laws, that a divorce ſhall be given, or by any public judgment to declare a diſſolution of marriage. For neither legiſlators nor judges can, in any caſe, have a right to counteract the law and will of the SUPREME LAWGIVER and JUDGE. If they may counteract and ſuperſede the divine will in one, they may in all caſes; and, at once, diſcharge men from all obligation to the DEITY. This would be to deny the ſupremacy of the MOST HIGH, and to make themſelves the ſupreme legiſlators and judges. Hence the great queſtion is not, whether marriage be a civil contract, or a divine inſtitution? But what is the law of the CREATOR? What hath HE commanded, and what hath HE forbidden with reſpect to this relation? Let this be determined, and the matter will be decided, among all who maintain the divine ſupremacy. It will determine it not only with reſpect to individuals, but with reſpect to legiſlators and judges: For they may not, by law, public judgment, or any other means, countenance that, which is repugnant to the divine law. Both in public and private life, they are obliged, not only to avoid ſin themſelves, but, as far as may be, to diſcountenance and prevent it in others. There is, therefore, nothing at all, in the objection, to invalidate the preceding arguments. Theſe obſervations may ſerve as a general anſwer to the objection, and to ſhow that it is founded entirely in falſe principles and concluſions.

HOWEVER, as many ſeem to place their chief dependence, with reſpect to the ſupport of the doctrine of divorce, on the ſeveral matters contained

contained in this objection, no part of it shall be passed without particular attention.

WITH respect to the first part, That marriage is merely a civil contract, it is so far from the truth, that as to the essence of it, it is of a moral nature, founded in the morality or original fitness of things, antecedent to all positive law concerning it, either divine or human. It is also a divine institution, founded in the original morality, or fitness of the relation.

THE creation of mankind male and female indicates an original fitness and design that they should enjoy each other. But as they were rational creatures, capable of chastity and religion, of natural and moral affection towards their offspring, there was a moral unfitness in their having a common enjoyment of one another, as is the case with the irrational creation. It would have been contrary to chastity and reason. There was therefore, both a natural and moral fitness in marriage; that, in this institution, twain becoming one flesh, might have a chaste and rational enjoyment of each other. Without this there could have been no such thing as conjugal affection, or as the natural affection of a father; as no man could know that he stood in that relation to any child. There could be no union of parental love and care; no mutual exertions for the preservation, support and education of the human offspring. No parent could be known but the mother. All children would, in a sense, be fatherless. On the mother would lie all the burthen of support, education and government of her offspring; though, in nature, less qualified for either than the male. In the peculiar weaknesses, wants, dangers and distresses of the feebler sex, they could not have known the kindness and assistance of husbands, nor their tender babes the care and affections of a father. This would have endangered the life and prevented the increase of the human race. In this way there could have been no regular government or education of children, nor any seed of GOD, to build his church and plant the heavenly Jerusalem with redeemed creatures. This would not only have been exceedingly subversive of human happiness, but of the chief end of the creation of mankind. These are contrary to nature, reason and morality. Hence it is abundantly evident, from the light of nature, that there was originally, antecedent to all positive law, a moral fitness in marriage. It is founded in the moral law, in the law of chastity and love. This most effectually guards against the unfitnesses which have been mentioned. In this is founded all conjugal affection, and by this only is it maintained. This unites the affections of both the parents in their offspring, and most effectually calls forth their mutual love, care and exertions for their preservation, maintenance and education. It is one of the principal means of the preservation of the life of man, in his defenceless and tender years; of the comfort of individuals; of the peace and happiness of society; and, of training up a seed for the service and enjoyment of their CREATOR. There is

therefore

therefore, in all these respects, a great moral fitness in the marriage institution.

THAT it is of a moral nature, is further evident from the seventh commandment. This surely is a part of the moral law, or law of nature, founded wholly in the original moral fitness of things. This forbids the sexes the enjoyment of each other, in every other way but that of marriage. This shews, at the same time, that it was the original design of their creation, and founded wholly in morality, that they should enjoy each other in this and in no other way. As this commandment is wholly of a moral nature, and as its whole design and business is to honour, support and guard the institution of marriage, it evinces, that, as to the essence of it, it is wholly of a moral nature.

FURTHER, the words by which marriage was originally instituted, which contain the substance of the seventh command, shew that it is of a moral nature. The time, place and circumstances of its appointment, in paradise, in a state of innocency, when its principal ends could be only of a moral, or religious nature, that the holy pair might provoke and assist each other to love and praise, and that they might replenish the earth with a seed to serve the LORD, gives further evidence of its morality.

THE reasonings and commands of the prophet Malachi, of CHRIST and his apostles, their references to the original state and circumstances of things, when they treat on the subject, lead us to view it as a moral institution. The great TEACHER of men treats of marriage as a moral subject, in his explanation of the moral law. He reduceth it to the head of the seventh commandment, and shews that whoever is guilty of a gross violation of marriage, at the same time violates this moral precept. This, again, gives demonstrative evidence, that it is founded in the moral law. Indeed our SAVIOUR and his apostles taught nothing but morality. CHRIST made no civil laws, nor uttered any prohibitions of a civil nature. The laws therefore respecting marriage, are all moral, and the institution itself is moral.

IT is not only a moral, but a divine institution. It has GOD for its sole author. He instituted it in the primæval state, ordaining that the first pair should be one flesh, antecedent to all laws, obligations and institutions, but such as were purely moral and divine. It was prior to every other positive law or institution, either human or divine. Our SAVIOUR teacheth us, that this original law or institution is still the law of marriage. To this he refers all his disciples, that they may learn the nature, obligations and duties of marriage†. This irrefragably demonstrates that marriage is a divine institution; for that which hath GOD alone for its author, that which preceded all civil or human laws and institutions, cannot possibly be civil or human, but must be divine.

ALL

† Math. 19. 4, 5, 6. Mark 10. 6, 7, 8, 9.

ALL expositors which I have ever read on the subject, treat marriage as a divine institution, founded in the moral law. This appears to have been the opinion of Mr. Pool and his continuators; of Mr. Henry, and of Doctors Whitby, Guyse and Doddridge‡. Indeed I do not remember ever reading any divine, who maintained the contrary doctrine.

HENCE, as marriage is founded originally in the moral fitness of things, and is a divine institution, it neither is nor can be subject to the regulations of civil society, any further than those regulations are conformable to the moral law, and the divine institution. When therefore it is said in the objection, The legislature have a right to determine what shall be a legal marriage, the meaning cannot be that they have a right to act contrary to the law of nature, to the institution and the statutes of HEAVEN. No objector, I presume, will hold the objection in this point of light. This would be to maintain, that civil rulers, by their laws and traditions, have a right to counteract the law of nature, and make void the law of GOD; a conduct which the SAVIOUR severely reprimanded in the rulers of the Jews§. Indeed this would be for them, like the man of sin, to exalt themselves above all that is called GOD†. Therefore as the civil ruler may determine nothing respecting the legality of marriage, contrary to the divine institution, so neither may he determine that it shall be dissolved for any other cause than that which the divine law will warrant.

FURTHER, as marriage and the laws respecting it are of a moral and divine nature, they bind the makers and judges of law, in their public, no less than in their private character. As men in private life are under obligations to practise and encourage every moral duty, and divine institution, and to discountenance and flee all immorality, so are legislators, in their public character, so far as things of this nature fall under their province, legislation or jurisdiction. Both the legislator and judge are not only obliged to keep the Christian sabbath, but to make such laws, and to give such judgments respecting it, as shall encourage its sanctification, discountenance and punish its gross violations. In like manner are they not only under obligations not to kill, but to make laws for the preservation of human life, and to punish murder, and other gross violations of the sixth commandment. The common consent and practice of this and other states, nay, of mankind in general,

‡ See their expositions on the several passages of scripture which relate to marriage and divorce. Several of these have been quoted already. Mr. Henry on Genesis 2. 23, 24. observes, "The Sabbath and marriage were two "ordinances instituted in innocency. See here how great the virtue of a divine ordinance is; the bonds of it are stronger than those of nature. To "whom can we be more firmly bound than to the fathers that begat us, "and the mothers that bare us? Yet the son must quit them to be joined "to his wife, and the daughter forget them to cleave to her husband."

§ Matth 15. 3, 6. and Mark 7. 6, 13.

† II Thess. 2. 4.

general, vouch the truth of these observations. But as marriage and the laws respecting it, are equally of a moral and divine nature, they are under the same obligations to secure the rights of marriage, and to punish all gross infractions of them. The fitness of things and the divine will are equally obligatory in these cases. This part of the objection is both contrary to morality, and the common consent and practice of mankind in all similar cases. The whole objection indeed, appears to be entirely without foundation.

WITH respect to the objections against understanding our SAVIOUR's prohibition in the sense for which I have pleaded, made on this ground, that other prohibitions equally positive and universal are to be understood in a limited sense, as *Labour not for the meat which perisheth——Take no thought for the morrow——Swear not at all, &c.* It need only be observed, That it is no evidence that all prohibitions are to be taken in a limited sense, because some are thus to be understood. At this rate we should be obliged to understand the ten commandments in a very limited sense, as not prohibiting all idolatry, murder and incontinence. But the truth is, that all prohibitions are to be understood in their literal and full import, unless the connection in which they stand, the analogy, or some other part of scripture, teach the contrary. Whether the preceding arguments do not evince, that this cannot be pleaded with respect to the prohibition of the Christian LAWGIVER relative to divorce is submitted to the publick; and whether the alledging of them can be any thing to the purpose.

ON the whole we are persuaded that divorces for any other cause than incontinency, are not only contrary to the express commands of HEAVEN, but to the peace, honour, and welfare of families, the general order, peace and happiness of society. This church, therefore, and all other churches, ought in duty to their common LORD, and for the general good, to expel persons divorced for any other cause, with those who marry them, from their communion, and all the people should say, Amen, as when the curses were denounced from mount Ebal.

BUT we proceed to say with respect to the particular matter of divorce pending before this council, That it cannot be vindicated, on the footing upon which divines have put it, who judge it lawful in cases of total desertion. They maintain, that before the injured correspondent proceeds to a divorce, there should be long waiting, that all means for a reconciliation should be attempted, and it should also be known that the deserter will not be reconciled. The assembly of divines, with whom these churches profess to agree, say, "Nothing but adultery and such willful desertion, as can no way be remedied by the church or civil magistrate, is cause sufficient for dissolving the marriage bond *". They suppose that both the church and civil rulers must interpose, and use their utmost endeavours to heal the matter, and the case must be absolutely desperate, before a separation

* Confession of Faith Capt. 24. of marriage and divorce.

ration is warrantable. But doth any thing of this nature appear in the present case? The husband doth not appear to have left his wife on account of the least disaffection to her; but to escape the officer, the disgrace and hardships of imprisonment for debt. In less than three years he made her a visit, at which time it seems from what has been deposed, that although it was with great difficulty she could be persuaded so much as to see him, and though contrary to what is written, *The wife hath not power of her own body, but the husband: Defraud ye not one the other*, she excluded him her bed, yet in the morning, when he was about to leave her, he put a gold ring upon her hand. After he was gone, he sent her presents of clothing. These it is true were small, but as much for a poor man, as a large sum would have been for a man of fortune. Neither the church nor civil magistrate made any attempts to prevent a separation, nor doth it appear that the woman attempted any herself. The desertion appears neither to have been on the footing of disaffection, nor total at any one time for three years †. Before the expiration of three years from the time he made her a visit, and in still less time, from his last presents, she obtained a divorce, and became one flesh with another man. Does this appear at all like the case described by the Assembly of divines? Has it not still much less of the appearance of the case described by the apostle in his epistle to the Corinthians? Had she attempted all the means which he recommends to retain her husband? Nay, had she ever attempted any? Did she give him no occasion of grief and discouragement, when he made her his last visit? Did she not receive and countenance the visits of another man, previously to her divorce from her lawful husband? Have they not conspired to obtain a divorce, by an ex parte hearing, without any citation of the other party or his friends in so private a manner, that those who wished to oppose them, had no knowledge of the affair? Under these circumstances, though they and a few of their peculiar friends, told their own stories and had none to contradict them, or offer a word on the other side of the question, they but just obtained a divorce. One of the judges openly opposed it, and the chief judge declared, "That it was a very doubtful case "and had one word been said against it, the divorce would not have "been obtained."

This, Reverend Fathers, and gentlemen of this venerable council is the case before you. The pastor and brethren of this church view *this man*, as having *committed adultery*, in marrying her, who has been put away without a warrantable cause, and *this woman* as an *adulteress*, in putting away her husband, and in becoming one flesh with another man.

As

† The law requires total desertion for the term of three years. State Law, book p. 41. Not three years during a man's life; but at one time, which had not been the case in this instance

As the apostle therefore hath written to us *Not to keep company, if any man, that is called a brother, be a fornicator, with such an one no not to eat*, we have refused to eat with them. We have done it with seriousness, mature deliberation, and a great degree of unanimity. We are persuaded that we are acting for CHRIST, pleading for his institutions, and the general happiness of human nature.

WE intreat our fathers and brethren seriously, and without prejudice, to enter fully into the spirit of our plea. We beseech you not to suffer any prepossession, the custom of human courts, nor the desire of pleasing the world, to warp you from duty. You well know how CHRIST hath said, *Whosoever shall break one of these least commandments, and shall teach men so, he shall be called the least in the kingdom of heaven; but whosoever shall do and teach them, the same shall be called great in the kingdom of heaven.* If you will plead for his institutions, and strengthen the hands of your brethren, who are struggling against sin, quietly and faithfully attending on the discipline which CHRIST hath commanded, you will do yourselves honour in the sight of GOD, and glad the generation of his children. Your decision on this point will probably do much good or evil. Should you determine against divorces, as our SAVIOUR hath done, and fix them on a scripture foundation, you will teach men to revere his word; do something to prevent perfidy and wantonness, to secure some of the most important enjoyments of men, and to serve the general interests of the REDEEMER's kingdom. But should you finally determine, that persons may be divorced in the loose manner which has been practised in this state, and especially should you judge the divorce under consideration to be agreeable to the divine word, and justify the previous courtship, you will, in our opinions, put your sanction upon the loose constructions which have been palmed upon the most express and determinate declarations of the KING of Zion. You will justify the present practice of divorces in its utmost latitude. Will you not, in this way, contribute to the purposes of scepticism and infidelity, and as far as your opinion can have influence, contribute more and more to break down the sacred inclosure, with which heaven hath compassed the seventh commandment, and the most tender and important rights of human nature! Will you not counteract the sentiments and practice of the most ancient and renowned states and kingdoms, and of the church of CHRIST in the first and pure ages! You will grieve this sister Church, and give us occasion to take up that mournful language of the ancient church, *The watchmen that went about the city found me, they smote me, they wounded me.* You will, as far as your influence can effect it, throw a happily united and harmonious church and people into division, tumult and confusion.

BUT we submit the event to him whose government is perfect and universal. We are sure that he will take care of his own cause, and amply reward those who suffer for his sake. We pray, that if he should put the honour upon us, we may conduct with submission, meekness

and

and patience. Whatever human courts and councils may determine, we hope ever to be thankful and rejoice, that we have the more sure word of prophecy: and while we find it unalterably written in the STATUTES of HEAVEN, *What GOD hath joined together let not man put asunder; whosoever putteth away his wife, except it be for fornication, and marrieth another, committeth adultery, and he that marrieth her that is put away committeth adultery;* we say AMEN.

APPENDIX.

EXHIBITING a general View of the Laws and Customs of the STATE *of* CONNECTICUT, *relative to Divorce; and of their deficiency, as it is apprehended, that they neither properly secure the rights of Marriage, nor the State from guilt and corruption: Also a comparative view of Connecticut respecting this point, with New-England, with itself, the Jewish and Christian Church, in their purest ages; with other States and Kingdoms, and with Rome pagan for several centuries. It concludes with a general invitation to attempt an immediate reformation.*

WHENEVER the laws of a state are repugnant to the divine; they can, by no means, be vindicated. When they are such in their nature, or become such, by construction and practice, as to render the most important rights of individuals, or the public insecure, it must be granted that they are very defective. When by law, or general custom, men may be deprived of important interests, or of their dearest enjoyments, by an ex parte, or superficial hearing, there is something entirely contrary to liberty and justice, to the law of GOD and nature.

FURTHER, the law must be deficient, when it makes no adequate provision for the prevention or punishment of capital offences, and to guard the community against a general depravation. In these respects, it is presumed, that the laws and practice of Connecticut, respecting divorce, are deficient and faulty.

IT is not always possible for the legislator to determine what will be the effect of particular laws. The design of them may have been good, and at first, they may have promised fair, and yet upon trial it may be found, that their influence is pernicious and intolerable. Sometimes laws may be good in themselves, and yet, for the want of a proper guard and caution, through misconstruction and the influence to custom, become highly detrimental to community. At other times, laws are enacted and long continued, through mistake, which are wrong in themselves; and yet the mischief they operate is so gradual, and so grows into custom as it increaseth, that the evil which they effect, though is

may

may be great, escapes the notice both of the lawgiver and judge. From some, or all these causes conjointly, and not from any ill design in the legislature, it probably is, that the laws respecting divorce, are so imperfect and defective, in the points which have been mentioned.

If the preceding reasonings be conclusive, the law itself is entirely repugnant to the general statute of the Christian Lawgiver. It ought therefore to be immediately repealed.

Should it be contended that the law is not in itself repugnant to the divine; yet in its present construction and practice, it can admit of no vindication. According to these, neither men nor women have any security against a divorce, without ever being heard on the subject. The court often hear the case, and give judgment against the party absent, though he hath never been cited, nor had the least intelligence of the process. Hence the judges, in some instances, have been grossly imposed on; in others, it has appeared afterwards, on the return of the parties who had been absent, that they had misjudged through want of information. By their judgments women have been divorced from their first husbands, and their families have been broken up; yet upon their return, after a full hearing before the General Assembly, the same women have been separated from their second husbands, whom they had newly married, and sent back to the husbands whom they had put away. Thus family after family hath been broken up and ruined. Hath not iniquity, in these cases, succeeded iniquity? The women who had put away their husbands and gone into second marriages returned to the very men whom they had put away: in direct opposition to the divine prohibition, *Her former husband which sent her away, may not take her again to be his wife, after that she is defiled: for that is abomination before the* Lord. Two notorious instances of this have happened, within a few years, in this vicinity. These abominations are the unhappy fruits of the laws and customs of Connecticut.

The instances of divorce on ex parte hearings, are very numerous. In cases of desertion, I believe, they are generally obtained in this way. If the absent party have not some known place of residence, in the state, the law requires no measures to be taken to give information of the suit, nor any suspension of it for that purpose. No notification is given to the absent party, no attorney, relative, or any other person is provided to speak on his or her behalf. This is also the case, in some other instances, in which the persons are in the state. Either they are not served with a citation, through some pretended difficulty, or if a citation be served, the party is not obliged to appear, and in fact, in many instances makes no appearance, in court. The action nevertheless proceeds, and a bill is given entirely on the representations of the party suing for a divorce.

These I term ex parte hearings. If they be not, I am unable to determine what will bear that denomination. I cannot but imagine they are incompatible with all ideas of justice. They are subversive of the essential rights of men: for it is an essential right of every man

to

to be heard in his own defence. To deny him this, is inconsistent with the very design of law and civil courts. This is, that every cause may have a fair and full hearing, and be issued on the principles of justice. When therefore sentence proceeds without such hearing, there is on the most candid supposition, either through the prevalency of custom, through error, or want of information, iniquity in the place of righteousness †. That was a pertinent challenge, *Doth our law judge any man before it hear him, and know what he doth?* Nor less pertinent was the reply of the heathen magistrate to the priests and elders of the Jews, *It is not the manner of the Romans to deliver any man to die, before that he which is accused have the accuser face to face, and have licence to answer for himself concerning the crime laid against him.*

THE custom respecting divorces is contrary to the law and practice in other cases of far less importance. In the affair of the distribution and settlement of insolvent estates the matter must be publicly notified, six, ten or eighteen months, before a creditor can be debarred from bringing in, and recovering a debt, even of five shillings *. In the case of absent or absconding debtors, provision is also made that agents shall answer for them; and, that beside leaving citations at the places of their last or usual abode, that the court shall be adjourned from time to time, that the attorney, factor or agent, may have opportunity to notify his principal ‡. Is it not indeed admirable, that when the law makes such provision for the security of property of the least amount, that no such provision shall be made, to prevent the ruin of whole families, and to guard the most essential interests and bonds of human society? Is not this a defect which calls upon the legislator for an immediate remedy? Ought the husband and wife to be more easily separated, than the creditor may obtain the most familiar cause, or be thrown out of a shilling? This is verily the present state of the case One who petitions for a divorce may come in, on the last days, just at the heel of the court, and in a few hours, without ever having cited the absent party, or given notice to a single friend of his, obtain a divorce §. A case of property to the amount of six pence, cannot be thus decided between persons who are both natives of the state. I am persuaded, that, in this matter, the law and usage of Connecticut have not a parallel upon earth.

I WISH to compare them with the laws and usages of one of the loosest kingdoms, respecting marriage and divorce, in all Europe. Such an one, so far as I can learn, is Prussia. Her laws admit of divorces in many cases, and, under certain restrictions, of what they term left hand marriages, concubinage, or plurality of wives. They admit of divorce in cases of desertion; but before the action can be raised against a deserter it must be proved, that the desertion was malicious and

† Eccles. 3. 16. * State Laws, P. 105. ‡ Page 35.
§ This was the case in the instance, which hath given such trouble to the church and people of North-Haven.

and with a design to abandon the deserted correlate. Then they make provision, that the fugitive spouse shall be summoned, and that if the place of his residence be unknown, that he shall be cited by a public edict. They further provide, that if the fugitive do not return, that an attorney be named to manage his defence *. If on a full hearing the fugitive correlate is found guilty, all his, or her effects are forfeited to the innocent party for life; and the delinquent is laid under a prohibition of marriage, without a dispensation from the crown †.

How widely different is this from the law and usage of Connecticut? Here nothing can be done suddenly. No action can be commenced till there is full proof of malicious and designed desertion. Nothing can be obtained without the most public notice. No ex parte hearing can find the least toleration. The delinquent must be found and punished.

In cases where the parties are willing to be divorced and make a mutual demand of it, the Prussian law provides, "That the proceed-"ure in the affair be only gradual. First endeavours shall be used "to reconcile the parties, and all the motives that ought to deter-"mine them to this, shall be proposed; observing if it be necessary "to call a clergyman to give them a suitable exhortation. If these "steps prove ineffectual, they shall be separated from bed and board for "one year. If at the years end, there remain no more hopes of re-"conciling the parties, and they persist in their petition, the mar-"riage may be dissolved ‡."

Here every remedy is provided against a separation. The law takes care that those remedies be applied and that proper time be given for consideration: nay, it interposeth and punisheth the parties, and finds the case absolutely desperate, before it will suffer a divorcement. This is doing everything which the *Westminster* Confession makes necessary, before it shall be lawful to proceed to a divorce. Happy would it be, did the laws of Connecticut make the like provision. Desertions and divorces would doubtless then be comparatively few §. Under such regulations they would be much more tolerable. Does not the nature of the case, the great importance of preserving the rights of marriage, the peace and order of families, and the sacred inclosure with which Heaven hath encompassed the seventh commandment, demand these regulations?

Further

* Frederician code, vol. I. P. 126, 127. † P. 127.

‡ F. C. vol. I. 125.

§ A suspension of the matter, and giving the parties time for consideration, would in many instances prevent the sin and unhappy cousequences of a separation. No man, perhaps, was ever more engaged in obtaining a divorce, or more loudly complained of his unhappiness in the conjugal relation, than the famous John Milton; yet as the laws of his country would admit of no divorce, he became reconciled to his wife, and lived happily with her ever afterwards. Many who have put away their companions, and made it matter of lamentation, all the future part of their lives, had the matter been delayed, would have been prevented, and they and their families would have enjoyed honour and peace.

Further, is there not a peculiar propriety in making them, in Connecticut, as the ſtate and theſe churches have adopted this confeſſion, as agreeable to the divine word, and as a rule of faith and practice, which, in all ſuch caſes demands them?

It is apprehended that no divorce ought ever to be given till all proper meaſures for a reconciliation have been attempted without ſucceſs; nor without bringing the parties, if poſſible, to anſwer face to face before the court. There ought to be a moſt thorough examination and diſcovery of the whole ſtate of the caſe; ſo that divorces may not be given without ſcripture warrant, and that when they are given the delinquent may be found and ſuffer deſerved ſhame and puniſhment.

Though they be cited, yet if they be not obliged to appear, and here be not a thorough inveſtigation of the caſe, a divorce may be obained by a colluſion. The parties may agree to a ſeparation: that ne ſhall ſue for a divorce, and that the other ſhall not anſwer, to conradict any repreſentations which the petitioner ſhall make. In this ay, all perſons deſirous of a ſeparation, may obtain a divorce. It reuceth the matter at once, to this, that neither the law, nor the marage vow, can prevent a ſeparation of the ſpouſes at their pleaſure.

Indeed on ſuppoſition that one of them is unwilling, the other ay, either by rewards or threats, or by both conjointly, prevent the ppearance of the other, and ſo obtain a bill, by groſs miſrepreſentaon, when it can, by no means, be warranted. There is reaſon to lieve that there have been inſtances of divorce, in both theſe caſes, warrantable either by religion, morality, or good order. Numeus inſtances, doubtleſs, will take place in future, unleſs effectual proions be made againſt all ex parte hearings, and that ſufficient time be ven, and means uſed for the fulleſt information. That this proviſion not made, in a caſe of ſuch magnitude as the diſſolution of the marge bond, eſpecially, ſince it is made in matters of far leſs importce, appears to be a grand defect in our ſyſtem of laws.

There is another, perhaps ſtill greater than this. No proviſion is de, in caſes of divorce, for the puniſhment of the delinquent. enever there is a juſt occaſion of divorce, one party hath been guilty an high miſdemeanor. He, or ſhe, hath been guilty of violating greateſt bonds of human ſociety: been guilty of a breach of the riage vow. This can be nothing leſs than premeditated and habitperjury. One or other of the parties in ſome inſtances have actucommitted adultery, and the divorce is granted on this footing. ll other inſtances the delinquents, agreeably to the expreſs declaon of the Christian Lawgiver, either cauſe others to commit aery, or commit it themſelves. *But I ſay unto you, that whoſoever th away his wife, ſaving for the cauſe of fornication, cauſeth her to it adultery. And I ſay unto you, whoſoever ſhall put away his wife, t it be for fornication, and marrieth another committeth adultery.* ſe are capital crimes; crimes to be puniſhed by the judge.

Perjury,

Perjury, in civil and criminal caſes, is puniſhed with fines, payment of damages, ſitting in the pillory, diſability of ſwearing in any court; and, in ſome inſtances with death: But the wilful, habitual and perſevering violation of the marriage contract, or vow, in which there is a moſt ſolemn appeal to the Omniſcient Creator, is treated as innocent and harmleſs. In the eye of the law, this great wickedneſs, the ſubverſion of the peace and order of families, the vitiation of community, and the expoſing of it to the divine rebukes hath nothing criminal or miſchievous.

That which is commonly termed adultery is puniſhed as a capital offence. By the law of Moſes the puniſhment is death; by ours, whipping, branding and the perpetual wearing of a halter†. But that which the Chriſtian Lawgiver hath declared to be adultery, which, in many inſtances, may be much more criminal than the other, paſſeth without puniſhment, threats or frowns. In the former caſe it may be committed on ſome ſudden and violent temptation, without any conſideration of the conſequences, or deſign of future and perpetual treachery; but, in the latter, the delinquent proceeds to it with deliberation; with a fixed perſevering determination, ever to violate all marriage duties, towards the lawful correlate.

Is it not admirable, that while the legiſlature is clothed with vengeance, and the law ſpeaks fines, diſabilities, impriſonment, halters and death, in caſes of ſimilar enormity, that they ſhould be ſilent and without a frown with reſpect to theſe? The public face beholds them ſerene as ſummer evenings, placid as the face of the deep when there is not the gentleſt breeze in motion.

The ſacred books claſs covenant-breaking, violation of oaths, and adultery amongſt the blackeſt crimes. They declare, that *becauſe of theſe the land mourneth, and the wrath of GOD cometh on the children of diſobedience.* They are great offences, both againſt God, and againſt ſociety. They have a great tendency to a general corruption of manners, and to ſubject a community to the moſt awful viſitations.

Is it therefore poſſible that this ſhould be right? Can it be honourable to a Chriſtian Legiſlature, that, in caſes like theſe, the law ſhould inflict no fines, no diſabilities, no forfeitures, nor marks of public ſhame and diſapprobation? Can it be conſiſtent with ſound policy? Doth not this require that the beſt proviſion be made to puniſh the vicious, and to ſecure the public peace and ſafety? Surely it does. The civil magiſtrate, acting in character, *is a terror to evil works.* He *beareth not the ſword in vain: for he is the miniſter of GOD, a revenger to execute wrath upon him that doth evil.*

In every view we can take of the law, in theſe points, whether religious or political, I cannot but be perſuaded, that there is a capital defect. So far as I can learn this is not the caſe in the other American States, nor in the looſeſt kingdoms in Europe.

Even

† State Laws P. 8.

EVEN in Pruſſia, where there are, as has been obſerved, great indulgences, in theſe matters, the delinquent is ſubject to forfeitures and diſabilities. He, or ſhe, cannot contract a ſecond marriage without a licence from the crown. If this be not attended, the ſpouſes are puniſhed as bigamiſts†.

SUCH puniſhments and public ſtigmas have great effect to render divorces ſhameful and odious, and to ſecure the rights of marriage. But, in Connecticut, the ſilence of the law, in this point, the foſtering of perſons of this character in the boſom of the public, without a frown, or the leaſt mark of diſapprobation, give them countenance, and cauſe vice to walk with a bare face and a ſtretched out neck. The great facility with which divorces are obtained, and the multiplicity of them, are a further encouragement. Such people keep themſelves in countenance by their numbers, by the cuſtom of the country, by the opinions and examples of great men, be they ever ſo erroneous and deſtructive. The ſilence and ſanction of law, in a ſpecial manner, are ſuch ſoothing cordials, ſuch effectual opiates, that no flaſhes, nor thunder, from the divine word will alarm their conſciences.

THESE are, doubtleſs, ſome of the principal reaſons, why we are ſo much degenerated from the practice of our anceſtors, and become ſo unlike to all other churches, whether Jewiſh or Chriſtian, in their pureſt ages; and alſo to all proteſtant ſtates and kingdoms. Nay, theſe are ſome of the reaſons, why we even exceed ſome of the moſt polite and poliſhed heathen, in that great ſin of putting away, which the LORD GOD of Iſrael hateth. Theſe have all united their influence, and, with the luſts of the human heart, have co-operated in the production of that kind of madneſs, for divorce, which, like a contagion, ſpreads over the ſtate.

CUSTOM, law, the countenance of great men, eſpecially if they are eſteemed good men, will make any vice faſhionable. Theſe made divorces in Rome, ſo frequent, that among their beſt men, it was matter of great lamentation. It had flouriſhed ſix or ſeven hundred years, without a ſingle inſtance of divorce. But as ſoon as divorces became cuſtomary, and as ſoon as perſons of figure and influence fell into the practice, Seneca and Tertullian lament, that no body bluſhed at them†. Let the law be ſilent, and let it once become cuſtomary

† Frederician Code Vol. I. P. 127.

† Obſervatur non raro quingentis amplius annis, ſexcentis volunt aliqui floruiſſe Rempublicam Romanam, ſine divortii uſu, (quod tamen legibus toto illo tempore permiſſum) uſque ad notiſſimum illud Spurii Carbilii Rugæ, qui ſterilitatis cauſa primo uxorem dimiſit. Poſtmodum vero Repudium et votum fuit quaſi matrimonii fructus, ut ait Tertullianus juxta ac Seneca, Numquid jam ulla repudia erubeſcit, poſtquam illuſtres quædam ac nobiles feminæ, non conſulum numero, ſed maritorum annos ſuos computant, et exeunt matrimonii cauſa, nubunt repudii. Tamdiu iſtud timebatur, quamdiu rarum fuit. Selden, Vol. III. P. 768. Et Romani, cum nulla lex repudium vetaret, annos tamen 700 ſine exemplo repudii egerunt. Poli Synopſis, Vol. IV. P. 163.

customary to practise the grossest instances of injustice and murder, and people will commit them in open day, without a blush. Of this we have sufficient evidence, in the late numerous payments, in Continental currency, not equal in value to a fifth, or tenth part of the original debt; and the frequent instances of deliberate murder, in dueling, where the practice is tolerated, and grows into custom. These things are mentioned to show the pernicious influence of bad precedents, and the necessity of making effectual provision, by law, for the punishment of such capital misdemeanors, as the violation of the marriage bond.

To give still clearer conviction in these points, and exhibit a full view of our degeneracy, I shall now compare Connecticut, in its present state, with New-England and with itself, for the first half century; with the Jewish and Christian churches in their purest ages; with other states and kingdoms; that, in this comparative view, we may blush at our own features, and be roused to an immediate reformation.

First, let us make the comparison between ourselves now, and New-England and Connecticut, the first half century. For nearly sixty years, from the settlement of New-England, I find but one instance of divorce‡, and no law by which it might be obtained. More than forty years, from the settlement of this state, elapsed, before any such law was in existence†. No divorce was given by virtue of the law, till the year 1692. After this divorces were, for many years, very sparingly given. But as they became customary, as there were no punishments for delinquents, and as the shame decreased with the growth of the practice, they have, within this few years, had a rapid increase. In less than a century, four hundred and thirty nine pair, eight hundred and seventy eight persons, have been separated by divorce. This whole number, forty eight couple excepted, have been divorced in the short term of fifty two years, Between twenty and thirty pair, forty and fifty people, are now annually separated by divorce, in the Superior Court, besides those put asunder by the General Assembly. About twenty times as many are now divorced annually, as were in almost sixty years after the first settlement of the state; and about half as many as were divorced through the whole first century. Seventeen pair have been divorced the last circuit. How unlike is Connecticut to her former self?

Next, let Connecticut be compared with the Jewish and Christian churches, in their purest ages. For the term of seven hundred years from the promulgation of the law of Moses, there is not to be found so much as an example, nor even the mention of a divorce§. Indeed there was

‡ This was given, by a sovereign act of the General Assembly of Connecticut, August 12th, 1657.

† In the Massachusetts and Connecticut codes, printed at Cambridge 1672, there is no law respecting divorce. The law of Connecticut relative to it was made five years after, Oct. 11, 1677.

§ In Fœdere vero Veteri per septingentos a lege lata aut circiter annos divortii mentio nullibi occurrit. Selden's U. E. Vol. III. P. 764.

no complaint or reproof of the Jews, on this account, till the time of the prophet Malachi, considerably more than a thousand years from the giving of the law. What a striking contrast is here, between Connecticut, under the full blaze of the gospel, and the Jewish church, under a dispensation, which in comparison with it had no glory at all?

In the Christian Church divorces were condemned, and divorced persons excommunicated, at least for the first three or four centuries††. Besides it seems that the severest corporal punishments were, for many centuries, inflicted on those who were found to be the faulty causes of divorce‡‡. How widely different are these matters conducted in Connecticut? How deformed and fallen is its appearance when compared with the church in the primitive ages?

But little better will it bear a comparison with other states and Protestant kingdoms, or even with Rome pagan in her best days. The difference between Connecticut and Prussia hath in some measure been shewn already. In that kingdom, I suppose, divorces are given more easily and frequently than in any other Protestant kingdom; yet the matter is vastly better guarded than in this state. For this reason it is to be presumed that they are much less numerous, according to the number of the people than they are in Connecticut. Besides the difference which hath been noticed between Prussia and Connecticut, there are several other things in which there is a great difference. In Prussia the law forbids persons who have obtained a divorce and gone into a second marriage, from ever returning again to the correlate which hath been put away*; and so it effectually guards against the abomination which God hath so expressly forbidden, as causing a land to sin, and making it abominable|| But in Connecticut the party putting away, and which hath gone into a second marriage, is by public authority taken from the second husband and sent back to the first, In Prussia all cases on which divorces may be obtained are particularly stated, and the whole process directed and guarded†‡. But this is far from being the

†† Selden Vol. III. P. 344. Quoted above.

‡‡ Sed in repudio culpaque divortii perquerenda, durum est legum veterum moderamen excedere. Ideo constitutionibus abrogatis, quæ nunc maritum, nunc mulierem matrimonio soluto præcipiunt pœnis gravissimis coerceri. Selden, Vol. III. U. E. P. 831.

All the Saxon churches, and most of the Protestant churches, in Europe, their consistories and judges, it seems, maintain that the violators of the marriage bond ought to be punished, and do severely punish them. Et adulteri et adulteræ, et desertores et desertrices condemnantur voce docentium in ecclesiis, et judicum consistoriis: et a magistratibus severé puniuntur. Harmony of Confessions, P. 258.

* Frederician Code, Vol. I. P. 127.

|| Deut. 24. 4.

†‡ F. Code, Vol. I. from page 122 to 135.

The Prussian law takes away the children, in all cases of divorce, from the delinquent, and gives them to the innocent correlate. If the husband be the guilty party, he is obliged to maintain both the wife and children, according to his fortune and quality. P. 131, 132.

the case in Connecticut. The law respecting desertion is construed, and acted upon, with great liberality. Cases which cannot, by any means, be brought under this description, are carried to the Assembly, where persons wishing for a divorce are treated with the same attention and generosity as in the other court. Between them both divorces are so multiplied, as to be matter of great grief, so far as I can learn, to almost the whole body of the clergy, to many good people in the state; and so as to give great trouble and perplexity in some of our churches.

No better will Connecticut bear a comparison with the church and laws of England. These admit of no total divorce§§. It is true that some of the nobility, and people of the first quality, have of late years, in some few instances, by a sovereign act of the king and parliament, obtained a divorce, in cases of adultery: But it is with great difficulty that divorces are obtained even in these cases. The common people cannot be at the expence of them.

The Waldenses and Norwegians, I have shewn, excommunicated all persons guilty of divorce: and that it is the doctrine of the Protestant churches of Europe, in general, that they ought to be severely punished: and, that, in fact, punishments are inflicted upon them.

The State of New-York, from its first settlement till the year 1787, for the term of about one hundred and seventy years, affords no instance of divorce. Indeed, till that time there was no law in the state which admitted of divorce in any case whatsoever†. In the southern states they are rarely, if at all, admitted. In comparison with Connecticut, there are but few in any of the other parts of New-England. To whom then can we be likened for this great wickedness of putting away? Will even pagan Rome present us with an equal? No, with respect to this, for the term of five, six, or seven hundred years, she stands forth as an uncontaminated virgin. During this long period she had not once done that, which every year, in numerous instances, is perpetrated in Connecticut. Is it possible, in this view, that we should not be convinced of something amiss? Does not the example of our ancestors reprove and condemn us? Do not the sacred books, the examples of all good men which they have recorded, the Jewish and christian church, in their purest ages, testify against us? Do not the laws and customs of the most ancient and politic kingdoms, and even those of our sister states, reprove us, both in point of policy and religion? Will they not with one consent rise up against us in that day when the kingdoms and judges of the world shall appear before his tribunal who is higher than the highest?

Is

§§ Blackstone Vol. I. P. 441.

† March, 1787, a law was enacted in the state of New-York, by which a divorce may be given in case of adultery; but it ordains, that after the dissolution of the marriage has been pronounced, "It shall not be lawful for the party convicted "of adultery, to remarry any person whatsoever, and that every such marriage "shall be null and void."

Is it not then time to stop, and consider? High time, unitedly, to attempt a reformation? If matters are suffered to run on, in their present channel, shall we not soon become like the nations of the world before the giving of the law, when marriages were only for moons, or years, as suited the parties? Or will it not be as it was in Rome, after divorces grew into fashion, that married people will separate at pleasure †? Will it not come to the very thing which Seneca laments, in his day, that there will be few or no marriages without divorce? As he judiciously remarks, people, by hearing and seeing it, will learn the practice *. We shall soon, under the light of the gospel, become like the Jews and heathens in their most corrupt and degenerate state. Should not Christians lament, fear, and by all means, guard against a wickedness which a wise heathen lamented?

DOUBTLESS it is a question of serious importance, whether the civil fathers of the state, or the ministers of righteousness, can be innocent if they neglect to employ their abilities and influence for the suppression of so dangerous and growing a mischief? Is it not worthy of consideration whether the supreme judge will not view the sin of putting away as not barely the sin of the individuals actually engaged in it, even as a public abomination? To be sure while the public look on without a frown, or the least provision for its prevention or punishment?

IF the legislature or judges connive at rather than punish it; if they suffer such laws and customs as countenance rather than discountenance it, as make it fashionable rather than dishonourable; and if the ministers of the gospel acquiesce rather than reprove and remonstrate; will not their JUDGE treat them as accomplices in the same wickedness? Will not the community become guilty before him, and lie open to public chastisement? Nay, if the watchmen will not warn the wicked, and they perish in their wickedness, of whom shall their blood be required?

IMPORTANT is it therefore, that there should be a general exertion to prevent this growing wickedness.

IT is respectfully proposed, whether the legislature ought not to repeal the law respecting divorce in cases of desertion? Can they be sure that in continuing and acting upon it, according to the present custom, they are not acting against the express statute of the Christian LAWGIVER, and against the general order, peace and happiness of society? If the case be only doubtful, is it not much the most safe and prudent to repeal the law, and desist from the present practice? If the Christian LAWGIVER has indeed prohibited divorce, in all cases but those of incontinency, it must be an instance of high presumption and criminality, in the greatest human judges to decree, that the husband and

† Ita nec maritus, solum uxorem, sed uxor maritum, pro libitu dimittebat apud Romanos, ac sponsalitio nuptialique contractui uterque pro arbitrio renunciebatur. Selden's U. E. Vol. III. P. 763.

* Quia vero nulla sine divortio acta sunt, quod sæpe audiebant facile dedicerunt. Dr. Whitby's Annot. Vol. II. 147.

and wife ſhall be put aſunder in any other. For duſt and aſhes to enact laws againſt the ſtatutes of the MOST HIGH, and to determine and pronounce, that they ſhall be ſeparated, whom HE hath ſaid LET NOT MAN PUT ASUNDER, is a matter too ſerious and awful to be treated with lightneſs and inconſideration. On the other hand, there is no divine precept, that a divorce ſhall be given in any caſe. All that can be pleaded is a bare permiſſion. In caſes of deſertion, I preſume, it is not capable of demonſtration, that the general good of ſociety demands any law or cuſtom by which the huſband and wife may be ſeparated. Prudence and ſafety therefore appear to be on the ſide of repealing the law and giving up the preſent practice.

FURTHER, it appears, from the repreſentations made above, that the law, in its preſent conſtruction and practice, is contrary to the ſentiments and practice of the chriſtian church, in the firſt ages; and to the proteſtant churches in general. Indeed the ſentiments, policy, and practice of the moſt ancient, experienced and politic proteſtant ſtates and kingdoms ſeem to be againſt the law and practice of Connecticut in this matter. Should not this, at leaſt, create a doubt whether they are not wrong both in point of morality and policy?

BESIDES there are reſpectable numbers of gentlemen in the miniſtry and in civil liſe, who, in their conſciences, believe the law, as it now ſtands, to be entirely repugnant to the law of our SAVIOUR reſpecting divorce, to the great law of love, and general good of ſociety. They are grieved, put to fear and diſtreſs, on the account of the law and practice, in caſes of divorce. They are perſuaded, that, by theſe means, the land is defiled and made abominable; are grieved for the diſhonour, which, in their view, is done to the DIVINE MAJESTY, and fear the tokens of his diſpleaſure on the community.

IN ſhort, by theſe means, churches are brought into great trouble and difficulty; and if the law be continued they will, probably, be more and more troubled, rent and divided, on that acccount. Are not theſe ſerious and weighty reaſons for its repeal?

SHOULD not the legiſlature vouchſafe to repeal the law, it is humbly propoſed and earneſtly deſired, that, in their great wiſdom and goodneſs, effectual proviſion might be made againſt all ex parte hearings, and that no caſe relative to divorce be allowed a hearing in court, till proper time has been given and all probable means of reconciling the parties have been attempted, and the caſe appears deſperate: That they would ordain, that, in all caſes, in which it can poſſibly be done, the parties ſhall be obliged to anſwer face to face in the court, ſo that if there be colluſion, or other wickedneſs, it may be diſcovered, and the delinquent found: That, when one of the parties is not in the ſtate, he, or ſhe, ſhould be cited by a public edict, and that ſufficient time be given, for the abſent party to be certified that the ſuit is commenced: and, that in caſe of non-appearance, an attorney or agent be provided to manage the caſe, in behalf of the party abſent

sent; that there may be a thorough investigation of it, and the court may proceed on the fullest information.

IT is also proposed, with due submission, that provision should be made, by law, for the punishment of delinquents, in every case of divorce. That when a divorce is given in case of adultery, order should be issued for the immediate arrest and punishment of the adulterer or adulteress†; and, that, in other cases, disabilities and punishments be appointed adequate to the offence of the party in default.

FURTHER it is proposed whether provision may not, and ought not to be made, by the legislature, for the restraining and punishment of contention, abuse and wicked conduct in husbands and wives, and to prevent, as far as may be, such conduct as may lead to a total alienation of conjugal affection, to desertion and divorce. This is the case in some protestant states, at least in Prussia.

IF one of the correlates be found guilty of abuse, and the affair has proceeded so far that ministers and other friends could not effect a reformation, the delinquent is punished by a separation from the bed and board of the other for the term of one complete year. This punishment the law will not remit, even though the delinquent make promises, and give security, of good behaviour for the future*.

IN this state the law makes provision for the good conduct of individuals, of parents and children, servants and masters, and takes care that gross misdemeanours towards each other be restrained by condign punishment. It is apprehended, that, in the same way, provision might be made to prevent gross abuse between the husband and wife; and that were the wisdom and goodness of the legislature employed in this, and

† There have been about an hundred instances of divorce for the express cause of adultery, yet I cannot find, that, in a single instance, there has been any punishment inflicted, or so much as a prosecution commenced. Can it be true indeed, that in Connecticut adultery is justified by prescription? Or will any venture to say that there was no sufficient evidence of the fact, after the judges have given a bill for the express cause of adultery? Does the chief court in the state condemn and record persons as adulterers, and break up families, on this footing, without any proper evidence of the fact? Or will it be said that no complaints have ever been exhibited? Is not this saying, that it is the custom, or common law, of Connecticut, That adulterers shall escape with impunity? The chief judges of the state, and the state's attorneys are acquainted with the facts, and what else can be the construction of the public conduct? How have the laws and customs changed from one extreme to the other? By the first laws of Connecticut, adultery was punished with death. Colony Records, Vol. I. P. 92. This was the case in New-Haven. See the Records of that Colony. This seems to have been the law throughout New-England. Some were executed upon it. Gov. Hutchinson's History, Vol I. 441. The instances of execution took place on those males only who had been guilty of incontinence with married women. It seems to have been their idea that adultery in the male always implied incontinency with a neighbour's wife. Perhaps this is the true scripture idea. This therefore furnisheth an important reason for the Christian Lawgiver's using the word PORNEIA, which is expressive of all kinds of incontinency, which can be committed within the bands of wedlock, rather than any other.

* Frederician Code, Vol. I. P. 131.

and the various ways, which they might devise, to prevent ill conduct, between those near correlates, and their final separation, it would tend much more to the preservation of chastity, the happiness of families, and the health of society, than the present multiplication of divorces.

IN these views, it is with becoming deference, proposed to my Reverend fathers and brethen, in the ministry, whether it be not their duty to unite in an humble petition and address to the honourable General Assembly, to take these matters into their serious consideration, and to make such further provision for the preservation of conjugal chastity and fidelity, as their wisdom shall direct. This may be done by particular associations, or more properly, perhaps, by the general association, in the name of the whole.

THE united exertion and influence of the clergy, in this matter, would have weight with the legislature, do much for the divine honour, the good of the church and commonwealth.

ALL gentlemen of character and influence, and the community at large, are earnestly invited to pay such attention to these matters, as their nature and importance demand, and to exert themselves to obtain such regulations respecting them, as shall be most consonant to the divine word, and subservient to individual, domestic and public happiness.

EVERY person may do much in his private capacity to promote these great purposes. If every husband and wife would conduct in character. This would be an effectual remedy against all divorce. The motives for doing it are great and numerous. Nothing can lay a more sure foundation for immortal friendship, honour and bliss among relatives. Besides, the laws of marriage cannot be violated without a violation of the law of nature, the divine institution, and an abuse of all the goodness of the common PARENT of the universe, in the provision he hath made by it for the preservation of the life and chastity of men; for the honour and comfort of families in the present state, and their exaltation and bliss in the future. By a violation of the institution of marriage men violate all those precepts which guard and enforce it. GOD hath said, *Let thy fountain be blessed: and rejoice with the wife of thy youth. Let her be as the loving hind and pleasant roe, let her breasts satisfy thee at all times, and be thou ravisht always with her love. Husbands love your wives, even as* CHRIST *loved his church. So ought men to love their wives as their own bodies: he that loveth his wife loveth himself. That they teach young women to love their husbands. Wives submit yourselves to your own husbands as is fit in the* LORD. *Husbands love your wives, and be not bitter against them. Let every one of you in particular, so love his wife even as himself; and let the wife see that she reverence her husband.* These commands, and all others of like import, are but so many explanations of the law of nature, and of the marriage institution. These indispensibly bind all

Christians

Christians to the obſervation of it. In like manner doth the ſeventh commandment, and all other commands reſpecting the duty of chaſtity. In theſe views how vaſt is the guilt of thoſe who groſsly violate the marriage contract? Let theſe conſiderations have their juſt weight. Let it alſo be conſidered that the examples of good men recorded in ſcripture are univerſally againſt divorce. They furniſh us with no examples of it. Reflect on its miſchievous conſequences to families, and how many, on the account of it, have afterwards gone mourning to their graves. Though people may ſometimes triumph in it for a while, yet; does it not terminate like the triumph of Satan after the deception of our firſt parents, in hiſſing and grief, as unſavory as ſoot and aſhes†. The laws and judgments of men cannot make the leaſt alteration in the laws and inſtitutions of the SUPREME LAWGIVER. *Till heaven and earth paſs, one jot or one tittle ſhall in no wiſe paſs from the law till all be fulfilled.* Should human legiſlators ſolemnly enact, That the tide ſhall no more ebb and flow, that ſummer and winter, ſeed time and harveſt ſhall no more ſucceed each other, the tide would nevertheleſs ebb and flow, and the ſeaſons roll on invariably as they had ever done. Juſt ſo let them enact what they pleaſe reſpecting the moral law and moral inſtitutions, they will remain the ſame. Obligations to obey them can neither be vacated or diminiſhed, by human ſtatutes. Though men may eaſe their conſciences, by the countenance of them, in their breach of covenants and violations of chaſtity, at preſent, yet they will give them no relief in the preſence of their JUDGE. It is of the higheſt importance that it be deeply fixed in the heart of man, that not the fallible laws of mortals, but the LAW of GOD, is to be the rule of final deciſion. HE hath ſaid, The word that I have ſpoken, the ſame ſhall judge him in the laſt day.

† So having ſaid, awhile he ſtood, expecting
Their univerſal ſhout and high applauſe
To fill his ear, when contrary he hears
On all ſides from innumerable tongues
A diſmal univerſal hiſs, the ſound
Of public ſcorn.——
Chew'd bitter aſhes, which th' offended taſte
With ſpattering noiſe rejected——
With hatefulleſt diſreliſh writh'd their jaws
With ſoot and cinders fill'd.——

Milton, Book X.

ERRATA.

Page 4, after *conjointly* and *languages*, and p. 9. l. 4. from the bottom, after *husb-and*, periods are uſed, which read with commas. P. 7. l. 10. from the top, read *ſup-oſitoi-*. P. 40. l. 4. *u* is inverted in *mentioned*. P, 37. l. 10, read *pureſt*. P. 39. l. 5. from the bottom read *of* before *cuſtom*. Ib. bottom l. read *it* inſtead of *is*. P. 40. l. 18. read *their* inſtead of *heir*.

The Well-Ordered
FAMILY:
OR,
Relative DUTIES.

BEING THE
Subſtance of ſeveral SERMONS,

About {
Family Prayer.
Duties of *Husbands* & *Wives*.
Duties of *Parents* & *Children*.
Duties of *Maſters* & *Servants*.
}

By Benj. Wadſworth. A.M
Paſtor of a Church of CHRIST *in* Boſton, *N.E.*

Pſal ci.2.7.— *I will walk within my houſe with a perfect heart.— He that worketh deceit, ſhall not dwell within my houſe* ——

Joſh. xxiv. 15. *As for me and my houſe, we will Serve the Lord.*

Gen. xviii. 19. — *He* (that is, Abraham) *will command his Children and his houſehold after him, and they ſhall keep the way of the Lord.*

BOSTON: Printed by *B. Green*, for *Nicholas Butſolph*, at his Shop in Corn-Hill. 1712.

Preface.

GOod Order in any Society, renders it beautiful and lovely. The upholding of Good Order in it, tends to promote the benefit and comfort of all the Members of it. This is true of Families, as well as of other Societies. A Family wherein the true Worship of God, good pious Instruction and Government are upheld, is beautiful in the eyes of God himself; he delights to bless such. He blesseth the Habitation of the Just. *Every Christian (every Gospel Minister especially) should do all he can to promote the Glory of God, & the Welfare of those about him; & the well ordering matters in particular Families, tends to promote these things. I believe the Ignorance, Wickedness (& consequent Judgments) that have prevailed, & still are prevailing among us, are not more plainly owing to any one thing, than to the* neglect *of Family Religion, Instruction & Government; and the reviving of these things, would yield as comfortable a prospect*

of

of our future good, as almost any one thing I can think of. My Prayer to God is, that what I have here offered may be Instrumental to quicken Persons to Family Prayer, and to carry themselves agreeably to the various Capacities they sustain in Families. If what I have written, may promote God's Worship, & Good Order, in any one Family of these who shall Read it ; I shall not grudge the pains I have taken. Bnt if none should reap benefit by reading these my Endeavours, yet I hope I shall not repent of this my Essay ; for (as far as I know my own heart) God's Glory, and the Good of his People, were chiefly aimed at herein. The consideration that my Life is short and uncertain, makes me the more desirous, to do something that may be useful (if God bless it) to the Interests of Religion, after I am gone, and shall be here no more. I know the things I have here discoursed of, are matters of constant Obligation ; therefore the Inculcating of them, should never be tho't unseasonable. That God for Christ's sake would accept these my Endeavours, & make them successful to promote his Glory, and the good of Souls, is the Prayer of the Unworthy Author.

Benj. Wadsworth.

The

The Well-Ordered FAMILY:

OR,

Relative DUTIES.

1 Cor. VII. 24.

Brethren, Let every man wherein he is called, therein abide with God.

IT ſhould be the Study and Care of Chriſtians to Serve and Pleaſe God, in every Capacity and Relation they ſuſtain; this ſeems to be the plain Senſe and Import of our Text! In the three preceeding Verſes, the Apoſtle ſpeaks more particularly about *Servants.* If any while *Servants*, were call'd and converted to the true Chriſtian Religion, the Apoſtle would not have them be diſcontent with, or uneaſie at, their Servitude. *Art thou called being a Servant, Care not for it?* v. 21. Don't be caſt down at the thoughts of thy Servitude, don't murmur at it, but be

 quiet

quiet in it. Thus he directs them, though at the ſame time he grants, that freedom and liberty are rather to be deſired than *Servitude* ; if a man might have his choice The Apoſtle further declares, that there is no difference between *Freemen* and *Servants* ; as to *Spiritual* Priviledges or Duties. If a *Servant* to men is a *true Chriſtian*, he is the *Lord's Feeeman* ; he's free from the guilt and tyranny of Sin, and is an Heir of Eternal Glory. So one that is a *Freeman* (not Servant to any man) if he's a true Chriſtian, he's the *Lord's Servant* ; he's as much oblig'd as any elſe, to obey all the Commands of Chriſt, *v.* 24. So that as to Spiritual Priviledges and Duties, there is no difference between *Freemen* and *Servants*. *There is neither Jew nor Greek, Bond nor Free, Male nor Female ; for ye are all one in Chriſt Jeſus*, Gal 3 28. When therefore the Apoſtle in the 23. *v.* of our Context ſays, *ye are bought with a price, be not the Servants of men* ; the meaning is not, that Servants ſhould quit the Service of their Maſters, but that they ſhould *not ſerve the luſts nor corruptions of men.* They ſhould not ſerve nor pleaſe men in any thing that's inconſiſtent with their ſerving and pleaſing of Chriſt, who has bought them with a price, and whoſe Servants therefore they are. Inaſmuch as Chriſt has bought them with a price, they are not their own, but ſhould glorifie him with their Bodies and their Spirits which

which are his, 1 *Cor* 6 20. Having ſaid theſe things, the Apoſtle adds in our Text, *Let every man wherein he is called, therein abide with God.* Whether he is a *Freeman*, a *Servant*, or in what *Capacity* or *Relation* ſoever he is, yet being *Called* (being Converted to the true Chriſtian Religion) he ought therein *to abide with God*; that is, he ſhould pleaſe and ſerve God, act as becomes a Chriſtian, in that Condition or Relation which Providence has plac'd him in. We might note by the way, that *the Chriſtian Religion does not diſſolve or deſtroy, thoſe various Relations or Capacities, which are common among men.* It does not diſſolve the Relation between Husbands and Wives, Parents and Children, Maſters and Servants, Rulers and Subjects: It is ſo far from diſſolving, that it rather confirms thoſe Relations, and the Duties thence ariſing. It teaches the Duties of thoſe Relations, and preſſeth the performance of them. Social Duties and Comforts, are not hindred but furthered by Chriſtianity. The more practical Chriſtianity prevails in any Society, ſo much the better Relative Duties will be performed, & ſo much the more Relative Comforts will be promoted. But paſſing this Note, the *Doctrine* to be inſiſted on from the words, is this.

DOCT

DOCTRINE

Christians should endeavour to Please and Glorifie God, in whatsoever Capacity or Relation they Sustain.

Under this Doctrine, my design is (by God's help) to say something about *Relative Duties*, particularly in *Families.* I shall therefore endeavour, to speak as briefly and plainly as I can, about. (1) *Family Prayer.* (2) *The Duties of Husbands and Wives* (3) *The Duties of Parents and Children* (4) *The Duties of Masters and Servants.* Therefore according to this Method, something is to be said.

I. *About Family Prayer.* Now here I shall endeavour: (1.) *To show that Family Prayer is a Duty.* (2.) *To answer some Objections, that are too apt to be made against this Duty.* (3) *To add something by way of Use.* We are therefore,

1. *To show that Family Prayer is a Duty.* Indeed, all particular persons, should maintain a constant practice of *Secret Prayer.* They should enter into their Closets, and having shut their door, *they should pray to their Father which seeth in secret*, Mat. 6. 6. And as particular persons should thus Pray in Secret, so *Families* should Pray to God too. The Families should get together Morning and Evening, and when together, the Head of the Family

mily ſhould Pray to God with them, and for them. That 'tis the Duty of Chriſtians thus to do, ſeems evident.

1. *From the very light of Nature.* That there is a God, that his Providence governs the World which he has made; that Providence beſtows Benefits, & inflicts Evils; are things evident from the Light of Nature: therefore this God ſhould be Prayed to and Served. God's Providence governs the Affairs of *Societies*, as well as of *Particular Perſons*; therefore *Societies* (of which a *Family* is the firſt and ſmalleſt ſort or kind) ſhould acknowledge God, both by way of *Prayer* and *Praiſe*. A Family ſhould pray to God, for Family Mercies which are needed: and praiſe him for Family Benefits which are Enjoyed. Theſe things ſeem very evident from the Light of Nature. And hence the very *Heathen* had, not only publick Temples, Altars and Sacrifices; but alſo their *Penates* their *Houſhold gods* which they were wont to Worſhip in their Particular Families. It's likely thoſe *Mariners* with whom *Jonah* was in a Storm at Sea, were *Heathen*, or not well Inſtructed in the Knowledge of the true God, for they cried every one *to his god*; yet their hazard continuing, and being equally in eminent danger, they *Joined together in Prayer*, ſaying, *We* beſeech thee, O Lord, *we* beſeech thee, let us not periſh, *Jonah* 1 5. 14 That *Ships Crew* were of the nature of a *Family* (as every Ships Crew

Crew is) and the very Light of Nature taught them, *jointly and together to pray to God* for needful deliverance.

2. *It has been the practice of the Godly to Pray with their Families.* *Joshua* said, Josh. 24. 15. *As for me and my House we will Serve the Lord.* He was resolv'd, that he and his House, his Family, would Serve and Worship, Pray to, and Obey the only living and true God. This resolution should be imitated, by all Christian Housholders. If there was no Family Prayer in *Adam's* and *Noah's* Family, then for no one knows how long, no Worship was paid to God, but only in secret, which is not probable. We read of *Davids blessing his Houshold*, 2 Sam. 6 20. He had been worshipping God in Publick with the people; and then besides that, he worship'd God in private with his Family, even by *Family Prayer*; which seems the thing intended by *blessing his Houshold.* 'Tis said of *Cornelius*: Acts 10 2. *He feared God with all his House---- and prayed always.* Fearing of God, comprehends the *worshipping* of him; he being a devout man, *worship'd God with all his house*: he *pray'd always*; that is, he maintain'd a *constant course* of Prayer. It seems 'twas his usual practice, together with his Family to pray to God. Yea, our Lord Jesus pray'd with his Family. His Disciples, his Apostles, while abiding with him were his *Family*, and he pray'd with them, *Luk* 11. 1. He was

Praying

Praying in a certain place, when he ceased, *One of his Disciples* said to him. &c. When he had ended Prayer, one of his Disciples, of his Family (whom he had been praying with) took occasion to say, what there follows ; So Luk. 9 18. *As he was alone praying, his Disciples were with him.* He was praying with his Family, his Disciples ; and said to be *alone*, because at that time none but his Disciples were present. Thus tis plain, that our Lord Pray'd not only *for*, but *with* his *Family* ; and we are bid, to *follow his steps*, 1 Pet. 2. 21. *to do as he has done*, Joh. 13 15. and to *walk as he also walked*, 1 Joh. 2 6. Those therefore who neglect Family Prayer, seem to say by their practice ; they won't imitate Christ, they won't follow his Example, nor do as he bids them. Oh ! let men consider, how wicked the language of their practice is, when they neglect Family Prayer. Again, That Family Prayer is a Duty, seems evident.

3. *From Scripture Precepts.* Christians are bid, *to pray with all prayer*, and to watch thereunto *with all perseverance.* Eph. 6 18. *All Prayer*, surely comprehends *Family Prayer*, as well as *Secret* and *Publick* Prayer. And they should *persevere* or *hold on* in all *Prayer* ; that is, maintain a *constant course* and practice of Family Prayer, as well as of Secret Prayer, and of Publick, at the proper seasons of it. The Apostle says to Christian *Masters*, Col. 4. 2. *Continue in prayer* ; in the preceeding verse, he

mov'd

mov'd them to do their *Duty to their Servants*, and then adds, *Continue in Prayer*; it seems to intimate, that *Masters should pray with their Servants* (as well as *with* the rest of their Family) else they could not do all their duty to them. Yea, he says, v. 3. *Praying also for us.* The word here rendred *also*, sometimes signifies *jointly, conjunctly* or *together*, Mat. 13. 29. 'Tis sometimes translated, *together*, as Rom. 3 12. 1 Thes. 4. 17 And if 'twere so rendred in this Text, then 'twould run thus, *praying together* (or jointly and conjunctly) *for us.* Husbands and Wives are bid to live quietly and lovingly together, *that their prayers be not hindred*, 1 Pet. 3 7 Family Prayer seems there especially intended, for if there be jarrings and contentions between Husband and Wife; it's apt to hinder Family Prayer, or at least hinder the right performance of it.

4. *Christian Housholders should promote true Religion in their* Families; *therefore they should Pray with them.* They should promote the true Religion in their Families. They should *Command them to keep the way of the Lord*, Gen. 18. 19. They should bring up their *Children in the nurture and admonition of the Lord*, Eph. 6. 4. They should do all they can, that all in their Families may be truly Religious: Now Family Prayer is very proper, in order to promote true Piety. Oh! Christian Housholder, thou shouldst Pray with thy Family, and by thy Example shouldst teach thy Family,

mily, with what holy fear and reverence, with what brokenness of heart in confessing of sin, with what earnestness & fervency, they should pray to God for Pardon, Grace, Glory, for all benefits, outward or inward which they need Family Prayer is one methed very proper to spread and propagate true Religion; and those who neglect this Duty, seem little or nothing concerned for the Spiritual Good of their Families, or for the maintaining of God's Cause in the Wo ld.

5 *The neglect of Family Prayer, exposeth to God's Displeasure.* Jer 10. 25 *Pour out thy fury upon the Heathen that know thee not, and upon the Families that call not on thy Name.* On this Text, Mr. *Reyner* says,

'Observe how the Prophet couples *Heathen* 'and the *Families that do not Pray*, together, 'as being alike. Mr *Perkins* saith, the Fami-'lies in which God is not worshipped, are no 'better than Companies of Atheists; for this 'is one property of an Atheist *not to call upon* '*God*, Psal 14 4.

Indeed, though that fore-mentioned Text, *Jer.* 10 25. seems more immediately to refer to Heathen Nations; yet in proportion it may well extend to *Particular Families.* Surely, those who would avoid the Out-pourings of Divine Fury on their Families, should pray with their Families. If thou neglectest Family Prayer, thou seemest to lay thy Family open, naked, exposed to Divine Vengeance.

Bruit Creatures, *Hens* and *Birds* will place themselves so, as to keep off the Storms of Heaven from their young ones; but while thou neglectest Family Prayer, thou dost not use all proper means to keep off God's fury from thy Family. But possibly thou wilt say, God's fury does not overtake thee nor thine, though thou neglectest Family Prayer; thou hast as much health and prosperity, as those that Pray in their Families; therefore thou designest to continue Prayerless. 'Tis easy to reply, thou dost but verify what *Solomon* says, Eccles 8 11. *Because sentence against an evil work is not executed speedily, therefore the hearts of the sons of men are fully set in them to do evil.* God does not presently blast and destroy thee, no, he gives thee time and space to repent and reform; but if thou continuest to despise the riches of his goodness & forbearance, thou mayst expect that in his time (which is hastening) he'll pour out his vengeance on thee. Sometimes the Wicked have great Prosperity in this World, but notwithstanding that, if Repentance and Reformation prevent not, they must perish in Hell for ever. Though many more things might be added by way of proof, yet what has been said, plainly shows, that Family Prayer is a Duty, and ought to be attended and practised by Christians. But according to the method propos'd, we proceed.

2. *To answer some Objections too apt to be made against this Duty.* Object. 1

Object 1. *I was never brought up in a Praying Family. therefore I may be allow'd to Live as I was Educated, and to follow the Example set before me.*

Ans. III. Examples should never be followed, let them be set by whom they will. Exod. 23. 2 *Thou shalt not follow a multitude to do evil.* If those in whose Family thou hast been brought up, had been *Drunkards, Thieves,* profane Swearers, or the like; would this excuse thee in acting like them? No indeed, neither will their neglect of Family Prayer excuse thee, if thou dost follow their wicked example. *The wages of Sin is Death,* Rom. 6 23. If thou wouldst not be Damn'd in Hell, for fashion, custom, or company sake; then don't Sin for fashion, custom, or company sake: Don't follow others in sin, if thou wouldst not follow them to misery.

Obj 2. *I am ashamed to pray before others, therefore I neglect to pray with my Family.*

Answ. Tis indeed a shame to make such an Objection. We should be ashamed of Sin, and of our selves for Sin, but should not be asham'd of Duty. The Apostle was *not asham'd of the Gospel of Christ,* Rom 1 16 Neither should we be asham'd of it, or of any Duty it requires If *God is not ashamed to be called our God,* Heb 11. 16. (as he is not, if we sincerely serve him) then surely we should not be ashamed, in and with our Families, to own, acknowledge, and pray to him as such.

To pray in our Families, is no ſhame; to neglect it, is a ſhameful grievous crime. Nay further. let us conſider what our Saviour ſays, Mark 8 38. *Whoſoever therefore ſhall be aſhamed of me and of my words, in this adulterous and ſinful generation, of him alſo ſhall the Son of man be aſhamed, when he cometh in the Glory of his Father, with his Holy Angels* One would think, if thou hadſt any tolerable ſenſe of Spiritual Things, this Scripture would drive thy ſinful fear of ſhame from thee To be *aſham'd* of Chriſt and his ways before men, ſeems interpreted to be a *denying* of Chriſt before men; and ſuch *Chriſt will deny* in the Day of Judgment, *Mat.* 10. 33. If thou art aſham'd to own God and Chriſt, by keeping his Commands before men, before a few men yea, before a few perſons in thine own Family; then Chriſt will be aſham'd of thee before all the world; all men and Angels in the Day of Judgment. He'l then act, as if he was aſham'd of thee, he'l not own thee for his; but rather ſay, 'Thou wouldſt not own 'me in the day of thy life, now I wont own 'thee in the day of thy trial; I know thee 'not, thou art none of mine: thou didſt diſ-'approve of me, and my ways before a few 'men on earth; I now declare that I diſap-'prove of thee and thy ways, even before 'all men and Angels: depart from me thou 'worker of Iniquity, *Luk* 13 27 Oh! Conſider this, ye that forget God, ye that are a-ſham'd sham'd of Christ, of his ways, of your own duties; lest he tear you in pieces, and there be none to deliver you; lest he load you with shame, pain and misery in Hell, among the Prayerless Devils for ever.

Obj 3 *I have not the gift of Prayer, such a variety of words, and plenty of expressions as many have, therefore I don't pray in my Family.*

Answ. 1. *There's no need of Rhetorical Strains, or florid Expressions in Prayer.* Thou dost not need them, nor does God require them. There's no strain of Humane Rhetorick in those words, which God himself puts into our mouths Hos 14 2. *Take away all Iniquity, and receive us graciously.* God likes no one's prayer the better, for the sake of those florid expressions which some mens fancies are much taken with. Neither is a *great length* in Family Prayer necessary; nay, tis seldom convenient, lest it make the Duty wearisome; Our Lord condemns the *Heathen*, for thinking they should be heard for their *much speaking*, Mat. 6 7.

2 *A few plain Petitions from a broken heart, will be very pleasing to God.* Sincere, spiritual, penitential Groans, cloathed with the plainest expressions, will be pleasing to God; while the greatest variety of words, or finest oratorical expressions, coming from a vain hearted Hypocrite, will be loathsome to him. *The Sacrifices of God, are a broken spirit; a broken & contrite heart, O God, thou wilt not despise*, Psal.

51. 17 The *Publicans* Prayer, Luk 18 13. *God be merciful to me a Sinner*, was very acceptable unto God. If thou dost call thy Family together, and with brokenness of heart makest sincere confession of Sin, and dost pray for needful blessings, and give thanks for benefits receiv'd (though with the plainest expressions that can be) God will accept thee thro' Christ. This would be ten thousand times more pleasing to God, than thy neglecting of Prayer, meerly because thou hast not those gifts which thou dost think some others have. If we would but seriously study our own *wants*, and God's *Promises*, this would doubtless supply us with matter and words for Prayer. If we did but seriously consider, that by reason of sin, we and our Families deserve *Sickness*, *Pain*, *Poverty*, *Death*, *Hell*, even all manner of misery; and did also consider, that *God is nigh to all that call on him in truth*, Psal 145 18 *That he will regard the prayer of the destitue, and not despise their prayer*, Psal. 102 17 Would not this supply us with matter and words for Prayer? Yea, doubtless it would If thou wast in some outward danger and distress, doubtless thou couldst find words to ask for help and relief; and why not then, to ask for Spiritual Blessings, which are most needed? If thou wast to pay a *fine* of *five*, *ten*, or *twenty pounds*, for every omission of morning or evening Prayer in thy Family, would not such a penalty make thee

thee careful, not to omit this Duty; Doubtless such a penalty, would make thee find words and matter for Prayer; and shall not the honour of God, the Spiritual Welfare of thee and thy Family, make thee do as much? *Daniel* was once cast in the *Lions Den*, for *Praying to God*, Dan *ch.* 6 But if all such were to be cast to the *Lions*, who neglect Family Prayer, would not this danger make thee Pray in thy Family? doubtless it would. And what, wouldst thou fear the *rage of Lions*, more than the *outpourings of God's fury*? Is a *Lions Den* so terrible, as the pit of Hell? Oh! make no more vain excuses, that thou hast not the gift of Prayer; that thou wantest words and expressions for such a duty. Indeed, thou hadst better at least for a while, to use some Godly *Form of Prayer*, expressing it with sincerity of heart, than to neglect that Duty. The *using* a Form of Prayer, is not in it self unlawful, though the *imposing* one seems groundless. If thou wast duly affected, with a sense of thine and thy Families wants, and of God's gracious Promises, couldst thou not call thy Family together, and with them address thy self to God after some such manner as this?

'O Lord our God, thou art infinitely great 'and glorious; thou art Holy, but we are sinful: We are filthy and guilty as we proceed 'from Fallen *Adam*; our personal transgressions also are many and great, we therefore 'deserve

' deserve thy Wrath, and Curse on our Bo-
' dies and Souls, in time and throughout E-
' ternity. We are of our selves unworthy of
' any favour, unable for any duty; but thou
' hast graciously declar'd, that through Jesus
' Christ there's forgiveness with thee, that
' thou mayst be feared; and thou hast bid us
' in every thing, by prayer and supplication
' with thanksgiving, to make known our re-
' quests unto thee; we therefore humbly pray,
' that for Christ's sake thou wouldst pardon all
' our Sins, sanctifie our Souls, strengthen us
' against all our spiritual enemies, supply all
' our outward wants; help us to serve thee
' faithfully, and constantly, and let us be ever
' under thy merciful protection. We offer
' to thee also our humble and hearty praises,
' for all mercies outward and inward, hither-
' to bestow'd upon us; Lord, let thy mercies
' ingage us to love thee; make us faithful in
' Serving of thee, till thou shalt take us to
' Endless Glory in Heaven, through Jesus Christ,
' to whom with God the Father, and God
' the Holy Spirit, be given the Kingdom,
' the Power and Glory, for ever, *Amen.*

Mightest thou not after some such manner as this, pour out thy Petitions to God? Surely if thou wast rightly concern'd for the Spiritual Good of thy self and Family, thou wouldst not want matter and words for Family Prayer.

Obj 4. *I am so hurried and taken up with much*

much business that I have no time to Pray with my Family.

Answ. 1. *Tis a shame thou shouldst make this Objection.* Hast thou time to Eat, Drink, Sleep, to follow thy Outward Affairs; and canst thou spare no time to Pray in? Canst thou find time to receive God's mercies, and none to pray for them, or to give thanks for them? Possibly thou dost spend as much or more time than what's needful for Family Prayer, at the Tavern, in idleness, in needless chatting or diversion. And what, canst thou find time thus to throw away, and none to pray with thy Family in? If thou dost not Pray with thy Family, tis not really because thou hast no time for it, but rather because thou hast no heart for it. If thou art so hurried with business, as not to find time for Family Prayer; thou seemest to be a wicked Worldling, and to have thy heart overcharg'd with the cares of this life, and to be hastening to Endless Misery for thy practical Atheism. If thou canst not find time to serve God, do not think that he'l find time to Save thee.

2. *Thy honest lawful business will not suffer, for thy taking time for Family Prayer.* Thou shouldest *Pray* as well as Work for thy daily Bread. *In all thy ways acknowledge him* (that is God) *and he shall direct thy paths*, Prov. 3 6. Tis God alone can prosper thee in thy lawful Business; *Diligence* without *God's Blessing* cannot make any rich, *Prov.* 10 4. 22. Wouldst thou

thou prosper in thy Lawful Occasions? Then *pray* for it *In every thing make known thy request by prayer*, Phil. 4 6 Don't enter on thy daily business, without asking God's smiles & blessing. He can do more for thee in an hour or a minute, than all thy own cunning and labour can, in an whole day or much longer time. Wilt thou not spend a short time for Family Worship, but hurry hastily into thy business? Alas, God can by a thousand unthought of Accidents, clog and frustrate thy indeavours, for many hours & days together. Tis of the Lord, that men labour in the fire, and weary themselves for very vanity, *Hab* 6 2 13. Or if thou art *Prayerless* and yet *prosperous*; tis fit to consider, whether thou art not one of those fools whom prosperity destroyeth.

Mr. *Reyner* says,

'Mark what I say, Cursed is that Gain, 'Pleasure or Honour, that is gotten with neg- 'lect of Duties to God in Families.

Mr. *Flavel* says,

'Take it for a clear truth, that which is not '*prefaced* with *Prayer*, will be followed with 'trouble.

The *Turks* will *pray* (as tis storied of them) *five times a day, let their business be never so urgent*. Writers say, that the *Brachmans* among the *Indians*, and the *Magies* among the *Persians*, never began any thing without praying unto God. The Lessons of *Pythagoras* and *Plato*,

Plato, began and ended with *Prayer*. Oh. how will ſuch *Heathen* riſe up in Judgment againſt thoſe *Chriſtians*, who neglect *Family-prayer*, pretending *they have not time for it?* Oh Chriſtian, conſider, Mat 6 33. *Seek firſt the Kingdom of God and his righteouſneſs, and all theſe things ſhall be added.* Therefore don't ſay, you have no time. Do you think this Objection will excuſe you, in the Day of Judgment? Surely it wont, therefore you ſhould not allow it now.

Having thus anſwered theſe Objections, we are now:

3 *To add ſomething by way of Uſe.* What we have heard may ſhow us:

1. *That the neglect of Family prayer is a great ſin.* Many Heathen may riſe in Judgment, to condemn Chriſtians that neglect this Duty. Indeed thoſe who neglect this Duty of Family Prayer, ſeem to have but little regard to the Glory of God, to the good of their own Souls, or the Souls of their Families, or to the maintaining and propagating Religion in the World.

2. *Thoſe who have neglected this Duty, ſhould Repent and Reform.* They ſhould heartily & bitterly bewail, their ſo long neglect of this great Duty; and ſhould for the future ſet about it, and maintain the conſtant practice of it. Maintain Family Prayer, if you would eſcape Gods Judgments, and obtain his Bleſſings. Yea, make a daily practice

alſo,

alſo, of Reading ſome portion of the Scriptures, the Holy Word of God in your Families. So *Ship-maſters* alſo, ſhould call their Company together (being as it were their Family) & pray with them; they ſin greatly if they neglect it.

3 *Thoſe are blame worthy, who though they pray with their Families, yet they do it but ſeldom.* It may be ſome will Pray in their Families, but tis only on *Saturday Evenings* or on *Lords-days*; they wont ſpare time for this Duty at other Seaſons; but alas, they ſin grievouſly. Their Families need God's mercies *every day*, therefore they ſhould *daily pray* for them. Give us *this day* our *daily bread*, Mat. 6. 11. They *daily receive* mercies, & therefore ſhould *daily give thanks* for them. It may be others will Pray with their Families, but not more than *once* a day; it may be they pray only in the *Evening*, they wont ſpare ſo much time from Worldly Buſineſs as to pray to God in the *Morning*: Such are wicked Worldlings indeed. The Jews were wont to ſacrifice to God, *every morning and evening*, Numb 28 3 4. So Chriſtians ſhould offer the *Sacrifice of Family Prayer and Praiſe, every morning and every evening* How reaſonable and becoming is it, in the morning to bleſs God for the mercies of the night paſt, and to ask his needful favours for the enſuing day? And ſo in the evening, to bleſs God for the mercies of the day paſt, and to ask his protection and favour

to

to them in the ensuing night? When the Apostle says to *Masters of Families*, Col. 4 2 *Continue* in Prayer; it's probable he alludes to the *continual* Burnt-offering, that was offered *every morning*, and *every evening*. The same Apostle says, 2 *Tim*. 1 3. I thank God, whom I serve *from my Fore fathers* with pure Conscience, that without ceasing I have remembrance of thee in my prayers *night and day*. In this place, *night and day* seem to signifie *evening and morning*; so often he us'd to pray, and that according to the practice of his *Forefathers*, even of the *godly Jews in former Generations*. Psal 92 1, 2. *It is a good thing to give thanks to the Lord*,---to shew forth thy loving kindness *in the morning*, and thy faithfulness *every night*. Family Prayer should not be omitted, neither morning nor evening; if therefore the *Master* of the Family be necessarily absent, then the *Mistress* or some other person, should supply his place, as to this Duty of Family Worship.

4. *Family* Prayer *should be perform'd in due season*. We should indeavour that *all the Family be together* to join in God's Holy Worship. And therefore ordinarily (if it may be) Family Prayer should be attended, *before* any go abroad to their Day Labour; and before their minds begin to be hurried with Worldly Business, that so with the more sedateness of Spirit they may Worship God. In the Evening also Prayer should be attended, before

persons are overtaken with sleep and drowziness. How unfit are persons to serve the Living God, when through sleepiness they scarce know what they say themselves, or what is said by others? Therefore Young Persons, Children and Servants, should not be suffered to be abroad from the Family late at night; much less should Heads of Families (unless necessity require it) be out late and unseasonably, lest Family Prayer be thereby neglected, or very sluggishly performed.

5. *When Parents put out their Children to Service, they should take care to put them into Praying Families.* If you should put your Children into Prayerless Families, they'l have ill examples set before them; and will be in danger, of being greatly hurt thereby as to their Spiritual Concerns. Take heed therefore, that you dont thus expose or indanger your Children. I shall now add no more on this first General Head proposed, but only say, let us mind what has been said about Family Prayer, and practice agreeably thereto; resolving like him, Josh. 24 15 *As for me and my House we will serve the Lord.* We may therefore proceed to speak.

II. *About the Duties of Husbands and Wives.* Concerning the Duties of this Relation, we may assert a few things; and then draw some inferences therefrom. Concerning *Husband* and *Wife*, we may therefore assert.

1 Th

I. 'Tis their duty to cohabit or dwell together with one another. By God's own Ordinance, Husband and Wife are brought into the nearest Union and Relation to each other; God's Word calls them *one flesh*, Gen. 2 24 *A man shall leave his Father and his Mother, and shall cleave to his Wife; and they shall be one flesh.* Mat 19 5. *They twain shall be one flesh.* Being thus nearly *United*, surely they should *dwell together.* The Apostle says to men concerning their *Wives.* 1 Pet 3 7 *Likewise ye Husbands dwell with them.* The Greek word signifies, to *dwell in an house together*, or keep house together. If one house can't hold them, surely they're not affected to each other as they should be Indeed mens necessary Occasions often call them abroad, and sometimes (Seamen especially) to be absent for many weeks or months together; and when necessity requires such an absence of Husbands from their Wives, there ought to be a willing compliance with the call of Providence. But they should not separate nor live apart, out of disgust, dislike, or out of choice; but should *dwell together* as constantly, as their necessary affairs will permit. The Scripture says, *Let not the Wife depart from her Husband, and let not the Husband put away his Wife,* 1 Cor. 7. 10 11. They should leave their Fathers and Mothers (rather than fail) to live with one another. Psal 45 10 *Hearken O Daughter and consider, and incline thine ear: forget also thine own people, and thy fathers house.* *Rebekah* left her *Fathers House*, to go and dwell with *Isaac*, whom she had consented to have for her *Husband*, Gen. *ch* 24. *Rachel* and *Leah* left their Native Country and Fathers house, to go and dwell with their *Husband*, where God's Providence call'd him to be, *Gen.* 31. *ch.* The Duties of Husband and Wife one to another, oblige them to dwell together as much as may be: *To avoid fornication, let every man have his own wife; and let every woman have her own husband. Let the Husband render unto the wife due benevolence, and likewise also the wife to the husband. The wife hath not power of her own body, but the husband; and likewise also the husband hath not power of his own Body, but the wife: Defraud not one the other;...that Satan tempt you not for your incontinency,* 1 Cor. 7. 2...5. See also *Prov* 5. 15...20 Thus tis plain from Scripture, that Husband and Wife ought to dwell together; if therefore they quarrel, and so live separate from each other, then they sin very greatly, they act quite contrary to God's plain commands. If any have thus done, they ought heartily to repent of it, and fly to the Blood of Jesus for pardon.

2 *They should have a very great and tender love and affection to one another.* This is plainly commanded by God Eph 5 25. *Husbands love your wives, even as Christ also loved the Church.* That is, with a great, steady, constant,

constant, operative love. So *v.* 28 *so ought men to love their wives as their own selves, he that loveth his wife, loveth himself.* Col 3. 19 *Husbands love your wives, and be not bitter against them.* So *Wives* are required to *love their Husbands*, Tit 2.4. This duty of love is mutual; it should be perform'd by each, to each of them. They should endeavour to have their affections really, cordially and closely knit, to each other. If therefore the *Husband* is *bitter against his wife*, beating or striking of her (as some vile wretches do) or in any unkind carriage, ill language, hard words, morose, pevish, surly behaviour; nay, if he is not kind, loving, tender in his words and carriage to her; he then shames his profession of Christianity, he breaks the Divine Law, he dishonours God and himself too, by this ill behaviour. The same is true of the *Wife* too. If she strikes her Husband (as some shameless, impudent wretches will) if she's unkind in her carriage, give ill language, is sullen, pouty, so cross that she'l scarce eat or speak sometimes; nay if she neglects to manifest real love and kindness, in her words or carriage either; she's then a shame to her profession of Christianity, she dishonours and provokes the glorious God, tramples his Authority under her feet; she not only affronts her Husband, but also God her Maker, Lawgiver and Judge, by this her wicked behaviour. The indisputable Authority, the plain Command of the Great God, requires Husbands and Wives, to have and manifest very great affection, love and kindness to one another. They should (out of Conscience to God) study and strive to render each others life, easy, quiet and comfortable; to please, gratifie and oblige one another, as far as lawfully they can. When therefore they contend, quarrel, disagree, then they do the Devils work, he's pleas'd at it, glad of it. But such contention provokes God, it dishonours him; it's a *vile example* before Inferiours in the Family; it tends to prevent *Family Prayer.* The Apostle urgeth to a kind carriage between Husband and Wife, for this reason among others, *that their prayers be not hindred,* 1 Pet 3 7. Contention between these Relatives, tends to obstruct almost all *Duties* and *Comforts* too; tis a very extensive mischief, and draws innumerable sins and sorrows after it. Kind or unkind carriage between Husband and Wife, often renders this Relation the *most comfortable or most miserable* of any in the World. The *Heathen* at their *Marriage Festivals,* were wont to take the *Gall* out of the Beast to be sacrificed; intimating that there should be no *bitterness in that Relation.* They should be so mutually kind and loving, as to delight in each others company: if the contrary prevails, many mischiefs ensue. Though they should *love* one another as has been said, yet let this caution be minded, that they dont

love

love inordinately,becauſe death will ſoon part them. *It remaineth, that they that have Wives be as though they had none,* 1 Cor 7 29.

3. *They ſhould be chaſt, and faithful to one another.* The Seventh Commandment requires this, *Exod* 20 14. *Thou ſhalt not commit Adultery.* .So the Apoſtle tells us, the man muſt have *his own wife,* and the Woman *her own Husband,* 1 Cor 7 2. They muſt have nothing to do with any but their *own,* Prov. 5. 18,--- 20. *Rejoyce with the wife of thy youth,---let her Breaſts ſatisfie thee at all times, and be thou raviſh'd always with her love. And why wilt thou my Son, be raviſh'd with a ſtrange woman, and imbrace the boſome of a ſtranger?* 1 Theſ 4 3, 4. *This is the will of God, even your Sanctification, that ye ſhould abſtain from fornication: that every one of you, ſhould know how to poſſeſs his veſſel in ſanctification and honour,* As for Chriſtians, their Bodies as well as Souls belong to Chriſt, and that by ſpecial dedication *Rom* 12 1. T'is therefore a moſt vile aggravated wickedneſs in thoſe that call themſelves Chriſtians (tis bad in any, but worſe in them) to commit *fornication* or *adultery.* 1 Cor 6 15 *Know ye not that your bodies are the members of Chriſt? ſhall I then take the members of Chriſt, and make them the members of an harlot? God forbid.* There's a ſolemn Covenant between *Husband & Wife,* God is witneſs of it, and obſerves when any treacherouſly break it, *Mal* 2. 14. And he himſelf will avenge ſuch wickedneſs (if ſpeedy, hearty,

hearty repentance and reformation prevent not) though possibly tis committed so secretly, that men cannot punish it. Heb 13 4 *Marriage is honourable in all, and the bed undefiled, but Whoremongers and Adulterers God will Judge.* Tis the Undefiled Bed that is honourable; but God will Judge those that defile the Marriage Bed, that break the Marriage Covenant. *Adulterers* are to be *kept out of Heaven*, 1 Cor 6 9, 10 and *turned into the lake that burns with fire and brimstone*, Rev 21.8. Their *burning lusts*, are preparing them for a *burning Hell.* Let these things be seriously consider'd, to prevent all manner of Uncleanness, Fornication, Adultery. The Husband and Wife.

4. *Should be helpful to each other*, Gen. 2 28. The Lord said, it is not good that the man should be alone, I will make him *an help meet for him.* The Wife should be a meet help to her Husband; he also should do what he can, to help forward her good and comfort. They should do one another all the good they can.

1. *As to Outward Things.* If the one is sick, pained, troubled, distressed; the other should manifest care, tenderness, pity, compassion, & afford all possible relief and succour. Kind *Elkanah*, spake with tenderness and compassion to his Wife under her sorrows and troubles. 1 Sam. 1. 8. *Why weepest thou? why eatest thou not? And why is thy heart grieved? Am not I better to thee than ten Sons?* Husband & Wife should bear one anothers burthens, sympathize

thize with each other in trouble; affording to each other all the comfort they can. They should likewise unite their prudent counsels and endeavours, comfortably to maintain themselves, and the Family under their joint care. *He that provides not for his own, especially them of his own house; he hath denied the faith, and is worse than an Infidel,* 1 Tim, 5 8 *Jacob* took care for to provide for his own house, *Gen.* 30 30. Tis said of the Husband with respect to his Wife. *Exod.* 21. 10. *Her food, her raiment, and her duty of Marriage; shall be not diminish.* The Husband should indeavour, that his Wife may have Food and Raiment suitable for her. He should contrive prudently, and work diligently, that his Family, and his Wife particularly, may we well provided for. The Wife also in her place should do what she can, that they may have a comfortable support. The Apostle requires, *that wives be faithful in all things,* 1 Tim. 3 11. *keepers at home,* Tit. 2 5. and *that they guide the house* (manage matters well within-doors) *give none occasion to the adversary to speak reproachfully:* he condemns those that are Idle, wandring from house to house, and not idle only, but tatlers also, and busie bodies, speaking things which they ought not, 1 *Tim.* 5 13, 14. When Women go idling and tatling abroad, neglecting their houshold affairs; the Apostle says, they give occasion to the adversary to speak reproachfully

fully. They expose the profession of Christianity to reproach, by their idleness, as well as by their being tatlers and busie bodies, therefore diligence in business is part of the Wives duty, as well as the Husbands. *Prov.* 14. 1 *Every wise woman buildeth her house; but the foolish plucketh it down with her hands.* Tis said of the Vertuous Woman, *The heart of her Husband doth safely trust in her, so that he shall have no need of spoil; she will do him good and not evil, all the days of her life. She seeketh wool and flax, and worketh willingly with her hands; she riseth early while it is yet night, and giveth meat to her houshold, and a portion to her maidens; she considereth a field and buyeth it, and with the fruit of her hands she planteth a Vineyard, she layeth her hands to the spindle, and her hands hold the distaff,* Prov. 31. 11, 12, &c. These things that have been mention'd show, that Sloth & Idleness either in Husband or Wife, are sinful and shameful; therefore they should avoid the same, and diligently endeavour to do all the good they can to each other (as well as to their whole Family) even as to Outward Things. They should be helpful to each other.

2 *As to Spiritual Things.* They can't show greater love or kindness, than by prudently, earnestly, diligently indeavouring each others spiritual everlasting welfare. Therefore if one of them seems to have little or no regard to Religion; the other should by serious counsels,

ſels, and a godly example, indeavour to win him or her over to the ſaving knowledge and practice of the truth. *What knoweſt thou O Wife, whether thou ſhalt ſave thy Husband? Or what knoweſt thou O Man, whether thou ſhalt ſave thy Wife,* 1 Cor 7 16. *Likewiſe ye wives be in ſubjection to your own Husbands, that if any obey not the word; they may alſo without the word,* be *won* by *the conver ſation of the* wives, 1 Pet. 3. 1. By Husbands that ob y not the word, it's likely are here meant *Heathen, Infidels,* thoſe who did not own and profeſs the true Chriſtian R ligion; and the Wives of ſuch being Converted to Chriſtianity, were to ſtrive by a pious, godly behaviour, to win their Husbands to the true R ligion alſo. Surely then, if Husbands that call themſelves Chriſtians, are vain, wicked, ungodly; their pious Wives (if ſuch they have) ſhould by a meek wining Converſation, inde vour their ſpiritual & eternal Good. Husbands alſo that are p ous, ſhould indeavour the like, as to the ſpiritual everlaſting Welfare of their Wives. Art thou willing O man that the Wife of thy boſome ſhould periſh in Hell for ever? Art thou willing O Woman, that thy Husband ſhould periſh in Hell for ever? If not, then by prudent counſels, cautions, exhortations, and a winning, obliging heavenly carriage, indeavour to further each other in thoſe ways of Holineſs, which lead to Eternal Glory. Indeavour to live, *as heirs together of the Grace*

of

of life, 1 Pet. 3. 7. You should join your hearts, heads, hands, your counsels and indeavours together; to promote the outward, but especially the spiritual welfare of one another. and of the whole Family under your care. You should diligently indeavour to be mutual Helps and Blessings. Husband and Wife,

5 *Should be patient one towards another.* If Husband and Wife are both truly pious, yet neither of them is perfectly holy. It may be through Satans Temptations, and their own Corruptions, such words and actions may sometimes happen, as may be displeasing and offensive to each other: now in such Cases, a patient forgiving, forbearing spirit, is very needful. Tis the duty of Christians in general, with all lowliness, meekness and long-suffering, to forbear one another in love. *Let* bitterness *and wrath, and anger, and clamour, and* evil *speaking* be *put away from you, with all malice*: *and* be *ye kind one to another, tender-hearted*, forgiving *one another*, even *as God for Christ's sake hath* forgiven *you*, Eph. 4. 31, 32. *Col* 3. 12, 13. Much more then is it the duty of Husband and Wife, to be of a patient, forbearing, forgiving spirit to one another; for God has made them *one flesh*. You therefore that are Husbands & Wives, dont aggravate each others faults; dont aggravate every error or mistake, every wrong or hasty word, every wry step, as though it were a wilful designed

intol

intollerable crime; for this would ſoon break all to pieces: but rather put the beſt conſtructions on things they'l bear, and bear with and forgive one anothers failings: dont let every indiſcreet word and action, make a flame, breach or broil between you. If you have any regard to the Glory of God, to the Honour of our dear Lord Jeſus, then carefully avoid ſtrife and contention; live and love as God commands you: You are *one fleſh* by his Law, live as becomes ſuch. If a man's head, hand, foot is uneaſy or pained, he is not for beating it, or cutting it off, but uſeth means for it's eaſe and recovery. So if ſome uncomfortable things happen between you, dont let them ſet you on ſcolding, quarrelling, fighting; don't let them make you croſs, ſullen, humourſome, to get pouting alone, not to ſpeak or be ſpoken to; don't let them make you live ſeparately, nor lodge ſeparately neither: for if it once comes to this, Satan has got a great advantage againſt you, and tis to be fear'd he'l get a greater. Impreſs an awful ſenſe of God's Authority, and of his Eye, on your Conſciences; and dont dare to live quarrelling or contending. If therefore any ſtrife happens between you at any time (which indeed never ſhould) let the matter be finiſh'd and made up in love as ſoon as poſſible. Oh be of a patient, forbearing, forgiving ſpirit to all perſons, but eſpecially to one another. Husband & Wife,

6 *Should honour one another.* Tho' Husband and Wife are *one flesh*, yet *the Head of the woman is the man*, 1 Cor 11. 3 The Husband being the Head, the chief respect and honour is to be put on him. Eph 5 33 *Let the Wife see she reverence her Husband.* God here requires, that the Wife should reverence and honour her Husband. *Sarah* honour'd her Husband, and call'd him *Lord*, Gen. 18 12. The Apostle mentions this *in her praise*, and for the *imitation of others*, saying, 1 Pet 3 6. *Whose daughters ye are as long as ye do well.* Both in *words* and *actions*, Wives should honour and reverence their Husbands. The Vertuous *Shunamite* shewed respect in *speaking* to her Husband, 2 *King* 4 22. Send me, *I pray thee* one of the Young men, &c She did not speak in an imperious, commanding, domineering way; but in a courteous, obliging, respectful manner *In her tongue was the law of kindness*, Prov 31 26 The very *Heathen* did conclude and establish it as a Law, (and a just one too) *that all the Wives should give their Husbands honour, both to great and small*; and their despising or contemning their Husbands, was justly reckon'd a great evil, *Esth.* 1. 17.--20 And as Wives should honour and reverence their Husbands; so Husbands should put respect upon their Wives too. *Giving honour to the Wife as to the weaker vessel*, 1 Pet. 3 7. Though the *Wife* is the *weaker vessel*, yet *honour* is to be put upon her in her Infe-

feriour

riour Station. 'Tis said of the V rtuous Woman. *Prov* 31 28 *Her Children rise up and call her blessed; her Husband also, and he praiseth her.* 'Tis plain indeed, that Husband and Wife should put respect and honour on each other; though the Husband is ever to be esteem'd the Superiour, the Head, and to be reverenc'd and obey'd as such. Though they should by no means allow or approve of what is sinful in one another; yet they should not needlesly expose each others failings, indiscreet words or actions, but rather cover them with a mantle of love: they should be tender of each others credit and reputation. It's bad, when there's strife and discord between Husband and Wife; but very bad indeed, if this strife comes to be bl z d and nois'd among the Neighbourhood. That which reflects shame and dishonour on one in this Relation, commonly does more or less on both of them, for both are one. They should not despise, but respect and honour each other.

7 *The Husband's Government ought to be gentle and easy, and the Wifes Obedience ready and chearful.* The Husband is call'd the *Head of the Woman*, 1 Cor. 11. 3. It belongs to the *Head*, to rule and govern The very *Heathen* establish'd it as a *Law* (and a j st one too) *that every man should bear ru e in his own house*, Esth 1 22. Yea, the Word of God plainly requires that a man should *rule well his own*

 house,

house, 1 Tim. 3. 4 Wives are part of the House and Family, and ought to be unde the Husbands Government: they should O *bey their own Husbands, Tit.* 2 5. Though the Husband is to rule his Family and his Wife yet his Government of his Wife should no be with rigour, haughtiness, harshness severi ty; but with the greatest love, gentleness kindness, tenderness that may be. Thoug he governs her, he must not treat her as a Servant, but as his *own flesh*: he must love her as himself, *Eph* 5 33. He should make his government of her, as easie and gentle a possible; and strive more to be lov'd than fear'd; though neither is to be excluded On the other hand, Wives ought readily and chearfully to obey their Husbands Col 3 18 *Wives submit your selves to your own Husbands.. be in subjection to them,* 1 Pet 3. 1. Thoug the Husband and Wife are *one flesh,* yet th Husband is the *Head,* and the Wife is requi red to obey him, and that by God's p ain Command: *She may not usurp authority over the man,* 1 Tim 2. 12, but must *obey him in all things,* Eph 5 24. that is, in all lawful things Having thus shewed from the Word of God, how Husbands and Wives should carry it to one another, we may proceed t draw a few Inferences from these things, *viz*

1. *These Husbands are much to blame,* w *dont carry it lovingly and kindly to their Wive* O man, if thy Wife be not so young, beau

fu

ful, healthy, well-temper'd and qualify'd as thou couldst wish; if she brought not so much Estate to thee, or cannot do so much for thee, as some other women brought to or have done for their Husbands; nay, if she does not carry it so well to thee as she should: yet she is thy Wife, and *the Great God Commands thee to love her*, not to be bitter, but kind to her. What can be more plain and express than that? Eph 5 33 *Let every one of you in particular, so love his Wife even as himself.* How vile then are those, who dont love their Wives, can't abide to be with them, loath their Company, hate them call them vile names, curse them, reproach, defame and belie them; beat and strike them: will fume, vex, fret, fling and threaten as though they would rend all to pieces before them; so that their Wives can scarce ever have a quiet hour with them? Such Husbands carry it more like bruits, than what becomes men: they deserve sharp reproof and severe punishment too. O man, it may be thou art idle, lazy, dost take no care to provide Necessaries for thy Wife and Family; but instead of this, dost take to Tipling, Gaming, Ill Company, dost tarry out very late and unseasonably, and then comest home drunk, vomiting, or raging like a furious beast; if tis so, thou art exceeding vile and wicked. But possibly thou dost not run this great length of wickedness, yet if thou dost purposely grieve and vex thy Wife, twit her of any deformities, or unwilful Infirmities, twit her of her mean Parentage, mean or vicious Relations, dost twit her of her Poverty when she came to thee, of her mean abilities of body or mind; or if thou at any time strivest purposely to displease, fret or provoke her, then thou art base, vile and wicked in so doing: For herein thou dost not only abuse a Woman, a Creature, part of thy self; but thou dost affront and provoke the Great God, in trampling his Holy Laws under thy feet. He's a witness of thy base carriage to thy Wife, and will reckon with thee for it, *Mal.* 2. 14 Nay, if thou dost not diligently indeavour, to provide suitably for thy Wife, if thou dost not manifest tender love to, and care for her, striving to render her life quiet and comfortable; even thy omission in these things, is highly criminal and provoking to God, tis contrary to his plain Commands.

2 *Those Wives are much to blame, who dont carry it lovingly and obediently to their own Husbands.* O Woman, if thy Husband be not so young beautiful, healthy, so well temper'd and qualified as thou couldst wish; if he has not such abilities, riches, honours, as some others have; if he does not carry it so well as he should; yet he's thy Husband, and the Great God Commands thee to love, honour and obey him. Yea, though possibly

possibly thou hast greater abilities of mind than he has, wast of some high birth, and he of a more mean Extract, or didst bring more Estate at Marriage than he did; yet since he is thy Husband, God has made him thy Head, and set him above thee, and made it thy duty to love and reverence him. If therefore thou dost hate or despise him, revile or dishonour him, or disobey his lawful Commands; if thou dost usurp authority over him, much more if thou dost lift up thy hand to strike him (as some shameless wretches will) then thou dost shamefully transgress the plain Commands of the Great God: thou dost trample his Authority under thy feet. Nay, if thou dost twit thy Husband of his mean birth, abilities, Estate, Relations (if they are mean) if thou dost by being cross, pouty, sullen, humoursome, put the Family out of order, and so grieve and displease thy Husband; if thou dost so vex, fret, contend, that he can scarce have any quiet in the house, or comfort in thy Company, then thou sinnest very greatly indeed. If thou art proud and haughty, and aspirest to spend more, or live higher, than thy Husbands Incomes will allow of; and so causest contention in the Family, this is a very great crime in thee: For the man to labour and toil hard, to venture Estate and Person too, to get money; and for the Woman foolishly and prodigally to spend what s thus gotten, is very blame
worthy

worthy indeed, Thou shouldst be a meet help to thy Husband, but if thou dost carry thy self like a spend-thrift, like a fret & scold; thou art rather a cross and. tryal to him. *It is better to dwell in the corner of the house top, than with a brawling woman in a wide house: ... It is better to dwell in a wilderness, than with a contentious and angry woman*, Prov. 21 9 19 *The contentions of a wife are a continual dropping*, Prov 19 13 *A continual dropping in a very rainy day, and a contentious woman are alike*, Prov. 27 15. O Woman, great is thy wickedness, if thou dost so carry thy self as. to deserve such a Character as this: If thou dost carry it basely and wickedly to thy Husband, thou dost not only abuse man, but thou dost affront God himself, in trampling on his Holy Commands. It may be thy discontent, fretting, scolding, quarrelling, makes thy Husband weary of the house, he can't abide to be at home, he has no quiet nor peace there; this makes him idle away his time, get into bad company, stay out late at nights, take to Tipling, Gaming, and other ill practices; which tend to bring shame, poverty, misery on him, on thy self and Family. Has not thy ill undutiful carriage, been a great occasion of thy Husband's naughtiness? If it has, though this won't excuse him, yet it greatly condemns thee

3. *Husbands and Wives should humble themselves before God, for their short comings in Duty*

to each other. Though they owe duty to one another, yet tis God's Law that declares and prescribes what that duty is; when therefore they fail in duty, they not only wrong each other, but they provoke God by breaking his Law; and therefore should be humble before him for it. And who is there that does not fall short of Duty, even in every Relation and Capacity which he sustains? If those of us who are (or have been) in a Married State, do examine our own hearts, affections, actions, doubtless we shall find we have fallen far short of those Duties, which this Relation requires. Have we done what we could, to render each others life quiet and comfortable; especially to further each other in the ways of true Holiness? Have we liv'd as *heirs together of the grace of Life*? So far as we have fallen short of these things, we have sinned, and should be humbled for it; and should pray that God would help us to carry it aright for the future, in every Relation we sustain.

4. *Those sin greatly, who strive to make or maintain any breach or contention between Husband and Wife.* Since the Union between these Relatives is so near, and so much mutual love and kindness incumbent on them; it must needs be a great crime for any to make or maintain discord between them. Those who would set Husband or Wife at variance, or keep them so; are doing the Devils

their lives long. They ſhould eſpecially *be much in Prayer to God*, that he would lead, guide, and bleſs them in this weighty affair. *Solomon* ſays, Prov. 19 14, *A prudent Wife is from the Lord.* Tis ſuch a Wife he ſpeaks of, Prov. 18 22, *Whoſo findeth a Wife, findeth a good thing, and obtaineth favour of the Lord.* There is indeed much of the favour and mercy of God, in providing a ſuitable Husband or Wife; and therefore God ſhould be earneſtly ſought to in ſuch an affair. Thoſe who have deſirable, comfortable Husbands or Wives, ſhould be very thankful to God for ſo favouring them. And thoſe who have wicked, vicious Yoke-fellows, and ſore afflictions thereby, ſhould be humble before God under their trials; and ſhould earneſtly pray that they may have grace to do their duty, notwithſtanding the temptations they meet with, and that they may be ſpiritual gainers by all that is uneaſy to them.

6. *Parents ſhould act wiſely and prudently, in the Matching of their Children.* God ſaid to his people, concerning the *Heathen*, Deut 7. 3. *Neither ſhalt thou make Marriages with them; thy Daughter thou ſhalt not give unto his Son, nor his Daughter ſhalt thou take to thy Son.* This plainly ſhows, that Parents ſhould be concerned in the Marrying of their Children: they ſhould endeavour that they may Marry with ſuch, as may be moſt proper for them, moſt like to be Bleſſings to them. *Abraham*

was

was follicitous, that his Son might not Marry one of the *Canaanites*, but a Person of more Vertue & Religion, Gen 24 *ch.* *Naomi* sought a good Husband for *Ruth* her Daughter in-law; that she might have *rest*, & it might be *well with her*, *Ruth.* 3 1. And as Parents should indeavour, that their Children may be well Married; so they should strive, that their Children may be Blessings to their Relatives in the Married State. Therefore they should bring them up vertuously and piously; and also give them the best directions they can in the weighty affair of seeking a Yoke fellow. I have met with this saying, of a pious Gentlewoman who had many daughters, *viz.*

'The care of most people is, how to get 'good Husbands for their Daughters; but my 'care is, to fit my Daughters to be good 'Wives, and then let God provide for them. Mr. *Philip Henry* (an Eminent Minister of Christ) would say to his Children (as to their choice of a Yoke-fellow in Marriage) *keep within the bounds of Profession*) (he would have them seriously regard Religion) & *look at suitableness* in Age, Quality, Education, Temper, *&c.* Having given these directions, he would say to them, *Please God and please your selves, and you shall never displease me.* And as Parents should be concern'd, to see their Children married to suitable persons; so Children should have great regard, to the consent and advice of Parents in this great affair.

Isaac took her for a *Wife*, whom his *Father* had provided, Gen. 24. ch. *Jacob* obey'd Father and Mother, in seeking a Wife, *Gen.* 28. 1, 2, 5. Tho' *Jacob* loved *Rachel*, yet he would not take her without *her Father's consent*, Gen. 29. 18. When *Sampson* lov'd a Woman, he would not marry her without the *consent of his Father and Mother*, Judg. 14 2. Children should indeed have great regard to their Parents advice, in this weighty affair of Marriage; and Parents should be as careful, that they dont abuse their power in this matter, in imposing on their Children contrary to their Inclinations, or in needlesly and unreasonably crossing of them. But having thus mentioned the Duties of *Husbands & Wives*, we proceed to say something,

III. *About the Duties of Parents and Children.* And here twill be proper to speak, (1) *About the Duties of Parents to their Children* (2.) *About the Duties of Children to their Parents.*

As to the first of these, I shall indeavour, (1) *To show what are the Duties of Parents to their Children.* (2) *To give some directions about the doing of them.* (3) *To mention some motives, to quicken and stir up to the doing these Duties.* I shall therefore indeavour,

1. *To shew what are the Duties of Parents to their Children.* And here I might say,

1. *They should love their Children, and carefully provide for their Outward Supply and Comfort,* whil

while unable to provide for themselves. The very Light and Law of Nature requires, that Parents should *love their Children*; Scripture demands it also. *Mothers* should *love their Children*, Tit.2 4 So should *Fathers* too. *Like as a Father pitieth his Children*, Psal. 103 13. *Abraham* was not only a strong Believer, but a tender Father too, he *loved* his Son *Isaac*, Gen 22 2. Parents should nourish in themselves, a very tender love and affection to their Children; and should manifest it by suitably providing for their outward comfort. Here I might say, as soon as the Mother perceives her self with Child, she should be careful, not to do any thing, injurious to her self or to the Child God has formed in her A *Conscientious* regard to the Sixth Commandment, (which is, *Thou shalt not kill*) should make her thus careful. If any purposely indeavour to destroy the fruit of their Womb (whether they actually do it or not) they re guilty of Murder in God's account. Further, before the Child is born, provision should be made for its comfort when born. Some observe concerning our Saviour's Mother (the Virgin *Mary*) that tho' she was very poor and low, and far from home when deliver'd of her Son; yet she had provided *Swadling Cloths to wrap her Son in*, Luk.2,4- 7. Mothers also if *able*, should *Suckle* their Children. Tis said, Lam.4 3. *Even the Sea monsters draw out the breast, they give suck to their young ones.*

 Surely

Surely, Women ſhould not be worſe than ſuch Monſters. Among many ſorts of bruit Animals, wiſe Providence has provided this method for the *nouriſhing their young ones*, even the *giving of them ſuck.* Infinite Wiſe Providence has provided the ſame method, for the *nouriſhing of young Children. Sarah* (though a great & rich woman, *Wife* to a *Mighty Prince* Gen. 23.6) *gave ſuck to her Son Iſaac*, Gen 21 7,8 *Hannah* did ſo, to her Son *Samuel*, 1 Sam. 1 23. Thoſe Mothers therefore, who have *Milk* and are ſo *healthy*, as to be *able* to *ſuckle* their Children; and yet thro' *Sloth* or *Niceneſs* neglect to ſuckle them, ſeem very criminal and blame-worthy. They ſeem to diſlike & reject that method of nouriſhing their Children which God's wiſe, bountiful Providence has provided as moſt ſuitable. Having given theſe hints about *Mothers*, I may ſay of *Parents* (comprehending both *Father* and *Mother*) they ſhould provide for the Outward Supply and Comfort of their Children. They ſhould *nouriſh and bring them up*, Iſa. 1. 2. They ſhould endeavour that their Children may have *Food* ſuitable for quality and quantity; ſuitable *Raiment* and *Lodging*. In caſe of *Sickneſs Lameneſs*, or other Diſtreſs on Children; Parents ſhould do all they can for their help, health or relief. *He that provides not for his own, eſpecially thoſe of his own houſe, hath denied the faith, and is worſe than an Infidel*, 1 Tim. 5. 8. Our Saviour takes it for granted, that Parents

rents will *give good things to their Children*; Luk. 11.13. God wont suffer his Children, *to want any good thing*, Psal. 84 11. Christians should be *Followers* (that is, *Imitators*) *of God* as far as they can, *Eph.* 5.1. Therefore if they can help it, they should not suffer their Children to want any thing that's really good, comfortable and suitable for them, even as to their Outward man. Yet by way of Caution I might say, Let wisdom and prudence sway more than fond indulgent fancy, in *Feeding* and *Cloathing* your Children. Too much niceness and delicateness in these things is not good; it tends not to make them healthy in their bodies, nor serviceable and useful in their Generations, but rather the contrary. Let not your Children (especially while young, and unable to provide for themselves) want any thing needful for their outward comfort.

2. *Parents should bring up their Children, to be diligent in some lawful Business.* It's true, time for lawful Recreation now and then, is not altogether to be denied them. Even when Jerusalem is a City of Truth, an *Holy Mountain*; it shall be full of *Boys and Girls playing in the streets*, Zech. 8.3 5 Yet for such to do little or nothing else but play in the streets, especially when almost able to earn their living, is a great sin and shame. They should by no means be brought up in Idleness, or meerly to learn Fashions, Ceremoni-

ous Compliments, and to dress after the newest mode, &c. Such folly as this ruins many Children. *Boys and Girls* should be brought up diligently in such business as they are capable of, and as is proper for them. *Adam* (our First Parent) brought up his two Sons (we first read of) one to *keep Sheep*, the other to *till the Ground*, *Gen.* 4 2 Nay when *Adam* himself was Innocent, God allow'd him not to be *Idle*, but set him to *dress* and *keep the Garden*, Gen. 2. 15. *Jacobs* Sons *kept Sheep*, their *Occupation* was about Cattle *from their Youth*, *Gen* 37 12. & 46. 33, 34 They were not brought up *Idly when young*, but were imploy'd in business. *David* was at his *Calling*, his business, *keeping Sheep*, when God sent to *Anoint him King*. 1 Sam 16 1 3, 11. *Elisha* was *Plowing in the Field*, when God call'd him to be a Prophet, 1 King. 19 19 - 21. *Gideon was threshing*, when call'd him to *deliver Israel*, Judg 6 11, 12. *Amos* was taken from his *Particular Calling*, from *following the Flock* & *gathering Sycamore fruit*, to be a Prophet? *Amos* 7. 14, 15. *Peter, Andrew, James aud John*, were call'd by Christ from following their *Particular Occupation*, to be *Apostles*, Mat. 4 18.---22 These Godly men, these eminent Saints, were not lazy, idle drones, they had their *Particular Callings*, Trades, were Imploy'd in lawful business; and were so diligent therein, that they would not leave the same to set a Preaching or Prophesying, till they had a plain clear

clear call from God so to do. And from these Instances we might learn by the way, that for men to be diligent in their own proper Calling, Trade or Business, acting suitably in their own Sphære; is the way to meet with God's Blessing, and to be advanc'd by God, to be great Blessings to others. *Prov.* 22. 29 *Seest thou a man diligent in his business, he shall stand before Kings, he shall not stand before mean men.*

Again, Christians are bid to be, *not Slothful in business?* Rom. 12 11. The *Slothful*, is called *Wicked*, Mat. 25 26 If any *would not work, neither should they eat,* 2 Thes. 3 10. *Drowsiness shall cloath a man with rags,* Prov. 23. 21. Christians are required, *to work with their hands the thing that is good, Eph* 4 28. To *do their own business, and work with their own hands,* 1 Thes. 4. 11. And if Christians should be thus diligent in business, surely they should be brought up to it *while Young. Train up a Child, in the way wherein he should go,* Prov 22 6 This may well refer, to things of a *Civil and Secular*, as well as to those of a religious nature. Would you have your Sons or Daughters, live as lazy, idle drones, as useless, nay, pernicious persons when grown up? If not, then don't bring them up in Idleness. Bring them up to business, some lawful Imployment or other; though you have never so much Estate to give them. It may be they may lose their Estates, (the World is full of such Instances)

Instances) and how miserable will they be then, if unacquainted with, and uncapable of business? Nay, if they're brought up idly, though they should retain their Estates; it's not likely they should be Serviceable, but very likely they will be hurtful, to the Publick. Therefore let them be brought up to diligence. And when you put them out (if you do put them out) to some Trade or Calling; to be sure see that tis a lawful Calling; and such as suits (as much as may be) the Abilities and Inclinations of your Children. Put them into *Religious Families*, the Heads whereof will say with him, *Josh* 24 15. *As for me and my House, we will serve the Lord.* Charge them also to be *dutiful and faithful*, to those under whose care they must be. Some are more fit for a *Studious* Life, to serve the Publick with their Heads, Pens, Tongues; and some for a more *Mechannick* Imployment. If you're careful to bring them up diligently in proper business, you take a good method for their comfortable subsistance in this World, (and for their being serviceable in their Generation) you do better for them, then if you should bring them up idly, and yet leave them great Estates. Under this Head I might further add, Parents should (if able) give some portion of Worldly Goods to their Children. *Abraham* did so by his Children, *Gen* 24 36 & 25 5, 6. The Apostle says, 2 *Cor.* 12, 14 *Parents ought to lay up for their Children.*

When

When Children first Set up for themselves, their Parents if able, should give them some Stock, something to begin with, that they may live comfortably, and not be discouraged. When the *Hebrews* set an *Hebrew* Servant at Liberty, they were to give him something to begin with. *When thou sendest him out free from thee, thou shalt not let him go away empty; Thou shalt furnish him liberally out of thy Flock, and out of thy Floor, and out of thy Wine-press: of that wherewith the Lord thy God hath blessed thee, thou shalt give unto him*, Deut. 15. 13, 14 And if Servants were to be furnish'd at Setting up for themselves, much more should *Children* have Incouragements of this nature. By a prudent *Will*, Parents should also provide, that after their Decease, their Estates may be suitably divided among their Children. I don't mean, that they must needs give all they have to their Children; if their Estates are plentiful, they would do well to give something to pious and publick Uses. *David* had many Children, yet having a great Estate, he left very considerable for the *Building of the Temple, and furtherance of God's Worship*, 1 Chron 29. 3 5.

3. *Parents should teach their Children good Manners.* A civil, respectful, courteous behaviour, is comely and commendable; & Children should be taught such a Carriage. *Abraham* shew'd his good breeding, when he stood up, and bowed himself before the people of the

the Land. *Gen.* 23 7 *Jacob's* Wives and young Children (little Boys) were so well taught, as to bow themselves when they came before *Esau*, *Gen* 33 6,7. *Elihu* let those that were Elder than himself, speak before he did, *Job* 32 4 6 The Apostle *Paul* show'd Good Manners, when he said to the Governour, *Most Noble Festus*, Acts 26 25 *Fastus* was an ill man, yet being a Governour, being Cloathed with Authority, the Apostle gave that respectful honourable Title to him. These things plainly show, that those who wont put suitable marks of civil respect and honour on others, especially on Superiours, or those in Authority; dont imitate the commendable Examples of the Godly recorded in Scripture: their rudeness, and affected unmannerliness, is a plain breach of God's Law. For God's Law says, Lev. 19 32 *Thou shalt rise up before the hoary head, and honour the face of the Old man* This is good Manners, the contrary is mention'd as a Curse. Isa 3 5 *The Child shall behave himself proudly against the Ancient, and the base against the Honourable.* Solomon says, *Stand not in the place of Great men, for better is it that it should be said unto thee, come up hither, then that thou shouldest be put lower*, Prov 25 6, 7. Our Saviour adviseth that if we're bidden to a Feast, we should not sit down in the highest room, but rather in the lowest; that others (and not we our selves) may advance us, *Luk* 14 8 -- 10 These things

things plainly intimate, that we ſhould be modeſt, reſpectful and mannerly in our Carriage: Children therefore ſhould be ſo Inſtructed; for they ſhould be, not riotous or unruly, *Tit.* 1. 5. Whatſoever things are of good report, if there be any vertue, any praiſe, think on theſe things, *Phil* 4 8. Therefore Parents, teach your Children to be *Mannerly* and *Reſpectful* to your ſelves, to Civil Rulers, to Eccleſiaſtical Rulers, to all Superiors in Age or Office. Yea, teach them to be civil and reſpectful to all perſons whatſoever, according to their Rank and Station: Dont ſuffer them to be *rude, ſaucy, provoking* in their words or actions unto any; for this would be a ſhame to your Children, and to you too. Nay, ſuffer not your Children to be *Imperious or Domineering*, ſo much as to the *meaneſt Servants* in your Houſes, for ſuch a baſe indulgence, may imbolden them to an ill carriage to others alſo. But though you ſhould teach your Children to be Mannerly, I dont mean, that they ſhould ſpend all or great part of their time, in nicely, curiouſly, critically obſerving thoſe various, changeable, ceremonious punctilio's of carriage, which ſome very fooliſhly affect: this would be time very ſinfully ſpent. A Child may avoid ſuch fooleries and fopperies, and yet be very civil, courteous, mannerly in his words and geſtures.

4. *Parents ſhould Inſtruct their Children, in the only true Religion taught in the Scriptures.* You ſhould

ſhould bring them up, *in the Nurture and Admonition of the Lord*, Eph. 6 4 Acquaint them as plainly and throughly as you can, with the great eſſential fundamental points of Religion. Indeavour that they may underſtand & believe, that there is but One Living & true God, ſubſiſting in Three Glorious Perſons, the Father, the Son, and the Holy Ghoſt; that the Bible is the Holy Word of God, the only Rule of Faith and Practice; that by *Adam*'s Fall, he and all his Poſterity became ſinful and miſerable; that Chriſt Jeſus, God's Man Mediator, is the only Saviour of Sinners; that none can be Saved without true Repentance of Sin, and Faith in Chriſt. Inſtruct them as particularly and diſtinctly as you can, about the Perſon, Natures, Offices of Chriſt, about the nature and end of his Death, Reſurrection, Interceſſion; about the true nature and neceſſity of Faith & Repentance. Teach them to keep Holy the Sabbath Day; the Power of Godlineſs can never be maintain'd without this. Teach them the nature and uſe of the *Sacraments*, *Baptiſm* and the *Lord's Supper*; and the *Covenant-Obligations* they lie under, to love and ſerve Jeſus Chriſt ſincerely. The Jews were bid to teach their Children, the meaning of the *Paſſover*, that Divine Inſtituted Ordinance, *Exod.* 12 26,27 This plainly implies, that you ſhould regularly ſeek *Baptiſm* for your Children; you ſin greatly if you neglect it. *Moſes* had like-

to

to have lost his life, for not getting the Initiating or first Seal of God's Covenant, applied to his Son, *Exod.* 4 24, 25. You should teach your Children the great Truths and Duties of *Religion*, of *Piety*, and press and urge them to act agreably thereto. You should also teach them *Second Table duties*, namely to be sober, chast, temperate, not by word or deed to wrong any one in his person, name or estate; but to be Just to all, and bountiful to the Indigent as they have opportunity and ability. In a word, you should teach your Children to live soberly, righteously and godlily, in this present World; and to adorn the doctrine of God our Saviour in all things. Something more may possibly be said, about instructing Children in Piety, and bringing them up *Religiously*; under the *directions* & *motives* by and by to be mention'd

We therefore proceed to say,

5. *Parents should govern their Children well, Restrain, Reprove, Correct them, as there is occasion.* A Christian housholder, should *rule well his own House*, 1 Tim. 3. 4. Children should not be left to themselves, to a loose end, to do as they please; but should be *under Tutors and Governours*, not being fit to govern themselves, *Gal.* 4. 1, 2. Children being bid to obey their Parents in all things, *Col.* 3. 20. Plainly implies, that Parents should give suitable precepts to, and maintain a wise government over their Children; so carry it, as their Children may both *fear* and *love* them. You should *restrain*

your Children from Sin as much as possible, th neglect of this in *Eli*, brought sore Judgment on his house, 1 *Sam* 3 13. You should *Re-prove* them for their faults; yea if need be *Cor-rect* them too. *Prov.* 13. 24 *He that spareth th rod, hateth his Son; but he that loveth him, chasten-eth him betimes.* *Solomon* reckon'd it a sign o *love*, to *chasten* a child (when he deserves it and a sign of *hatred* to *neglect* it. *Prov.* 23 13 14. *Withhold not correction from the Child; fo if thou beatest him with the rod, he shall not die* (It may by Gods blessing be instrumental, to *prevent his eternal Death*, as the next words seem to intimate) *thou shalt beat him with the rod, and shalt save his Soul from hell. Foolishness is bound up in the heart of a Child, but the rod of correction shall drive it far from him*, Prov 22. 15 *Chasten thy Son while there is hope, and let not thy Son spare for his crying*, Prov. 19 18. *The rod and reproof give wisdom: but a child left to himself bringeth his Mother to shame*, *Prov* 29. 15. These divine precepts plainly show, that as there is occasion you should *chasten* and *correct* your Children; you dishonour God and hurt them if you neglect it. Yet on the other hand, a Father should *pitty his Children*, *Psal.* 103. 13 *You should not provoke your Children to wrath, lest they be discouraged*, Eph. 6. 4 Col. 3 21. You should by no means carry it ill to them, you should not frown, be harsh, morose, faultin and blaming of them, when they dont deserv it, but do behave themselves well. If you fau

an

and blame your Children, show your selves displeas'd and discontent, when they do their best to please you ; this is the way to provoke them to wrath and anger, and to discourage them ; therefore you should carefully avoid such ill carriage to them. Nor should you ever correct them upon *uncertainties*, without sufficient evidence of their fault. Neither should you correct them in a *Rage* or *Passion* ; but should deliberately indeavour to *convince* them of their fault, their sin ; and that tis out of love to God's honour and their good (if they're capable of considering such things) that you correct them. Again, you should never be *cruel* nor *barbarous* in your corrections ; and if *milder* ones will reform them, more severe ones should never be us'd. Under this head of *Government* I might further say, you should restrain your Children *from bad company*, as far as possibly you can. *Prov.* 13 20. *A companion of fools shall be destroyed.* If you would not have your Sons and Daughters destroyed, then keep them from ill company as much as may be. Prov, 4 14 15 *Enter not into the path of the wicked : and go not in the way of evil men. Avoid it, pass not by it, turn from it and pass away.* Here are plain, strict, reiterated, *repeated* precepts ; to *avoid ill company* ; surely then there's *great danger* in keeping such company, therefore you should use utmost care, that your Children avoid it, lest it ruine them for ever. You should not suffer your Children, needlesly to frequent

Caverns, nor to be abroad *unseasonably on nights*. lest they're drawn into numberless hazards and mischiefs thereby: you can't be too careful in these matters.

6. *Parents should endeavour to see their Children well dispos'd of, well settled in the World.* They should seek to have them *well Married* if they can. In this matter (as well as others) Parents should seek to promote their Childrens welfare. *Abraham* sought a *good Wife* for his son *Isacc, Gen. 24 ch. Naomi* said to her *daughters in law*, Ruth. 1. 9. *The Lord grant that you may find rest, each of you in the house of her Husband.* And she afterwards said to *Ruth*, concerning the same matter, Ru h 3 1. *My daughter, shall I not seek rest for thee, that it may be well with thee*? But having already said something of this matter, in the close of my discourse about the duties of *Husband and Wife*; I shall add no more at present about it.

7. *Parents should pray for their Children.* They should earnestly desire the good of their Children, both in Body and Soul, in time and throughout Eternity; therefore it must needs be their duty to pray unto God (the fountain of all good and grace) that he would sanctifie and bless them: that he would make them holy and useful on earth (as well as grant them outward supplies) and make them happy in heaven for ever. *Job* did *pray* to God *for his Children*; yea he made a usual custom and *practise* of so doing, *Job*. 1. 15. *Abraham* pray'd

pray'd for his Son, saying to God, Gen. 17. 18 *O that Ishmael might live before thee.* Surely those Parents have little or no true love to their Children, who do not daily, constantly, heartily and earnesty pray to God for his blessing of them, especially with Spiritual and Heavenly blessings. Having given these general hints, about the *duties of Parents to their Children,* we may

II. *Give some* Directions *about the doing of them.* Yet the *Directions* (as well as following *Motives*) which I shall mention; shall be chiefly about *Religion,* and what concerns the *Souls* of their Children. I would therefore say to Parents, by way of *Direction,*

1. *See to it, that you instruct* Every one *of your Chi dren in the things of God.* The Apostle says, 1. *Thes.* 2. 11. 12. We charged *every one of you* as a *Father doth his Children,* that ye walk worthy of God. Parents should teach *every Child they have,* to know, love, obey God and Jesus Christ. O Parent, look on thy Children, on all thy Sons and Daughters (if thou hast sundry of them) consider their Bodies, consider their Souls; and think, is there any of them, thou couldst be willing should be a Slave to the Devil, an object of divine wrath, a firebrand in hell for ever: couldst thou be willing it should be thus, with any of thy Children? If not, then let not any one of them live uninstructed.

2 *Begin* **Betimes** *to teach your Children.* You have the opportunity, the advantage (and tis a great one) *early* to teach them; before they can learn of any one else. As soon therefore as they are capable of instruction, be sure let them have it. And take care in this one great point, that they be taught *to Read* as soon as ever they are capable, that they may be able to consult God's mind in his written Word. *Timothy* knew the Scriptures *from his Childhood*, 2 Tim 3 15 Writers tell of a *Young Person* suffering Martyrdom for Christianity, who said, *He had sucked in the Doctrine of Christ with his Mothers Milk*; Indeavour that your Children may do so too. Indeavour to infuse good principles, great truths into them, as soon as ever they are able to receive them; and before they have opportunity to suck in errors from ill examples, ill companions, or false teachers. While you lay them in your bosomes, and dandle them on your knees, try by little and little to infuse good things, holy truths into them. Why should you not teach them such things, as soon as you can teach them any others. The longer you delay, the more backward they'll probably be; besides this, you know not how soon death may part them and you asunder. *Boast not thy self of to morrow, thou knowest not what a day may bring forth*, Prov 27 1.

3 *Take your Children with you to God's Publick Worship* Grown up Christians, should attend God's Publick worship, *not forsaking the assembling*

bling themselves together, Heb 10 25. Well, Children should be *train'd up in the way they should go*; even in that way which they should not depart from when *old*, *Prov.* 22 6 Therefore they should be *train'd up*, in the practice of *attending God's publick Worship*. Joel. 2. 16 -- *Assemble the Elders, gather the Children, and those that suck the breasts.* We find that the *law was read* in the hearing of *little ones*, as well as of *Men* and *Women*, Josh' 8. 34, 35 We find not only *Men & Women*, but also *Children* attended on a *religious account*, *Ezra* 10 1. *Moses* said to Israel, ye stand *this* day all of you before the Lord your God---- *your little ones*, your wives--- that thou shouldest enter into Covenant with the Lord thy God, *Deut.* 29. 10--12. Tis therefore a great sin and shame, that many Parents keep their Children so long as they do, from God's publick worship, you should bring your Children to God's publick worship, to his House, as soon as they can be kept so quiet there, as not to make a disturbance; that so they may be early inur'd to an holy practice, taught in religious truths, and have a reverential regard to divine things, begotten in their minds.- 'Twould be very proper also, when they come from hearing the *word Preached*, to ask them *what they remember* of it; that so they may be quicken'd to mind the great matters of Religion. Yea when you thus inquire of them, you may very properly take occasion to give them holy counsels, and inculcate and impress divine truths upon them.

4. *Teach*

4. *Teach your Children the Catechism.* *Catechismes* are design'd, as an easy short and useful way, to instruct persons (young ones especially) in the great truths and duties of Religion. Many *Catechismes* are useful for this end, but I know none better than that commonly us'd, *Scil.* The *Assemblies Cathechism.* I know not a better book (of humane composure) in the world, for a short and speedy instructing of youth, in the fundamentals of our holy Religion, with care and diligence it may be soon learnt; tis worthy to be learn'd by young ones, and remembred by the oldest of us all. When young persons learn it, tis pitty but that they should mind to *remember* it as long as they live. You should particularly teach your Children, the *Ten Commandments*, that divine rule of practice; and the *Lord's Prayer*, that divine direction for the offering our Petitions to God. T would also be very proper, to teach them that summary belief, commonly call'd the *Apostles Creed.* It might do very well also as they become able, to incourage them to get some *Psalms* or *Chapters*, or some special select portions of Scripture *by Heart*; this might be of great use to them as long as they live.

5. *Indeavour that your Children may rightly* **Understand**, *the great truths and duties of Religion.* Tho' you should inculcate divine things on them as soon as may be, yet when they are capable of more knowledge; you should indeavour that they may *understand the true meaning*, of

of those things which are taught them. Our Saviour when teaching said, hearken to me every one of you and *understand*——he *expounded* to his disciples, *Mark* 7. 14. & 4 34 *Philip* said to the *Eunuch*, Acts. 8 30 *Understandest* thou what thou readest ? so when you speak to your children about religious things, indeavour that they may understand them. Therefore God requires you, to teach them *diligently*, *Deut.* 6 6. Some observe the word signifies, to *whet it upon them*, when a man is *whetting a tool*, he takes *many Strokes* in doing it, diligently minds what he's about, that his tool may have a good edge. So you should use *diligence, care, industry* to teach your Children; you should make *a business of it*, yea and a great business too, and not do it carelesly as a thing by the by.

6 *Dont be over tedious, too long at once ; but be frequent in teaching your Children.* If you are over long and tedious in teaching and catechising of them, this may make them weary of, and loath the exercise ; therefore be more short but *very frequent*, in this work of instructing them. The Scripture intimates, that you should do something at it when you *lie down*, and when you *rise up*, when you *walk by the way*, and when you *set in the house* Deut 6 6 7. When you are *dressing* or *undressing* your Children morning and evening, you might very properly say something to them about religion, for the good of their Souls ; according as they are

are capable of receiving it: you would not *lose time*, but they might *gain advantage* by this. If the Text last mentioned dos not plainly require, that you should teach them *every morning and evening*; yet it undeniably requires *great frequentcy* in the work. You may very well take frequent transient occasions, to promote their pious knowledge and practice; but besides this, you should be sure to have your *stated and fixed times for their instruction*; and no Sabbath day should pass, without your doing something at it. You might do well also by some *small rewards* and Incouragements, to quicken them in learning the truths and duties of Religion; you might as well grant them such Incouragements in such a case, as in others.

7 *You should keep your Children as much as may be, from those who would poyson their Souls by erronious Doctrines.* We read of some *That creep into Houses, and lead captive Silly women... that subvert whole Houses, teaching things that they ought not*, 2 Tim. 3 6 · Tit. 1. 11. Therefore keep your Children as much as possible, from those who are known to have erronious tenets, such as tend to destroy Faith and Godliness. Keep them also as much as may be, from reading vain, foolish, erronious Books; lest thereby they drink in ill principles, or lest some ill Impressions are made on their affections. Indeed there are too many books in the world, which seem greatly fitted

and

and adapted to ſerve the Devils Intereſt; they deſerve *Burning* rather than *Reading*; let not young ones meddle with ſuch Books.

8 *Warn them particularly againſt thoſe Sins you ſee them moſt peculiarly prone to & in danger of.* If you ſee them peculiarly prone to *raſh anger, Revenge, Pride, Calling ill Names, Profane Swearing, Playing on the Sabbath-Day, Stealing* &c. You ſhould very particularly warn them againſt thoſe Sins. Where you ſee the greateſt danger, you ſhould uſe the greateſt care to oppoſe it, yea, warn them againſt thoſe evils, which many are apt to count *Small* ſins, or it may be *no* ſins at all. Poſſibly ſome will count, tis no fault for *Children* to quarrel and *fight*; but ſurely tis, and you ſhould warn them againſt it. Poſſibly ſome will think, tis ſcarce a ſin for *Children to rob Orchards and Gardens*, to get fruit for preſent eating; but ſurely tis, and if Children are indulg'd in it, it may lead them to greater tranſgreſſions. Neither is this contrary to the Indulgence, in *Deut.* 23 24. Where there was *Plenty* of what was common; and perſons have wanted refreſhment.

9. *Take occaſion from the diſpenſations of Providence, to give good Inſtruction to your Children.* How often have you proper opportunities for this? If you hear of great loſſes any meet with in their eſtates, how properly might you tell your Children, of the *uncertainty* of earthly Injoyments; & that they are not to be eagerly deſir'd, nor at any time truſted in? When you hear of the

the *Death* of others, especially *Sudden* Death; more especially the sudden Death of *Young Ones*, how suitably might you say to your Children, 'What would have become of you, if you had 'been thus suddenly snatch'd away? Would 'your Souls have gone to Heaven, or to Hell; 'which of them? Well, prepare speedily for 'Death, you dont know but that you may both '*Speedily and Suddenly* be turned into Eternity.

10, *Solemnly charge and Command your Children to Serve God; yea Seriously expostulate with them about it.* Deut. 32 46. *Command your Children, to observe to do all the words of this law.* You should *exhort* and *charge* them, to walk worthy of God, 1 *Thes.* 2. 11. 12 *David* did so charge his *Son*, 1 *Chron.* 28 9. *Know thou the God of thy Father, and serve him with a perfect heart and a willing mind* 1 Kings. 2 3. *Keep the Charge of the Lord thy God, to walk in his ways, to keep his Statutes, and his Commandments, and his Judgments, and his Testimonies, as it is written in the law of Moses*, &c. Imitate this holy man, Solemnly warn, charge, command your Children, to know, trust in, love and obey God and Jesus Christ; charge them to do this, as they will answer the contrary at the day of Judgment. Yea, Seriously *Expostulate* with your Children, about their duty and their Eternal Salvation. *Prov* 31, 2. *What my Son? And what the Son of my Womb? And what the Son of my vows?* Mothers and Fathers both might Expostulate with their Children about

their

their ſpiritual good, and ſay, 'What, will 'you not love, ſerve and obey God, the God 'that has made you, preſerv'd you, loaded 'you with benefits hitherto? Will you be ſo 'wicked, as to neglect and rebel againſt, this 'moſt gracious God? What, will you not 'ſeek firſt the Kingdom of God and his righ- 'teouſneſs? We have taught and charg'd 'you, to believe in Chriſt, to obey God; we 'long, cry and pray for your Converſion, 'your true Sanctification, that you may be 'Saved for ever; and ſhall all be in vain? 'Will you diſregard, the Commands of God, 'the commands of your Parents, and your 'own eternal welfare? We have taken great 'care of you, great pains with you, and will 'you ill requite us by going on in Sin, to the 'diſhonour of God, to our ſhame and grief 'will you bring our heads with Sorrow to the 'Grave? Will you make us grieve & mourn, 'that ever we had ſuch Children as you? 'Will you our dear Children, pieces of our 'ſelves (for whom our bowels, our hearts, 'our ſouls are concern'd; yea greatly and 'fervently concern'd) will you forget God, 'and neglect the bleſſed Jeſus, whom we dear- 'ly love, and to whom we have conſecrated 'you? Will you neglect Heaven, deſpiſe 'Grace and Glory; run your ſelves into hell, 'and become a prey to devouring Devils for 'ever; how can we bear the thoughts of this? 'Nay, will you not intirely give up your 'selves to Christ, and live wholly to him; 'that our Souls might rejoyce and be com-'forted by you?

To this purpose, you might pathetically expostulate with your Children, striving to make abiding Impressions, of the weightiest matters on their Souls Let them plainly see that your very Souls are fervently concern'd for their everlasting welfare.

11. *Follow your Children with wholsome Counsels, tho' they are grown up.* Tho' they are grown to be Men and Women, yea tho' they're Married, and live in Families of their own, and you see them but now and then; yet still you are their Parents, and twould be proper that you shou'd drop your holy counsels on them. Put them in mind of former Instructions, quicken them to Serve the God of their Fathers; do you all you can (as long as you and they live) to further them in an holy heavenly Life.

12. *Besure to set good Examples before your Children.* Prov. 20 7. *The just man walketh in his Integrity, his Children are blessed after him.* Walk in Integrity, in Uprightness, setting a blameless heavenly example before your Children; if you would have them blessed after you. Other methods of Instruction, probably will not do much good; if you dont teach them by a godly Example. Dont think your Children will mind the good Rules you give them, if you act contrary to those Rules your-selves

selves. If you bid them *Read*, *Pray in Secret*, *attend on God's Ordinances*; and yet neglect these things your selves: if you bid them avoid ill Language, and yet use it your selves; if you thus do, what reason have you to think, that your Counsels and Instructions will do them any good? And you that are Fathers and Mothers, see to it, that you do not quarrel nor contend with one another; and that you dont oppose or contradict one another, in commanding of your Children. If the Father should bid the Child do one thing, and the Mother require another thing at the same time; alas what an ill example would this be? This would tend to confusion indeed. If your Counsels are good, and your Examples evil; your Children will be more like to be hurt by the latter, than benefitted by the former. See to it therefore, that you dont in word or deed set an ill example before them; but that you may be very blameless and exemplary, and may be able to say, as, 1 Cor. 11. 1. *Be ye followers of me, even as I also am of Christ.* Having given these *Directions*, we may (as was propos'd)

3. *Mention some* Motives, *to quicken and stir up Parents to do their Duty to their Children: especially to do their utmost, that their Children may be truly and practically Religious.*

Here consider,

1. *God's plain Command requires you that are Parents, Religiously to Instruct and Educate your Children*

Children. Deut. 6 6, 7. These words which I command thee this day, shall be in thine heart; and *thou shalt teach them diligently to thy Children.* Here, Parents are plainly and strictly required, to teach God's Commandments to their Children. *Train up a Child in the way wherein he should go,* Prov. 22. 6. *Bring them up in the nurture and admonition of the Lord,* Eph. 6. 4. See also, *Psal.* 78. 5.—7. Parents, here are repeated divine Precepts, as express and plain as can be, for your teaching your Children in the Truths, Ways, Worship, Ordinances of God. If such plain commands of the Lord God Almighty, the Maker and Judge of all Men, will not move and quicken you to the religious Educating of your Children; then, what will do it? what can do it? Possibly you Read, Pray, keep Sabbaths, attend on Ordinances, *&c.* and why so? why do you these things? Possibly the reason you would give (which indeed is the best reason that can be) is, because God commands you to do so. Well, there's the same reason for your religious Educating of your Children, for *God Commands* this as plain as any thing in Scripture. How dare you then neglect it? 'Tis not a small light thing, a matter of indifferency, whether you bring up your Children Religiously or not; no, tis an indispensible duty. You are guilty of gross, plain, horrible disobedience to God, if you neglect it. Well then, if you have any Conscience, any sense

sense of spiritual things; let the express Authority, the plain repeated Precepts of the great God, move and quicken you to bring up your Children, in the knowledge, fear and service of God.

2. *Tis absolutely necessary for your Children to be truly Religious.* They're Children of wrath by Nature; they can't escape Hell, without true Faith and Repentance; such faith they cannot have, without some doctrinal knowledge of Christ. *How shall they believe in him, of whom they have not heard?* Rom. 10. 14. Therefore it's absolutely necessary that they be Instructed, in the Truths & Duties of the Christian Religion; they can't escape Hell nor obtain Heaven without it. Now it's your indispensible Duty, to indeavour the welfare of your Children, you're worse than Infidels if you neglect it, 1 *Tim.* 5. 8. Twould be barbarous, inhumane, worse than bruitish, if you should neglect the Bodies of your Children; and thro' sloth and carelesness suffer them to starve and die: how much greater then is your barbarity and wickedness, if you take no care to prevent the everlasting ruine of their Souls? For the Soul is more worth than a World. *What shall it profit a man if he gain the whole World, and lose his own Soul? or what shall a man give in exchange for his Soul?* Mark 8. 36, 37 And will you then have no regard, to the precious Souls of your Children? Again, you were instrumental

 of

of bringing your Children into a State of Sin and Misery; as they came from you Sinful Parents, they were *Shapen in Iniquity and Conceiv'd in Sin*, Psal 51. 5. And wont you do your best, to deliver them from Sin & Misery? Will you bring them into a miry slow, a Sea of Misery, & leave them perishing there, without using means to Save them? Where's your Religion? Where's your love to Christ, your tender regard to the honour of his Name; if you dont use utmost care, that your Children may know and serve him? When your Children are dangerously Sick, you'r commonly much concern'd for them, you'll send for Physitians, ask the skill, direction, help of any that are likely to be Serviceable; you do what you can for the recovery of their Health: and will you do all this for their Bodies, and not take as much pains for their Souls, which are a thousand times more worth? Your Children are Sick, their Souls are Sick of a dangerous disease, they re in danger of falling into an eternal Fever, into the eternal fire of divine Vengeance; Christ is the only Physitian that can heal and cure them, and wont you do your utmost that they may be cured by Him? We read of a Man that came to Christ kneeling down and saying, *Lord have Mercy on my Son, for he's lunatick and sore vexed, oft times he falleth into the fire, and oft into the water*, Mat 17 14 15 We read of a Woman, who cryed to our Lord Jesus saying,

Have

Have Mercy on me O Lord thou Son of David, my Daughter is grievously vexed with a Devil, Mat. 15 21, &c. And will not you be as much concern'd, for the precious Immortal Souls of your poor Children as these were for the Bodies of theirs? The Souls of your Children, are naturally dead in trespasses and in sins; they are sorely vex'd and wounded by their Spiritual enemies; they are slaves to Satan: their lusts often *meritoriously* throw them into the waters, the floods of divine fury, and into the fire of divine vengeance; and are you not concern'd, to have them deliver'd from this woful, sinful, miserable condition? Oh dead Affections, flinty Souls, rocky Hearts, if you can see the Souls of your poor Children, torn to pieces by Satan's malice and their own lusts; if you can see them *languishing, dying, perishing, sinking into eternal flames,* and yet not teach and instruct them, in the one only way of Salvation. Many will provide suitable food for their *Dogs, Horses,* and other *Beasts,* that they mayn't want what's proper for them; but you are worse to your poor Children, if you dont take utmost care to Save their Souls, than such are to their bruit beasts. Oh Parents, let the *Miserable State,* the *Great Necessity* of your poor *Children,* move your bowels towards them, and put you on doing your utmost to Save their Souls. Shall your Children perish thro' your neglect? Will you bring forth Children for the devourer, the

destroyer

destroyer of Souls? Shall the devouring Lion of Hell, prey upon your Sons and Daughters? The Children which you carried with care and pain, which you brought forth with pangs sorrow and trouble, which you fed with the Milk of your own breasts, which you oft imbrac'd in your tender Parental arms; shall these be crush'd in Satan's clutches, & plagu'd in the Jaws of his Malice for ever? Shall Hell it self be the more throng'd and crouded, for any of your Family? Oh! Indeavour to prevent it. God's *Authority* (which was the *first* Motive) and your Childrens great *Necessity* (which is the second Motive) should quicken you to do your utmost; to bring up your Children Religiously.

3. *Amazingly great will your guilt and danger be, if you neglect the Religious Education of your Children.* We have already proved, that God *requires* you to Educate your Children Religiously; well, the great God will not be mocked. If you trample on his Authority, you'l incur his displeasure. God theaten'd to bring on *Eli's* house such judgments, as should make both the Ears of them that heard them to *Tingle*; and what was this terrible threatening for? Why God says, 1 Sam. 3 13. *For the Iniquity which he knoweth, because his Sons made themselves vile, and he restrained them not.* He did not instruct, warn, charge restrain his Children as he should; therefore God brought such judgments. Nay consider,

th

Sixth Commandment says, *Thou shalt not Kill*; this not only *forbids* our Murdering any Person, but also requires that we should do what we can, to *prevent* his being killed. If a man did not restrain his Ox, known to be unruly, but suffer'd him to kill a man; the Owner of that Ox was then to *die as a Murderer*, Exod. 21. 29. He was to suffer as a *Murderer*, because he did not do what he might and ought to have done, to *prevent* his Neighbour's death. You may easily apply the matter to the present case; if you dont do what you can to Save the Souls of your Children, you are (in some sort) guilty of Murdering them. If your Children should starve to death, by your carelesly neglecting to give them necessary food, you would be plainly guilty of Murdering their Bodies. And are you not as plainly guilty of Murdering their precious Souls, if you carelesly & slothfully neglect, to give them those pious Instructions, Counsels, Warnings which they need? How dreadful then is your guilt and danger before God, if you neglect the Souls of your Children? When God made Inquisition for blood, he said to Cain, Gen 4 9. *Where is Able thy Brother?* So when God makes Inquisition for the blood of Souls, and says, Where are those Children I committed to thy care and charge, What's become of them; What Answer canst thou make, if thou dost neglect their pious Education? The charge God gives thee concerning thy Children, seems the same for substance, with that, 1 King. 20.

39. *Keep this man, if by any means he be missing, thy Life shall go for his Life.* If therefore you neglect to take care of the spiritual good of your Children, you will be highly guilty before God. I believe it will be a very black, heavy, damning charge against Multitudes of Parents in the Judgment day, *That they neglected the Pious Educating of their Children.* *Ministers* are made *Watch-men for Souls,* and must *give an account* of them, *Heb.* 13. 17. If the wicked go on and die in their Sins, because their Watch-men did not warn them to repent and reform; then their blood will be required at their Watch-man's hand, *Ezek.* 3. 18. As I am a Watch-man therefore I am oblig'd, for my own safety, and that I may be free from the blood of your Souls; to tell you, that the Pious Religious Education of your Children, is your duty, your great duty, & great is your guilt and danger if you neglect it. I have often put you in mind, of Piously Instructing and Educating your Children, tis a duty of vast Importance: And I do now again, solemnly charge and warn you in God's Name, (as you will answer it to Him in the Great Day) to bring up your Children for God. I would deliver my own Soul, I beseech you to deliver yours; therefore dont neglect the Souls of your Children, lest you bring dreadful guilt on your selves.

4 *Your Children belong to God, therefore you should bring them up for Him.* God is the Maker

ker, Preserver, the Sovereign Lord Proprietor of all Persons; He says, Ezek. 18 4 *All Souls are Mine.* Tis God has made your Children, you should therefore bring them up in their Maker's Service. Put them upon *Remembring their Creator in the days of their Youth,* Eccl. 12. 1. Say of your Children, as *Hannah* of *her Son.* 1 Sam. 1. 11. *I will give him unto the Lord, all the days of his Life.* But further, the most of your Children belong to God *by Covenant.* When God takes *Parents* into Covenant with Himself, he takes in their *Children* also with them; he did so by *Abraham,* Gen. 17. 7. And the *blessing of Abraham is come upon the Gentiles,* Gal. 3. 14. Those therefore that are born of Covenant Parents, are God's Covenant Children; He calls them *His. Thy Sons and thy Daughters, whom thou hast* born unto Me — *Their Sons whom they* bare to Me, Ezek. 16 20 & 23. 37. You Parents, you call God *Your God:* You profess Christ to be *your Prince and Saviour.* The most of you have been *Baptized,* and if any of you have not, tis your great sin and shame, that you dont sincerely and diligently seek after it. I suppose the most of your Children have been Baptized; the *Seal,* the Mark of Gods Covenant has been set upon them; they belong to Him by Covenant; they have been solemnly consecrated to his Service: and what, will you not bring them up for him, to whom you have thus solemnly consecrated them? Surely you

you ſhould do all you can, that thoſe who have been given up in Covenant to God, ſhould know, love, fear and ſerve him You ſhould indeavour, that every man ſhould have his right and due; much more that the Great God ſhould have his right & due, and that his Covenant ones may yield Covenant Obedience to him. When *Hagar* ran away *from her Miſtreſs*, an Angel of the Lord bid her return and *ſubmit to her Miſtreſs*, Gen. 16 9. When *Oneſimus* ran away from his Maſter, the Apoſtle *Paul* ſent him back *to his Maſter* again; as his Epiſtle to *Philemon* ſhows. Surely then you ſhould do your utmoſt, that God's Covenant Children & Servants, ſhould not run from nor quit his Service; if they do, you ſhould do what you can, to make them return to it again.

5. *The Examples of the Godly, ſhould quicken you to bring up your Children for God.* God ſaid concerning *Abraham.* Gen. 18. 19. *I know Abraham, that he will Command his Children and Houſehold after him; and they ſhall keep the way of the Lord.* The Perſon here commended is *Abraham*, famous for Faith and Obedience. He that commends him, is God, the Great God, the Alſeeing Jehovah, whoſe Judgment is always true, right and good. The thing he commends him for is, *His Commanding his Children and Houſehold*, that they might *Keep the way of the Lord.* Not only his *Children*, but his *Houſehold*, all his *Servants*, were charg'd to

Know

Know and *Serve God.* Remember therefore, that as you should bring up your *Children*, so you should your *Servants* too; in the Fear and Service of God. Let the Directions and Motives already mention'd, forward you in Religious Educating your *Servants*, as well as your *Children*. You are equally oblig'd by God's Law, to keep *Servants* as well as *Children*, from *Profaning God's Sabbath*, Exod. 20. 10. Therefore you should teach *Servants* the Laws of God, the Truths and Duties of Religion, charge them to obey God; how else can you prevent their doing amiss? The Apostle says. Gal.4. 1,2. *The heir as long as he is a Child, differeth nothing from a Servant — but is under Tutors and Governours.* This plainly shows that *Servants* as well as *Children*, should be under Tutors and Governours; they should be taught and charg'd, to know and serve God. I mention these things about *Servants*, that none may think that if they instruct their *Children* well, they are excus'd tho' they neglect their *Servants*: let none think so, for tis a great mistake. Again, consider *Joshua's* resolution (recorded for his honour and our imitation) Josh. 24. 15. *As for me and my house, we will Serve the Lord.* He resolv'd to instruct and charge his *House*, all his Children and Servants to Serve the Lord. *David* did *Instruct* his *Son Solomon*, who says. Prov. 4. 3 — 5 *I was my Fathers Son— he taught me also, and said unto me, Let thine heart retain my words: keep my Commandments*

mandments and live. Get wisdom, get under-standing: forget it not, neither decline from the words of my Mouth. *David* was a great King, had abundance of business lying on his hands; yet he did not neglect the teaching of his Son, he found time for that most necessary business. As for *Timothy*, he knew the Scriptures *from a Child*, 2. Tim. 3. 15. How could this be, if he had not been early taught and instructed? He was doubtless thus taught, by his Godly *Mother Eunice*, and *Grand mother Lois* (whose unfeigned faith the Apostle commends 2 *Tim* 1. 5) Thus we see, the Godly are recorded and commended in Scripture, for religiously Instructing and Educating their Children. Now these things being written afore-time, were *written for our learning*, Rom 15 4 There-fore *be ye followers of those, who thro' faith and patience inherit the Promises*, Heb. 6 12. As God *commends* Householders, for the Religious teaching and governing their Families, so he *blames* those that *neglect it*. *Eli* is charg'd with *despising* God, with honouring his Sons more than God. 1 *Sam*. 2. 29, 30. The reason is, *his Sons made themselves vile, and he restrained them not*, 1 Sam 3 13 If you dont imploy your Opportunities & Abilities your Authority and Power, to bring up your Children in the knowledge and fear of God God then reckons, that you *dishonour* and *despise* him, and that's bad and vile indeed.

Consider,

6 *The better you Instruct your Children at home, the more likely they'll be to profit by Publick Preaching.* Doubtless many good Sermons are almost lost on many Persons, and that for this reason, because they dont understand what's Preached. If the Minister useth such words as these, *Regeneration, Conversion, Effectual Calling,* the *Old* or *New* Covenant, *Assurance, Perseverance,* &c. Your Children ordinarily wont know what's meant hereby, unless they're instructed in their Catechism, and well taught at home. If a Minister useth the plainest words and expressions he can think of, yet he must necessarily use many; which Young Persons probably will not understand, if they're not well Instructed in Private. Dont think it enough therefore, that your Young Persons attend on God's Publick Worship (tho' that is their undeniable duty) but teach them well at home, Instruct them well there; that they may be the better able to understand and be benefitted by, what's Publickly Preached.

Consider,

7. *The Pious Educating of Youth, is the best way to continue and propagate the true Religion to future Generations.* We own (and that on good grounds) the Christian Religion, to be the best, the only true Religion in the World; surely then, we should do our best, that it may be continu'd and propagated among others after we are dead. *He appointed a Law in Israel, which he commanded our Fathers, that*

they should make them known to their Children. That the Generations to come might know them, even the Children which should be born, who should arise and declare them to their Children, &c. Psal. 78. 5 — 7 Thus God plainly requires, that we should indeavour the Propagating the true Religion, even among Children *not yet born*, that is, in all future Generations The Godly Israelites were concern'd and fearful, lest their Posterity, (not then born) should cease from, or fail of, Serving the Lord, *Josh.* 22 25. The Apostle *Peter*, speaking about the truths and duties of Religion, says, 2 Pet. 1. 15. *I will indeavour that you may be able* After my Decease, *to have these things always in Remembrance.* So you should teach and charge your Children, that they may know and serve God *after your Decease*, after you are dead and rotten in your Graves. Nay, dont neglect giving wholesome Instructions and Counsels to your Children, tho' they seem heedless and regardless of them now; for possibly God may bring these counsels to their Minds, and make them Instrumental of saving good to them, even after you are dead and rotten. Seed often continues hid, unseen under the clods a pretty while; and after that, springs up and brings forth fruit. Indeed the upholding of Family Instruction and Government, is one of the best methods can be taken, to Propagate the true Religion to after Generations. In a Christian State, when Persons are brought up

Igno

gnorantly and Irreligiously *while Young*, they often prove naught as long as they live : they often prove *Plagues* and *Pests* to the *Families*, *Churches, Towns, Countrys*, where they live. They commonly retain thro' their whole life time, the ill Opinions, Ways, Practices they were brought up in. *Can the Ethiopian change his skin ? or the Leopard his spots ? than may ye do good, that are accustomed to do evil*, Jer. 13.23. When Persons have been *accustomed* to do evil, tis no easy thing to break that custom. If you would not have your Children Ignorant, Profane, Irreligious when they leave your Houses, or after your Death, then dont suffer them to be so while under your Family care. Would you have your Children when grown up, to walk in the right way ? Then *Train them up* in it, *Prov* 22. 6. Catechise and counsel them well while Young, if you would have them Godly and Useful in their Generations. History tells us, that by *virtue of Catechising*, there was never a Kingdom but receiv'd alteration in their Heathenish Religion, within fourty years after Christ's Passion. *Julian* the *Apostate* (thought to be the *wisest Enemy* the Church ever had) when he went about to suppress Religion, did *not use Torments* (as many others had done) but (as tis storied of him) *put down Schools and all Catechising.* Indeed the Devil could not have prompted him to a more likely way, to root out the Christian Religion, than to hinder Youth from being

Instructed and Educated in it. Many talk much about *Reformation*, about maintaining and *Propagating* the true Religion; they prescribe means for it, such and such things must be done, *Magistrates* must do this, *Ministers* must do that, they lay much blame on others; but possibly they prescribe no means to, they think little or nothing is amiss in, themselves. But if we are serious and in earnest for Reformation, for Propagating Religion; then let every Housholder Reform his own Heart and Life, and religiously Instruct, Charge & Govern his own Family. This is the way, if we would have Religion revive and flourish. I make no doubt, but that the *Decay of Religion* of *Practical Godliness* among us, is not more owing to any one thing, than to the *neglect of Family Instruction and Government*. Without *Family care*, the labour of Magistrates and Ministers for Reformation and Propagating Religion, is likely to be in a great measure unsuccessful. It's much to be fear'd, Young Persons wont much mind what's said by Ministers in Publick, if they are not Instructed at home: nor will they much regard good Laws made by Civil Authority, if they are not well counsel'd and govern'd at home. One says,

'Give us the *best Magistrates*, let them Enact the *best Laws*, and back them with the *Strictest Execution*; yet Societies *will be naught*, while governours of Families neglect their duty in Religious Education. Well then,

bring

bring up your Young Ones for God. Our Fathers left a pleasant Land, pleasant Worldly accommodations, and came to this Place, (a Wilderness not sown) that they might injoy Gods Ordinances in their Purity, that they might teach and practise the true Religion without being molested; and might leave the same as the *best Portion to their Children*: and shall this Religion languish & die in our days, (Oh how greatly is it decay'd already as to the power and practice of it!) or shall it die in the next Generation, thro' our neglect in this? God forbid that it should. Therefore God forbid, that Family Instruction or Government, should be slacken'd or neglected. I'm fully satisfied, That that man has not one jot of true Religion in his heart, who is willing that the true Religion should die, when he himself does: and I'm as fully satisfied, that the Religious Educating of Youth. is one method as good as can be taken, to Propagate the true Religion to future Generations.

8. *It will be much for your own benefit, Religiously and Conscientiously to Educate your Children.* If your indeavours prove successful, and your Children become truly conscientious and religious, then,

1. *This will be for your outward profit and advantage.* For if your Children are truly conscientious, you may put trust and confidence in them, leave much of your business and care with them; they'l. be diligent & faithful in what

what you set them about: this will be to your profit and advantage. Whereas many Children are so false, careless, negligent; that their Parents can't trust them with any business, can scarce believe any thing they say, but are almost impoverish'd by their ill practices.

2 *This will make you Joyful. A wise Son maketh a glad Father*, Prov. 15. 20. *The Father of the Righteous shall greatly rejoyce: and he that begetteth a wise Son shall have joy of him*, Prov. 23. 24 It must needs be pleasing and joyful to Christian Parents, to see their Children modest, sober, blameless, useful in their Places; especially to see them practically Godly. But if thro' your negligence, your Children prove vile, wicked, scandalous; this (if you have any Grace, nay any moral principles such as are often found in Heathen) must needs be a grief unto you. *A foolish Son is a grief to his Father, and bitterness to her that bare him*, Prov. 17. 25. Such a *foolish* Son, is the *calamity of his Father — and the heaviness of his Mother*, Prov. 19 13 & 10. 1.

3. *This will be for your honour.* If your Children are truly Pious and Conscientious, they'l manifest love, respect, obedience to you, this puts honour on you; but if they're disobedient & irreligious (thro' your neglect) this reflects dishonour on you. We read of a *Son that causeth shame*, Prov. 17. 2. And what Children are they that cause shame to their Parents? Why commonly such as are *left to themselves*,

selves, (Prov. 29 15) not well taught nor govern'd. If Family governours neglect duty to their Young Ones, no wonder if they're dishonoured by them. *Nabal* was so churlish & ill carriag'd in his Family, that he became contemptible ; one of his own Servants said of him, *he was such a Son of Belial that a man could not speak to him*, 1 Sam. 25. 17. Nay further, the wickedness of Children often brings them to a *miserable End*, which must needs be a grief and *shame* to their Parents ; if they have any natural affections in them. We read that *little Children mock'd the Prophet Elisha, saying, Go up thou bald head Go up thou bald head* ; but God sent *two She bears that destroy'd fourty two of them*, 2 King. 2. 23, 24. Their wickedness brought them to a miserable end, which doubtless was very distressing to their Parents. But you may be sure those Children were *not well Educated*, they were of *Bethel*, a Place of great *Idolatry*, they mock'd at a *true Prophet* for his Infirmity of Age, being *bald* ; and very likely also for his *Religion* and *Office*, being so taught by their *Idolatrous* Parents : for *Idolaters* were no friends to faithful Prophets. By the way, never suffer your Children to laugh or jear at natural defects in any, at *deafness, blindness, lameness*, or any deformity in any Person ; but teach them rather to admire God's Mercy, that they themselves dont labour under such inconveniences. Indeed the wickedness of Persons, has sometimes brought them to open

shame,

shame, capital Punishment, to the *Gallows* where they have confess'd, that the neglect of Family Instruction & Government, has been the occasion of their wicked practice & shameful end: this must needs bring shame & grief to Family Governours, whether Parents or Masters. Therefore bring up your Young Ones for God, lest you are filled with shame, sorrow, and grief for neglecting it; by the miseries they bring on themselves. If your indeavours to bring up your Young Ones for God, are *Succeeded*, twill be for your own *Profit*, *Joy* and *Honour*, even here in this World.

And I may add,

4. *If your're faithful and conscientious in the Religious Educating of your Children, 'twill yield you comfort when Death parts you from them.* Such parting time will soon come, and if you neglect your Childrens Souls, how grievous will it be to part? If you were Sick, & look'd on your selves as dying, how grievous would it be to reflect on your negligence, & to think, 'I'm 'going to leave my poor Children, in a wide 'wicked World full of Snares & Temptations; 'and I have not fortifi'd them against the 'same, by suitable constant Instructions, War'nings & Exhortations; and now I'm going, 'and can do no more for them? Again,

If Death takes your Children from you, how bitter will it be to reflect and think, 'Alas, 'they are dead, they are gone to an endless 'Eternity and I know not whether to Heaven 'or 'or Hell; I have not diligently taught and 'govern'd them, nor daily & earnestly pray'd 'for them as I should have done; I dont know 'but they're gone to Hell thro' my negligence; 'and now they're past the reach of my In-'structions, Tears, Prayers, I can do no more 'for them for ever O wretched Creature that 'I am, I have been cruel, barbarous, merciless 'to their Souls in basely neglecting of them: 'alas, how bitter must such reflections as 'these, needs be to those that feel the sting of 'them?

But on the other hand, if you are conscientious in Educating your Children, and can appeal to God as witness of your sincerity, diligence, fidelity (notwithstanding your unavoidable bewail'd Infirmities) then you may part with your Children when Death comes, and that with Peace and comfort. If your Consciences testify for you, twill be matter of rejoycing to you. Therefore if you would *part comfortably* from your Children, then *Conscientiously & Religiously teach* and govern them. Nay, if out of Conscience to God you religiously Educate your Children, Indeavouring that they may be truly holy, then God will accept and reward such your indeavours, whether he gives the Success you desire or not. *Every man shall receive his own reward, according to his own labour*, 1 Cor 3 8. Tis not said, according to his *Success*, no, possibly he had little or no Success in his work; but according

to

to his *Labour*, his care, diligence, faithfulness. Faithful Ministers are a sweet Savour unto God, in them that *Perish*, as well as in them that are *Saved*, 2 Cor. 2. 15, 16. So if you diligently do what you can, with conscientious care, to bring up your Children in the knowledge and fear of God; God will then accept and reward you for ever, tho' your Children should prove never so vile and scandalous. Let these great and weighty Motives which have been mention'd, quicken Parents to use utmost care and diligence, religiously to Educate their Children.

Having said thus much, about the *Duties of Parents to their Children*, we are now to say something,

2. *About the Duties of Children to their Parents.* And here I shall mention a few things.

1. *Children should love their Parents.* Parents & Children should love mutually, love one another; if they dont, they're *without natural affection*, which is mention'd among the worst crimes of *Heathen*, Rom. 1. 31. and *Hypocrites*, 2 Tim. 3. 3. If Children duely consider, they'l find they have abundant cause to *love* their Parents, they are very base & vile if they neglect it. Unless they *love* their Parents, they can't do other duties which they owe to them, as they should.

2. *Children should fear their Parents.* Lev. 19. 3. *Ye shall fear every man his Mother and his Father.* God requires that *every Person* should fear

fear his Parents, not only his *Father*, but also his *Mother*. Yea the *Mother* is here mention'd *first*, possibly because Persons are more apt to disregard their *Mothers*, tho' they stand in some awe of their *Fathers*. But Children should *fear both*, fear to offend, grieve, disobey, or displease either of them. The great God of Heaven, bids *Children fear their Parents*; if therefore they fear them not, they rebel against God.

3. *Children should Reverence and Honour their Parents.* Exod. 20 12. *Honour thy Father and thy Mother.* This is one of those commands, which the great God uttered immediately with his own Mouth. Our Saviour repeats this Precept, *Matt.* 15. 4. And so does the Apostle, *Eph* 6. 2. They should in their *words*, put resp ct and honour on their Parents; by no means speak rudely or sawcily to them. They should by way of respect, acknowledge the *Relation* between them and their Parents, As *Isaac* did, *My Father*, Gen. 22 7 And *Solomon* said, *My Mother*, 1 King. 2. 20. They did not disown their Parents, they did not scornfully call them, the *Old Man*, or the *Old Woman*, but *respectfully* said, *My Father*, *My Mother*. *Rachel* spake very *respectfully* to her *Father*. Gen. 31. 35. *Let it not displease my Lord.* Children should not only in *Words* but also in bodily *Gestures*, put honour on their Parents. The Children of the vertuous Woman, *rise up* and call her blessed, *Prov* 31: 28.

They *rose up*, showing reverence therein; and call'd her *blessed*, they *spake* respectfully and thankfully to her. *Solomon* even when *King*, did *rise up* to meet his *Mother*, he *bowed* himself to her, 1 *King*. 2. 19. *Joseph* tho' greatly advanc'd, the second man in *Ægypt*, yet *bowed himself* to his Father, *Gen*. 48. 12 It becomes Children of what *Age*, *Sex*, *Quality* or *Dignity* so ever; to show respect and reverence to their Parents, both in *Words* and *Gestures*. And wo to them that despise, contemn or abuse their Parents. *He that smiteth Father or Mother, shall surely be put to Death*, Exod. 21. 15 'Twas not death, a capital crime, meerly to smite another Person; but God's law made it a capital crime, for any to smite Father or Mother. So, *Lev*. 20. 9. *He that curseth Father or Mother, shall surely be put to death*. Prov. 30. 17. *The eye that mocketh at his Father, or despiseth to obey his Mother; the Ravens of the valley shall pick it out, and the young Egles shal eat it*. That is, such an one shall come to a shameful and untimely Death; die so shamefully, as that the birds of prey should feast upon him. Children therefore should take heed that they dont dare to *Mock* at Parents, or *despise* to obey them. *A foolish man despiseth his Mother*, Prov. 15 20. Persons are often more apt to *despise a Mother*, (the weaker vessel, and frequently most indulgent) than *Father*; yet if any man does despise his Mother, God calls him a *fool* for it; God counts him

him and will treat him, as a vile, ſcandalous wicked Perſon. *Deſpiſe not thy Mother when ſhe is old*, Prov. 23. 22. If Parents are grown *Old, Crazy, Infirm, Sickly* ; able to do little or no buſineſs, but need much tendance ; if they'r weak or ſhatter'd in the abilities of their minds ; nay if they're chargeable with evident Sinful failings & infirmities ; yet Children ſhould *not deſpiſe* them, but *honour* them ſtill. Tho' Children ſhould hate their Sins, yet they ſhould love & honour their Perſons. *Noah's* Drunkenneſs was a great Sin in him; yet twas baſe for his *Son* to *Mock* or Jear at him (as *Ham* probably did) and twas commendable in *Shem* and *Japhet*, to cover and hide as far as lawfully they could, what might expoſe their Father to further ſhame or contempt, *Gen.* 9. 21. — 25. Oh its a very great and dangerous crime, for Children to deſpiſe or diſreſpect their Parents. Deut. 27: 16 *Curſed be he that ſetteth light by his Father or his Mother, and all the People ſhall ſay Amen.* All the People ſhould reckon, and ſay, that he deſerves to be curs'd of God, who ſets light by his Parents ; who ſlights, diſreſpects, deſpiſeth or diſhonoureth them. Children ſhould be ſo deſirous to honour their Parents, that they ſhould even hide and conceal their Sinful failings, ſo far as they can do it without Sin in themſelves : they ſhould never deſpiſe their *Perſons*, but always honour them.

4 *Children should give diligent heed, to the wholesome Instructions and Counsels of their Parents.* Prov. 1 8 *My Son, hear the Instruction of thy Father, and forsake not the Law of thy Mother.* Prov 6 20 *My Son, keep thy Fathers's commandment, and forsake not the Law of thy Mother* Psal. 44 1 *We have heard with our Ears, O God our Fathers have told us what work thou didst in their days, in the times of old* It seems they heard, minded, remembred what their Fathers had told them about the wondrous works of God, which should quicken them to fear and serve him Tis said, Prov. 13. 1. *A wise Son, heareth his Fathers Instructions.* Therefore those are *Fools*, very *Wicked*, who won readily, heartily, thankfully receive and retain, the wholesome counsels of their Parents. Oh Children, the great God of Heaven bids you hearken to the good Instructions and Counsels of your Parents; if you neglect disregard or despise them, you therein disobey God himself.

5. *Children should patiently bear, and grow better by, the needful Chastisements and Corrections their Parents give them.* Heb. 12 9. *We ha Fathers of our flesh which corrected us, and we gave them Reverence.* Children should *Reverence* their Parents, in patiently bearing deserv'd corrections, and in growing more dutiful and obedient thereby. They should not be proud stout, stubborn, refractory, refusing the corrections their Parents would justly give them

or

or refusing to be *mended* and reformed thereby. Prov. 29. 17 *Correct thy Son, and he shall give thee rest : yea he shall give delight to thy Soul.* Children should see to it, that their Parents may have *rest*, quiet and *delight of Soul*, in the *good fruits* of their *Corrections*. Oh Child, if thou art not bettered by the Correction of Parents, thou art in danger of being terribly destroyed. Prov. 15. 10 *He that hateth reproof shall die.*

6. *Children should be faithful and obedient to their Parents.* They should be faithful to their Interest, and not wrong them in their Estates. It may be some Children are apt to think, that what's their Fathers is theirs; and so will make bold to take almost what they please of their Fathers Estates, without their Fathers leave; and will spend, give or game away the same as they list. But those who are thus free with their Parents Estates, thus wast and diminish them without their Parents leave; they Sin greatly. Prov. 28. 24 *Whoso robbeth his Father or his Mother, and saith, it is no transgression; the same is the companion of a destroyer.* Prov. 19 26. *He that wasteth his Father, and chaseth away his Mother, is a Son that causeth shame and bringeth reproach.* Well then, let Children be true and faithful to their Parents, not defrauding or wronging of them at all in their Estates. What their Parents give them they should be thankful for, but they should not take what's their Parents, without their

knowledge and good liking. And as Children ſhould be *faithful* to their Parents Intereſt, ſo they ſhould *obey their Commands*. Our Holy Lord Jeſus was *Subject to His Mother*, and to *Joſeph* his Mothers Husband, *Luk*. 2 51. God ſays, Eph 6. 1. *Children, obey your Parents in the Lord, for this is right*. Col. 3. 20 *Children, obey your Parents in all things*. That is, in all *Lawful* things; for if Parents ſhould bid their Children *Lie, Steal, Swear falſely*, or do any thing that's Sinful, they ought not to obey them therein. God is our Supream Lawgiver and Judge, therefore if any ſhould bid us act contrary to his Laws, we ought not to obey them therein. Our Saviour ſays, Mat. 10 37. *He that loveth Father or Mother more than me, is not worthy of me*. We muſt never diſpleaſe Chriſt, to pleaſe any Perſon whatſoever. But Children ſhould obey their Parents, in all lawful things. Children, if you find your hearts ready to riſe, and rebel againſt your Parents; then read theſe plain commands of God now mention'd, wherein your Maker requires you to obey your Parents. In this very caſe (as well as in a thouſand more) Indeavour to impreſs an awful ſenſe of God's Authority on your Conſciences. When you diſobey the lawful commands of Parents, you diſobey God himſelf. The *diſobedient to Parents*, are numbred among the *worſt of Heathen and Hypocrites*. Rom 1. 30 2 Tim. 3 2 To *obey Parents*, is *right*, tis *well pleaſing to the Lord*,

Col.

Col. 3 20 therefore to *disobey* them, must needs be *wrong*, it *provokes* God. Oh Children, consider these things, they are not light or small matters; lay them seriously to heart. It may be your Parents bid you go to work, bid you do these or those things; but you wont, you disregard what they say. It may be you idle away your time, you'l be abroad very late on Nights, very unseasonably; you'l get into ill Company, frequent Taverns, take to Gaming and other ill practices, and all this quite contrary to the plain commands of your Parents. is it so? If it is, then you disobey and rebel against God himself. Tis no small evil you're guilty of; you greatly provoke the Holy God, your're in the way to ruine. Consider that awful place concerning the Sons of *Eli*, 1 Sam. 2 25 *They hearkened not to the Voice of their Father, because the Lord would slay them.* When Children are stubborn and disobedient to Parents, they're under awful Symptoms of terrible ruine. When Children are disobedient to Parents, God is often provok'd to leave them to those Sins, which bring them to great shame & misery in this World, as well as to endless Plagues in the other. The Father and Mother of a *Rebellious Son*, were to bring him forth to the Judges for *open Punishment*, and say, Deut. 21 20. *This our Son is stubborn and rebellious, he will not obey our voice; he is a glutton and a drunkard* If he *wont obey his Parents*, then he's left it seems

(and

(and how often does it prove so?) to *Gluttony* and *Drunkenness*? and at length dies by the hand of Justice for his great Wickedness. We read, Ezek. 22. 7. *In thee, have they set light by Father and Mother.* Then follows an account of *Oppression, Contempt of holy things, profaning the Sabbath, Murder, Idolatry, Incest, Adultery,* &c. Some seem to think, that *disobedience to Parents*, was *leading* to all those other abominations there mention'd. Alas Children, if you once become disobedient to Parents, you dont know what vile abominations God may leave you to fall into. When Persons have been brought to die at the *Gallows* for their crimes, how often have they confess'd, that *Disobedience to Parents* led them to those crimes? As for my own part, except what's openly irreligious and profane, scarce any thing is more grating and roiling to me, than to see Children rude, sawcy, unmannerly, and disobedient to their Parents. When the Prophet would set forth the great wickedness of God's People, he mentions these things as *plain evidences* of it. Mic 7 6 *The Son dishonoureth the Father, and the Daughter riseth up against her Mother.* The Apostle describes *Perillous times*, from this (as well as many other things) 2 *Tim.* 3. 1, 2. that Persons are *disobedient to Parents.* The fifth Commandment is, *Honour thy Father and thy Mother*; the Apostle calls this, the first Commandment *with Promise*, Eph. 6 2. Indeed a gracious God

God often bestows, singular outward (as well as other) blessings on those, that are conscientions in honouring and obeying their Parents. God was much pleas'd with the *Rechabites*, and promised singular favour to them; because they were careful to *Obey the Commandment of Jonadab their Father*, Jer. 35 18, 19. On the other hand, God often brings even outward shame and misery on those, who are disobedient and rebellious to Parents. When therefore disrespect and disobedience to Parents, becomes common and prevailing, then the *times are Perillous*, they're very Sinful, and like to grow worse till ruine comes. On let Children mind these things, lay them deeply to heart, apply them close to their own Consciences; lest they provoke the Lord, to pour out his terrible Indignation upon them.

7 *Children should be very willing and ready, to Support and Maintain their Indigent Parents.* If our Parents are Poor, Aged, Weak, Sickly, and not able to maintain themselves; we are bound in duty and conscience to do what we can, to provide for them, nourish, support and comfort them, *Mal* 3 17.— As a man spareth *his Son that serveth him.* Children should be *Serviceable*, useful, comfortable to their Parents. History tells us, *Æneas* was called *Pious*, for delivering his *Aged Father* when in great danger. When *Jacob* was *Old* and *Famine Prevail'd*, his godly *Son Joseph* did provide for and *nourish him*, and his Family too, *Gen.* 47 21.

When

When he ſent his Father a *Preſent*, he ſent him *the good things of Egypt*, as well as *Corn, Bread, Meat, Gen.* 45. 23. He ſent him not only *neceſſaries* to ſupport Life, but what might alſo be for conveniency, comfort and *delight*: he was willing his Father ſhould ſhare in the *beſt things* he had. This was a noble commendable example, and condemns thoſe, who would put off their aged or poor Parents with the *meaneſt things*. When *Sampſon* gat ſome *honey*, he gave of it to his *Father* and his *Mother*, *Judg.* 14. 9. He was willing to *feed them* as well as himſelf. When *David* and his *Kindred* were in danger from *Saul's fury*; he took care for the *ſafety and comfort* of his *Father and his Mother*, 1 *Sam.* 22 3, 4. *Rahab* was ſolicitous for the welfare of her *Parents*, when ſhe agre'd with the *Iſraelites Spies*, ſaying, Joſh. 2. 12, 13. — *Swear unto me by the Lord — that ye will ſave alive my Father and my Mother, and my Brethren and my Siſters*, &c. If our Parents are in any danger, we ſhould do what we can for their ſafety, as *David* and *Rahab* did. *Tully* (a very Heathen) could ſay, *We are not born for our ſelves, but partly for our Country, partly for our Parents, and partly for our Children. — It conduceth much to the welfare of our Country, that Children be Pious to their Parents.* Doubtleſs many *Heathen* will condemn thoſe *Christians*, who are backward to relieve and ſupport their Parents. Our bleſſed Redeemer when in great pain, when *hanging*

hanging on the Cross, even *then* recommended his *Mother* to the *care of his beloved Disciple*; who *from that hour took her to his own home*, Joh. 19. 26, 27. Our Saviour also *condemn'd* those, who would allow *Children* (tho' under a pretence of *Devoting their Estates to Pious uses*) *to withhold suitable maintainance from their Parents.* To *maintain Parents* if they are needy, is part of the *honour* we owe them; therefore our Lord calls the *withholding maintainance from them*, a *making the word of God of none effect*, Mat. 15. 4. — 6. Mark 7. 11. — 13. Twas said to *Naomi* concerning her *Grand-son*, Ruth. 4. 15. *He shall be unto thee a restorer of thy life, and a nourisher of thine old age.* Some read it, to *feed* thine old age. Indeed Children and Grand-children, should be ready to feed, nourish, comfort their aged Indigent Parents, and Grand-parents. The Apostle says, 1 Tim. 5 4. *If any Widow have Children or Nephews, let them learn first to shew Piety at home, and to requite their Parents: for this is good and acceptable before God.* v. 16 *If any man or Woman that believeth have widows,* (if their Mothers or Grand mothers are Widows) *let them relieve them, and let not the Church be charged.* The word here rendred *relieve*, comes from a word that signifies (and is sometimes translated) to *suffice*, Joh. 14 8. to be *enough*, Mat. 25. 9. to be *sufficient*, 2 Cor. 12 9 Indeed Children should not be coveteous & niggardly, in supplying their Parents; but (if able) they,

they should readily afford what may suffice, be enough and sufficient for them. For if they dont requite and relieve their Parents; they are *not Pious*, they neglect what's *good & acceptable to God.* In a word, it's vile and abominable in Children, to suffer their helpless Parents to want what's for their necessity and comfort, if they are able to supply them. What care did our Parents take of us, when we were little things, when we could not *do* nor *speak* for our selves? How often, and how long a time, did they *feed & cloth* us? And they did it gladly and cheerfully. How tender were they of us, in our Sickness & Wants; how ready to do all they could for our welfare? Surely we can't sufficiently requite them; we should think nothing too much that we can do, for their real comfort. We dont deserve food our selves, if we are not willing to grant part of it to our Parents, if they need it. Let us consider what has been thus offer'd, from the plain word and law of God; and be quickened hereby to do our duty to our Parents, as long as they and we shall be continu'd in the World.

Having thus set forth in some general heads, the Duties of Parents and Children; we are (according to the method propos'd) in the last place,

IV. *To say something about the Duties of Masters and Servants.* Under the title of *Masters, Mistresses* also may be comprehended; for they are to be *submitted to*, Gen 16 9. They are to have an hand *in guiding the house* and governing the Family, 1 *Tim.* 5 14 And by *Servants* we may understand, *Male* and *Female*, both Men Servants & Maid Servants; for both the one and the other should be under government, and in subjection, *Exod.* 20. 10. Under this last head therefore I shall say something, about, (1) *The Duties of Masters to their Servants.* (2) *The Duties of Servants to their Masters.*

1. *About the Duties of Masters to their Servants.* Here I shall say,

1. *Masters should suitably provide, for the bodily Support and Comfort of their Servants.* Servants, are of their household; and if they provide not for such, they're worse than Infidels and have denied the faith, 1 *Tim* 5. 8 The vertuous Woman allows to her household, both *food and raiment*, Prov 31. 15, 21. It's true, sometimes by bargain or agreement, the Servants themselves (or their Parents or Guardians) are to provide them *Cloths*; when tis so, then the Master is free from that care and charge But when Servants are wholly at the finding and allowance of their Masters, then their Masters should provide them *suitable food, raiment, lodging* such as may be for their

health and *comfort*. And in case of *Sickness* or *Lameness*, such *Physick* and *careful tendance* as are needful; should be granted to them. When the good Centurion had a Servant Sick, he besought the Lord Jesus (the best Physitian for Soul and Body) *to heal him*, Mat. 8. 5, 6. He did not treat his *Sick Servant* like a worthless dog (or as the *barbarous Amalekite* left his Sick Servant to perish, 1 *Sam.* 30. 13.) but shew'd a *tender care* of and concern for him: the same is the undeniable duty of all Masters and Mistresses, in the like case of Sickness on their Servants. For any to pinch their Servants (tho' *Negro's*, *Indians*, or any *Slaves*) not allowing them such *Food*, *Raiment*, *Sleep* (and careful tendance in case of Sickness) as are needful for them; is an unmerciful, wicked, and abominable thing.

2. *Masters should keep their Servants diligently Imployed.* Indeed they should allow them sufficient time to *Eat*, *Drink Sleep*; and on proper occasions some short space for relaxation and diversion, may doubtless be very adviseable. To be sure Servants should be allow'd time, for *Secret Prayer*, *learning their Catechism*, *reading the Bible*, and other good Books for their Spiritual benefit. Those Masters dont show much Religion, who wont allow their Servants time for such things as these. But tho' time should be allow'd for these things, yet we may say in general, Servants should be kept diligently imploy'd in

busines.

business Tis said of the vertuous Woman, Prov 31 27 *She looketh well to the ways of her household, and eateth not the bread of Idleness.* She wont be *Idle* her self, nor suffer her household to be so neither; she'll keep them well to their business: She shew'd her *vertue* in this; all Masters and Mistresses should imitate her herein. Idleness is the Devils School; Satan finds work for those. who are not imploy'd for God No good comes of Idleness. Dont suffer your Servants to be *Idle*, oversee them carefully and inspect their carriage, to prevent their unfaithfulness On the other hand, *dont be Ægyptian Task masters to them*, dont put them on work beyond their Power and Ability (nor on work improper and unsuitable for that sort of Service they ingag'd for) and dont require an *unreasonable measure* of work from them.

3. *Masters should defend and protect their Servants* Since their Servants are under their care, and imploy'd in their business; if any would wrong or injure them, they should indeavour to protect and defend them. This is *just and equal*, right and reason require it; now Masters should do for their Servants, that which is *just and equal*, Col. 4 1. Masters themselves should not abuse their Servants, nor suffer (if they can prevent it) others to injure them.

4 *Masters should govern their Servants well.* They should charge them to obey God's com-

mands, to live soberly, righteousl & g dlily. They should use their authority, in furthering their Servants in a blameless behaviour; and in restraining them from Sin. They should not suffer *Man Servant* nor *Maid Servant*, to profane the Sabbath, *Exod* 20 10. By the same rule, they should restrain them from all other Sin as far as possibly they can. Therefore they should chasten and correct them, if need so require. *Judgments are prepared for scorners, and stripes for the back of fools*, Prov. 19 29. *A Servant will not be corrected by words, for tho' he understand he will not answer*, Prov 29 19 If he's so fool hardy, high and stout as not to be mended by words; then correction should be us'd for his reformation. Yet you should not correct them (as we said before of Children) in rage and passion; nor upon uncertainties, unless you are sure of their faults nor should your corrections be cruel and unmerciful; if milder ones will do, more severe ones should ever be avoided. Masters should not be tyrannical to their Servants, nor act as tho' they had an Arbitrary unlimitted power over them. They should *not oppress* them *Deut.* 24 14. Nor *rule them with rigour*; Lev. 25 43 The Apostle says to Masters concerning their Servants. Eph. 6 9 *Forbearing threatening.* The word rendred *forbearing* some translate, *moderating*. Threatening should never be immoderate, nor exceed what the crime deserves. Masters should not frown

and

and threaten, when Servants are not in fault; nor for every ignorant slip or mistake neither. Masters should not affect an harsh, rough, rigorous way of speaking to their Servants; as tho' they were another sort of Creatures different from themselves. Masters should be *good and gentle*, 1 Pet. 2 18. As Masters should govern their Servants well, restraining them from Sin as much as may be; so they should incourage and commend them when they do well. Our great Lord (the Master of us all) will say to the faithful, Mat. 25 21. *Well done* thou good and faithful Servant. Surely then, we should say to our Servants, *well done*; we should *commend* and incourage them when they deserve it. Again, when Masters or Mistresses make *Promises* to Servants, they should faithfully and exactly fullfill them. If we would have Servants faithfull to us, we should be so to them And I might here say as to *hired Servants*, their *Wages* should be duely honestly and seasonably paid them. Col. 4. 1. *Masters give to your Servants that which is just and equal; knowing that ye also have a Master in heaven.* If we should wrong our Servants in Word or Deed, possibly in some cases they would scarce know how to right themselves; but shall their helpless condition imbolden us to wrong them? God forbid. We have a Master as well as they, even God in heaven, and we are accountable to him how we carry it to our Servants.

God will relieve the oppressed, he will recompence wrongs; the fear of his holy displeasure therefore, should restrain us from any way injuring our Servants. Tho' we are now their Superiors, yet they and we shall soon stand on a level before the Throne of our Judge; who will give to every one according to his ways. Let us not therefore wrong the meanest Servant we have; but give what is just and equal; and hear what they can reasonably plead for themselves in any matter. *Job did not despise the cause of his Man Servant or Maid-Servant, when they contended with him*, Job 31. 13 We should give to Servants (as well as others) what's their right and due. If we keep back the *Wages of Hirelings*, or defraud them of their due; their cries will enter into the ears of the Lord of Sabbaoth (the Lord of hosts) and great will our guilt and danger be. Jam 5 3, 4 *At his day thou shalt give him his hire — lest he cry against thee to the Lord, and it be Sin unto thee* Deut. 24 15. *The wages of him that is hired, shall not abide with thee all night, until the Morning*, Lev. 19 13. No, it should be paid presently. This indeed seems to refer to *Day Labourers*; but the law in proportion, may extend to Servants hired for some longer time, wages should be paid them as soon as they are due. God says, Mal 3 5 *I will be a swift witness against those, that oppress the hireling in his wages.* Let those conscientiously consider this text, who are back-

backward to pay those whom they hire to work for them.

5 *Masters should Teach and Instruct their Servants well.* When Masters take *Apprentices*, to teach them some particular Trade or Occupation; they ought in duty and conscience, to give them all the skill and insight they can, in such their Occupation. If they dont faithfully Instruct them therein, they're unjust and unrighteous to them. But by the way, Masters should not allow themselves in any unfair practices in their Callings, nor teach their Servants so to do. If Masters are hired to *Work by the Day* (as in some Trades they often are) they should not be *lazy and idle* (if they are, they do but *Steal* in taking the whole of the Wages agre'd for) they should not do their work slightly or fallaciously; nor teach or suffer their Servants so to do. They should not for the *getting of more custom* (and grasping much more work into their hands) make *fair Promises*, which possibly they have *no prospect nor design to accomplish*; nor should they teach or allow their Servants, in such a vile wicked abominable practice? Masters should communicate to their Servants, all the honest skill to be us'd in their Trade, but no ill tricks or cheating fallacious practices. Well, but should not Masters take care of the *Souls of the Servants*, and teach them the *Truths and Duties of Religion* ? Yes indeed they should, tis their indispensible duty so to do

do; but this was spoken to before under the head of *Parents bringing up their Children Religiously*. The things there offer'd, should direct and move Masters, to bring up their Servants in the knowledge, fear and service of God. If you suffer your Servants to be ignorant, irreligious, vicious; they may do unspeakable mischief to the Souls of your Young Children, if you have any such in the Family. Would you have your Children truly Religious? Then strive that your Servants may be so too. Nay if by God's blessing on your pious indeavours, your Servants become truely conscientious and religious; they'll be the more pr fi able to you. They'll then be trusty, faithful, diligent in your absence as well as in your presence; they'll be great blessings to you. *Abraham* had a *Religious Servant*, and he betrusted him with a weighty affair (the getting a Wife for his Son *Isaac*) and that Servant prov'd both *Prayerful* and *Successful* in the matter, *Gen ch.* 24. The affairs of *Laban* were *blessed* for the sake of *Jacob*, his religious godly Servant. *Gen.* 30 27 The affairs of *Joseph's* Master, were blessed for the sake of *Pious Joseph*: being conscientious, he was faithful to his Master; and would not be unchast with his Wife, tho' strongly tempted thereto. *Gen.* 39 3, 8. 9 *Onesimus*, before conversion, was an unprofitable Servant, a base fellow, he ran away from his Master; but after he was converted, and truly Pious,

Paul

Paul said of him to his Master *Philemon*, v. 11. *Now he is profitable to me and thee.* Indeed a religious Praying Servant, is a very great blessing and should be so esteemed. Therefore do what you can, that your Servants may be such. By no means discourage them, from any thing that's vertuous and pious; but by good Instructions, counsels, and a blameless example set before them, do your utmost to make them truly religious. Keep them as much as possible from ill company, pray hard for them. You should thus strive that they may be truly religious, for the sake of your own credit, comfort and profit, for the sake of their precious Souls, for the promoting Gods glory by the Propagating of Religion in the World. Having thus hinted at the *Duty of Masters to their Servants*, we may,

2 *Say something about the Duty of Servants to their Masters.* And here I might say,

1. *Servants should fear their Masters.* God says, Mal. 1 6 *If I be a Master where is my fear?* This plainly intimates, that Servants should *fear* their Masters; yea they're bid to obey them with *fear and trembling*, Eph. 6 5 To be subject to them *with all fear*, 1 Pet. 2 18. They should therefore stand in awe of their Masters and Mistresses, and be afraid justly to offend them in any thing.

2 *Servants should Honour their Masters.* 1 Tim 6 1. *Let as many Servants as are under the Yoke, count their own Masters worthy of all honour;*

honour: that the Name of God and his doctrine be not blaspheméd. Servants are bid, Tit. 2 9. *Not to answer again*; the word signifies, *not contradicting.* Servants should in their words and actions, put respect and honour on their Masters; they must not give sawcy, impudent, contradicting Answers to them. If those Servants who pretend and profess to be Christians, are rude and unmannerly to their Masters, carry it as tho' they were their equals; if they are sullen, surly, humoursome so as scarce to give an Answer when spoken to; or if they give ill language, cross provoking impudent words; I say if they do thus, then they expose the Christian Religion (which they profess) to be blasphem'd and ill spoken of. Those who dont honour their Masters, they dishoncur God by breaking his plain commands.

3 *Servants should Obey their Masters, be diligent and faithful in their Service and to their Interest.* The word of God is very plain & express for this. Col. 3 22; 23 *Servants, obey in all things* (that is, all *lawful* things, as was before hinted about Children obeying their Parents) *your Masters according to the flesh: not with eye service as men pleasers, but in singleness of heart, fearing God, and whatsoever ye do, do it heartily as to the Lord, and not to men.* Tit 2. 9, 10. *Exhort Servants to be obedient to their own Masters, and to please them well in all things, not answering again. Not purloyning* (that is, not

not Stealing from them, or defrauding them in their Estates) *but shewing all good Fidelity, that they may adorn the doctrine of God our Saviour in all things.* Eph. 6 5 — 7. *Servants, be obedient to them that are your Masters according to the flesh, with fear and trembling, in singleness of your heart as unto Christ: not with eye Service as men pleasers but as the Servants of Christ, doing the will of God from the heart; with good will doing service as to the Lord and not to men.* You that are *Servants*, take your Bibles, frequently read these plain commands of the Great God; that out of obedience to his Supreme indisputable Authority you may be mov'd and quicken'd, conscientiously to obey your Masters, and be faithful to their Interest. And you that are *Masters*, if your Servants are disobedient or unfaithful to you, then read to them these plain commands of the Great God, indeavouring to impress on their Consciences, a sense of Gods Authority and their own duty. Tell your Servants not passionately but seriously, that in disobeying your lawful commands, they disobey not only men but God also; because God requires them to obey you. But to proceed, these things plainly show, that Servants should be obedient and faithful to their Masters. Yea they should carry it thus to their Masters, *not only to the good and gentle, but also to the froward,* Pet. 2 18. Servants, are your Masters or Mistresses *froward*, are they pevish, fearful,

passionate,

passionate, unkind, unreasonable in their carriage to you? If they are, that's their Sin, and for it they are accountable to God, their Master and yours too; yet God requires you to obey their lawful commands, and do what you lawfully can to please them, notwithstanding their ill carriage to you. If they dont do their duty to you, yet you should indeavour to do your duty to them. Tho' when you think they act unreasonably, you may sometimes humbly and modestly suggest your thoughts in the matter, as *Naaman's* Servants did, 2 *King*. 5. 13 yet their lawful commands you ought to obey. You therefore that are Servants, take heed,

1. *To obey All the Lawful commands of your Masters and Mistresses.* Art thou a Servant, and art thou set about some mean, servile, laborious work? Then remember, 'tis God set thee about it; for God bids thee obey thy Master. Dont scornfully think, that that work is below or beneath thee, which God sets thee about. When thou disobeyest the lawful commands of thy Master, thou disobeyest God himself, and despisest his Authority: that's vile indeed.

2. *Obey your Masters, willingly, heartily, cheerfully.* God bids you obey your Masters, with the *heart*, and with *good will*, Eph. 6 6, 7. If therefore you mutter, grumble, find fault, are sullen, and show a backward unwilling mind to do what you're set about; you then break

the plain Commands of the Great God: you rebel against and dishonour him. Therefore be hearty, cheerful, willing, in obeying your Masters & Mistresses; indeavour to *please* them well in all things, God bids you do so.

3 *Obey God in obeying your Masters.* That is, obey your Masters for this reason, because *God bids* you obey them. If this principle prevails (as it should) in your hearts and consciences, twill prompt you to obey *all* the lawful commands of your Masters; and to be as diligent and faithful in their absence as in their presence, behind their backs as before their faces. The Scriptures but now menti-on'd show, that you should obey your Masters, in *singleness of heart, not with eye service as men pleasers,* you should do it *heartily as to the Lord and not to men,* you should do it as *unto Christ.* When your Master or Mistress bids you do this or that, *Christ bids you do it,* because he bids you obey them: therefore do what's bidden, out of obedience to Christ, as to him and for him. If you act from this principle, you may really please & honour Christ, while you're doing the meanest work you are set about. It may be you sometimes think, that *Magistrates* and *Ministers* and those in Publick Stations, have an Opportunity to bring much honour to God; (tis true, they have so) but as for you poor underling Servants, you can do little or nothing for God's honour; but this is your mistake. If you obey your Masters,

are faithful in their Service, and that *out of obedience to God* (as has been said) you then honour & glorifie God; he's as well & really pleas'd with what you thus do, as with any thing that's done by those in Publick Stations. You honour God, by conscientious obedience to your Masters, therefore he'll take his time to honour you too. For he has said, 1 Sam. 2. 30. *Them that honour me, I will honour.* Nay, if you obey your Masters after the forementioned conscientious manner, Christ will reward you in heaven for it. It may be when you do your best, froward Masters & Mistresses will not be pleas'd with what you do, you can't give them content; but if tis so, yet if you're faithful and conscientious, Christ will be pleas'd with you and reward you *Of the Lord ye shall receive the reward of the Inheritance; for ye serve the Lord Christ*, Col 3 24. *Whatsoever good thing any man doth, the same shall he receive of the Lord, whether he be, bond or free*, Eph. 6. 8. These things were spoken by the inspired Apostle, more immediately & directly, to *quicken Servants* conscientiously & faithfully to obey their Masters. And what greater incouragement can you have than this, to obey your Masters out of obedience to Christ? Dont think strange of what I'm going to say, if out of obedience to Christ, you obey your Masters or Mistresses, in *working in the Shop, or in the Field, in making a Fire, Sweeping the House, washing the Dishes*, or in the *meanest business* you

you can be set about; verily the Lord Jesus will take notice of it, remember it, acknowledge it, and *Reward it in Heaven hereafter.* Having thus shewed, that Servants should honour and obey their Masters, and be faithful to their Interest. we may (before we proceed to other distinct heads) draw a few Inferences from these things. Scil.

1. *Servants act very wickedly, when they dishonour or disobey their Masters.* It may be some Servants, by telling false tales and stories out of the house, do greatly hurt their Masters and Mistresses in their Credit, Reputation and Business; such are wicked Servants, they disobey and dishonour God, in thus dishonouring those that are over them. Possibly some Servants are very high, proud, stout, they'll scarce bear to be commanded or restrained: they are for much liberty. They must have liberty for their tongues to speak almost what and when they please; liberty to give or receive visits of their own accord, and when they will; liberty to keep what company they please; liberty to be out late on nights, to go & come almost when they will, without telling why or wherefore; such liberty they contend for, they wont be rul'd, govern'd, restrain'd: or it may be the work they are set about, they reckon 'tis beneath and below them, they wont stoop to do it, but will rather disobey Masters or Mistresses; such Servants are very wicked. They are daring in their plain dis-

 obedience

obedience to God, their abominable rebellion against him: they trample Gods law, his Authority, under their feet.

2. *Servants are very wicked, when they are Lazy and Idle in their Masters Service* The *Slothful* Servant, is justly call'd *Wicked*, Mat. 25. 26 When *Abraham* sent a *faithful Servant* about a weighty affair, that Servant being arriv'd at the place designed; he would not so much as *Eat* till he had *told his Errand*; and having finish'd his business, he was for *hastening home* as soon as might be, *Gen.* 24. 33, 35. He was not for *loytering and playing by the way*, as many Servants are. Faithful *Jacob* took care of his Masters affairs, *Night and Day*, tho' he met with great difficulties therein, *Gen.* 31, 38 — 40. *Joseph* was so *diligent and faithful a Servant*, that he was soon *betrusted* with the *whole of his Masters affairs*, Gen 39. 5. — 8. These things are commendable, but when Servants are lazy, idle, santering, slothful; they then break the plain commands of God, they greatly dishonour him.

3 *Servants are very wicked, when they Cheat their Masters, or hurt them in their Estate or Interest.* When Servants will take *Money, Victuals, Drink, Cloths*, or any goods, any thing belonging to their Masters or Mistresses; and will sell them, give them away, or imploy them in Junkets and Merry meetings, they do very wickedly therein. This is *Theift*, this is *Purloyning*, and *not shewing all*

good

good fidelity, as they should, *Tit.* 2 10 Those also do very wickedly who will entertain or incourage Servants in such vile practices.

4 *Servants do very wickedly, when they run away from their Masters* When Servants run away from their Masters or Mistresses, and quit and forsake their Service, this must needs be a very great wickedness; for it's directly contrary to those commands of God before mention'd. The Apostle *Paul* did *send home* a run-away-Servant, Scil. *Onesimus*, as his Epistle to *Philemon* shows. An *Angel* of God, *sent home* another such *Run-away Servant*, Scil. *Hagar*, Gen. 16 9 The holy Apostles, the holy Angels, thought it wickedness for Servants to run from their Masters or Mistresses. So when upon the *beating of a Drum*, *Servants* will list themselves *Volunteers*, and quit their Masters Service, without the knowledge or consent of their Masters; therein they do very wickedly. They rebel against God's Authority, which requires them to be faithful and obedient to their Masters. Indeed if Servants are *Impress'd*, to go into the War, the case is quite different; that power which does Impress them is Superior to the power of their Masters, and they ought to submit to it; but for them of their own accord to list *Volunteers*, and quit their Masters Service, is plain disobedience to God. God has set up Authority and Government in Families, those who throw it off or run from it, rebel against him. Ser-

vants are not proper judges, who is fit to go into Publick Service; others are more proper than they, to determine in ſuch a caſe. Tis not true courage or Publick-Spiritedneſs, that makes *Servants* (ordinarily) liſt *Volunteers*; but tis a looſe humour, a refractory Spirit, they would be from under the yoke of Family Government. Thoſe Servants who have thus quitted their Maſters Service, ſhould be deeply humbled before God for their great Wickedneſs, they ſhould heartily repent of it. Having thus ſhewed, that Servants ſhould honour and obey their Maſters; and having mention'd a few Inferences there from, we may proceed to ſay,

4 *Servants ſhould patiently bear, any deſerved Chaſtiſements their Maſters inflict on them.* When they are juſtly chaſtened for a fault, they ſhould bear it patiently, and ſhould reform. Nay if their Maſters thro' miſtake or paſſion, ſometimes chaſten them wrongfully; they ſhould yet ſtrive to bear it as patiently as they can. The Apoſtle ſays, 1 Pet 2 19, 20 *For this is thank worthy, if a Perſon for conſcience towards God, endure grief, ſuffering wrongfully. For what glory is it, if when you are buffeted for your faults, ye ſhall take it patiently? But if when you do well, and ſuffer for it, you take it patiently, this is acceptible with God* If ſuch patience ſhould be ſhown under *undeſerved* puniſhments, then ſurely thoſe that are *deſerved*, ſhould be born with great patience indeed.

deed. 'Tis true, if Masters make a trade of being cruel or unreasonable, in inflicting groundless punishments on their Servants; 'tis fit such Servants should be reliev'd and help'd by Civil Authority, and that their Masters should be punish'd by the same.

Once more,

5. *Servants should Pray for God's blessing, on their Masters affairs.* *Abraham's* pious faithful Servant, did so, *Gen.* 24.12. And obtain'd Success in the business his Master set him about. The example of this *Praying Servant*, is fit to be imitated by all Servants. Thus I have mention'd sundry Duties, arising from the various Relations or Capacities, which Christians very often sustain; would to God these Duties might be duely consider'd and practis'd. 'Tis commonly said, those are not *really good*, who are not *Relatively good*. If we would be *good Christians*, we should obey *All* the commands of Christ, and do the Duties of those several Capacities or Relations he has set us in: then (according to our Text) *wherein we are called, therein we do abide with God.*

Soli Deo Gloria.

FINIS.

The Contents of this Book.

THe Text opened. Doct. *Chriſtians ſhould indeavour to pleaſe and glorifie God, in whatſoever Capacity or Relation they ſuſtain.* The deſign under the Doctrine, is, to ſpeak of *Relative* duties, particularly in Families; and therefore to ſpeak about, (1) Family Prayer, and then about the duties, (2) of Husband & Wife. (3) of Parents and Children. (4) of Maſters and Servants.

1. Family Prayer, is prov'd to be a duty, from (1) the light of Nature. (2) the example of the Godly on Scripture record. (3) Scripture Precepts. (4) the obligation of Family-Rulers, to promote Religion in their Families. (5) The neglect of Family Prayer's expoſing Perſons to God's diſpleaſure Then follows an *Anſwer* to thoſe objections. (1) I was not brought up in a Praying Family (2) I'm aſham'd to Pray before others. (3) I have not the gift of Prayer, ſuch a variety of words as others have. (4) I'm ſo hurried with buſineſs, I have not time to Pray Uſe. in theſe Inferences. (1) Neglect of Family-Prayer, is a great Sin (2) Thoſe who have neglected it, ſhould repent and reform. (3) Thoſe are blame worthy, who tho' they Pray in their Families,

Families, yet 'tis but seldome. (4) Family-Prayer should be perform'd in due season. (5) When Parents put their Children to Service, they should put them into Praying Families.

2. About Husbands and Wives, we may say 'tis their duty, (1) To cohabit or dwell together. (2) To love one another intirely. (3) To be chast, and faithful to each other. (4) To be helpful to one another. (1) As to outward. (2) Spiritual things. (5) To be patient towards one another. (6) To honour one another. (7) The Husband's government should be gentle, the Wives obedience cheerful. Use, in these Inferences, blame belongs; (1) To Husbands that dont carry it well to their Wives. (2) To Wives that dont carry it well to their Husbands. (3) Husbands and Wives should be humble before God, for short comings in duty to each other. (4) It's a great Sin, to make or maintain a breach, between Husband and Wife. (5) The duties of the Married state should be well consider'd, before Persons enter into it. (6) Parents should act wisely in matching their Children.

3. About Parents and Children we may speak distinctly, and say, that Parents should, (1) Love their Children. and provide for their outward comfort. (2) Bring them up *diligently* in lawful business (3) Teach them good manners. (4) Instruct them in Religion (5) Govern them well, rebuke and correct them

way to propagate Religion. (8) Twill be much for your own benefit, piously to educate your Children; if your indeavours are Succeeded, you'll have, (1) Joy. (2) Outward profit. (3) Honour. However, if you are faithful in doing duty to your Children, then, (4) You'll have Peace when death parts you and them asunder.

About the duty of Children to their Parents, we may say, Children should, (1) Love their Parents. (2) Fear them. (3) Honour them. (4) Give diligent heed to their Instructions. (5) Patiently bear their deserved corrections. (6) Obey them. (7) Relieve and maintain them if need requires.

4. As to Masters and Servants, we shall speak, first, of the duties of Masters to their Servants, and say, Masters should, (1) Provide suitably for the bodily comfort of their Servants. (2) Keep them diligently imploy'd. (3) Defend and protect them. (4) Govern them well. (5) Instruct them well. Then, secondly, As to the duty of Servants, they should, (1) Fear their Masters. (2) Honour them. (3) Be faithful and obedient to them. They should obey, (1) *All* their lawful commands (2) They should obey *Willingly*, and do it, (3) Out of obedience to God. Therefore Servants are very wicked, when (1) They dishonour or disobey their Masters. (2) They are idle in their Service. (3) Runaway

---

THE

Educational Directory:

Designed for the use of Schools and Private Families.

The former part of it being an address to parents and teachers respecting the education of children, specifying many lessons which parents may choose to teach their children, which may be done by the use of this part of the treatise.

With a supplement recommendative of literature (or learning) addressed to studious pupils; in which virtue, morality, religion and Politeness are represented as conducive to present peace, joy and happiness

The peculiar advantages of several important arts, are minutely stated, with an epitomal grammar, and miscellaneous moral precepts.

Although these hints most parents have not seen,
Yet children's children may their time redeem,
And learn their children vicious ways to shun,
And teach their offspring what their sires might well have done.

Train up a child in the way he should go, and when he is old he will not depart from it. *Prov.* xxii. 6.

By ENOS WEED.

Finted for the Author, and for Six Merchants, and Nine Teachers of Schools. *Price* 25 Cents each, or 18*s.* per doz.

N. B. Those who wish to become purchasers, may enquire for them at Daniel Smith's near the Bear-Market, at Mr. Brown's, No. 70 Water Street, or at Mr. Moore's, all book-binders in N. York city;—Or, at Peter A. Johnson's book-binder, Morris-Town or at Moses M. Comeses, Newark, New-Jersey.

RECOMMENDATIONS.

Extract of a Letter to the Author from Mr. Donald Fraser, Author of the "Columbian Monitor," "Remarks on the Times," "Mental Flower Garden," &c. Teacher of an Academy in the city of New-York.

SIR, New-York, April 4, 1803.

Having perused your book, entitled "EDUCATIONAL DIRECTORY," etc. I find that it contains a number of good moral and scientific maxims for youth. It is not dressed in so very elegant a style as some critics might desire; yet, it is calculated, in my opinion, to prove a good assistant to parents, and an useful school-book.

That you, and all those engaged in the arduous and important duties of cultivating the minds of the rising age, may be amply rewarded, both here and hereafter, is the sincere desire of, Sir,

Yours, etc.

D. FRASER.

Extract of a letter to the Author, from Mr. Dennis Mac Gahagan, late Teacher of an Academy, now resident in the city of New-York.

SIR, New-York, April 5, 1803.

I have read your "EDUCATIONAL DIRECTORY," etc. I am satisfied with the morality and good sentiments it contains, and believe it worthy the attention, and close perusal, of Parents and Teachers, more particularly those residing in the country, who have not an extensive recourse to books and company. I wish you all happiness, and that God may preserve your health, to proceed further with the good work you are engaged to promote. I am of further opinion, that every child, capable of reading, ought to have one of the books to use at school and at home.

DENNIS M'GAHAGAN.

Extract of a Letter from Mr. J. B. Brewer, Teacher of a respectable and large school in the city of New-York.

SIR, New-York, April 5, 1803.

Having been presented with a copy of your "EDUCATIONAL DIRECTORY," in the perusal of which, I find many good sentiments and moral instructions, worthy the attention of Parents and all such as have the care of youth,—As such it appears to be a good school-book, calculated to suit the young and tender mind.

That this, and every laudable pursuit may meet with due merit and suitable encouragement, is the sincere wish of your friend and Humble Servant,

J. B. BREWER.

ADDRESS TO THE READER.

ALTHOUGH some may not immediately perceive the necessity of putting a book into the hands of a clild, the first part of which seems to have been designed for the use of parents and teachers, yet none can reasonably object against using the second part of it for children, since the whole is addressed to studious pupils, and is calculated to stimulate and encourage them in the pursuit of literature, morality, and true virtue.

Let such consider that children will soon become men and women, and the most part of them parents, and many of them teachers of children.

Where indeed can they learn these useful and elementary precepts better than at school; and at what age will they more easily imbibe, or more willingly retain them? Will it be wise to leave children, in a great measure strangers to these principles of duty and happiness until they have contracted an intimacy with men of corrupt minds; and until their vicious habits are established? Is it to be presumed that they will more readily attend to these precepts after they become heads of families, and are anxiously engaged in laborious pursuits in order to obtain the necessaries of life for themselves, and for their children?

Let us suppose for once that children are neglected and left to do as they list—that they are suffered to read such books—keep such company, and imitate such examples as profligate and unprincipled men may chose to set before them, and never attend to instuctions of this nature.

To what alarming degrees of vice and infamy may we not apprehend that our children must reach if they should be left to the dictates of unguided nature, and to the influence of those adults who are inveterately established in the most vicious principles, and pursuing the most unwarrantable practices?

If it be granted that these educational directions are worthy to be remembered, and to be reduced to practice by parents and teachers, and that they ought to be qualified for educating children before they have children under their care; who can object against our using all the means in our power to establish such principles in the minds of children as may fit them to act a most useful and important part in society.

Or who can blame us for endeavoring, while it is in our power, to communicate to the rising generation, and through them, to the latest posterity, such sentiments of action as may contribute greatly to meliorate their condition here on earth, and to secure and enhance their felicity in a future world.

N. B. It is presumed that the judicious teachers of schools will cause their pupils to peruse, repetedly, this directory, and that they will suffer them to read each a sentence, in connection with others classed with them; or, if one read alone, a suitable number of sentences for each exercise; and likewise it will be strictly necessary that the pupils have an opportunity to commit to memory a large proportion of this treatise, according to their capacity of retaining sentenses in their memories.

PREFACE.

I AM far from concluding that the sentences contained in the following treatise, will be satisfactory to every class of citizens ; neither do I conclude that I am qualified to instruct my learned superiors, in those arts which they are better versed in than myself, but in consequence of an entire neglect of the learned to instruct the ignorant, and unexperienced Parents, Tutors, and Teachers of children, concerning the most suitable methods to be observed in the education of the young and rising generation under their care, and in consequence of the many erroneous methods pursued by young and unexperienced teachers, and likewise the many prevailing evil habits which have been established, and are still establishing in the young and rising generation, by the neglect af Parents and Tutors, and by the unreasonable requirements of the above hinted Guardians of children, and since I have no prospect that any of my learned superiors are about to publish instructions, which might be far superior to any contained in the succeeding sheets ; I have concluded that the following treatise may be of use for a part of my Fellow-Citizens, who may choose to peruse and put in practice the following incorrect and unheard of instructions. I earnestly request my learned superiors who may choose to criticise on the impropriety and incoherency of many of the sentences published in the following sheets, to pardon what they may find amiss, and blame themselves for not furnishing the public with a far superior work than what appears in the succeeding treatise. If by publishing the following instructions, I may be a means of contributing any useful ingredients to the Instructors of youth in general, and to my Fellow-Citizens who have the more especial care of children, and if the young and rising generation may receive any lasting impressions of virtue, which may have influence over their minds, and which may have a tendency to encourage them in the pursuit of virtue, and restrain them from many vicious practices which otherwise they might have pursued; then the author hereof will have no just occasion to blame himself for thus exposing himself to public view, notwithstanding a few may choose to load him with reproaches and censure him for his vain attempts thus to stand up in opposition to the prevailing customs and opinions concerning the education of youth. And although some may be disposed to censure and disbelieve, concerning some of the methods recommended. I have only one request to such, viz. please not to judge before a proper attention to evidence, nor condemn without making proper trial.

EDUCATIONAL, &c.

A sound mind, in a sound body, is a short but full description of a comfortable state in this world. He that has these two, has little more to wish for; and he that wants either of them, will be but little the better for any thing else. Mens comfort or disquietude are most part of their own making. He whose mind directs not wisely, will never take the right way; and he whose body is unhealthy and feeble, will never be able to advance in it. I confess, there are some men's constitutions of body and mind so vigorous and well framed by nature, that they need not much assistance from others; but by the strength of their natural genius, they are from their cradles carried towards what is excellent; and by the privilege of their happy constitutions are able to do wonders.

But examples of this kind are but few; and I think I may say, that of all men we meet with, nine parts of ten are what they are good or evil, useful or not, by their education. It is that which makes the great difference in mankind. The little, or almost insensible impressions on our tender infancies, have had very important and lasting consequences: and there it is, as in the fountains of some rivers, where a gentle application of the hand turns the flexible waters into channels, that make them take quite contrary courses; and by this little direction given them at first in the fountain, they receive different tendencies, and arrive at last at very remote and different places.

§ 2. I imagine the minds of children are as easily turned this or that way, as water it self; and though this be the principal part, and our main case should be about the inside, yet the clay cottage is not to be neglected. I shall therefore begin with this case, and con-

Health } sider first the health of the body, as that which perhaps you may rather expect from that study I have been particularly engaged in, and that also which will be soonest dispatched, as laying, in very little compass.

§ 3. How necessary health is to our business and happiness; and how requisite a strong constitution, able to endure hardships and fatigue, is to one that will make any figure in the world, is too obvious to need any proof.

§ 4. The consideration I shall here have of health, shall be, not what a physician ought to do with a sick or crazy child, but what the parents, without the help of physic, should do for the preservation and improvement of any healthy, or at least not sickly constitution in their children: And this perhaps might be all dispatched in this one short rule, viz. that gentlemen should use their children as the honest farmers, and substantial yoeman do theirs. And here for the consideration of all, I may with propriety assert in general,

Tenderness. } that most children's constitutions are either spoiled or at least harmed by pampering & tenderness.

§ 5. The first thing to be taken care of, is, that chil-

Warmth. } dren be not too warmly cloathed by day, or too much covered by night, either in Winter or Summer.

The face of a child, when new borne, is no less tender than any other part of the body: It is use alone that hardens it, and makes it more able to endure the cold: our bodies will endure almost any hardship, either in being exposed to cold, heat or wet, if from the begining we have been accustomed to them.

Be careful therefore and not clothe children with too warm cloathing in winter. As soon therefore as nature has covered their heads with hair, and strengthened them with a year or two's age, be willing to let them run about by day without a cap, it is best also that a child should lie without one at night, there being nothing that more exposes to Headach, Colds, Catarrhs, Coughs, and several other Diseases, than keeping the head too warm.

Feet. } It will be found advantageous also to accustom your Children to the washing of their Feet in warm water frequently at night before they go to bed, & let their feet be free from dirt and scurf at all seasons of the year: in all other alterations from our ordinary way of living, the changes must be made by gentle and insensible degrees; and so we may bring our bodies to almost any thing without pain or danger, also if the shoes of Children are constructed so as to leak in water it will not be found injurious to but beneficial to them, but the Rules are more especially suited to boys than girls; but with a little alteration will suit the constitution of girls especially when they are young; the Poor People set us an example by suffering their Children without distinction of sex or season in the year to go without shoes or stockings, or very frequently with very poor ones, and frequently with such as the rich are ready to lay by as unfit for use, and yet under all these seeming disadvantages their Children are much more Healthy than the Children of their most wealthy neighbours. The washing their feet in cold water occasionally if their feet be not subject to coldness, beside all the other advantages attending, it will prevent Corns and procure a certain degree of Hardiness and of Health not to be obtained by any other means.: Also bathing will in many instances be found advantageous according to the known Practice of the Jews in the cold climates of Germany and Poland at all seasons of the year. The Irish and Scotch practise washing their Childrens feet in cold water, and bathing their whole bodies in cold water while in infancy or while they are quite young, especially the Scotch in the midst of Winter and they find that cold water does them no harm even when there is ice in it.

Swimming } § 8. When boys have arrived to a suitable age, the learning of them to swim especially in the Summer Season, will be found of great advantage respecting their health, if they are cautioned never to go into the water when exercise has at all warmed them, or left any emotion in their Blood or Pulse, and may be a means of saving their lives in some future time.

Air } § 9. It has been found by experience that the accustoming Children to the open air, and to be as little as may be by the fire even in Winter, and also the using them to Heat and Cold, Shine and Rain, (even while young,) will be the most likely methods to fit boys for the hardships they are likely to pass through, if they live untill they are men and for that necessary business which they will have to attend unto in order to obtain the necessaries of life: so likewise if you suffer both Boys and Girls to be out and continue at their business, or play without any covering on their heads, said practice will be found to be a means of promoting their health, and will occasion no inconvenience to them, except their being sun burnt or their having the appearance of a darker skin than they otherwise would have had.

§ 10. One danger only accrues to Children by their being suffered to play in the open air, which is when they are heated with exercise, they may perhaps sit or lay down on the cold earth, this I grant and drinking cold drink when hot with exercise, brings more people to the grave, or to the brink of it, by fevers, and other diseases than any thing I know of. Therefore since Children are not always under the eye of their tutors or parents, they should very early be accustomed to strict rules of forbearance from the dangerous practice of exposing themselves to sudden colds and innumerable other dangers which originate from the too sudden change of the body from heat to cold.

§ 11. The destructive practice of strait-laceing girls when young, in order to the well forming their bodies, is very injurious to them and doubtless in some instances will be a means of very much shortening the time of their continuance on this stage of action.

Clothes.

§ 12. For example, the women of China have been accustomed to have their feet only pinched and unreasonably bound even from their infancy, which is doubtless the cause of their feet and even their whole bodies being so uncommonly small, their lives also very short; while the men in those parts are of the ordinary stature of other men, and live to a proportionable age. How much more dangerous then must it be to compress those parts of the body which contain the heart and seat of life.

§ 13. A plain simple diet will be found to be of great advantage, always being carefull that bread be eaten with every thing; all sorts of meat are to be used very sparingly. Perhaps children under three or four years of age, would do best without any; they would breed their teeth much easier in infancy, and lay a foundation for a more healthy and strong constitution. Plain beef, mutton, veal, &c. using only one sort at a meal, and that with not much sauce, but hunger and no meat will be found good especially for children but once a day, and every sort of food ought to be chewed well to avoid indigestion and the many diseases which proceed from it.

Diet.

§ 14. For breakfast and supper, milk, milk-pottage, water-gruel, flummery and twenty other things of the like nature, without being mixed, viz. using but one sort at a meal without much sweatening, salting, or spicing, which tend to increase thirst and inflame the blood. A piece of brown bread well baked, sometimes with and sometimes without butter or cheese, would be often the best breakfast for children. Nothing but dry bread alone should children use between meals; by this practice they will be in love with bread, and will not be likely to eat more than nature requires. Also, too frequent eating will be found injurious. In some parts of the world they have only one set meal a day towards night, and in other parts, two meals except a little dry bread alone and some raisins, &c.

Meals. } § 15. The time of eating meals should be varied, viz. no set hour for breakfast, dinner, or supper. Children will never be in danger of starving if they are suffered to eat bread alone between their general meals, even if the time of their eating them should be much varied.

Drink. } § 16. Their drink should be no better than small beer, and that too they should be suffered to have only between meals or after they have eat a piece of bread. The reasons why I say this, are these.

§ 17. More fevers and surfits are brought on to people by their drinking when they are hot, and by resting too long after exercise in cold air, than by any one circumstance I know of. Thefore if by play or other exercise, children are hot, then dry bread will ill go down, and so if they cannot have drink, but upon that condition they will be forced to forbear, for if they are hot, they should by no means drink, excepting a very small quantity at a time, before at least a good piece of bread first be eaten, will gain time to warm the bear or water blood-hot, which then they may drink safely. If they are very dry, it will go down so warmed and quench thei thirst better; and if they will not drink it so warmed, abstaining will not hurt them. Besides this will teach them to forbear, which is an habit of greatest use for health of Body and mind too.

§ 18. Take care and establish no habits of eating or drinking either by night or day, which will not be likely to prove beneficial to them when they are grown up. The too frequent drinking even of water will be found to be not only troublesome to those who have the care of Children, but very injurious to them.

Strong drink. § 19. Above all, care should be taken that Children very seldom if ever taste any wine or strong drink, except it be when they need strong drink as a cordial or medicine. They never ought to be suffered to drink it in private or with servants.

Fruit § 20. All kinds of fruit should be used with caution, and according to rules of reason and temperance especially Melons, Peaches, and most sorts of Plumbs and grapes, are for the most part to be avoided, and neither these nor any other fruit will be suitable upon a full stomach: but a little time before eating or between meals: and some times full ripe Strawberries, Cherries, Gooseberries, or Currants may be used for breakfast. These with some other summer fruits being in some measure suited to the season in which they are produced, may refresh our languishing stomachs, therefore a too rigorous restraint, and a too strict forbidding them the use of fruit, will but increase theirdesires after them, & they like our first parents will the more be exposed to an excessive use of them, when they are free from those restraints which they have been under, and they may be the procuring cause of their own natural death, all fruits ought to be eaten when, or not untill they are fully ripe: Apples and Pairs may be eaten pretty freely, apples especially after the beginning of September. Sweetmeats of all kinds are to be avoided, they being very expensive and exceedingly unwholesome, but fruits dryed without sugar are very wholesome.

Sleep. } § 21. Nothing is more to be indulged in Children than sleep.. In this alone they are to have their full satisfaction when young; but some time between the age of seven years and ten, they are to be called up in the morning when they seem to be disposed to indulge themselves too much in sleep, but care ought to be taken to accustom Children to rise early in the morning, even while young, so that they may not be used to take the most unprofitable and unhealthy hours for sleep, and the most profitable and healthy hours for exercise, beside the early rising may prevent them when they are grown, from going into bad company which assemble and continue together untill late hours, which to one that is used to early rising will be burdensome. Great care should be taken in awakening Children with a low call or some pleasant or agreeable sound.

Time of their sleep should be limited to about eight hours, that being time enough for healthy grown persons to sleep in, but never ought Children to be frightened or terrified while they are sleepy, with loud or disagreeable noises and severe threats and such like treatment, as will be disagreeable to them untill they are fully awak'd.

Bed } § 22. Their bed ought to be rather composed of quilts than feathers, for hard lodging strengthens the parts, and contributes very much towards a sound constitution, whereas a downy bed is often the cause of weakness and the keeping the reins too warm, is many times the means of the stone, and the forerunner of an early grave.

Costiveness } § 23. To prevent costiveness, accustom children ro go to stool regularly at least once in twenty four hours, and the time best suited for this is in the morning immediately after eating, and thus custom will help nature or become a second nature, and will be a means at preventing many disorders which proceed from a neglect of this nature, one among the many reasons of this time being the most suitable, is that they will be more likely to remember it before they become engaged in their pursuits of learning play or exercise, and for this reason it is a custom, that for the most part all even grown persons would do well always to observe.

§ 24. The tender constitutions of Children should have but little done for them, and that according to the absolute necessity the case requires. A little of experienced good medicines with ease and abstinence from flesh, often puts an end to several distempers in the beginning, which by too forward applications to Physicians might have been lasting diseases, when such a gentle treatment will not stop the growing mischief, nor hinder it from turning into a form'd disease, then it will be necessary to apply to some sober and discreet physician.

Physick

§ 25. And thus I have done with what concerns the body and health which reduces itself to these few and easy observable rules. Plenty of open air, exercise and sleep, plain diet, no wine or strong drink, and very little or no physick, not too warm and strait cloathing, especially the head kept cold, and the feet not too warm or too cautiously kept from being wet even in cold water.

Mind

§ 26. Due care being had to keep the body in strength and vigor, so that it may be able to obey and execute the orders of the mind; the next and principal business is to set the mind right, that on all occasions it may be disposed to consent to nothing but what may be suitable to the dignity and excellency of a rational creature.

§ 27. The difference to be found in the manners and abilities of men, is owing more to their education than to any thing else, therefore the greatest care is to be taken in the forming Childrens minds, and giving them that seasoning early which shall influence their lives always after.

§ 28. As the strength of the body lies chiefly in being able to endure hardships, so also does that of the mind. And the principal and chief foundation of all virtue and worth is placed in this. That a man is able to deny himself his own desires, cross his own inclinations. and purely follow what reason directs, as best though the appetite lean the other way.

§ 29. The greatest mistake which parents are apt to be guilty of in the education of their Children, is in suffering them while young to do according to their wrong desires and inclinations, because they are young, but they never ought thus to live at loose ends, but to be trained up while their minds are tender and pliable in the ways of virtue, in order thus to lay the foundation for their conduct through life.

§ 30. They who choose not to comply with this caution, will to their sorrow find that although their Children while young might have been forced to obedience with ease, yet if neglected untill four, seven, fourteen or twenty years of age, they are not to be conqured but perhaps will ever after go on towards the ruin of body and soul.

§ 31. We are generally wise enough to begin the tutoring creatures of the brute species while they are young, and neglect only our own. If the child must have grapes or sugar-plumbs when he has a mind to them, rather than make the poor baby cry, or be out of humour; why when he his grown up, must he not be satisfied too if his desires carry him to wine or women. They are objeets as suitable to the longing of one of more years as what he cried for when little, was to the inclinations of a child.

§ 32. It is to be wondered at that there are any footsteps of virtue remaining, since Children are not only put out of the way of virtue, but are absolutely taught vice, before they can go alone they are principled with Violence, Revenge, and Cruelty, give me a blow that I may beat him, is a lesson which most Children hear every day, because they have not strength to do hurt, but does not this corrupt their minds.

§ 33. Again a Child is set a longing after a new suit for the finery of it, thus the little girl when finely dressed, is taught to admire herself by being call'd a little Queen, Princess &c. thus the little ones are taught to be proud of their clothes before they can put them on, and thus they continue in the course of pride being taught it while young, and strongly inclined to it by nature for ever afterwards.

§ 34 Lying and equivocal excuses, but little different are put into the mouths of Children, and apprentices and young people, when considered as an advantage to their parents or masters. Gluttony with all the many disorders and evils attending it, is virtually recommended to Children, when the eating dainties and such kinds of food as are most agreeable to our appetites, is become so common a business of life, and the reserving that part of our meals which is most calculated to tempt the appetite to excess for the taste, & if the stomach happens to be too full to receive it with an appetite, then a glass of wine is thought best to arouse the cloyed appetite, and help digestion although it only serves to increase the surfit. Likewise when Children are a little out of order, the urging them to eat and also the cramming their stomachs, are evils to be guarded much against, when if nature was suffered to be at leisure to correct and master the peccant humors, it would be many times the best remedy against an impending disease which otherwise will unavoidably attack them.

§ 35. Children should be accustomed while young to deny themselves of every thing that will be any way injurious to them, and should never be suffered to have any thing which they cry for, or for the obtaining of which they discover such a great degree of impatience and loud crying, but they should be suffered only to have a sufficient supply of those things which are thought fit for them, if Children were thus to be continually tutored while young, they would no more cry for those numerous unnecessary things than they would cry for the moon.

§ 36. I am not for having Children crossed in every thing, nor is it to be expected that while they are in coats, they should have the wisdom or consideration of counsellors, what I am contending for is, that they should not be suffered to have or do any thing that will be injurious to them, however importunate they may be for them, but harmless play things &c. which will not injure them, they are to have without importuning for them. I have seen Children at a table, who whatever was there, never asked for any thing. but contentedly took what was given them; And at another place I have seen others cry for every thing they saw; must be served out of every dish and that first too: What made this vast difference but this; that some were accustomed to have what they called or cried for, the other to go without it? The younger they are, the less are their unruly appetites to be complied with. Whatever is denied them ought never to be given to them how much soever they cry for it.

§ 37. Be sure to establish the authority becoming

Early. a father tutor or master, as soon as your Child is capable of submission, and can understand in whose power he is, if you would have him stand in awe of you, imprint it in his infancy and as he approaches more to a man, admit him nearer to your Familiarity, so shall you have him your obedient subject, (as is fit,) whilst he is a child and your affectionate friend when he is a man.

§ 38. This awe thus established must be gradually abated as the Child increases in years, and the severe brow of the father tutor or master is to be smoothed, and the necessary severity exercised towards them while young, mixed with as much indulgence as they make not an ill use of, and not by beating chiding, or other servile punishments, they are for the future to be governed as they grow up to more understanding, according to the rules of mildness reason and love.

Self denial. § 39, He that has not a mastery over his inclinations, he that knows not how to resist the importunity of present pleasure or pain, for the sake of what reason tells him is fit to be done, wants the true principle of virtue and industry, and is in danger of never being good for any thing. This temper therefore so contrary to unguided nature is to be got betimes; and this habit as the true foundation of future ability and happiness is to be wrought into the mind, as early as may be even from the first dawnings of any knowledge or apprehension in Children, and so to be confirmed in them by all the care and ways imaginable; by those who have the oversight of their education.

§ 40. Whereas, if the mind be curbed and humbled too much in Children; if their spirits be abased and broken much by too strict a hand over them, they loose all their vigor and industry, and are in a worse state than the former, but those who are possessed of a lively and sprightly spirit, come sometimes to be set right and so make able and great men

But dejected minds, timorous tame and low spirits, are hardly ever to be raised, and very seldom attain to any thing. To avoid the danger that is in either hand is the great art; and he that has found a way how to keep up a Child's spirit easy active and free, and yet at the same time can restrain him from many things he has a mind to, and also draw him to things that are uneasy to him; he I say that knows how to reconcile these seeming contradictions, has in my opinion got the true secret of education.

§ 41. The usual short and lazy method of preferring chastisement, and the rod in restraining Children from vicious actions, and also forcing them to the observance of those that are necessary and virtuous, is of all other methods the most carefully to be avoided. This kind of punishment contributes not at all to the mastery of their natural propensity, to indulge corporeal and present pleasure, will only excite them to avoid pain at any rate, and rather encourages it, and thereby strengthens that in them, which is the root from whence spring all vicious actions, and the irregularities of life; for from what other motive, but of sensual pleasure and pain does a Child act by, and drudges at his book against his inclination, or abstains from eating unwholesome fruit that he takes pleasure in only out of fear of whipping? He in this only prefers the greater corporeal pleasure, or avoids the greater corporeal pain. By this method of correction those principles are cherished in Children, which it is our business to root out and destroy. And therefore I cannot think any correction used to a Child whose shame of suffering for having done amiss, does not work more upon him than the pain.

§ 42. This sort of correction, naturally breeds an aversion to that which it is the tutors business to create a liking to. How frequently do we see Children hating those exercises which at the first were much in love with, after they have been obliged contrary to their inclinations at some times to do certain acts, the which if they neglect, they have been wipped chid or teazed about them, thus for instance, play is an exercise which Children are in the general most in love with, but if play be enjoined on them as a task, and if they are obliged to attend on a single play untill they are weary at it, and so of a second and a third, untill you go through with all their beloved sorts of plays, and it be enjoined with a proper authority, and a severe punishment be threatened, and even inflicted on those who refuse to obey, Children would in a very short time have as great an aversion to their plays, as they now have to their necessary studies, which have very inconsiderately and without any just reason or probability of success been enjoined on them with the like severity, all severe punishments are to be avoided on common occasions, and never ought to be used but on extraordinary ones, and then not except it be in a case of real disobedience to well known commands, on the other hand to flatter Children, to perform their little tasks by giving them those sweet morsels which they most love, or by giving them a suit of clothes, or some fine ornament or a piece of money, as a reward for their application to any of those exercises you would wish to have them continue in, is by no means to be practised, if you wish to have your Child become virtuous and useful to himself or others in the world, but to teach them willingly to cross their wrong and unruly appetites on all occasions acccording to reason and justice, is the great business of education.

§ 43. I say not this because I would have Children crossed in their innocent desires, but I would have their lives made as agreeable to them as may be provided these conveniences, be not bestowed on them as any particular reward, but only on account of their being esteemed by their parents or tutors.

§ 44. I grant that good and evil rewards, and punishments are the only motives to a rational creature; I would have parents and tutors always treat Children as reasonable creatures.

§ 45. The pains and pleasures of the body, used as the means of guideing Children in the ways they should go, for if you redeem their desires of one pleasure by the proposal of another, you lay no principle of virtue in Children, but you thereby inlarge their appetites and instruct them to wander. By this way of proceeding you, foment and cherish in them that which is the spring from whence all evil flows which will be sure on the next occasion, to break out again with more violence, give them stronger longings and and your self more trouble.

¶ 46. The rewards and punishments then which of all others are the most usefull in the education of Ch ldren, are esteem and disgrace, if their minds can but once be brought to relish them: If therefore the father tutor or mother caress and commend them when they do well, shew a cold and neglectfull countenance to them upon doing ill; and this accompanied by a like carriage of all others that are about them, such a method will be of much more service than threats and blows, that have become common and are of no use when shame does not attend them.

¶ 47. In order to make the sense of esteem and disgrace sink the deeper, those things which are agreeable should constantly accompany those who are in a state of esteem; so likewise, should disagreeable accompany those who are neglected, and in a measure dispised on account of their untoward conduct and seeming disobedience, and thus if you can shame them out of their faults, for besides that, I would willingly have no punishment inflicted, and make them in love with the pleasure of being well thought on, you may turn them as you please, and they will be in love with all the ways of virtue.

¶ 48. Here a strict watch should be kept over servants and all others who are about Children, lest they by a contrary course of conduct frustrate all these methods, and render them abortive.

¶ 49. Whenever Children have offended, they ought not to be immediately restored to favor, after their receiving a few blows, which has been before intimated should very seldom be used, lest the too frequent use should become so common as to be of no use, as all other methods of punishment cease to be beneficial after they have become common.

¶ 50. Although reputation be not the true principle and measure of virtue, (for that is,) the knowledge of a mans duty, and the satisfaction it is to obey his maker, in following the dictates of that light God has given him, with the hopes of acceptation and reward, yet it is that which comes nearest to it: And being the testimony and applause that others give to virtuous and well ordered actions, it is the proper guide and encouragement of Children, untill they grow able to judge for themselves and find what is right by their own reason, and by that light which hath to all men appeared, and which is that grace which bringeth salvation and saves those who obey it.

Reputation.

¶ 51. Either chiding or scourging Children for their faults, ought to be performed in private, and in such a calm manner as to make no show of an angry passion, but on the contrary a show of love and concern for their welfare, but when they are praised for their suitable actions it ought to be in publick, so as to restrain them from evil and encourage them in the ways of virtue.

¶ 52. The trifleing playish temper and disposition observable in most Children, should rather be encouraged, it being beneficial to them, as long as they remain Children, provided it be under the restraint of their parents or tutors, so as they dont injure any creature by it, nor discommode any person, yea the chief art is to make all that they have to do sport and play too.

§ 53. And here let it be remembered that the

practice of charging Childrens memories upon all occasions, with rules and precepts which they do not understand nor can possibly remember, is very far from being advantageous to them, but if you would learn a child any action let it be done over and over again, repeatedly untill it be established into a habit, and then it will not depend on memory only; thus bowing to a gentleman when he salutes him, and looking in his face when he speaks to him, is by constant use as natural to a well bred man as breathing; it requires no thought no reflection. Thus you may plant what habits you please in Children.

§ 54. Let therefore your rules to Children be very few, each of them well established by becoming a habit before another be proposed, and thus add one rule after another as they advance in age.

§ 55. But after all that has been written above, about rules, precepts and habits, the natural abilities of children, ought very strictly to be attended to, so that nothing be required of them but what they can perform, and whenever they forget seemingly what has before been taught them, let them be reminded of it in a calm and sedate manner, and not by harsh words and chiding as if they were willfully guilty, always being cautious about requiring too much of them at one time. We never need to expect that we can alter any one's genius, although we can much improve and mend untoward dispositions, but it is in vain for any creature to attempt the planting in children's minds, quite opposite dispositions which seems to be the work of the creator alone.

Dissembling.

§ 56. Children should never be suffered to dissemble, especially in gestures, words or manners, but always to speak and act according to the true sentiments of their hearts. Thus a courteous address ought never to proceed from one that does it merely for show and not from affection. They should be taught how to act on all occasions, which acts ought to be performed first in the presence of a skillful tutor, so that any impropriety which may attend said actions, may be rectified by observation, and thus not leave children to judge of rules for themselves.

Manners. § 57. Concerning manners, but a very little care is necessary to establish them in children, especially the heaping on them a large number of rules about their putting off their hats, or making legs, or courtesies, and such like punctillioes of outward gesture to the neglect of their minds, which should be stored with the kind sociable affections, which will lead them to a becomeing behavior in riper years, which will be learned best by their observance of the common tokens of civility among those who are well bred.

§ 58. Children should be kept from associating with wicked and illbred servants or others, who will be likely to learn them their ill words and actions; yea and give them such counsel as will encourage them in acts of disobedience, and thus lessen the authority that parents justly claim over their children.

§ 59. Children should feel always easy in the company of their parents or tutors, and should receive all those things which please them from their hands, but servants ought not to be suffered thus to make court to, and flatter children into their company, by which means they will learn their vices. Thus strong Drink, Wine, Fruit, play-things, &c. children should never receive from the hands of servants.

§ 60. Good principles of morality breeding and a becoming gracefullnes, is not generally to be learned by children at school, among a disorderly herd of boys, and where they can be under the eye of their master, but a small part of the twenty-four hours in each natural day, but may be learned with more ease at home, under the immediate care of their parents or tutor. Virtue, real virtue is the main point to be aimed at in education, and not a forward pertness, nor the many little arts of trifling.

§ 61. Nothing ought to be done, nor any liberty taken in the presence of Children which you would forbid in them, nor will it be good to excuse yourself by saying it is suitable for one of my age and not fit for Children, you will thereby increase their desires the more to imitate you, neither can Children reasonably be corrected for what they see their parents or tutor perform, since they are so exceedingly prone to imitate what they see others do.

§ 62. Children should never be punished with a rod for childishness, or whatever time and age will of itself reform, to which if we add. Learning to read. write, Arithmetic and Book-keeping, foreign languages, &c. as under the same privilege viz. not to be beat into them by blows, we shall have but little occasion for them or any force in an ingenious education, the right way to teach them those things, is to give them a liking and inclination to what you propose to them to be Learned, and that will engage their industry and application which may be easily done with the observance of what is written above, and the following rules.

§ 63. None of those things that Children are to learn, must be imposed on them as a task for it will be found, that any of their beloved plays may be made burdensome to them after they have been obliged to play, thus by commanding a child to perform any one play that he shall choose, without changing or varying the play untill he is really unsuited with it, or really weary of it, you can cause him in this manner thus by putting him to one play after he is weary of another, untill he will be weary of all his plays or of any thing which you

Task.

want to set him against: yea, these and such like requirements ought to be made a punishment, even for disobedience. On the other hand, those things which you would have your Children learn, ought to be made a recreation to their tasks of play, after a seaming unwillingness has appeared to the child in his parent or tutor to learn him, the which privilege should be granted him after he has shewn a great desire to learn, and repeatedly asked for an opportunity at his book or any thing else you want him to learn, but if a degree of aversion appear in your child to these exercises, you must carefully endeavour to cause him or her to wish for an opportunity, by telling them the great advantages they will have if they can be suffered to learn at the same time, instance to them the real privileges which some of their acquaintances are in possession of in consequence of their having learned it, and when they are very much engaged in study or appear desirous to learn, (lest they continue so long in exercise as to be cloyed,) they ought to be frequently obliged to look off, and then while they are obliged to look off of their books in school, then let others that are in the same class be advised to take the advantage of them that look off by attending closely to their books, and so on which methods will be found to be of unspeakable advantage.

§ 64. From what is above written, it appears evident that Children should not be indulged in a lazy dull listless temper and disposition, but should be obliged to be reasonably active about some thing, therefore it will be of use to make such, do something; but take great care that those things you want them to learn be not enjoined at this time, but any exercise that you dont want them to learn may be urged upon them so as to have their minds fixed and steady, and thus it is that they will learn to take their minds off from one pursuit and fix them on an other with ease and pleasure, which habit will be of more advantage to them th-n to learn Latin or Logick or most of those things Children are required to learn.

Correction. § 65. Frequent chiding as also the frequent use of the rod on every occasion, and for every little slip or neglect for the want of memory in the child is the ready method to render all such requirements inefectual and abortive in subjecting the child: yea, so far from establishing your government over a child, you will but encourage it in its beloved disobedience: a look or nod is enough on such occasions, but the use of passionate ill language will doubtless teach the child to use the same, since a child acts altogether from a desire of imitating especially those who are much older than himself, a severe and unremitted correction with a rod ought to be used as the last remedy, and that for nothing but obstinate wilful disobedience to well known commands, (intermingled with suitable reproofs and reasons, shewing the shame and disgrace that such conduct persisted in, will expose them to,) at the same time shewing the danger of everlasting punishment in another world if they repent not and for sake their sins; and let the parent or tutor express a sorrow that they have occasion thus to put them in pain: with a suitable degree of pity and tender compassion.

§ 66. Calm and suitable reproofs for the little heedless miscarriages of Children with instructions what you would have them to do often repeating them when you have any reason to believe that their faults are the effects of forgetfulness, and not willful neglects, will gradually reclaim them from all those little miscarriages, and as they advance in age they will improve in manners and in unreserved obedience to the wishes of their parents or tutors; especially if they fear and love and wish to have the good will of the parent or tutor.

Reproofs.

Reason and } § 67. Children should on all occasions example. } be treated as reasonable creatures, such plain reasons as are suitable to their age and capacity should be used with them, and not lengthy discourses which scarcely a grown person can understand, and the best and most sure methods to reclaim them from wrong or unsuitable practices, even to fortify their minds against the temptations to them is to show them the examples which it may be they have knowledge of; yea! the exceeding ill consequences attending ill or bad actions, and, the good and agreeable consequences attending suitable actions, which they are to learn from real examples set before them

§ 68. The first appearance of vice in a child, any incfination to transgress any of those good rules which you would have him observe, should be treated by you as a matter of wonder and amazement. At the same time, informing him you was far from expecting such conduct, and carefully avoid the unseasonable, forbiding too much practised by parents and tutors, which will prove to be injurious to them, and will serve only to excite, yea, and even increase desires in Children to do those very things which they were forbidden to do, when perhaps otherwise those desires never would have been in them: this is true respecting ourselves, as well as in Children viz. those acts which we are forbidden to do we most desire to perform, if we have no apprehension of evil in those acts which Children are so much addicted to, then there will be no use for the rod on such occasions: the rod as before odserved should be the last remedy, and that in cases only of extremity, and even that not very soon after the crime is committed, not untill you have had time for cool reflection so as to judge what method to take, and what measure will be necessary, for no one ought ever to correct a child, in a passion of anger or wrath.

§ 69. It perhaps will be objected, that some Children would never learn if they were to be tutor'd according to what is above written, to which I answer if none of the mild methods will prevail on him to begin to learn which will very seldom if ever happen, and if he refuse it after it be enjoined with authority, then it is obstinacy for which he may be corrected in the manner above described, but this should be made no general rule but only an exception to it.

Rules for teaching letters advantageously. } § 70. Print one two, or at most three letters either on a small piece of paper (ornamented,) or on the pupil's nails, with a pen and ink, or with the point of a pin. Call him often and teach him the names of the letters, and let any one of the schollars or byestanders do likewise: and after he or she has obtained a desire for to study, suffer him to look on a short time as a privilege or recreation granted him instead of being obliged to play contrary to his inclination: for I would have him set against his play or plays before he has learned the alphabet, I say play or plays because he should not be suffered to attend on more than one at a time, and let him be obliged to pursue that one, perseveringly as a task untill he be weary of it before he be suffered to play any other, and so on let him after being commanded so to do as above hinted, exercise himself in one at a time, then after he is cloyed fully of that one play, let him choose another instead of that, and then another play &c. untill he shall have no inclination to any one.

At all times the teacher of Children should without falsifying truth according to the scripture, ("as deceivers and yet true.") Show an apparent unwillingness that his pupil should have an opportunity to learn, but especially be apparently unwilling to grant liberty for his pupil to look on the book, and after a short time even while he his most engaged in study command him to look of and put away if it be a piece of paper with two or three letters printed on it or a book, and if there be time enough oblige him or her to return to their task of play, and after repeated requests for leave to look on suffer him to look on again, but let it here be remembered that no one student should be suffered to look on or attend to his or her study so long that it becomes a disagreeable exercise, but he should be obliged to look off before he is in the least weary of his pursuit.

A pupil should be able to name the first two or three letters (as above hinted,) in any word before he be suffered to look on any other, and then after he has fully learned the first two or three letters, give him two or three more to look at, then after he has fully learned them, let him take two or three more &c. untill he become fully acquainted with the whole small alphabet, then show him the similar letters which perhaps is not completely fixed in his mind, such as b d q p f s &c. * then the compound letters such as ct, st, fl, sl, &c. then let the two or three first tables of syllables be compleatly fixed in the pupils mind, so that he or she can repeat every sylable in order as in the tables out of book or any one of them separate in any word. Then teach the capital letters, then words of two letters, then words of four letters, then teach words of five, then words of six letters &c. And let it here be remembered that a child should spell over each parcel of syllables or words so loud as to be heard, (and that should be a small number not exceeding forty or fifty,) untill he can spell every syllable or word

* *Moreover those scholars who are ingorant of the letters, should have a regular place in a class and move as in the other clases.*

perfectly right, for untill a child can spell his lesson every syllabel or word of it right, he should never be suffered to study it to himself, for if he should spell a lesson over an hundred times wrong it will do him more harm than good; because he has first to unlearn all that he has been habituated to spell wrong before he can be learned the true pronunciation of those syllables or words, but after he has learned the pronunciation of syllabels words, &c. then he may be suffered to look on a short time after first obtaining liberty from his parent or tutor, and but a short time until he or her should be obliged by an authoritative command to put by the book, for a child should never be suffered to hold a book in his hand except it be for the sake of useing it for to learn out of it, and that with an earnest desire so to do.

Moreover it would be much for the advantage of convenience of the teacher, (and perhaps much more so for the employers,) to insist on it as a rule not to be broken that every scholar must have clean hands, a clean thumpaper and pointer, a smooth thin piece of board or shingle to hold under the book, so that each scholar may continually keep his place and observe the exact place in the book, and if each scholar in the class spell each one or two words, (or if it be thought best by the teacher to pronounce each word before it be spelled, and each scholar be requested to spell or name each letter in the word a little after the teacher and after it is thus spelled the teacher is to pronounce the word again first, and then all in the class as one are to pronounce the word again,) in either case the scholar can easily observe the place in the book, but if through inattention he should loose the place in the book, then as a punishment he should be obliged to move below one in the class, or some other trifling penance should be imposed on him for his neglect. For in no case should a child be whipped or ferriled for looking off his book, or for mis spelling or for erroneous pronunciation: In no case should a child be thus corrected excepting only for absolute disobedience to well known commands; I say welknown because a child should have all rules for practice as well as those which he is commanded to obstain from often repeated to him; or he should often repeat them so as to have them comlpeatly fixed in his mind before he be liable to stripes for a breach of them. Therefore the literary rules for teaching letters advantageously may be thus expressed.

Rule 1. § 71. Let the teachers always seem to be unwilling to teach, or that his pupil should have an opportunity to learn in the book, or study or spell over repeatedly those sylables or words which he has been teaching him to pronounce.

Rule 2. Let the teacher speak often to his pupil, of the many advantages he is to expect on the account of his being suffered to spell in the book, or to study, and in this way becoming a man or woman of great learning, of honor, pleasure, profit, &c. and here, it would be good for the teacher to quote living examples in contrast, of the advantages &c. of being learned, naming such a one, and such a one, that the pupil has knowledge of, and also the disadvantages attending those who are ignorant, likewise naming particular persons who are known to the pupil.

Rule 3. Let the good conduct of the pupil, entitle him to the privilege of being learned, and also to the privilege of an opportunity of spelling over his small number of sylables or words to himself, and for his misconduct, let him be obliged to miss of an opportunity of being teached, or of a time to study, at the same time let him know that others are all the while taking double advantage of him, and that it will be very difficult for him to regain this lost time.

Rule 4. Let all those civil and harmless amusements, which the ignorant and mean delight in, be enjoined as a task, and be obliged to continue in one or other of them untill he is very weary of it, I say of it, because he should not be suffered to play only one play at a time, and let him choose that one sort and so from time to time, first let him be obliged to continue in that play of his first choice, much longer than he is really willing so to do, and so he must choose play after play. untill he be cloyed with every sort of play or exercise; the which he need never to learn, as above written.

Rule 5. Whenever a pupil is suffered to study, let it be where he was last learned to spell, so that by repeatedly spelling the words which he can spell and pronounce, (for none other should he be suffered to studdy in this way,) he may the sooner learn to read.

Rule 6. Let premiums be often given to the pupil, or some one ornament or token of victory, be fixed on the one which out does all the rest in the same class; perhaps a medal to be worn for a few minutes may suit, or untill the next time of trial, or untill some one else shall out do the bearer of the medal, the methods of trial are, spelling out of the book where they were last learnd, or by reading two or three words the quickest beginning first, with the two lowest in the class, both of them are to stand up and try which can read two three or four words of the colums quickest. then the one that has pronounced them quickest, continues standing and the other is to sit down below the one that has pronounced quickest, & then the next in order that is higher in the class is to stand up and try with the one that has out done the one which sat down lowest in the class, & thus continue the tryal through the class, two or three times round; the methods of these kinds of trials may be varied according to the knowledge of the class. From pronouncing two words quickest, twice told to the pronouncing three, four, five, six or more words quickest untill the trial is ended.

N. B. Methods of trial may be suited to each class, according to their knowledge; even those Children, who do not know the letters may stand up by the teacher two, three, or four at a time, and all look on while the teacher is pointing to a single letter, and the one which sounds the letter the quickest is to move above, if any one be above him or her in the class, thus may such literary trials be continued as often as shall be found convenient, after the literary class has a pretty general knowledge of the letters, the similar letters should be very critically attended to, yea, let the teacher here mind to point first to one then to the other letters, which have the nearest resemblance to each other by way of comparison, thus, when any one in a class which are very expert, while spelling, if any one or more sounds a letter wrong, let him or them immediately, or after the exercise of the class is ended, be called to the teacher and be exercised, by looking at and naming all the similar letters in comparison, in this way the pupil will soon have the idea of each similar letter fixed in his mind.

Rule 7. Whenever scholars are most engaged while studying, oblige them to look off their books, sometimes a single scholar, then another, and soon after another; at the same time suffer a part of the same class to studdy, and often remind them while studdying that now is the best time to studdy while the others are obliged to look off, and that now is the time to take advantage of those who are now not suffered to studdy. Likewise let none be allowed to look on their books very long at a time, neither suffer them to hold their books in their hands to play with them, but frequently oblige them to put their book out of their hands as before observed.

Rule 8. If any pupil appears to be very backward, dull & very unwilling to learn, or seem to have no desire to studdy, oblige him to play the more, and that with those who are like himself; such should not be suffered to play with the willing and active students; (lest they mislead those who have been well tutored,) neither should boys and girls be suffered to play near to each other, but should always be obliged to play at a distance from each other, while under the tuition of their tutors at school.

Rule 9. Let every scholar be well instructed in the first and easiest rudiments of literature before he be burthened with such syllables, words or names which are too hard for him to learn with ease and pleasure. According to the above introductory hints to those who begin to teach Chidren the sounds of syllables, &c. after the pupil can name all the letters.

Moreover let each scholar be learned to read each table, or part of a table which has been used for one exercise before another part be begun upon, and thus from part to part, according to the regularity in the book which is used for teaching; let each small part or portion of syllables, or words, which the teacher shall judge suitable. For one exercise be repeatedly taught the pupil from time to time; and after the pupil can pronounce every word perfectly right, then according to the above rules for studying, let him spell it over thirty, forty, or fifty times to himself according to his need, in order to learn to read those syllabels or words quick and easy, without spelling them at the time of reading.

Thus will it be found by experience, that scholars will obtain more lasting knowledge, by studying where they have been learned last, as above hinted, with that degree of willingness which will be excited in them, by striving with others than otherwise they could have done by spelling over the same words a few times loud, within the hearing of their teacher, for in this way, they may have time to spell over the words learned, twenty, thirty, forty, or fifty times to themselves, (while the teacher is attending to the other classes) and thus scholars will very soon become good readers of those easy words, and likewise they can in these ways, learn to read those words called hard, and which are composed of many syllables.

Rule 10. Oblige every scholar, which appears to have any wish to play, to continue long at this exercise, untill he be very weary of it, and let it be enjoined as a punishment for some ill act done, or because his teacher is apparently unwilling that he should become proud of learning so fast as he would do, if suffered to look on as much or as long as he wishes to according to that which is above written.

Rule 11. Let scholars know and understand every rule for the division of syllables and also for the spelling, accenting and pronounciation of words and all other rules of art which are necessary to be learned in the school, to which the pupil is sent for instruction as soon as they can comprehend them, (which will be much earlier than is in common believed,) and let the teacher first name every letter in each word, while exercising a class each of them saying after him, let also the teacher be carefull to sound the accented syllables in words or names of two or more syllables much louder than any other syllables in the same word or name; and at the beginning of every exercise let the pupils be learned to put the accent on the accented syllable before they proceed to spell, and let the teacher pronounce each word before he begins to spell it; for I would advise all teachers at least, a part of the time to spell each and every word with the class, the teacher should name each letter before any one in the class, so that each of them first hear the teacher name each letter and each of them say after the teacher, and so of syllables and words, the teacher always to be the first to sound the letters and syllables and also to pronounce the words, the whole word to be pronounced before it be spelled and after it has been spelled, which will be a ready method to fix the sounds of words in the pupils minds) some times also, let the teacher pronounce, one, two, or more syllables and each one of the class in rotation, from the highest to the lowest in the class, and other syllables each scholar to sound the syllable or syllables which have been sounded by the teacher, adding only one syllable for example, let the teacher spell or pronounce thus, e,x or ex, the scholar say a,m am ex,am, the teacher is to say p,e,l, ex-am-pel or thus let the teacher say, c,o,n, con, the scholar is to say,s,t,i, sti con-sti,the teacher to say t,u,tu con-sti-tu, the scholar is to say, tion-shun, con-sti-tu-shun, &c.

Rule 12. Never Should a scholar be whipped or ferriled for misnameing letters or for any error in pronounciation, but only for a transgression of or for disobedience, too well known commands. If a scholar be obliged to move one lower in a class for loosing his place in the book or for misnameing a letter,it will be enough for every error of this kind.

Moreover if any doubt of the utillity and propriety of the above particular rules, let them attend to their own experiences concerning the many acts which have been required of them while they were young and under the tuition of their parents, and also of the many pursuits, which they were commanded to abstain from, and I doubt not of the witnessing of the greater part of the people, so far in favor of the above statement of rules for teaching letters advantageously, that they will be ready to acknowledge, that those acts which their parents tutors or schoolmasters, enjoined on them as a task, were thereby made very disagreeable to them, and those pursuits which they were commanded to abstain from, they had the stronger desires to pursue, and this disposition seems still to be rooted in all men, namely an unwillingness to obey commands, and a great desire to do those acts we are forbidden to do. And that which may likewise serve as a circumstance to confirm us in a belief of this bias fixed in our own nature, is a report concerning the Children of the portuguese, thus expressed by Mr. John Locke. "It is so much a fashion and emulation among their Children to learn to read and write, that they cannot hinder them from it: they will learn it one from another, and are as intent on it as if it were forbid them. I remember continued he that being at a friends house, whose younger son, a child in coats, was not easily brought to his book, (being taught to read at home by his mother,) I advised to try another way, than requiring it of him as his duty.

We therefore in a discourse on purpose amongst ourselves, in his hearing, but without taking any notice of him, declared that it was the privilege and advantage of heirs, and elder brothers, to be scholars; that this made them fine gentlemen, and beloved by every body; and that for younger brothers, it was a favor to admit them to breeding: to be taught to read and write, was more than come to their share; they might be ignorant bumkins and clowns if they pleased. This so wrought upon the child, that afterwards he desired to be taught; would come of himself to his mother to learn, and would not let his maid be quiet untill she heard him his lesson." I doubt not but some way like this might be taken with other Children; and when their tempers are found, some thoughts might be instilled into them, that might cause them to desire learning of themselves, and make them seek it as another sort of play or recreation. But then as I said before it must never be imposed as a task, nor made a trouble to them. There may be dice and playthings with the letters on them, to teach Children the alphabet by playing; and twenty other ways may be found suitable to their particular tempers, to make this kind of learning a sport to them. Thus Children may be cozened into a knowledge of the letters; be taught to read without perceiving it to be any thing but a sport, and play themselves into that which others are whipped for.

Children should not have any thing like a task in literature required of them; neither their minds nor their bodies will bear it, it injures their healths, and their being forced and tied down, to their books in an age at enmity, with all such restraint has I doubt not, been the reason why a great many have hated books, and learning all their lives after: "It is like a surfuit, that leaves an aversion behind not to be removed." Thus far the celebrated Mr. John Locke.

Reading. § 72. Moreover, I must here object against the too common methods of suffering Children to spell and read both in the space of an hour, or for one school exercise; and I must believe that the arrangement in some spelling books of tables, of monosyllables, of columns of two syllables, then more lessons for reading, then after these a table of columns of three syllables, then after that lessons for reading &c. All which easy lessons serve as means to fill the young ignorant and unexperienced pupil, with wrong and erroneously high notions of his ability, to read before he has half learned to spell, and thus it is that scholars tutored in these methods, never become good spellers, nor are they while thus exercised, likely to learn to advantage, nor in this way to become good readers, for they will think it far below their rank in knowledge to be employed about spelling, and much less are they willing to attend to the spelling over those words which have been spelled in the hearing of their teacher, (to themselves,) the most speedy and advantageous method of learning to read, but I think it would be best to keep all books for reading out of the reach of Children, untill they are good spellers, yea! so expert at spelling that they can pronounce the most difficult and lengthy words in any spelling book with ease, and as quick as any one need to read in any book, and without stopping to spell one syllable of them, thus I think that children should be learned to read before they know that they can read, by a positive experiment in a common book.

Neither does reading, ever ought to be imposed as a task, nor does a child ought to be too much limited or confined to just such books as his well informed, parents or tutors would wish, at least they should take care, that they do not show themselves too much engaged while they are employed in enumerating books for their pupils, but the putting such books in their way as will be likely to inform them of what they ought to do, and avoid likewise those books that are calculated to impress on their minds the fear of, and love to their creator, their duty to their superiors, and inferiors, and also their duty to all mankind, and that will be calculated to deter them from all vicious actions and encourage them in the ways of virtue must be the books that may with propriety be put in their way, if they are not positively required to read them, likewise those little books which are calculated to show them the shapes and natures of beasts, birds and fishes, and other entertaining and true story books may also be of use to them, but their reading as well as all other useful exercises, should be attended on cautiously with respect to the time employed in them, never should a useful exercise of this nature be continued in, untill the mind becomes tired and weary of it, so that I must believe, that a seeming unwillingness in the parents or tutor, for to indulge the pupil in his beloved exercise of reading would be of great use to the pupil, since it would be a means of increasing his desires after books, and of reading and attending to what he has or can have an opportunity of reading.

Writing. § 73. After a child has learned to read expeditiously and according to grammatical exactness, then if the pupil has an earnest wish for to learn the use of pen ink and paper, let him first be taught how to hold his pen, and how to move it advantageously before he be suffered to use paper; and here I choose to approve of the method of holding the pen, so as not to lean to the right nor left, the elbow should be held close to the body, the pen should be so leaned as to have the top part of it directed to shoulder, the point of the pen should be about three quarters of an inch beyond the end of the middle finger, which should be placed at the right side of the pen, while the fore-finger should be held on the top of the pen stretched out strait, the end of the thumb should be held so as to be directed to the inside, trans-mark of the first joint of the fore-finger, the next finger to the little finger, should just be laid on, the little finger and should be supported on the end of it, and the heel of the hand, should be held at a considerable distance from the paper, the pen should be moved without moving the hand from its place on the paper, by the motion of the thumb and two fingers only, and the paper should be moved gradually towards the left hand, by the fore and middle fingers of the left hand, and the paper should be compressed, kept steady and square before the writer, by the same two fingers of the left hand; then after the pupil has learned to hold his pen and move it in any direction by his thumb, fore and middle fingers, of his right hand, and has made a few strait but sloping marks, and also, some with regular turnings, resembling the upward hair-strokes, of the h, m, n, &c. then let him proceed to the moving his pen, without any ink in it, over two or three of the first letters in the alphabet, then let him try to make them according to copy; in this method let him use several sheets of paper, untill he has in this method learned from observation, and absolute practice to begin and make all the letters in the alphabet, then let his chief exercise be to make all the letters in the alphabet, using for his coppy pretty full and large letters, engraved on paper, with a copper plate, for I think for the most part these coppeys should be used for the convenience of the teacher, and for the good of the school and profit of the learner, for I must believe that the pupil will, in this method, much sooner have regular and fixed ideas of the perfect shapes or figures of the letters, than he could from the best and most numerous coppys, wrote by the most expert teachers, for they will vary the shapes of letters, aud do not write always alike, and beside much loss will be experienced by the employers by the change of teachers, if each teacher is as they say, to set all the coppys, but if copper plate coppys be only used, then those inconveniences will be dispenced with—After the pupil has learned to write all the letters well, then he may be learued the method of joining them, then a little time may be spent to learn to join syllabels, then words, and afterward sentences may be written, but all these exercises should be after large hand copper-plate coppys, then a few days before the pupil is to quit his daily writing exercises, and before he undertakes to learn arithmetick and book-keeping, he should be learned to make all the figures and should be well versed in the art of writing correctly, without the use of rule or plummet.

After the scholar has learned to read & write well, perhaps it may be suitable that he be taught Arithmetic; but in this art also, as in all others, it ought to be the care of the teacher, to make every circumstance attending the pupil while he is endeavoring to learn, as agreeable to him as possible, and let him know and understand each rule, (and if it be not plain enough in the printed book, let the teacher explain, and illustrate it with easy and self-evident examples,) before the pupil attempt to proceed and always let the pupil well understand one branch of an art before he be exercised in another; and thus rule after rule, should be well explained, and the pupil should know the nature of the rule, and reasons why he is to do thus, and thus, in these methods. I conceive that the teachers would save themselves much trouble, and also the pupil would advance much faster in arithmetical knowledge than in the old methods, which are vexatious to the teacher, and unprofitable to the learner; while the teacher is employing a great part of his time to look over the sums as it is expressed; and thus it seems the teacher has to learn his pupil by shewing him exactly how to proceed in each new sum; when on the contrary, if a pupil was to understand the rules, he might set sums for himself; ask and answer questions in this art, and thus have it much better fixed in his mind and learn the art in a much shorter time.

Arithmetic.

Book-keeping.

§ 76. Common plain book-keeping, shuld no doubt be leaned immediately after the pupil is well versed in Arithmetic, because, the practice of keeping a regular book of accounts, is of so much more importance in our course through life, than perhaps the knowledge of any other art which has been taught instead of it; and next after arithmetic, and because it seems to have a strict connection with the art of numbers.

This art should, no doubt, be learned by girls as well as boys, for it seems to be of as much importance for farmers wives and daughters, to understand book-keeping as it is for the farmers themselves, or for their sons, since the charging of articles delivered, and the crediting articles received, seem to come more in the way of a farmers wife and daughter, than in the way of himself or his sons. And these observations also will hold good in many instances applicable to the merchants and mechanics; and these same reasons may be urged for to make appear the absolute necessity of educating girls with as much care & attention yea, more than is to be taken to educate boys; as the care in the educating children is more necessarily entrusted to the women, than to the men, since they are for the most part frequently from home and at a distance from their children, while the children are almost hourly in the presence of their mothers, who, if they have been well educated themselves, are capable of improving many opportunities for instructing their children in the arts and sciences, and also in the practice of virtue.

§ 77. The best and most expeditious methods of

Language. } learning any language are by attending to the very words that are daily used by any one that understands the language, thus, if a parent wishes for his child to learn French, Dutch, Spanish or any of those languages that are termed living languages; let him or her live with some sober and discreet person, which understands the language proposed, and who makes use of said language on all occasions and of no other. Thus a child may learn a language with a very little or no expence, while others are employing the chief part of their useful hours in each day, for years and at a great expense in the old traditionary methods of learning from books.

The dead languages may doubtless be learned in a much shorter time, and for much less expence by a strict attention to books, that are printed in the already known language, and in the language proposed to be learned either word against word in columns in contrast, or sentence against sentence; and thus perhaps any language may be learned by a young person of a sound mind, if he will read in such books only, and with a persevering attention, and if he will endevor to fix in his memory a very few words in each day, and especially such words which stand for the real objects of his dayly attention.

Moreover the language that each person has most occasion for should be most critticllay attended to, and no doubt, the prevailing custom of teaching Children the correct grammar of the toungue most in use in any country, is both reasonable and covenient, and likewise very profitable. Therefore the language should be first learned, and then the grammar of it.

Music. § 77. The prevailing (pretended religious,) custom of denying to Children the use of some one or more instruments of music, I think is very unreasonable, unscriptural, and so far from having a good effect on Childrens minds, that I think that quite the reverse from what is intended takes place viz. The child which is made to believe, that the loving parent of mankind has forbid to man the lawful & temperate use of those creatures, which are good and suitable for the use of man; I think that such restraints serves to increase the natural hatred in the human heart against the divine being, and the multiplication of crosses as I may say which the scriptures do not enjoin, is one way to serve and please satan instead of serving the all wise powerful and loving creator and preserver of all worlds.

I have no doubt but music, either instrumental or vocal, would be very useful in each family, it would no doubt be a means of preventing much vain and unprofitable conversation, and likewise much jarring and contention. Musick resembles the exercise of the Blisful Hosts above, who are according to the scriptures employed in sounding forth praises, and in using golden harps, it is also said of them, that they sung a new song, and no man could learn that song excepting those which were redeemed from among men, and again it is said of them, *Revelation*, xv. 3, "*And they sing the song of Moses, the servant of God and the song of the lamb, &c.* See also Psal. cl. 1. *Praise ye the Lord; praise God in his sanctuary; praise him in the Firmament of his power.*

2. *Praise him for his mighty acts; praise him according to his excellent greatness.*

3. *Praise him with the sound of the trumpet; praise him with the Psaltery and harp.*

4. *Praise him with the timbrel and dance; praise him with stringed instruments and organs.*

5. *Praise him upon the loud cimbals, praise him upon the high sounding cymbals.*

6. *Let every thing that hath breath, praise the Lord, praise ye the Lord.*

But lest I should be misunderstood, I shall here observe that I do not think it any way suitable for parents or tutors, to encourage or allow Children (neither do I think it right for grown persons,) to go to those schools of satan viz. Froliks for almost every exercise in them, is condemned in the scriptures of truth, such as revelling chambering wantonness, profaneness, gluttony, drinking to excess, &c. but it seems that music has become so rare, and so much has been said against the use of instruments of musick, that it is not to be heard except a rewaad is given to the mu sition, but if Children were suffered to use such instruments as they would choose at home, and if it was a prevailing custom for instrumental or vocal music, to be heard in each house, or by every family, and other circumstances being made agreeable by parents or tutors, about Children at their homes, then but very few of them would wish to go abroad into evil company to hear music, or to learn their pernicious and evil ways.

Themes. } § 78. Children should not be burthened with too many rules, nor be obliged to learn whole pages from the most approved authors, nor should they be obliged to form themes in manuscript for to be read in public, especially on subjects they do not understand, nor in any one language they are endeavouring to learn, nor before they have fully learned it.

But some particular sentences which contain some special rules for their conduct through life, either literary moral or divine may be learned.

§ 80. All children should be instructed deligently in the principles of true religion, and let these instruc-

Religion. } tions be such as agree with their capacity, and such as are calculated to excite love in them to the Divine Being, and to all his requrements which are the most reasonable suitable, and the best calculated for the present happiness of all human creatures, who are in possession of it, even in this transitory world ; none beside the only wise creator, either in heaven or in earth, was capable of forming such wise and good laws, so suitable to the nature of man, in all states and conditions of life : I have no dout but all those who are in possession of this pearl of great price, the one thing needful, the real presence of the spirit of God, (which is styled love,) in the heart and soul, which flows out towards God, his laws, and towards the true followers of Jesus Christ. I say whoever has thus tasted that the Lord is gracious, would choose to love God with full purpose of Heart, rather than serve sin, and Satan, if there was no Heaven nor Hell. He can truly say according to the scriptures that good understanding giveth favor; but the way of the transgressor is hard and he is ready to say, like the inspired psalmist David, in the XIX Psalm, after speaking of the law, testimonys, statutes, commandments, fear and the judgments of the Lord, said, they are true and righteous altogether.

More to be desired are they than gold, yea, than much fine gold; sweeter also than honey and the honey-comb.

Moreover by them is thy servant warned: and in keeping of them there is great reward.

The practice of obliging children to learn chatechisms, creeds and lengthy prayers by heart, as if all their duty consisted in these, I must think is not for the benefit of children neither is the highly commended methods of obliging children to hear others pray or read, nor the constraining them to go and attend public worship, contrary to their wishes will be likely to benefit them, but will no doubt be a means of prejudicing their minds against their Creator, and against his requirements. They should be instructed to do to all others, as they would be willing that others should do unto them. They should be taught that God sees and knows all that they think say or do, and that the Lord requires their hearts, & if they attempt to pray the should go by themselves in secret, and express only the true desires of their hearts: some short prayers for little Children which were composed by Dr. Wats, and what is styled the first Chatechism, or the principles of religion, and likewise the scriptural Chatechism, contained in the

Bibliographical Spelling-book. All these may with propriety be learned to Children, and it would be well for them to have these, well fixed in their memories.

Geography. } § 80. Geography is an art, which all who are endowed with common sense, and reason may have some knowledge of, & it will be a very pleasing study for Children, and will be very servisable to them when they become men and women, for I would have both boys and girls well educated, and I think of the two, girls should have the best education, if they are to undertake only a common employment, and more especially does girls ought to be learned to read and understand what they read, and likewise they should be taught the use of the pen, arithmetic and book-keeping, for how often does it hapen that a woman has need of exercising herself in those acts, even if she be only a common farmers wife, and how convenient would it be if the women were well educated for them to learn their Children, and since the Children is chiefly committed to the care of women; I therefore urge it as a reason, why girls should be well educated.

And since I am unwilling in the general to inculcate rules for the education of youth which are singular and are not likely to be beneficial to those who observe them, I will here quote the opinion of the celebrated John Locke verbatim.

"Geography, I think should be begun with." For the learning the figure of the globe, the situation and boundaries of the four parts of the world, and that of particular kingdoms and countries, being only an exercise of the eyes and memory, a child with pleasure will learn and retain them. And this is so certain that I now live in the house with a child. whom his mother has so well instructed this way in geography, that he knew the limits of the four parts of the world, could readily point being asked, to any country upon the globe, or any county in the Map of England; knew all the great Rivers, Promontories, Straits and Bays in the world, and could find the Longitude and Latitude of any place, before he was six years old."

Misrepresentation. § 81. None who have the care of Children, should ever misrepresent real facts to them; nor suffer others who live with, or are in company with them so to do. Therefore those methods of terrifying Children, (if they are a little cross or illhumored,) by telling them of Raw head and bloody bones, fearful sights and aparitions, which they may expect to see in the night time, or if they go into such a dark room, or pass by such a grave-yard in the night time, or go to such a house, which they may suppose has been haunted, &c. nor should any one inform them, that they will be carried of by a stranger which may be present at the time of their crying, and pevishness neither should they be informed that any one tame or harmless beast will hurt or kill them &c. All such methods of terrifying Children ought carefully to be avoided.

On the contrary, Children should be informed, that the chief inconvenience attending those which travel in the night, is they are in some danger of stumbling, or falling, because they are not able so well to see the things in their way, as they might in the day time: Therefore it becomes them to be careful how or where they walk in the dark.

Cruelty. § 82. Children should never be suffered to torture any one creature which they have under their power, such as flies, or insects, birds, or reptiles, &c since those practises are really evil, and beside, if they are suffered to torture harmless animals while they are young, they will thus be habituated to acts of cruelty after they arive to manhood even towards those of their own species.

Imperious-ness. } § 83. Children should never be allowed to contend with, or to rule over each other, according to their strength, or age, but all of them should be obliged to submit to all the reasonable requirements of their parents, tutors, masters or misresses, according to their several stations in life.

Justice. } § 84. Children should be taught to be just in their dealings, one with an other, (for they should be suffered to own some things which they have occasion for,) and they should be instructed how to obtain property lawfully, and how to use those things which they need, after they are in possession of them.

Children should frequently be reminded, that in all cases, and in every circumstance of life, they should do unto others, as they are willing that others should do unto them: This rule is applicable, to all we say or do respecting any human person on the face of the earth, and should never be dispensed with by any one.

Children should not only be told the absolute necessity of being just in their dealing with all, but should be informed of the advantages of being esteemed honest: They should also be informed of the disadvantages of being dishonest; for those who have showed themselves to be of a dishonest temper and disposition, are theirby put under many disadvantages, for who will trust a person a second time, who has once been cheated and defrauded by said person: dishonesty and circumvention, may seem to serve for the present opportunity, but never afterward, those who have knowlege of those dishonest persons will be shy of, oppose and stand in the way of them which have been guilty of such unrighteous acts.

Civility. } § 85. There are two sorts of in-civility; The one a sheepish bashfulness, and the other an unbecomcing negligence and disrespectful behaviour; both which may be avoided by observing this one rule, not to think meanly of ourselves, and not to think meanly of others.

We should teach children all those becoming methods of civility and good breading, according to their age and station, which they may be in need of, whenever they go into the presence of their superiors, inferiors or equals; and these particular habits of civility and good maners should be established in them, while they are under our tuition, and before we suffer them to go among such people; otherwise they will be under the necessity of judging for themselves.

Compassion } § 86. Children should be encouraged in acts of pitty, and tender compassion towards those which are in distress, and in want:—They should be taught liberality, and how to reconcile those acts of charity, which our Creator requires of us, with prudence and economy, according to the scriptures: "*He that hath pity upon the poor, lendeth unto to the Lord; and that which he hath given, will he pay him again, and he that receiveth a righteous man in the name of a righteous man, shall receive a righteous mans reward. As ye have therefore opportunity, do good unto all man, but especially unto them, which are of the household of faith.*"

Prov. xxviii. 27. *He that giveth unto the poor shall not lack: but he that hideth his eyes shall have many a curse.*

Company } § 87. Parents and tutors should be careful to restrain the children committed to their care, from every evil and vicious practice; and in order thus to tutor them, every circumstance about them, should be made agreeable to them, while they are innocently employed, and while they are in the presence of their parents or tutors, so that they may have a love to them and a wish to remain in their company: for this purpose, let all those things which children wish for be granted to them, if they are things which may be easily and lawfully obtained, and if in no case they are likely to injure their bodies or souls, nor no one else of the human race.

All parents and tutors should endeavor to win the affections of the children under their care, so that they may wish to remain in their company, and be ready on all occasions to hearken to their instuctions and willingly obey all their commands.

Children should be suffered to accompany their parents or tutors, when they make friendly visits, and thus the parents may introduce them among such companions as may be of use to them; and therefore it seems that parents and tutors, should visit such people as are well bred, have good principles, and are capable of instructing the ignorant in those ways, which are worthy the pursuit of all those who wish to be useful members of society, faithful citizens, and happy men, either in this present world or in a future state, after these clay-cottages, are dissolving in the cold earth.

Publick Worship. § 88. Parents and tutors would do well to suffer their children to accompany them to places of public worship, for I am of an opinion that all children who are capable of understanding what they hear, should go willingly to some place of public worship, (neither should they be kept at home, because they cannot be dressed so well as some others) for their minds are more susceptible of instruction, and they are more apt to retain in their memories what they hear than adults, and are much more likely to give an earnest heed to what they have heard while young, than they will do when old in sin; and because that light or grace, which hath to all men appeared, is present with them, to send home to their hearts, those instructions they may hear from those preachers, exhorters, or teachers, which they are suffered to hear, I say suffered, because none should be obliged to go to any particular place of public worship, while they are utterly averse to the teacher, which they expect to hear, for in such a case, good instructions will not be well received.

If in every little settlement, there should be some one pious instructor appointed to meet with children and teach them on the Lords day, the fear of the Lord, and what the Lord requires of them, and should diligently instruct them in the principles of religion and good manners, and should likewise endeavor to train them up in those ways which they should go. I have no doubt but the Lord would abundantly bless such laudable pursuits, and would more and more increase the convincing opperations of his grace, and thus we have reason to hope, that children may be restrained from many vicious practices, which they are adicted to, by means of being idle on the Lords day, and thus have their minds much biased in favor of religion and virtue.

In the life of the Rev. John Fletcher, may be found an extract in which is particularised an institution of his, which was complyed with, viz. he the said John Fletcher, advised to have places appointed (the number of which, if I mistake not, was six in one parish) for sunday schools, so that all those children which were in need of instruction, and were employed in the course of the week, so that they had no opportunity of attending on a school on a week day, (which was the case of apprentices and the children of the poorer sort of people) might have an opportunity of being learned to read and to write; and also might be instructed in the principles of religion, and if I mistake not, each teacher was to receive for his reward, one English shilling for his teaching per day.

Tasks and Recreations. § 89. Moreover, I think it will not be amis to urge the parents and tutors of children on all occasion, so to conduct towards them that whatever they wish them to learn may, be made agreeable to them, and whatever they would wish them to avoid, should be made very disagreeable to them, and let all those courses which children are most inclined to pursue while they are children, such as play and other unprofitable diversions, by which their time is wasted, and neither their boddies nor their minds bettered, be enjoined on them as a task separately, so that but one of those uuprofitable exercises be enjoined at one time, and that to be pursued under the eye of the parent, tutor or overseer, appointed for that purpose, to see that the child so employed, persevere without any lengthy intermission in that one exercise, untill he or she shall repeatedly ask for liberty to quit that one exercise, and manifest a wish to do some thing else, &c. as above more particular specified : And on the contrary, let parents and tutors on all occasions, so calculate for those pursuits, which they wish children to be trained up in, that the pursuits be made very agreeable ; so likewise, let the parents and tutors of children on all occasions, remember that the children under their care, are reasonable creatures, and thus should be ready to inform them of all the advantages, that will be likely to result to those who continue in the ways of well doing, and of the particular advantages, which may be reasonably expected from all the arts (which if they can but have the time and opportunity of learning) which they are to be instructed in, and likewise, let parents and tutors, very particularly point out all the dangers and disadvantages, which the ignorant, ill-bred and vicious, are liable to both in this world, and in that which is to come.

Talents. § 90. It is evident that the all wise an merciful Creator, has particularly fitted every rational creature for some noble purpose, by im parting into them some one or more talents or incli nations, which are of use to them, in order to obtain the common necessaries of life, and also which will enable them to do good to their fellow mortals, as accountable creatures, that must one day be called on to give an account to the Judge of the Quick and the Dead, of the improvements they have made, of the advantages they have enjoyed, while remaining in a probationary state.

Moreover it appears highly necessary for all parents and guardians of children, particularly to observe and try by all suitable means, to have a knowledge of the talents or inclinations of the children under their care, even while they are young, so that they may judge for the children what methods it will be most prudent for them to pursue, while employing their children, for the improvement of their bodies or minds, and let the parents who wish their children to do well for themselves and others, and who wish them to succeed in any particular calling, let the child be trained up in that calling which he is most inclined to pursue.

Trades. } § 91. Children and young persons are very unwilling to remain inactive, if they are not employed so as to obtain good to themselves or in doing good to others, they will be employed in doing evil: And although I have so much insisted on the exercise of play, and other unprofitable recreations being enjoined as a task, or as a punishment for some ill deed done; yet I would earnestly recommend to parents and tutors, to employ the children under their care, in such a manner, that they will learn no ill or vicious habits thereby, but let them learn to do such acts as are most likely to be benificial in life, and every exercise which they are to be engaged in, should be a kind of recreation to some other exercise: Thus may every employment be made agreeable; however to youth it will be strictly necessary to learn all rational persons, some one or more trades, so that they may be occasionly employed, and never be under the disagreeable necessity of remaining unemployed, nor of misspending their time with the vain, vicious, and idle pretended gentlemen and ladies, who so far from obtaining estates for themselves in their way of living, or of adding to those which have been amassed by their ancestors, that they are contriving methods to spend them ; and here it may be proper for the parents and tutors, to be engaged in shewing their pupils, (as may be said with a witness) that bad company tends to ruin.

Intricacy of the English language. § 92. Whereas the English language, abounds with many words which are sounded alike, but spelled differently, and also with many letters used, (in by far the greatest part of the words contained in said language,) which are entirely unnecessary, for the spelling of those words by means where of the language has become exceedingly intricate, even to the natives of the North American States, who as yet make use of that language, because no other language has been formed, for their use, instead of the English language, not withstanding, I conceive that a language might be formed for the use of the North American States, from the English language, which would be highly beneficial to them. And although many might object against an attempt like this, yet I am of an opinion, that such an event will take place, and the plan of such a language, regularly deduced from the English language may be published.

Change of Teachers disadvantageous. § 93. In consequence of the intricacy of the English language which is taught in the common schools of North America, and because the teachers of schools, (partly from their own neglects, but chiefly because they act in conformity to the wishes of their employers,) neglect to purchase copperplate coppys for the use of their schools, the frequent change of teachers has occasioned the loss of much money and increased the expenses necessary for the education of youth; and, because no fixed rules for the pronunciation of English words, has been agreed on in consequence of the impracticability of such rules if they were formed, and because it would be imposible for any man to form invariable rules for the division of sillables, and for the pronunciation of the English words in their present form.

Wherefore it seems each teacher employed by the Americans, has in many cases to conform to the fashionable pronunciation of English words, in order to please his employers, and each succeeding teacher may have a different opinion about the fashionable pronunciation of many words, and since said fashion of pronunciation is continually varying and not uniform in any two large towns in North America; therefore I conclude that if the Americans were under the necessity of changing the teachers of their schools once every quarter, (according to the voluntary practice of many school districts in North America,) one half of the money so expended for the education of Children would be lost, beside the unnecessary losses occurring to the Americans by the variation of the shapes of letters which are wrote by the teachers for coppys at different times, and the still greater variation of the forms of letters wrote for coppys by dfferent teachers. Supposeing nothing be reckoned for the disadvantages arising from the different methods in which Children are taught by the different teachers.

The American language how to be formed. § 94. If the Americans were of my opinion, they would make use of a language like the English, but differing from it in some few particulars.

And first, in order to form such a language, a number of new letters will be absolutely necessary: Because there are a number of sounds used in the English language, for which there are no letters used to express, and those sounds have been conveyed to us only by tradition.

Secondly, there should be a regular combination of letters in each word, so as to be expressive of it, each letter should have but one invariable sound, and it should be sounded in all words alike excepting only the vowels, which vary only with respect to what grammarians term quantity, and no quantity need be distinguished but long and short, and this might be understood, if their should be an invariable method of using them in syllabies and words without using the long or short accent.

Should it be asked, how many letters need be added to the roman alphabet, in order to form such an alphabet, by which all the necessary sounds in words may with propriety be expressed; perhaps it will be impossible to give a satisfactory answer, but thus much may be said, as many letters should be added as are absolutely necessary to spell all the sillables words or names used in the language. If it be asked how many letters should be expunged from the roman alphabet? I answer none excepting the long ſ, and that because of its near resemblance to the letter f: Some of the letters should have different names: It would be convenient also, for two of these four letters viz. b, d, p, q, to be omitted, and two other characters added in their stead, having the same names of those letters which might be omitted. The vowels, should always be sounded long, when placed alone or at the right hand of all the consonants in the same sillable; and always short at the left hand of any one or more consonants in the same sillable. There should be two other letters added to express two of the three sounds of the letter a, and c should never be sounded like k, g should never be sounded like j, but it should be always sounded hard; as in hebrew names

Moreover there are many words in the English language which are misspelled, and many words differently spelled but pronounced alike; if I should attempt to form a new language for the Americans, from the English language, I should thus proceed, after having a sufficient number of letters added to the roman alphabet, to express all the necessary sounds to be used in the language; I should have this fixed, as an invariable rule, that all words should be spelled as they are pronounced, and that no two words should have exactly the same meaning, or in other words every sound should have a different meaning.

In order to form this American language, out of the English; I should first select all the words in common use contained in the English language, which are truly spelled according to the above hints; and I should in the next place insert all the misspelled words in one column, and spell those words over again, exactly as they should be pronounced, and at the head of the columns of words spelled in the English method, I would have these words viz. English words erroneously spelled, and at the head of the other column of words, which are to have the same sound, and meaning should be these words, American words truly spelled, by this method, we might teach our Children to pronounce the many misspelled English words in a much shorter time, and consequently learn them to read English books printed according to the old method of spelling, with less expense than we possably could without the addition of these new characters. If then it be found by experience, that the misspelled English words can be sooner learned by the addition of these American words to be truly spelled in contrast with said English words; then it will be highly advantageous for us Americans, to have our, Children educated in the proposed two methods of spelling; and whenever a sufficient number has learned to read the American language, thus to be truly spelled; then no inconvenience need to occur to the Americans if the PRINTERS should choose to print the old books over again which they may easily do, and with much less ink and paper than would be necessary for the printing the same books, in which a much larger number of letters would be necessary to form the words contained in them, and the old books will still be read by those who have been learned to read in the old method of spelling, and the books which may be printed in the new method, can be read by those who have been learned to spell in this new method of spelling. Perhaps some may be ready to enquire what can be done with those words which are sounded alike, but spelled differently.

To which I answer, let the different methods in which these words are spelled, be critically attended to, and let them be pronounced exactly in conformity to the letters which compose them; then if this method should be agreed on, then almost all of these words may with propriety be sounded different from each other without spelling them over again; and those words which cannot be sounded differently by means of pronouncing them as they are spelled (for many words in the English language are spelled exactly alike, are pronounced differently and have different meanings,) should be spelled over again, and have new sounds affixed to them: And those words which have been spelled alike and pronounced alike, should have different sounds according to theirdifferent meanings, and for this last alteration there must be some differentnew sounds agreed on, which sounds have now no meaning affixed to them.

SUPPLEMENT

To the Educational Directory.

ATTENTIVE PUPIL! I have in the preceding part of this treatise, endeavored to advise thy parents, tutors, teachers or guardians, so to accommodate thee with food, cloathing, exercise, recreations and literary instructions, as will be best calculated, according to my opinion, to advance thee to honors, pleasures and a degree of contentment in this world. All those particular instructions to them respecting thy education, are particularly calculated for thy good and well-being, while thou livest in this world. And I have no doubt, if thy parents, tutors, guardians or teachers, should agree with me, and instruct thee according to the methods recommended to them, but thou wilt have reason to conclude, after being thus tutored by them, that it was love and affection in them towards thee, and an earnest wish in them, for thy future welfare, which has induced them to be thus careful about regulating thy actions, and also about advising thee to pursue those ways, which in their opinion, will be best calculated for thy real benefit, both in this world, and in that which thou wilt enter after leaving this stage of action.

When on the contrary, if they had suffered thee to pursue those things which thou wast most in love with, and if they had conformed to all thy wishes, then thou wouldest have been poor and miserable, yea despised and neglected, by those who are wise, learned and honorable. What advantage canst thou expect from idleness, or from those plays, which the mean and ignorant employ themselves in?

Canst thou reasonably expect to obtain food, or cloathing, or any of the conveniences of life, by means of such plays?

But if thou shalt in future, be in love with thy spelling, and other books, and shall use thy best endeavors, by spelling repeatedly all those words, or names, which thou hast not learned to read with precision and dispatch, until thou shalt be thus qualified to read them with pleasure, and expeditiously in any book; thy pleasures while thus employed, will very far exceed the pleasures of those, who are associating with the vain, vicious, wicked and ignorant; and while they are wasting their time, and spending their strength, in those pursuits which will not profit them, thou mayest pursue thy studies with pleasure; their exercises are fatigueing, disagreeable and unsatisfying, to well instructed children.

Moreover thou art to expect an increase of literary pleasure, as thou increasest in lerarning, and thy usefulness will also be increased as thy knowledge increaseth, if thou dost but make a good and right use of literary acquirements.

All the liberal sciences may be learned by those who have common sense and reason, and who prudently improve their time, while they are under the care and tuition, of those who are capable of teaching them. Science is knowledge, learning, and skill; properly that which is founded upon clear, certain and self-evident principles.

Do but consider my beloved pupil, how much better it will be for thee, to be endeavoring to learn all those arts and sciences, which thou art likely to have occasion for, than to be wasting thy time in those pursuits, which will do thee no good, and which will be likely to procure to thee much evil, poverty, want and disgrace. While we are endeavoring to learn any art, we should diligently consider all the advantages which we may reasonably expect by means of learning it; theretore, we should first endeavor to learn that art or science, which we have most need of, &c. and diligently improve the time allotted us, for our improvement.

Each one of us are composed of a body and a soul; each of which has its proper powers, parts or faculties, and it seems that our wise Creator, has qualified each of us, for a noble end and purpose, therefore it becomes each one of us who are capable, critically to observe those lawful and just inclinations, which are implanted in us by our Creator for the lawful obtaining the common necessaries of life, and for the general good of mankind;—for according to the faculties, or talents, which the Lord hath given us, so will he require us to act in this world; and by thus acting, we shall be using the most likely means for our honest, comfortable and decent maintenance while on earth: and in these pursuits if guided and led by the blessed spirit of Jesus Christ abiding in us, we shall partake of unspeakable happiness, in the present time.

Our bodies need daily new supplies of food, and constant defence against innumerable dangers from without, by cloathing, shelter and other conveniences. The charge of it, is therefore committed to a soul, endued with forethought, and sagacity, which is by far the noblest part in our constitution. The parts or powers of the soul, are all reducible to two classes, viz. the understanding, and will. The understanding contains all the powers which aim at knowledge: the will, all our desires, pursuing happiness, and shunning misery.

The seven liberal Sciences, are such as are noble and genteel, viz. Arithmetic, Grammar, Rhetoric, Music, Logic, Geometry, and Astronomy.

Arithmetic is a Science, which enables those who understand it, to account, and determine the value of several particulars, enumerated in an account of trade, or traffic, and all the powers and properties of numbers.

Grammar is an art, which enables those who understand it, to speak or write a language truly: or as some have expressed it, the Science of letters, or the art of writing, and speaking, properly and syntactically.

Rhetoric, is the art of speaking well and eloquently.

Music, is one of the Sciences termed liberal or genteel, belonging to the Mathematics, which considers the number, time and tune of sounds, in order to make delightful harmony; or the art of singing and playing on all sorts of musical instruments.

Logic is the art of thinking, reasoning, or making a right use of the rational or reasoning faculties.

Geometry, originally signified the art of measuring the earth, or any dimensions on, or within it; but now it is used, for the science of extension, abstractedly considered without any regard to matter.

Astronomy is a Science, which teaches the knowledge of the heavenly bodies, or Sun, Moon, Stars, &c. shewing their magnitudes, distances, order and motion.

Whenever thou hast learned to read all books correctly, and to write an eligible hand, endeavor to improve every opportunity thou hast, in committing to memory, words and their explanations, and for this purpose, it would be well for thee to select such words with their explanations, which thou wilt have the most need of, from some judicious compilation, or most approved dictionary, and write them in a book for thine own use, and commit a certain number of them to memory each day, or a small number at each time of learning them.

This rule will hold good, whenever thou shalt have occasion to learn, any particular sentence, or number of sentences, in any book; commit it or them to writing, and endeavor to learn only one line, or a line and a part, or at most, not more than two lines at a time, &c.

By these methods, thou wilt learn much faster, and remember those words or sentences of words much longer than thou wouldest, by learning large numbers or lengthy sentences; and after thou hast in part forgotten them, then thou canst find them in thy book, ready for thy re-perusal.

How canst thou understand words or sentences, in any book without first learning the meaning of those words which compose them? Now is the the time for improvement, while thou art suffered to go to school, and while thou art young, and before thou art obliged to pursue any regular employment, for thine own maintenance, or for the maintenance of any one, or more of those who will have a right to command thee to leave off thy studies, lay by thy books, and go to work, either in the field or shop.—Then thou wilt be denied the priviledges which thou now enjoyest. And if thou shouldest be suffered to take thy books or other instruments in hand, for improvement, thou wilt find it more and more difficult, to improve or increase in learning; because thy opportunities will be more and more shortened, and thy mind, as thou encreasest in years, will be more and more taken off from literary pursuits and improvements, and will be employed about devising means for thine own or others maintenance: therefore, now is thy time to advance in learning for thy literary advances, will be ever after more and more difficult.

Never waste or spend thy time in idleness or in any one exercise, which will never profit thyself nor any one else, for thy Creator and Judge, " *Will bring every work into judgment, with every secret thing, whether it be good, or whether it be evil.*" " *see Ecclesiastes, Chap. xii.* 14.

Never, therefore, shouldst thou speak contrary to the meaning of thine heart, by way of jest or in a fabulous manner. I advise thee to neglect reading all fables, lies and false sayings, in whatever book thou mayest find them printed. Neither shouldest thou ever keep company, with those children or grown persons, who speak ill or prophane language; nor with those who frequently employ themselves in vain jesting, joking, lying, or obscene speaking; nor with any one who willingly or wilfully disobey, any of the commands of the Lord thy God.

Moreover for thy directory in pronunciation, observe, while thou art pronouncing,

1. If thou accentest the most suitable syllable, in any word or name, then all the other syllables, in the same word, or name, may be easiest heard and understood.

2. While spelling those words or names which thou hast not learned the true pronunciation of, mind so to divide them into sallables, that thy spelling and pronunciation may perfectly agree.

N. B. The full accented syllyble in any word or name, is always to be sounded loudest.

Since it is indispensably necessary, for all those who can read and write, to understand, besides the true meaning of words, all the parts of speech, how to arrange them in sentences, and how to divide sentences and subdivide them; I have, therefore, here added some necessary hints concerning them, which will be exemplified in the following epitomal grammar.

In the English, or American Languages, there are ten kinds of words, or parts of speech, viz. Articles, Nouns, Adjectives, Pronouns, Verbs, Participles, Adverbs, Conjunctions, Prepositions, and Interjections.

An *Article*, is a part of speech set before nouns to fix their vague, or not established signification; as a man, the man, the tree, the house, the city, &c. An inch, an inlet, an inventory, &c. the article *an* is to be used before those nouns, which are begun with a vowel.

A *Noun* or *Substantive*, is the name of any person, place or thing; as Peter, or James, Philadelphia, Boston, Honor, Fame, Disgrace, Holiness, Unholiness, &c.

Nouns are distinguished by two numbers: viz. the *singular*, which specifies one; as a man, a dog, a tree, a troop: the *plural* which is expressive of two or more; as men, dogs, trees, troops, &c.

Nouns expressive of living animals, are either of the *Masculine** or *Feminine* † gender ‡ those of the masculine gender, denote the he kind, as a man, a prince, &c. and those of the Feminine gender; those of the she kind, as a woman, a princess, &c. nouns signifying things without life, are properly of no gender, as a pen, a table, &c.

Nouns of the Masculine, and Feminine genders are thus expressed.

Masculine.	*Feminine.*
1. ab-bot	1. ab-bess
1. ac-tor	1. ac-tress
2. a-dul-te-rer	2. a-dul-te-ress
2. am-bas-sa-dor	2. am-bas-sa-dress
4. ad-min-is-tra-tor	4. ad-min-is-tra-trix
1. bar-on	1. bar-on-ess
1. bach-e-lor	maid
boar	sow
boy	girl
1. bride-groom	bride
1. broth-er	1. sis-ter
Buck	doe
bull	cow
1. bul-lock	1. heif-er
cock	hen
count	1. countess
duke	dutch-ess
dog	bitch
1. dea-con	1. dea-con-ess
drake	duck

* From *mas*, the male kind.
† From *femina*, a woman.
‡ From *genus*, a sex, or kind.

N. B. A figure at the left hand of any word which is divided, is expressive of the accented syllable, in said word.

Masculine.	*Feminine.*
2. e-lec-tor	2. e-lec-tress
2. ex-ec-u-tor	2. ex-ec-u-trix
1. em-pe-ror	1. em-press
1. fath-er	1. moth-er
1. fri-ar	nun
1. gov-ern-or	gov-ern-ess
1. gan-der	goose
1. hus-band	wife
horse	mare
heir	1. heir-ess
1. hun-ter	1. hun-tress
jew	1. jew-ess
king	queen
lord	1. la-dy
lad	lass
1. li-on	1. li-on-ess
1. mas-cu-line	1. fem-i-nine
1. mar-quis	1. mar-chi-o-ness
man	1. wom-an
1. mas-ter	1. mis-tress
1. mil-ter	1. spaw-ner
1. ne-phew	niece
prince	1. prin-cess
proph-et	1. proph-et-ess
po-et	1. po-et-ess
pat-ron	1. pat-ron-ess
ram	ewe
son	1. daugh-ter
stag	hind
1. shep-herd	1. shep-herd-ess
1. tutor	1. tu-tor-ess
1. vis-count	2. vis-coun-tess
1. un-cle	aunt
1. wid-ow-er	1. wid-ow
1. wiz-ard	witch

Nouns have two cases, viz. the nominative [or naming] and the genitive case, which betokeneth property, or the possession of it, as men's women's, &c.

An Adjective is a word, which signifies the quality or nature of any person, place or thing; as a good man, a bad man, a great city, a small city, a fine house or a mean house, &c

There are three states, or conditions of an Adjective, viz. the positive, the comparative and superlative.

1. The positive is the simple and absolute state of the Noun, without referring to it in any other circumstance.

2. The comparative is that state or condition of the Noun when

its quality is somewhat increased or diminished, and it is formed by adding *r*, or *er*, to the positive.

3 The superlative is that state, or condition of the noun when its quality is mentioned in its highest, or lowest degree, and it is formed by adding *st* or *est* to the positive.

These degrees of comparison are frequently formed by the adverbs, very, infinitely, more, most, less, least, as more short, very short, most short, infinitely short; less common, least common, &c.

There are a few Adjectives, which are peculiar in their comparison, as good, better, best; bad, worse, worst, &c.

A Pronoun is a word used instead of a noun, to avoid the too frequent repetition of the same word, or of said noun ; as the man is merry, he laughs, he sings, instead of saying the man laughs, the man sings, &c.

The following pronouns (*it* only excepted), have three cases; viz. a *nominative, a †genitive and an ‡accusative case.

Singular.	*Plural.*
Nominative I	we
Genitive, mine, my	ours
Accusative, me,	us.
Nominative, thou	ye, you.
Genitive, thine, thy	yours, your.
Accusative, thee,	you.

SINGULAR.

Nominative.	*Genitive.*	*Accusative.*
he	his	him
she	hers, her	her
it	its	

PLURAL.

Nom.	*Gen.*	*Acc.*
they	theirs, their	them

* or naming.

† or possessive,

‡ From *Accuso*, to accuse, because this case requires the ce or accusatton of the verb.

Who, whosoever, and the pronominal adjectives, oné, other and another, are thus varied.

SINGULAR.		PLURAL.
Nominative,	thou	ye, you
Genitive,	thine, thy	yours, your
Accusative	thee	you

SINGULAR.

Nominative.	*Genitive.*	*Accusative.*
he	his	him
she	hers, her	her
it	its	

PLURAL.

Nom.	*Gen.*	*Accu.*
they	theirs, their	them

Who, whosoever, and the pronominal adjectives, one, other, and another, are thus varied :—

SINGULAR AND PLURAL.

Nominative.	*Genitive.*	*Accusative.*
who	whose	whom
whose	3. who-so-e-ver	3. whom-so-e-ver

SINGULAR.		PLURAL.
Nom	*Gen.*	
one	ones	ones
1. oth-er	oth-ers	
2. an-oth-er	an-oth-er	1. oth-er, oth-ers

The following have these variations.

SINGULAR.	PLURAL.
this	these
that	those
myself, ones-felf,ourself	ourselves
thyself, yourself	yourselves
himself, herself, itself	themselves

Those which follow, are further distinguished by their genders.

Masculine.	*Feminine.*	*No Gender*
he	she	it
his	hers	its
him	her	
himself	herself	itself

Pronominal adjectives, or such adjectives as partake of the nature of nouns, such as ten, eleven, twenty twenty-one, twenty-two, thirty, thirty-one, &c. fifty, sixty, seventy, eighty, ninety-ninety-three, &c. those of them which are expressive of one or more numbers of tens, seem to have a genitive case regularly formed by adding *s* to the nominative case thus ; ten tens ; twenty twenties.

A verb, is a word or part of speech, which is expressive of the acting or of the being of any person, any place, or any thing ; as the man calls, speaks, or sings, the city stands, or remains, the tree grows, stands, or falls.

The verb which signifies only being or existance, is a neuter verb, as I am, he is ; verbs which signify any kind of action, are termed active verbs ; as I speak, I write, I love, I hate, &c.

The noun or pronoun which stands before the active verbs in the above examples, may be called the agent, or actor, and that noun or pronoun which stands before the neuter verb, the subject of the neuter verb ; but the noun or pronoun which follows the active verbs, is called the object of the active verb.

There are four modes, * or methods of using the verbs ; the indicative, the imperative, the potential, and the infinitive.

The indicative † expresses the action or being, directly, and absolutely ; as I am, he loves, he walks, he runs, &c.

The imperative ‡ mode is expressive of command or anthority, and therefore is used to command or forbid ; as come, go, fear him, love him, serve him, &c.

The potential || expresses the action or being, as possible, or impossible, fit or unfit ; as I may love, I may walk, I may not love, I may not walk, &c.

The infinitive (*a*) expresses the action or being indeterminately ; as, to love, to hate, to be.

There are five tenses, or times ; the present, the imperfect, the perfect, the pluperfect, and the future.

---

* From *modus*, a manner.

† From *indico*, to show.

‡ From *impero*, to command.

|| From *potentialis* (*a possum*,) to be able.

(*a*) From *infinitivus* without bounds.

A

The present, expresses the time that now is; as I love, I hate, or I am loving, I am hating, &c.

The impertect denotes the time past indeterminately: as I loved, or was loving; or was hating, etc.

The perfect tense or time, is the past determinately; as I have loved, or have been loving.

The pluperfect tense, or time is the time past, as prior (or before) some other point of time specified in the sentence; as I had loved, I had walked; or, I had been loving, or I had been walking, etc.

The future tense denotes the time to come; as I will, or shall love or walk, I will or shall be loving or walking, etc.

A participle (b) is derived of a verb, and partakes of the nature both of the verb and the adjective. The participle, so far as it expresses the circumstance of the noun to which it is joined by the neuter verb, has the nature of an adjective.

There are two participles, pertaining to most verbs; the active participle which always ends in *ing*, and the passive participle which for the most part, ends in *ed*, as from the verb call, are derived the participles calling, and called; and also from the verb love, are derived the participles loving, loved.

If a verb ends in a single consonant preceeded by a single vowel bearing the accent, one more consonant of the same name is to be added; as commit, committing, committed, etc.

An Adverb * is a part of speech, joined to a verb, it is joined also to an adjective and sometimes to a participle yea, and sometimes to another adverb, to express the quality, or circumstance of a verb, an adjective, a participle, or an adverb; as he reads well; a truly good man; he is secretly plotting; he writes very correctly.

The adverbs in the preceding examples are well, truly, secretly: very, and correctly, are both adverbs.

Some adverbs admit of comparison; as often, oftener, oftenest; soon, sooner, soonest; and many of them are compared by the other adverbs, more, most, etc.

Adverbs have relation to time; as now, then, lately, etc. and to place; as here, there, etc. and to number; as once, twice, etc.

A conjunction † is a part of speech which joins words or sentences together; as albeit, although, and, because, but either, else,

---

(b) From *participo*, to partake.

* From *ad* to, and *verbum* a verb, but as implying the action of some agent, it has the nature of the verb.

† From *con* with, and *jungo* to join.

however, if, namely, neither, nor, or though, tho' therefore, thereupon, unless, whereupon, whether, yet.

The foregoing are always conjunctions; but these six following are sometimes adverbs; also, as otherwise, since, likewise, then; except, and save, are sometimes verbs; for, sometimes a preposition; and that, sometimes, a pronoun.

A preposition ‡ is a word or part of speech, set before nouns, or pronouns, to express the relations of persons, places, or things to each other; as he came to, and stood before the city.

Prepositions used in this sense, are such as follow. About, above, after, against, among, amongst, at, before, behind, below, beneath, between, beyond, by, for, from, in, into, of, off, on, upon, over, through, to, unto, towards, under, with, within, without.

An interjection ‡ is a word or part of speech which expresses any sudden emotion of the mind, transported with the sensation of pleasure or pain; as O! Oh! Alas! Lo!

---

‡From *pre* before, and *pono* to place.

‡ From *inter*, between, and *jacio*, to throw.

*SYNTAX.**

SYNTAX shews the agreement, and right disposition of words in a sentence.

The articles *a*, and *an*, are used only before nouns of the singular number; *an*, before a word that begins with a vowel; *a*, before a word that begins with a consonant; *an*, or *a*, before a word, that begins with *h*; as, "*A* christian, *an* infidel, *an* heathen, or *a* heathen." But if the *h* be not sounded, then the article, *an* is only used; as, "*An* hour, *an* herb."

A and *an* are indefinite: as, "*A* man, *a* house; *i. e.* any man, any honse without distinction. But *the* is definite, as, *The* man, *the* house; *i. e.* some one man, some one house in particular.

The is likewise used to distinguish two or more persons or things mentioned before; as *the* men (not the women). *The* senators (as distinguished from the representatives).

The verb ‡ agrees with its nown or pronoun, *i. e.* with its agent, or subject, in number and person; as the boys *write*; I *love*; he who *reads*.

In the complaisant style, it has been common to use *you*, instead of *thou*, when we speak to one person only; and in that case, it has a plural verb joined with it; as, you *are* my brother (properly, *thou art* my brother).

A noun of multitude, of the singular number, may have a vero either singular or plural; as, the people *is* mad; or, the people *are* mad. The latter expression seems to be the more elegant.

When two or more nouns, or pronouns, are connected together in a sentence, as joint agents or subjects, they must have a plural verb, though they should be each of the singular number; as, the man and his wife *are* happy—I and he *were* there—Richard and I *have been* very busy.

Sometimes a sentence, or an infinite mode, is the subject‡ of a verb; and then the verb must be put in the singular number and third person; as, the man and woman, appearing in public, *was* the cause of my going—to see the sun *is* pleasant.

When the agent and object of a verb are not distinguished (as in nouns) by different cases, the agent is always set before, and

* From *Syntaxis*, a joining.

‡ This agent, or subject, is always found by asking the question *who*, or *what*, on the verb; as, *who* write? the answer to the question, is *boys*; which word is the agent of the verb, *write*.

the object after the verb; this being the natural order, and necessary to determine the sense; as, *Alexander* conquered *Darius*. If Darius had been conqueror, it is plain that the order of the nouns must have been inverted.

The agent or subject is most commonly set immediately before the verb, or the sign of the verb; as, the *man* lives—the *city* hath stood a thousand years. In the imperitive mood, however, it is set after the verb; as, love *thou*—be *thou* happy. Also, when a question is asked, it is set after the verb, or between the sign and the verb; as, are *you* there?—doth the *king* live?

The pronouns *I*, *we*, *thou*, *ye*, *he*, *she*, *they* and *who*, are always used when they stand as the agent of an active, or the subject of the neuter verb; as, *I* see—*he* loves—*we* are—*they* go—that is the person who passed us yesterday.

The noun, or pronoun, which receives the force of the active verb, is most commonly set after the verb; as I love the *man*. But the relative, *whom*, or *whomsoever*, is always set before the verb; as, the man *whom* I love, is absent.

The accusative case of a pronoun is always used when it receives the force, or impression of the active verb, or active participle, or comes after the infinitive mode of the neuter verb; as, he calls *me*—she is beating *them* —I suppose it to be *him*.

When a pronoun is set alone in answer to a question, or follows the present or imperfect tense of the neuter verb, it must be put in the nominative case; as who did it? *me*, i. e. I did it—I was *he* that said so.

The passive participle, and not the past tense, should be always used when joined in a sentence with the neuter verb; as, it was *written* (not it was *wrote*) in Hebrew.

That form of the tenses in verbs, which is distinguished by the active participle is used with strict propriety when we would express the continuance of an action; as, I *have been writing* a long time—I *shall be writing* all the week.

The auxiliary signs, *do* and *did*, and their inflections, *dost*, *doth* or *does*, and *didst*, ought to be used only for the sake of emphasis; as, I *do* love—he *did* go.

Shall is used in the first person, barely to express the future action or event; as, I *shall* do it: but in the second and third, it promises, or commands; as, you *shall* do it. On the contrary, *will*, in the second and third persons, barely expresses the future action, or event; as, you *will* do it: but in the first it promises, or threatens; as, I *will* do it.

The terminations, *eth*, *ed*, and the participial form of the verb, are used in the grave and formal style; but *s*, *'d*, and the form of the past tense, in the free and familiar style; as (gravely), he *hath loved*—the man *hath spoken*, and still *speaketh*—(familiarly) he *has lov'd*—the man *has spoke*, and still *speaks*.

When two nouns come together with the preposition *of* between them, denoting possession, the latter may be made the genitive case, and set before the other; as, the property *of* the men—the *men's* property.*

Pronouns must always agree with the nouns for which they stand, or refer, in number, person and gender; as, the *sun* shines, and *his* race is appointed to him—the *moon* appears, and *she* shines with light, but not *her* own—the *sea* swells, *it* roars, and what can repel its force—*this* man—*these* women.

The neuter pronoun, by an idiom peculiar to the English language, is frequently joined in explanatory sentences with a noun or pronoun of the masculine or femanine gender; as, *it* is *I*—*it* was the *man*, or *woman* that did it.‡

When two or more nouns or pronouns of different persons are joined in a sentense, the pronoun which refers to them, must agree with the first person in preference to the second, and with the second in preference to the third; as, *thou* and thy *father* are both in the same fault, and *ye* ought to confess it—the *Captain* and *I* fought on the same ground, and afterwards *we* divided the spoil, and shared it between *us*.

When two or more nouns, or pronouns of the fingular number are joined together in a sentence, the pronoun which refers to them, must be of the plural number; as, the man and the woman had put on *their* clothes.

The genitive case of a pronoun is always used when joined to a noun to denote property or possession; as, *my* head and *thy* hand—the head of *me*, and the hand of *thee*, are inelegant ezpressions.

The genitive cases of the pronouns, viz. *my*, *thy*, *&c.* are used when joined with nouns; but *mine*, *thine*, *&c.* when put absolutely, or without their nouns; as, it is *my* book; or, omitting the noun, it is *mine*.

The same thing may be observed of *other*, and *others* in the plural number; as, the property of *other* men; or, without the noun, the property of *others*.

Mine and *thine* are frequently put for *my* and *thy*, before a word that begins with a vowel; as, *mine* eye, for *my* eye.†

---

* Nouns of the plural number, that end in *s*, will not very properly admit of the genitive case.

‡ Though this seems to be an indefinite use of the neuter pronoun, as expressive of some cause or subject of enquiry, without any respect to person or gender; yet in strict propriety, it cannot be so used with a noun of the plural number; thus, *It was they* that did it, is an impropriety.

† *Thou* is used to denote the greatest respect; as, O *thou* Most High! and likewise to denote the greatest contempt; as, *thou* worthless fellow!

Pronominal adjectives are only used in the genitive case, when put absolutely; as, I will not do it for *tens* sake.

The adjective is usually set before its substantive; as, the *second* year—a *good* man. Sometimes, however, for better sound's sake, especially in poetry, the adjective comes after its substantive; as, "The genuine cause of every deed *divine*."

When *thing*, or *things* is substantive to an adjective, the word *thing* or *things* is elegantly omitted, and the adjective is put absolutely, or without its substantive; as, who will show us any *good*? for, who will show us any *good thing*?

In many other cases the adjective is put absolutely, especially when the noun has been mentioned before, and is easily understood, though not expressed.

In forming the degrees of comparison, the adverbs, *more*, *most*, *less*, *least*, &c. are only used before adjectives when the terminations, *er*, and *est*, are omitted; as, *more* full—*less* beautiful.

For better sound's sake most adjectives ending in *ive*, *al*, *ful*, *ble*, *ant*, *some*, *ing*, *ish*, *ous*, and some others, must be compared by the adverbs, *more*, *most*, *less*, *least*, &c. "pensive, *more* pensive, substantial, *more* substantial."

When two *persons*, or *things*, are spoken of in a sentence, and there is occasion to mention them over again, for the sake of distinction, *that* is used in reference to the former, and *this* in reference to the latter: as,

"Self-love, the spring of motion, acts the soul;
"Reason's comparing balance rules the whole;
"Man but for *that* no action could attend,
"And but for *this* were active to no end."

That refers both to persons and things: as "The man *that* I respect; the thing, *that* I want, is not here."

The relative pronoun, *who*, *whose*, or *whom*, is used, when we speak of persons *only*; *which*, when we speak of things, or want to distinguish one of two, or more persons or things: as, "I am bound to respect a *man*, *who* has done me a favour; though he be chargable with *vices*, *which* I hate; *which* of the men? *which* of the roads will you chuse?

Who and *what* also are used in asking questions: *who*, when we inquire for a man's name; as, "*who* is that man? *what* when we would know his occupation, &c. as, "*What* is that man?"

The adverb is always placed immediately before the adjective, but most commonly after the verb; as. "A *very* pious man prays *fuequently*."

The comparative adverbs *than* and *as* with the conjunctions *and*, *nor*, *or*, connect like cases: as, "She loves *him* better *than me*; *John* is as tall *as I*; *he and I* went together; neither *he nor she* came; bring it to *me or her*.

The conjunctions, *if*, *though*, *except*, &c. implying a manifest doubt, or uncertainty, require the subjunctive form of verbs: as, Though he *slay* me, yet will I trust in him; I will not let thee go, except thou *bless* me; kiss the son, lest he be angry; if he but *speak* the word; see thou *do* it not.

Prepositions always govern the accusative case of a pronoun immediately after them; as, To *me*, for *them*, &c.

After verbs of *shewing*, *giving*, &c. the preposition *to*, is elegantly omitted before the pronoun, which notwithstanding must be in the accusative: as, I gave him the book, for, I gave *to* him the book.

The preposition *to*, is always used before nouns of place, after verbs and participles of motion: as, I went *to London*; I am going to town, &c. But the preposition, *at* is always used when it follows the neuter verb in the same case: I have been *at London*; I am at the place appointed. We likewise say, He touch'd, ariv'd, lives, &c. at any place.

The prepositon, *in*, is set before *countries*, *cities* and *large* towns, especially if they are in the same nation: as, He lives *in Boston*, *in Trenton*, &c. *At* is set before villages, single houses, and cities that are in distant countries: as, He lives at *Hackney*, &c.

The interjections, *O*, *Oh*, and *Ah*, require the accusative case of a pronoun in the first person: as, O *me*, Oh *me*, Ah *me*: But the nominative in the second: as, O *thou*, O *ye*.

No exact rules can be given for the placing of all words in a sentence: The easy flow and the perspicuity of the expression are the two things, which ought to be chiefly regarded.

MODES AND TENSES.

[After thou hast learned all the preceding hints respecting the parts of speech, and their arrangement in sentences; and hast an understanding of them, it will be necessary to commit to memory the following distinctions respecting the modes and tenses of verbs. etc.]

These modes* and tenses† are partly formed by the verb itself, and partly by the assistance of signs.

There are two modes formed from the verb itself: The indicative; as, I love; and the imperative; as, *love* thou. And like-

* From *Modus*, a manner or method.

† From *Tempus*, time, a variation of the verd, to distinguish the circumstance of time.

wise two tenses; the present; as, I *love*; and the past; as, I *loved*.

The auxiliary* signs are, *to do*, *did*, *have*, *had*, *shall*, *will*, *may*, *can*, *must*, *might*, *would*, *could*, *should*.

To, is a sign of the infinitive mode: as, *to* be; *to* love.

May, *can*, *must*, *might*, *would*, *could*, *should* and their inflexions,† *mayst*, *canst*, *mightest*, *wouldest*, *couldest*, *shouldest*, are signs of the potential mode.

Do, and its inflections, *dost*, *doth* or *does* are signs of the present tense.

Did, and its infiexons, *didst*, are signs of the imperfect tense.

Have, and its inflexions, *hast*, *hath* or *has*, are signs of the perfect tense.

Had, and its inflexion, *hadst*, are signs of the pluperfect tense.

Shall and will, and their inflexions, *shalt* and *wilt*, are signs of the future tense.

In verbs there is a reference to three persons in each number; as, singular, I *love* thou *lovest*, he *loveth*; plural, we *love*, ye *love*, they *love*. The second person of the verb in the singular number is formed out of the first by adding *est* or *st*; the third by adding *eth*, *th*, *es*, or only *s*.

St is added, instead of *est*, *th* instead of *eth*, to verbs ending in *e*; as love, lov*est*; prove, prove*th*; *es* to such as end in *ss*, *x*, and *o*; as, pass, pass-*es*; fix, fix-*es*; go, go*es*. When *est* or eth is added to a verb ending in a single consonant preceded by a single vowel bearing the accent, that consonant is doubled; as, *forget*, *forgettest*, *forgetteth*.

The first person speaks of himself; as, *I John* take thee Elizabeth.

The *second* person has the speech directed to him, and is supposed to be present; as, *Thou Harry* art a wicked fellow.

The third person is spoken of or described, and supposed to be absent; as, *That Thomas* is a good man.

The verb itself has but two terminations respecting time; as, *love* and *loved*; which last may be called inflexion of the preter or past tense: And when this inflexion of the preter tense is formed by adding *d*, or *ed*, to the person present tense, the verb is regular, and is declined after the following examples.

---

*From *auxilior*, to help.

‡ From *inflecto* to change (the ending.)

NOTE. The auxiliary signs seem to have the nature of adverbs.

Do, *have* and *will*, when they are not joined to verbs to distinguish the circumstance of time, are absolutely verbs: as, I *do* it, I *have* it, I *will* it.

INDICATIVE MODE.

Present Tense.

SINGULAR I love or do love, thou lovest, or dost love, he loveth or loves, or doth or does love. PLU. We love or do love, ye or you love or do love, they love or do love.

Imperfect Tense.

SING. I loved or did love, thou lovedst or didst love, he loved or did love. PLU. We loved or did love, ye loved or did love they loved or did love.

Perfect Tense.

SING. I have loved, thou hast loved, he hath loved. PLU. We have loved, ye have loved, they have loved.

Pluperfect Tense.

SING. I had loved, thou hadst loved, he had loved. PLU. We had loved, ye had loved, they had loved.

Future Tense.

SING. I shall or will love, thou shalt or wilt love, he shall or will love, PLU. We shall or will love, ye shall or will love, they shall or will love.

Some verbs in this mode will admit of a second future, especially such as signify the completing of any thing; as, *I shall or will have finished* to-morrow.

IMPERATIVE MODE.

SING. Love, do thou love, or love thou. PLU. Love, do ye love, or love ye.

POTENTIAL MODE.

Present Tense.

SING. I must, may, can, would, could, or should love, thou must, mayest, canst, wouldest, couldestd, or shouldest love, he must, may, can, would, could, or should love. PLU. We, must, may, can, would, could, or should love, ye, &c.

Perfect Tense.

SING. I must, might, would, could, or should have loved, thou must, mightest, wouldest, couldest, or souldest have loved, he must, might, would, could, or should have loved. PLU. We must, might, would, could, or should have loved, ye, &c.

The pluperfect tense, in this mode, is best expressed by the perfect; as, I *might have* loved her before the time you mention.

The future tense, of most verbs, in this mode, is best expressed by the present; as, I *may love* to-morrow.

There is a subjunctive* or conditional form which drops the personal terminations in certain tenses of this mode; as, though thou *love*, though he *love*.

INFINITIVE MODE.

PRESENT TENSE, to love; PERFECT, to have loved; FUTURE, about to love.

THE DECLENTION OF THE NEUTER VERB.

INDICATIVE MODE.

Present Tense.

SING. I am, thou art, he is. PLU. We are, ye or you are, they are.

Imperfect Tense.

SING. I was, thou wast, he was. PLU. We were, ye were, they were.

Perfect Tense.

SING. I have been, thou hast been, he hath or has been. PLU. We have been, ye have been, they have been.

Pluperfect Tense.

SING. I had been, thou hadst been, he had been. PLU. We had been, ye had been, they had been.

Future Tense.

SING. I shall or will be, thou shalt or wilt be, he shall or w be. PLU. We shall or will be, ye shall or will be, &c.

Second Future.

SING. I shall or will have been, &c.

IMPERATIVE MODE.

SING. Be, do thou be, or be thou. PLU. Be, do ye be, or be ye.

---

* From *sub*, under, and *jungo*, to join.

POTENTIAL MODE.

Present Tense.

SING. I must, may, can, would, could, or should be, thou must, mayest, canst, wouldest, couldest, or shouldest be, he, &c. PLU. We must, may, can, would, could, or should be, ye, &c.

Perfect and Pluperfect Tenses.

SING. I must, might, would, could, or should have been, thou must, mightest, wouldest, couldest, or shoudest have been, he must, might, would, could, or should have been. PLU. We must, might, would, could, or should have been, ye, &c.

The future tense in this mode, is best expressed by the present; as, I *may be* to-morrow.

The subjunctive form of this verb is thus distinguished;

Present Tense.

SING. Though I be, though thou be, though he be. PLU. though we be, though ye be, though they be.

Imperfect Tense.

SING. Though I were, though thou wert, though he were. PLU. Though we were, though ye were, though they were.

INFINITIVE MODE.

PRESENT, to be; PERFECT, to have been; FUTURE, about to be.

When the termination of the preter tense is not formed by addidg *d* or *ed*, to the first person of the present tense singular, the verb may be called irregular; but that irregularity being disco . - ered and observed in the preter tenses, the verb is declined in all other respects, as the regular verb.

The most common irregularity is when the *d* or *ed*, for better sound's sake, is changed into *t*; and this is, for the most part, the case, when the verb itself ends in *f, p*, and *x*: as *puft*, *wrapt*, and *mixt; for puffed*, *wrapped*, *mixed*, &c.

NOTE. The same irregularity, or contraction, frequently occurs in verbs of other terminations.

GRAMMATICAL ABBREVIATIONS.

A. Article—*N*. Noun—*Adj*. Adjective—*P*. Pronoun—V. Verb —*Par*. Participle—*Ad*. Adverb—*Con*. Conjunction—*Pre*. Preposition—*Int*. Interjection—*Nom*. Nominative—*Gen*. Genitive—*Acc*. Accusative—*Ind*. Indicative—*Imp*. Imperative—*Pot*. Potential—*Inf*. Infinitive—*M*. Mode—*S*. Sign—*S.in*. Sign of the indicitive mode—*S.i.m.* Sign of the imperitive mode—*S.p.m.* Sign of the potential mode—*S.i.m.* Sign of the infinitive mode—*S.pr.t.* Sign of the present tense—*S.i.t.* Sign of the imperfect tense—*S.p.t.* Sign of the perfect or past tense—*S.pl.t.* Sign of the pluperfect tense—*S.f.t.* Sign of the future tense.

GRAMMATICAL PARTS OF SPEECH EXEMPLIFIED.

GEN. XLV. 1, &c.

Then	Ad.	unto	Pre.
Joseph	Sub.	his	P.
could	S.p.m.	brethren	Sub.
not	Ad.	*VERSE* 2.	
refrain	V.	And	C.
himself	P.	he	P.
before	Pre.	wept	V.
all	Adj.	aloud	Ad.
them	P.	and	C.
that	P.	the	A.
stood	V.	Egyptians	Sub.
by	Pre.	and	C.
him	P.	the	A.
and	C.	house	Sub.
he	P.	of	Pre.
cried	V.	Pharaoh	Sub.
cause	V.	heard.	V.
every	Adj.	*VERSE* 3.	
man	Sub.	And	C.
to	S.i.m.	Joseph	Sub.
go	V.	said	V.
out	Ad.	unto	Pre.
from	Pre.	his	P.
me	P.	brethren	Sub.
and	C.	I	P.
there	Ad.	am	V.
stood	V.	Joseph	Sub.
no	Adj.	doth	S.p.t.
man	Sub.	my	P.
with	Pre.	father	Sub.
him	P.	yet	Ad.
while	Ad.	live	V.
Joseph	Sub.	and	C.
made	V.	his	P.
himself	P.	brethren	Sub.
known	Par.	could	S.p.m.

not	Ad.
answer	V.
him	P.
for	C.
they	P.
were	V.
troubled	Par.
at	Pre.
his	P.
presence.	Sub.

VERSE 4.

And	C.
Joseph	Sub.
said	V.
unto	Pre.
his	P.
brethren	Sub.
come	V.
near	Ad.
to	Pre
me	P.
I	P.
pray	V.
you	P.
and	C.
they	P.
came	V.
near	Ad.
and	C.
he	P.
said	V.
I	P.
am	V.
Joseph	Sub.
your	P.
brother	Sub.
whom	P.
ye	P.
sold	V.
into	Pre.
Egypt.	Sub.

VERSE 5.

Now	Ad.
therefore	Ad.
be	V.
not	Ad.
grieved	Par.
nor	C.
angry	Adj.
with	Pre.
yourselves	P.
that	C.
ye	P.
sold	V.
me	P.
hither	Ad.
for	C.
God	Sub.
did	S.i.t.
send	V.
me	P.
before	Pre.
you	P.
to	S.i.m.
preserve	V.
life.	Sub.

VERSE 6.

For	C.
these	P.
two	Adj.
years	Sub.
hath	S.p.t.
the	A.
famine	Sub.
been	V.
in	Pre.
the	A.
land	Sub.
and	C.
yet	Ad.
there	Ad.
are	V.
five	Adj.
years	Sub.
in	Pre.
the	A.
which	P.
there	Ad.
shall	S.f.t.
neither	C.
be	V.
earing	Sub.
nor	C.
harvest	Sub.

It wil be necessary, also, to commit to memory the following Eliptical Omissions of the several parts of speech, and the examples:

ELIPTICAL OMISSIONS, &c.

ELLIPSIS, as applied to grammar, is the omission of some word or words which must be supplied, either to complete the sense, or to make out the grammatical construction of the sentence.

The principal design of Ellipsis is to avoid disagreeable repetitions, as well as to express our ideas in as few words, and as pleasing a manner as possible.

In the application of this figure, great care should be taken to avoid ambiguity; for whenever it obscures the sense, it ought by no means to be admitted.

Almost all compound sentences are more or less elliptical.

The Ellipsis of the Article.

A Man, woman, and child, i. e. [that is] *A* Man *a* woman, and *a* child. *A* Father and son. *The* sun and moon. *The* day and hour.

The Ellipsis of the Noun.

A learned, wise, and good *man*; i. e. A learned *man*, a wise *man*, and a good *man*.

A prudent and faithful, *wife*. The *laws* of God and man. The safety and happiness of the *state*.

The Ellipsis of the Adjective.

A *delightful* orchard and garden, i. e. A *delightful* orchard and a *delightful* garden.

The Ellipsis of the Pronoun.

I love and fear *Him*, i. e. *I* love *Him*, and *I* fear *Him*.

My house and land. *Thy* learning and wisdom, *His* wife and daughter. *Her* Lord and master.

The Ellipsis of the Verb.

The man *was* old and crafty. i. e. The man *was* old and the man *was* crafty.

She *was* young, and rich, and beautiful. Thou *art* poor, and wretched, and miserable, and blind, and naked.

The Ellipsis of the Adverb, Preposition, Conjunction, and Interjection,

He spake and acted *wisely*. They sing and play *most delightfully*. She *soon* found and acknowledged her mistake. *Thrice* I went, and offered my service. That is, *Thrice* I went, and *thrice* I offered my service.

They confessed the power, wisdom, goodness, *and* love of their Creator. i.e. The power, *and* wisdom, *and* goodness, *and* love.

May I speak of power, wisdom, goodness, truth.

The entire ellipsis of the conjunction, as in the last instance, occurs but seldom: In some particular cases however it may have its propriety.

Though I love, I do not adore him. Though he went up, he could see nothing. i. e. Though I love him, *yet* I do not adore him.

I desire you would come to me. He said he would do it. i. e. He said *that* he would do it.

These conjunctions may be sometimes omitted; but, for the most part, it is much better to express them.

There are several *pairs of corespondent conjunctions*, or such as answer to each other in the construction of a sentence, which should be carefully observed, and perhaps never suppressed.

That, answering to *so*. It is *so* obvious *that* I need not mention it.

As answering to *so*. The City of *Bristol* is not near *so* large *as* that of *London*.

So answering to *as*. *As* is the Priest *so* are the People.

As answering to *as* She is *as* tall *as* you.

Nor answering to *neither*. *Neither* the one, *nor* the other.

Or answering to *either*. *Either* this Man *or* that Man.

Or answering to *whether*. *Whether* it were I *or* you.

Yet answering to *though* or *although*. *Though* she was young *yet* she was not handsome.

Prepositions are often suppressed.

He went *into* the Churches, Halls, and the public Buildings: *Through* the Streets and Lanes of the City; He spake *to* every Gentleman and Lady of the Place i.e. *To* every Gentleman and *to* every Lady.

I did him a kindness. He brought me the News. She gave him the Letters. i.e. She gave to him the Letters.

The Ellipsis of the Interjection is not very common.

O Pity, and Shame! *Milton.*

Moreover, it will be very convenient and profitable, for thee to exercise thyself very often, by endeavoring to designate the parts of speech contained in any sentence, which thy teacher or any other scholar may propose to thee; or thou mayest compose, or select sentences for thyself, and endeavour to distinguish the parts of speech according to the preceding method exemplified in the explanations of Joseph's speech to his brethren. Thus wilt thou establish grammatical distinctions in thy mind, and probably attain the advantages, which those possess who understand this necessary, and noble art.

Many are the advantages arising from a complete knowledge of letters, their combinations in words and names, and still greater are the advantages arising to those who can write an eligible hand, and can distinguish without looking on any grammatical book, all the parts of speech in the language which they have most need of, only by inspecting common sentences without a teacher to instruct, and those who are able to write correctly on any subject which they understand, have still greater advantages than either of the preceding pupils.

For those who are thus far instructed, are capable of expressing their thoughts, to those whom they have never seen.

They can send their requests to distant regions for those things which they need.

They are capable of forming books for the instruction of others, and many are able also to hire them printed, and they many times become rich by those means, and obtain an ample sufficiency of the necessaries, and conveniences of life, only by the means of writing.

Those who are good spellers, and of course, good readers, and writers, and who understand arithmetic, and are capable of teaching them, are employed to teach schools, and have a good reward for their servises; and they spend only a few hours, in each day, in order to fulfil their engagements, as school teachers. The rest part of their time, they can read, write, or study some other art or science, in order to qualify themselves, for more advantageous employments.

Those who have learned to keep a regular book of accounts, are employed as clerks for merchants, and afterwards when they become fit to transact business for themselves, and have obtained by their learning, any considerable property, they may if they find it most suitable, become merchants themselves, and often they enrich themselves by their trading.

But those who remain idle, and in a state of ignorance, are many times clothed in rags, suffer with hunger, and cold, and are exposed to many diseases, and are often in want; they are oftentimes cheated and defrauded out of their just earnings, because they have never been learned to read nor to write, nor have they learned arithmetic, or book-keeping.—Thus thou mayest perceive, in some degree, the disadvantages of being idle and ignorant.

The advantages of understanding the art of grammar, are many; if thou ever expectest to obtain lasting instructions, from the books thou art suffered to read, or perfectly to understand, those who read, or speak to thee, endeavor to have the rules of this art well fixed in thy mind, so that thou mayest be ready, on all occasions, to speak, or write correctly, and to answer all questions which may be asked thee, respecting said art, and to determine for thyself concerning any one word, which part of speech it is of, and also, how to form any sentence, exactly according to the most approved rules of said art. Whenever thou art thus far advanced in this art, thou wilt find a much greater degree of satisfaction, and pleasure, while reading, or while hearing others read or speak, than ever thou couldest have had by reading or hearing if thou hadst remained ignorant, of this noble, and advantageous art, yea thy knowledge of that which thou readest, or hast read or heard, will very far surpass, the knowledge which any good reader, can have without learning grammar.

Logic is another art very agreeable, and necessary to be learned, which is an art of reasoning with propriety.

Rhetoric, is a very agreeable art, by which one is enabled to speak in such a manner as will be best calculated, to persuade those who hear, therefore all those who expect to speak to any public assembly, or on any subject, before others, will find that this Art, will be very advantageous to them: yea, it will be of use on al most all occasions of life, therefore it is of importance, for all who are endowed with the reasoning faculty, and with a cultivation of it by logic, to endeavor to have some general principles of this art well fixed in their minds; those who are well versed in rhetoric are much admired, esteemed, and honoured by menkind in general; expert orators, frequently obtain a large income for their rhetorical performances.

If any one is in want of any necessary article, this will be of unspeakable advantage to them while endeavoring to obtain said article: I was almost ready to say, that this art will inspire those, who understand it, with suitable words and expressions on all occasions. An excellent orator may, by a well timed oration, sway the opinion of his audience whichsoever way he pleaseth: he can by one oration cause them to justify those very acts, which in a succeeding oration, he may cause them to condemn. It was because Herod made an oration to the people which caused them to shout and to say, It is the voice of a God, and not of a man; yet, nevertheless, because that Herod refused to give glory to God, for thus enabling him to speak excellently he was eaten of worms, and died. See Acts of the Apostles, Chap. XII. verses 21, 22, 23.

Moreover, attentive pupil, I would earnestly recommend the scriptures of truth as a book of more value than all the other books in the world for they (by the assistance of the spirit of Christ Jesus, which is the true light which hath to all men appeared) sheweth unto us the way of life and salvation. According to that notable passage, II. Tim. chap. III. verse 16. "And from a child thou hast known the holy scriptures which are able to make thee wise unto salvation hrough faith which is in Christ Jesus."

Be persuaded then to attend earnestly to the holy scriptures, read some part of them every day of thy life, and strive to learn by heart at least one verse every day. In this method, thou wilt have a treasure of knowledge which cannot be valued to its worth; it will be of unspeakable use to thee in years to come, if the LORD please to spare thy life so long. Please to read Exodus Chap, XX. verse 12. "Honor thy father and thy mother, that thy days may be long upon the land which the LORD thy GOD giveth thee." Ephesians chap. VI. verse 1. "*Children* obey your parents in the LORD; for this is right."

2. "Honour thy father and mother; which is the first commandment with promise;"

3. "That it may be well with thee, and thou mayest live long on the earth."

i. e. Thou shouldest obey all those who rule over thee if they are in the fear of the LORD, and if they enjoin on thee those acts which thou art made sensible of as being right, and agreeable to the scriptures, and to the teachings, of the spirit of Jesus Christ within thee.

Read, and commit to memory, that part of the Epistle of St Paul to Titus, Chap. II. verse 9, 10. &c. Exhort servants to be obedient to their own masters, and to please them well in all things; not answering again."

10. "Not purloining but shewing all good fidelity; that they may adorn the doctrine of GOD our Saviour in all things."

11. "For the grace of GOD, that bringeth salvation, hath appeared to all men."

12. "Teaching us, that denying ungodliness and worldly lusts, we should live soberly, righteously, and godly in this present world;"

13 "Looking for that blessed hope, and the glorious appearing of the great GOD, and our Saviour Jesus Christ;"

14. "Who gave himself for us, that he might redeem us from all iniquity, and purify unto himself a peculiar people, zealous of good works."

By these, and many more scriptures which might be quoted it very evidently appears that our Creator, and constant Benefactor, by the enlightning influence of his Spirit, shewed, and still doth continue to show to all mankind, as soon as they are capable of exercising the reasoning faculty, what thoughts, words, and actions are displeasing to him, and also those thoughts, words, and actions which are pleasing in his sight; for he is every where present, the darkness, and the light, are both alike to him; no human being can hide himself from the Almighty, and all-knowing Creator: he that hath formed the eye, surely he can see; and he that hath formed the ear, can surely hear; and he that hath created the heart, can discern all the thoughts of it, and the inmost recesses of the soul.

Read Jeremiah, chap. XVII. verse 10. "I the LORD, search

the heart, I try the reigns, even to give every man according to his ways, and according to the fruit of his doings."

Read also and commit to memory, a considerable part of the CXXXIX Psalm. especially the twelve first verses.

I will here inform thee more particularly about the cause of thy opposition of heart to this light of Christ Jesus, which reproves thee of sin, of righteousness, and a judgment to come; It is because thy heart, while in an unrenewed state, is opposed to GOD, to his laws, and to his true followers; but if thou shalt give an earnest heed, to the teaching of this spirit, and never oppose, quench, nor grieve it: but obey, and submit thyself unto its guidance, and teaching: this same grace will enable thee to repent of and forsake thy sins: this divine spirit, if received into thy heart, will change thy natural temper, and inclinations, in such a manner, that thou wilt find, by happy experience, that the service of GOD, is a happifying service: Thou wilt experience more pleasure while reading and commiting to memory the scriptures of truth: and while praying to thy father which is in heaven: and while hearing the gospel preached: or, in the acts of attending on religious exercises: than in all sinful courses: yea, much more durable satisfaction wilt thou attain unto if thy heart should be thus changed by this grace or light than it would be possible for thee to enjoy in the possession of all the material things under the sun. Nothing on earth can afford such real unspeakable, and heavenly joys, as thou wilt receive by thus being united to the divine spirit of Jesus Christ, by a living faith.

But if thou shalt refuse to submit to the teaching of the spirit of Christ within thee if thou shalt quench or grieve and continue in opposition to it, contrary to the witnessing thereof, and the testimoney of the scriptures of truth; thou wilt remain wretched, and miserable, and destitute of real, soul satisfying joy and happiness while thou livest on earth; and after death, thou wilt be punished for thy sins, with unspeakable horror woe, and misery.

Therefore, if thou ever expectest to be happy in this world, or after death, never think, speak, or act contrary to the teachings, of the divine spirit, which will instruct thee according to the truths contained in the scriptures (which thou canst know by comparing its teachings with them): It is a light, which will make thee sensible of thy sins, and lead thee in the way to escape the misery, which comes by sin, and to those joys which are unspeakable while on earth, and full of glory. But if this light is resisted; thou must expect nothing but tribulation and anguish in thy soul, while in the present time, and after death an unspeakable increase of thine anguish of soul for ever and ever, which is the second death.

TWENTY MIXED PRECEPTS.

1. Fear GOD, and by submitting to the teachings of his word, and spirit, believe in Christ, and thus be happy in this world.
2. Honour all men according to their several stations in life.
3. Revere, and obey thy parents, tutors, or teachers, if their requirments be agreeable to the scriptures, and to that light which hath to all men appeared.
4. Obey those, which have the rule over thee, so far as they direct thee according to the Scriptures.
5. Despise not those which are poor, or deformed, neither mock those, which have an impediment in their speach.
6. Show a becoming gracefulness, to thine equals, and never disoblige any one when thou art in company by exposing his faults, nor hurt his feelings, by utteing any bitter reflections, directed in direct opposition, to the known political, or singular, religious principles of any one present.
7. Pray very frequently according to the desires of thine heart and endeavor to read the scriptures daily, and try to commit a part of them to memory.
8. Endeavor to keep company with those which can teach thee, and which will not designedly entice thee into any error, or wickedness.
9. Hearken diligently to all good instructions.
10. Stay not long in the company of; nor imitate the wicked.
11. Improve every opportunity of advancing thy self in learning; and mispend none of thy time.
12. Love the well tutored scholars, and improve thine hours at school, while naughty boys are idle, or at their unnecessary plays.
13. Be always neat and cleanly, and never speak any unbecoming or disrespectful words to any.
14. Strive to be virtuous, and to excell thy companions at school in every art thou art endeavoring to learn.
15. Strive to live peceably with all, and neither provoke nor misuse any.
16. Love thy school-fellows, and remember that divine love, or grace in the heart, will cause happiness.
17. Strive to please thy teacher, thy parents, brothers, and sisters.
18. Play not with those which use ill words, or torture and afflict harmless birds, flys, or insects, nor with those who are more engaged in their plays, than they are in their necessary studies.
19. Always speak the truth, and never use any profane language, nor obscene discourse, and endeavor always to speak, or write with as much grammattical correctness, as thou wouldst wish to do, if every word was to be printed in a book.

20. Endeavor to act worthy of thy calling, and strive so to behave thyself in all companies, that none can have occasion to say any ill of thee.

DIRECTIONS FOR CHILDREN'S BEHAVIOR WHILE AT HOME.

If thou wishest to speak to thy parents or guardians, and hear them engaged in discourse with others, leave thy business until afterwards; but if thou must speak, be sure to whisper.

2. Use respectful, and corteous language to those who are servants, and never insult, or vex them, nor any one else.

3. As ye would that others should do unto you do ye even so unto them; never shouldest thou transgress this Scriptural command; see Mathew chap. VII. verse 12.

4. Quarrel not, nor contend with thy brothers, or sisters, but live in love, peace and unity.

5. Grumble not, nor be unreasonably discontented at what thy parents, or guardians appoint, speak, or do.

6. Bear with meakness, and patience, and without murmuring or sullenness, thy parents, or tutors reproofs; or corrections; yea though it should so happen, that they are causless or undeserved.

7. Let much of thy time be spent in reading, studying or exercise while at school, or in labour at home, while others are idle, or at play.

8. Forget not to pray unto, and seek the Lord, while thou art young, while in thy youthful days, so that thou mayest find him, and be made happy in his love. Enter into thy closet, and when thou hast shut the door pray to thy father which is in secret, and thy father which seeth in secret, shall reward thee openly. See Mat. vi. 6.

9. None are truly unspeakably happy in this world but those who love, fear and serve the Lord.

DIRECTIONS FOR CHILDREN'S BEHAVIOUR WHILE IN COMPANY.

1. Enter not into the company of superiors, (except it be for the transaction of some important business), except they invite thee, nor tarry long with them, if they treat thee with neglect, or appear to be uneasy in thy presence, nor sit down near to them without they invite thee.

2. Put not thy hand in the presence of others, to any part of thy body not ordinarily discovered.

3. Sing not, nor hum in thy mouth, while thou art in company.

4 Stand not wriggling with thy body, hither and thither, but stand steady and upright, with thy hands hanging down by thy sides.

5. Play not wantonly, like a mimic, with thy fingers or feet; it betokens absence of mind, and disrespect towards the company.

6. While coughing or sneeseing, make as little noise as possible, and always take care to turn thy face aside, if any victuals or drink be near to thee, and put thy handkerchief before thy mouth, or nose while so doing.

7. If thou canst not avoid yawning or gaping, cover thy mouth with thy hand, or handkerchief before it, and turn thy face aside.

8. When thou blowest thy nose, let thy handkerchief be used, and make not much noise in so doing.

9. Gnaw not thy nails, pick them not, nor bite them with thy teeth, but be careful to pare them close with a sharp knife, and never suffer them to grow very long.

10. Spit not on a clean floor, but in the corner, or if thou canst as well, go out and do it abroad.

11. Lean not on the chair of a superior, while thou art standing behind him.

12. Spit not on the fire, nor sit with thy knees far apart while thou art by the side of it.

13. Turn not thy back to any, but place thyself so that none may be behind thee.

14. Read not letters, books, nor other writings while in company, unless there be necessity, and after thou hast first obtained leave, except some one ask thee to read, and after thou hast perceived a willingness in the company to hear thee.

15. Touch not nor look upon the books or writings of any one, unless the owner invite or desire thee.

16. Come not near when another reads a letter, or any other paper, nor draw near, or attempt to listen to the conversation of any who discover a wish to converse without being heard by others.

17. Let thy countenance be moderately chearful, neither laughing nor frowning. Those who laugh loud, while in company discover too much vanity and ill manners.

18. Stand not before superiors with thy hands in thy pockets.—Scratch not thy head, nor be engaged in any other act, while thou art speaking to another, nor turn thy face one way, and thine eyes the other way, but modestly look strait before thee, or at the person to whom thou speakest.

19. While thou art walking with thy superior in the house, or garden, or on the common road, let him walk at thy right hand; walk not even with him, cheek by jole, but a little behind him,

yet not so far distant from him as to make it troublesome for him to speak to thee or hard for thee to hear.

20. Look not boldly, or wishfully, in the face of thy superior, as if thou wert about to draw his picture.

21. For any one to look upon another in company, and immediately whisper to another, is unmannerly.

22. Whisper not while in company, but if thou wishest to speak to any one and not be heard by the rest take him aside with thee.

23. Be not among equals, froward, [or fretful], but gentle, pleasant, peaceable, and affable.

24 Avoid the unmannerly, unreasonable, and indecent methods of those untutored persons, who, contrary even to the Scriptures, are wishing to be busy in other men's matters—they want to be informed of every particular circumstance of business respecting their neighbors, or those who live in the same town with themselves; yea, worse, for almost their first salutations to a stranger, are, What is your name?—or, Your name, Sir? if I may be so bold—Where did you come from?—What is your business to this place?—What is your occupation?—What business do you follow when you are at home, etc.

All which, seems to be contrary to true politeness, and even to that love of our neighbor as ourselves, which the Scriptures enjoin. Who is there among men that is willing that his neighbors should know all his methods and plans of business? or, who is there, being a stranger, that is willing on all occasions to answer all the above stated insignificant, and unmannerly questions.

25. Learn no sayings which will any way tend to bias thy mind in favour of vice, or the repeating of which will any way hurt the feelings of any present or do injury to the cause of truth and virtue.

26 Imitate not the wicked, nor be careful to repeat those pieces which will tend to excite the unlawful passions, or which will any way tend to mislead the minds of those who hear.

27. If thou shalt ever attempt to commit any sentence or number of sentences to memory, endeavour to learn those only which will tend to enlarge thy faculties, increase thy love of virtue, and which will tend to further thee in thy literary advances or mechanical operations, or which may serve to qualify thee for a greater degree of usefulness, to thy fellow mortals.

28. If thou wishest to be an agreeable companion to those who are wise, learned, and honorable, and to have the advantages of their assistance and advice, endeavour to establish in thyself habits of true politeness and abstain from all the opposite habits of scurrillity, prophaness and obscenity in thy conversation, gestures or apparel.

THE END.

Family in America

AN ARNO PRESS / NEW YORK TIMES COLLECTION

Abbott, John S. C. **The Mother at Home:** Or, The Principles of Maternal Duty. 1834.

Abrams, Ray H., editor. **The American Family in World War II.** 1943.

Addams, Jane. **A New Conscience and an Ancient Evil.** 1912.

The Aged and the Depression: Two Reports, 1931–1937. 1972.

Alcott, William A. **The Young Husband.** 1839.

Alcott, William A. **The Young Wife.** 1837.

American Sociological Society. **The Family.** 1909.

Anderson, John E. **The Young Child in the Home.** 1936.

Baldwin, Bird T., Eva Abigail Fillmore and Lora Hadley. **Farm Children.** 1930.

Beebe, Gilbert Wheeler. **Contraception and Fertility in the Southern Appalachians.** 1942.

Birth Control and Morality in Nineteenth Century America: Two Discussions, 1859–1878. 1972.

Brandt, Lilian. **Five Hundred and Seventy-Four Deserters and Their Families.** 1905. Baldwin, William H. **Family Desertion and Non-Support Laws.** 1904.

Breckinridge, Sophonisba P. **The Family and the State:** Select Documents. 1934.

Calverton, V. F. **The Bankruptcy of Marriage.** 1928.

Carlier, Auguste. **Marriage in the United States.** 1867.

Child, [Lydia]. **The Mother's Book.** 1831.

Child Care in Rural America: Collected Pamphlets, 1917–1921. 1972.

Child Rearing Literature of Twentieth Century America, 1914–1963. 1972.

The Colonial American Family: Collected Essays, 1788–1803. 1972.

Commander, Lydia Kingsmill. **The American Idea.** 1907.

Davis, Katharine Bement. **Factors in the Sex Life of Twenty-Two Hundred Women.** 1929.

Dennis, Wayne. **The Hopi Child.** 1940.

Epstein, Abraham. **Facing Old Age.** 1922. New Introduction by Wilbur J. Cohen.

The Family and Social Service in the 1920s: Two Documents, 1921–1928. 1972.

Hagood, Margaret Jarman. **Mothers of the South.** 1939.

Hall, G. Stanley. **Senescence:** The Last Half of Life. 1922.

Hall, G. Stanley. **Youth:** Its Education, Regimen, and Hygiene. 1904.

Hathway, Marion. **The Migratory Worker and Family Life.** 1934.

Homan, Walter Joseph. **Children & Quakerism.** 1939.

Key, Ellen. **The Century of the Child.** 1909.

Kirchwey, Freda. **Our Changing Morality:** A Symposium. 1930.

Kopp, Marie E. **Birth Control in Practice.** 1934.

Lawton, George. **New Goals for Old Age.** 1943.

Lichtenberger, J. P. **Divorce:** A Social Interpretation. 1931.

Lindsey, Ben B. and Wainwright Evans. **The Companionate Marriage.** 1927. New Introduction by Charles Larsen.

Lou, Herbert H. **Juvenile Courts in the United States.** 1927.

Monroe, Day. **Chicago Families.** 1932.

Mowrer, Ernest R. **Family Disorganization.** 1927.

Reed, Ruth. **The Illegitimate Family in New York City.** 1934.

Robinson, Caroline Hadley. **Seventy Birth Control Clinics.** 1930.

Watson, John B. **Psychological Care of Infant and Child.** 1928.

White House Conference on Child Health and Protection. **The Home and the Child.** 1931.

White House Conference on Child Health and Protection. **The Adolescent in the Family.** 1934.

Young, Donald, editor. **The Modern American Family.** 1932.